MW00333153

Speaking of Alabama

Speaking of Alabama

The History, Diversity, Function, and Change of Language

Edited by Thomas E. Nunnally

Foreword by Walt Wolfram
Afterword by Michael B. Montgomery

THE UNIVERSITY OF ALABAMA PRESS
Tuscaloosa

The University of Alabama Press
Tuscaloosa, Alabama 35487-0380
uapress.ua.edu

Copyright © 2018 by the University of Alabama Press
All rights reserved.

Inquiries about reproducing material from this work should be addressed to the
University of Alabama Press.

Typeface: Minion and Arial

Library of Congress Cataloging-in-Publication Data

Names: Nunnally, Thomas, editor.
Title: Speaking of Alabama : the history, diversity, function, and change of
language / edited by Thomas E. Nunnally ; foreword by Walt Wolfram ; afterword
by Michael B. Montgomery.
Description: Tuscaloosa : The University of Alabama Press, 2018. | Includes
bibliographical references and index.
Identifiers: LCCN 2018005493| ISBN 9780817319939 (cloth) | ISBN 9780817391980
(ebook)
Subjects: LCSH: English language—Dialects—Alabama. | English language—
Variation—Alabama. | English language—Social aspects—Alabama.
Classification: LCC PE3101.A2 S64 2018 | DDC 427/.9761—dc23
LC record available at https://lccn.loc.gov/2018005493

Contents

Illustrations

TABLES

Foreword

Walt Wolfram
North Carolina State University

Linguistics has a reputation, often well-deserved, for making the description of language into an abstract, arcane field of study that seems detached from the reality of everyday language use for communicative and social purposes. That is unfortunate. Notwithstanding the formal rigor and the technical metalanguage required to describe the structural details of language in a precise way, language is the soul of human and cultural existence. Accordingly, the examination of language should never be too far removed from our ordinary lives. As Ferdinand de Saussure, a theoretical pioneer whose ideas have had a monumental impact on linguistics as well as on literary and cultural theory, asserted a century ago:

> Of what use is linguistics? . . . In the lives of individuals and of society, language is a factor of greater importance than any other. For the study of language to remain solely the business of a handful of specialists would be a quite unacceptable state of affairs. In practice, the study of language is in some degree or other the concern of everyone (1916 [1986, 7]).

In an important sense, the thematic unity of *Speaking of Alabama* centers on the role of language as an essential, symbolic part of the cultural landscape of Alabama. As editor Thomas Nunnally observes in the preface, "Nothing is closer to the folk than the language coming out of their own mouths, whether the speaker is a Black Belt farmer or a Vestavia socialite." This observation sets the stage for the historical, regional, and cultural inclusiveness of different descriptions of the language brought together in this volume.

At the same time, this collection of essays is determined to break out of the tradition in which linguists direct their preaching to a small choir of professional linguists. The congregation for language description needs to be much more expansive, including audiences most affected by the use of language in their personal and social lives. Following Saussure's dictate, the authors seek to reach a broad-based audience with comprehensible information centered on the role that language plays in constructing regional, cultural, and personal identities—as participants within local communities in Alabama, as residents within the regional divides of the state, as members of different cultural groups, and as inhabitants within the overarching American South, an identity pervasive throughout Alabama.

There are several ways in which linguists can work with communities, state residents, and others interested in language in Alabama. First, they can work with community members to ensure that language variation is documented and described in a valid and reliable way. There is ample evidence of this ongoing documentation in a number of the essays in this collection, both in terms of varieties of English and in terms of languages other than English. Michael D. Picone's chapter on multilingual Alabama is an elegant overview that extends historically from the original Native American languages of the region, through the European and African languages in the Colonial and Antebellum periods, to the emerging role of Spanish and other languages in the twenty-first century. Robin Sabino's chapter on Tsalagi language revitalization complements the overall profile with a particular case study of language endangerment. She discusses the attempts at revitalization related to the significant Native American heritage of the original inhabitants, which personalizes a language narrative in a cultural context. Readers thus get both general profiles and particularized instances of language dynamics. Other chapters in the collection document variation in English, focusing on both the local and regional context of the English, or more properly, the Englishes, of Alabama. For example, chapters by Catherine Evans Davies, Crawford Feagin, and Thomas Nunnally and Guy Bailey highlight Alabama speech within the regional context of the South, whereas chapters by Rachael Allbritten, Anna Head Spence, and Jocelyn Doxsey focus on documenting language variation in the context of specific communities or subregions within the state. Clearly, this collection raises our consciousness about the past, present, and future state of language variation in Alabama, demonstrating the diversity of language in Alabama and the complexity of its language situations.

While there is ample documentation of language variation on a state and local level, the authors attempt to do more—to understand and to explicate the role of language in community life. For example, Allbritten probes the way that the production of vowels may project identity, J. Daniel Hasty examines attitudes of linguistic insecurity and self-deprecation that are sometimes associated with local and state dialect norms, and Kimberly Johnson and Nunnally examine the socioeducational and sociopsychological dimensions of code-switching for African Americans sometimes caught between local and external mainstream norms. So we see an effort to understand the reasons that we use language as we do—to situate ourselves socially, to project our identities to others, and to use language variation in the presentation of ourselves as we negotiate our varying communities of practice.

For the most part, the descriptions of language variation in Alabama are written in a way that is readily accessible to readers from broad-based backgrounds. For example, the historical overview by Picone and the introduction by Nunnally could be read by historians, folklorists, and even secondary students who are interested in the language history and variation within the state. These chapters demonstrate how linguistic knowledge can be framed in a way that piques readers' interests and provides information that is comprehensible to those who are not linguistic specialists. Sometimes the translation process for public audiences is difficult, but the general avoidance of technical linguistic terms combined with the provision of a glossary helps accomplish the goal of presenting linguistic material to public audiences.

The underlying impetus for this collection is the desire of researchers to be proactively engaged with the communities who provide linguistic resources for their research. As Cameron et al. (1992, 24) note, "If knowledge is worth having, it is worth sharing." At the very least, researchers should seek to share their insights with community members and to "give back" to the community, with the goal of empowering the community in some way. As John Rickford (1997, 315) observes, "The fundamental rationale for getting involved in application, advocacy, and empowerment is that we owe it to the people whose data fuel our theories and descriptions." In previous presentations, I have referred to this proactive engagement with research communities as the *principle of linguistic gratuity*. This principle challenges linguists to "pursue positive ways in which they can return linguistic favors to the community" (Wolfram 1993, 227).

The call for an engaged, public program of language study has been heard for more than a century now, but state-based initiatives like that undertaken in Alabama are still rare. Happily, Alabama is in the first wave of states striving to call attention to their rich, diverse linguistic heritage. In this respect, the South has taken a lead, with states such as North Carolina (Wolfram 2007c, Wolfram and Reaser 2014) and West Virginia (Hazen 2005) among the few states that have developed initiatives focused on raising awareness about language diversity. The state-based model offers obvious advantages for formal, school-based curricula as well as programs for state and local civic organizations. Perhaps just as important, it taps into a focus on "state pride" exhibited by many states in the South. There is an intrinsic connection between language and sociohistorical, sociocultural, and regional traditions and a level of consciousness about regional and sociocultural language variation that easily segues to the discussion of language diversity. In the South, language is one of the most frequent attributes associated with the region and often serves as a symbolic proxy for a whole range of behaviors considered to be "Southern" (Preston 1997; Tamasi 2000). "Speaking Southern"—or even "speaking Alabamian"—is a behavior that most Americans overtly recognize, so that it is natural to raise the issue of language variation in this context. The awareness of regional place in the South tends to be hierarchical, in that people identify strongly with their local community, the Southern state in which their community is located, and the overarching Southern region (Reed 1993, 2003).

Unfortunately, at the same time, this regional linguistic consciousness often evokes a concomitant set of stereotypes and prejudices about language and a relatively high level of linguistic insecurity among some Southern speakers—an issue addressed by some of the authors in this collection (e.g., Allbritten, Hasty, Nunnally, Nunnally and Bailey). Nonetheless, the high level of language awareness in the South provides a convenient opportunity to address language issues in a natural and convenient demographic, sociohistorical, sociocultural, and political context. In piloting various language awareness programs in North Carolina over the past two decades, my colleagues and I have found that the connection of language to community, state, and regional place has proven to be one of the strongest appeals of our programs (Wolfram, Reaser, and Vaughn 2008; Wolfram and Reaser 2014). *Speaking of Alabama* fits squarely within the state-based tradition of recognizing language as one of the prominent attributes of being Alabamian. The editor and the authors of the articles are to be congratulated for understanding how language portrays the cultural landscape of the state, its unique history, and its past and present cultural traditions.

At the same time, it is important to recognize that this book is just an initial step in the process of developing language awareness and that there is a wide range of activities and programs that need to be considered in engaging the residents of Alabama about language. These may range from opportunistic, teachable moments that spontaneously arise from current news events to specific programs for formal and informal education. Our outreach efforts in North Carolina (Wolfram 2007c), for example, have included a number of TV documentaries and DVDs that have aired on the state affiliate of the Public Broadcasting Service (PBS) (e.g., *Indian by Birth: The Lumbee Dialect* [Hutcheson 2001]; *Mountain Talk* [Hutcheson 2004a]; *Voices of North Carolina* [Hutcheson 2005]; *The Queen Family: Appalachian Tradition and Back Porch Music* [Hutcheson 2006]; *The Carolina Brogue* [Hutcheson 2009]; *First Language: The Race to Save Cherokee* [Hutcheson and Cullinan 2015]; and *Talking Black in America: The Story of African American Language* [Hutcheson and Cullinan 2017]) and audio CDs that combine dialect variation with oral histories and other cultural traditions (Childs, Wolfram, and Cloud 2000; Hutcheson 2004b, 2006b; Mallinson, Childs, and Cox 2006; Reaser et al. 2011). Outreach opportunities may also involve the construction of time-limited (Vaughn and Grimes 2006; Vaughn and Wolfram 2008) or permanent (Gruendler and Wolfram 1997, 2001) museum exhibitions. These exhibitions may be focused exclusively on language or contextualize language within other cultural and historical presentations. For example, an exhibit titled *Freedom's Voice: Celebrating the Black Experience on the Outer Banks*, constructed by the Language and Life Project at North Carolina State University (Vaughn and Grimes 2006), includes images, a play-on-demand documentary (Sellers 2006), interactive audiovisuals, artifacts, audio clips initially recorded as sociolinguistic interviews and reappropriated as oral histories, and informational panels that highlight African Americans' involvement in the history of coastal North Carolina. This exhibition combines history and culture through language in narrating the story of the "other lost colony" on Roanoke Island—the often-invisible role of African Americans in the maritime culture of the Outer Banks.

There are also other popular writing venues for presenting language variation related to a community or a state (e.g., Wolfram and Schilling-Estes 1997; Wolfram et al. 2002; Wolfram and Reaser 2014). It is possible, for example, to produce community-based dialect dictionaries with the members of a community (e.g., Locklear, Wolfram, Schilling-Estes, and Dannenberg 1999; Schilling-Estes, Estes, and Premilovac 2002). One team, under the direction of Albert Valdman, has been working with members of the Francophone community for more than a decade to compile the *Dictionary of Louisiana French* (Valdman et al. 2010) as well as a comprehensive CD that documents a comprehensive sampling of Louisiana's French dialects (Rojas et al. 2003). These projects are aimed primarily at the Francophone community rather than academics. In fact, subsidies for the project have made the cost of the dictionary affordable to the public. Dictionaries of indigenous language varieties are, in fact, one of the long-standing activities engaged in by linguists in documenting endangered language communities. Engaging communities in the compilation of local language and dialect dictionaries is one of the most collaborative language activities, since the resulting dictionaries are tangible products that a local community with minimal background in linguistics can understand.

One of our most ambitious outreach programs involves the development of formal curricular materials on language diversity for North Carolina's public schools. Unfortunately, formal education about dialect variation is still a relatively novel and, in most cases, controversial idea. Nevertheless, we have taught a middle-school curriculum in the same school on Ocracoke Island for the past sixteen years that links social studies and language arts (Reaser and Wolfram 2007a, 2007b) and piloted the state-based curriculum at various sites throughout the state (Reaser 2006). The examination of dialect differences offers great potential for students to investigate the interrelation between linguistic and social diversity, including differences grounded in geography, history, and cultural beliefs and practices.

Workshops on dialects for teachers and schoolchildren and special presentations at museums, civic groups, historical societies, and other community-based organizations are also common outreach venues for communicating knowledge about language diversity to the public. Lectures and workshops on dialect variation in different communities are not uncommon in Alabama now, thanks to the efforts of some of the authors of these chapters, who have traveled throughout the state providing information of the type reflected in the collections of this book, supplemented by audio and visual illustrations of language diversity. (See Davies's essay in this collection, an expanded version of her "Road Scholars" lecture for the Alabama Humanities Foundation, as an exemplar for linguists who want to reach out to their communities.)

But there is yet another reason for taking the message of language diversity public that may be even more critical than some of the reasons suggested in the preceding paragraphs, namely, the issue of equality and discrimination related to language. Most social and educational institutions in our society now claim to be committed to a search for fundamental truths about matter, nature, human society, and human culture. When it comes to language variation, however, there is an educational and sociopolitical tolerance of misinformation and folklore that is matched in few subject areas. There is an entrenched mythology about dialects, for example, that pervades our understanding of this topic, particularly with respect to the nature of standard and vernacular varieties. The most persistent challenge for the study of language in its social context continues to be the *principle of linguistic subordination* (Lippi-Green 1997), in which nonmainstream varieties of English are considered to be little more than illegitimate and unworthy approximations of the standard variety, with no inherent linguistic or social value. Such attitudes are often characteristic not only of dominant groups whose speech habits tend to conform to the standard variety but also, in a type of self-stigmatization, of vernacular-speaking communities who typically adopt the dominant language ideology as well—at least on an overt level. No region of the country is as accepting of an erroneous image of linguistic inferiority as the South (Preston 1997; Tamasi 2000; Hasty's essay in this volume). The social and personal stakes related to linguistic prejudice and discrimination are thus heightened in the South. Mitigating the effects of the dominant ideology is not done overnight or through instant conversion; it involves long-term, formal and informal (re)education on both local and broad-based levels. Communities that have been socialized into believing that their language variety is nothing more than "bad speech" present a significant challenge for the development of dialect awareness programs that celebrate rather than condemn local linguistic practices. Confronting negative linguistic self-images while working with communities to preserve and appreciate local linguistic heritage is the most critical challenge confronting researchers who work in nonmainstream community settings. At the very least, the educational system and society at large should assume responsibility for replacing the entrenched myths about dialects with factual information about the authentic nature of dialect diversity. This volume indicates that Alabama is taking an important step in confronting linguistic prejudice and discrimination related to the language differences of its citizens by celebrating *all* of its language traditions, past and present.

From a more positive, humanistic standpoint, learning about the natural basis of language diversity helps us understand similarities and differences in human behavior. It further offers an opportunity to see how language reflects and helps shape different historical and cultural developments. In this context, it is somewhat surprising that the current emphasis on multicultural education in the United States has rarely included linguistic diversity, since language is often an integral part of people's cultural identity. Linguistic intolerance and discrimination, however, are not limited to the uneducated. As noted in the *Economist* (January 30, 2015): "The collision of academic prejudice and accent is particularly ironic. Academics tend to the centre-left nearly everywhere, and talk endlessly about class and Multiculturalism. . . . And yet accent and dialect are still barely on many people's minds as deserving respect." The awareness of academic intolerance for language diversity on an institutional level has, in fact, generated programs such as "Educating the Educated," which targets the inclusion of language in diversity programs within higher education (Dunstan, Wolfram, Jaeger, and Crandall 2015). The imperative for informal and formal education about the status and role of language differences in American English is critical on a local, regional, and national level in order to initiate a positive shift in public and educational discourse about language diversity.

By practicing the celebration of linguistic diversity, this volume fulfills the admonition of Dwight Bolinger, former president of the Linguistic Society of America and Harvard linguist, that "language should be as much an object of public scrutiny as any of the other things that keenly affect our lives—as much as pollution, energy, crime, busing, and next week's grocery bill" (1979, 407).

Editor's Preface, Note to Linguists, and Acknowledgments

This volume revises and substantially enlarges the first sustained attempt to pub-
lish a body of linguistic research centered on the state of Alabama. Several years
ago, Joey Brackner, director of the Alabama Center for Traditional Culture, invited
scholars with links to the state to submit essays for an issue of *Tributaries: Journal
of the Alabama Folklife Association* to be dedicated to language in Alabama. Though
the subject matter departed from its usual concerns, the journal was certainly an
appropriate venue for linguistic research: nothing is closer to the folk than the language coming out of their own mouths, whether the speaker is a Black Belt farmer
or a Vestavia socialite, and it was the desire of the authors brought together for
the project to increase understanding of this most basic folkway. As guest editor
and contributor, it was my pleasure to work with Joey, Anne Kimzey, and Deborah
Boykin, the editors of *Tributaries*, to produce a double issue (Issue 10, 2007–2008).
The success of the endeavor with general readers and linguists alike persuaded me
to add to the collection and, through the aid and good graces of the University of
Alabama Press, to make it available to a national and international audience. To
the original eleven essays and three appendices (corrected, updated, and revised),
this volume adds more than one hundred pages of new material in three essays
available nowhere else.

We hope that three major themes running throughout the essays will enlighten
and intrigue all readers and especially Alabamians:

1. The history of language in Alabama throughout the state's amazing
   incarnations as a homeland to many indigenous peoples, a wilderness
   contested by European kingdoms and indigenous tribes, a woolly territory, an "instantly" populated and soon tremendously wealthy and powerful state, a decimated but defiant member of the failed secession, and
   now, a still-developing part of the New South;
2. the loss of language diversity in some respects and its concomitant
   growth in others; and
3. the flexibility and power of language, that most human of all human

abilities, to accommodate change within its user groups not only for communication but also for myriad social reasons.

We also hope that this book will not be the end of specialized research into language in Alabama but a spur to further investigation. We are well aware that much remains to be discovered and explained (many of the selections point the way to needed work), including further investigation of Alabama's once widespread Native American languages, the earlier stages of its Englishes recorded in rich but untapped stores of documentary evidence (see Montgomery's afterword), the specifics of African American English varieties across the state, and the development in the state of non-English languages being transplanted by new arrivals.

A NOTE TO LINGUISTS

Famed lyricist Oscar Hammerstein II wrote, "A bell is not a bell until you ring it." In the same way, basic facts about language cannot make headway against the many and harmful misunderstandings held by society at large, even by educated and fair-minded people, unless the ideas ring out clearly. In a reanalysis of the Southern English double modal ("I might could do it") for his dissertation, Daniel Hasty wrote: "I propose that there is an EPP feature on M that causes the subject to raise from the Spec of TP to the Spec of MP, which will yield the correct word order." For the specialist in generative grammar, his proposition is clearly expressed, but for the public in general, who generally and unfortunately believe that the double modal is merely incorrect English, even Daniel's reference to "correct word order" would be mystifying, though only that part of the quotation would appear to be comprehensible. In contrast, Daniel's essay in this volume, on attitudes of Alabama speakers toward their own dialect, can be understood by everyone, specialist and general reader alike, and goes a long way toward dispelling the curse of linguistic inferiority that dogs many.

For the linguist, then, I and the other authors present this volume not only to share our research findings but also to serve as a case study in trying to make linguistic findings both useful for specialists and accessible to nonspecialists. Although we believe that the essays further the field, we have endeavored to frame our findings in language of greater accessibility than would be necessary merely for scholar-to-scholar communication. To accomplish that aim, essays must sometimes cover background material that would not be needed in a professional journal article but that creates scaffolding for understanding. Also, I have asked some authors to include foundational material in their chapters beyond just their findings in order to further the context for other authors' essays, which I have cross-referenced. Furthermore, I have tried to make phonological/phonetic information accessible by using nontechnical spellings to suggest pronunciations when possible, also giving the more accurate phonetic spellings when they are necessary for finer points. An unfortunate and unresolved situation of phonological accuracy arose for me when trying to represent the sound [a] both by informal spelling (noting it is "something like 'ah'") and by its phonetic symbol. Neither representation of the low-central monophthongized allophone of the diphthong /aɪ/ can draw the intended sound from the internalized sound system of many non-Southern readers, even linguists, who do not possess the sound. English spelling has no means to distinguish the low-central "Confederate vowel" pronounced as a gradient between low-front [æ] in *cat* and low-back unrounded [ɑ] in *cot*, and vowel charts produced by non-Southern linguists often use [a] and [ɑ] without making the distinction. Readers who do not monophthongize /aɪ/ in any environments may lack the ability to hear the difference between, for example, rod [rɑːd] and monophthongal ride [raːd], a minimal pair to monophthongizing Southerners. But I hope most of my attempts at informal phonology are more successful. Finally, I have provided appendices that serve as an introduction to linguistic study. In taking these steps, I trust that the volume will be a self-contained whole to readers approaching the serious study of language for the first time, and I also hope that my professional colleagues will grant understanding if at times the exigencies of greater accessibility try their patience.

ACKNOWLEDGMENTS

It is always a pleasure to thank those who lent a helping hand. First and foremost, I thank Joey Brackner for initiating the issue of *Tributaries* devoted to language in Alabama and for his patience and help in seeing that large project through to completion. I thank Joey and coeditors Anne Kimzey and Deborah Boykin for graciously allowing me to serve as guest editor and Randall Williams of NewSouth Books, publisher of the journal, for his readiness to take on the presentational challenges of linguistic data. I further wish to thank the Department of English and the College of Liberal Arts at Auburn University, especially former department head George Crandell, for course reduction and travel support at crucial points; Guy Bailey, Michael B. Montgomery, and Walt Wolfram, for rounding out the revised collection; Michael, for helpful comments on original and new chapters; the University of Alabama Press's outside reviewers of the book project, for helpful input incorporated into revisions of the original set of essays; and the University of Alabama Press, for help in so many ways.

The authors of the journal issue's original selections join me in thanking Joey, Anne, Deborah, and Randall for comments and suggestions that helped keep our writing accessible to a general readership. And severally or together we acknowledge the contributions of and thank Jennifer Reid; Connie Eble; Michael Adams; María Johnson; Bethany Untied; and Natalie Weygand; Clark Center and Jessica Lacher-Feldman of the W. S. Hoole Special Collections Library at the University of Alabama; Russell M. Magnaghi; Jackie Eastman; Susan Piper; Monsignor Michael Farmer, Richard Chastang, Elizabeth Jones, and Neecee Matthews Bradshaw, for assistance obtaining a sample reproduction taken from the Fort Louis Registre de baptêmes; the Alabama Humanities Foundation; Chanoah Warren; with dedication of her essay, Crawford Feagin's late husband, James W. Stone, a fellow linguist whose support and critical mind and eye were essential to her work over the years; William Labov and the University of Pennsylvania Linguistics Laboratory;

Bert Hitchcock; Wayne Flynt; the people of Elba, Alabama, and of the Gulf Coast; John Singler, Greg Guy, Renee Blake, and the New York University Department of Linguistics; Kevin Roozen; with dedication of her essay, Kim Johnson's late grandfather, George "Butter" Luther McMath, who loved his family to the end; family, friends, and students who graciously allowed their speech to be recorded; and our students, for all they have taught us over the years.

Thomas E. Nunnally
Professor Emeritus of English, Auburn University

Speaking of Alabama

1
Exploring Language in Alabama

Thomas E. Nunnally

This book contains essays concerned with language and languages in Alabama. At the end of this essay, I give an overview of the volume and introduce the various articles, but first, because our goal is for our work to be accessible to specialist and nonspecialist alike, I thought it would be helpful to include an introduction to linguistics, which is the scientific study of language. Also, I provide three appendices: appendix A: The Sounds of English and Southern English is an explanation of the special alphabet and principles that linguists use to describe sounds (helpful for most of the essays); appendix B: A Glossary of Select Linguistic Terms, for ready reference, defines special terms that occur in the essays; and appendix C: Web Sources for Further Study annotates and directs you to interesting websites associated with the major topics of the volume.

What Linguistics Is About

Linguistics has a history both short and long. Linguistics of the past, or philology, was primarily interested in the past: classical languages, connections between languages, and the preservation of fading times. One outgrowth of this "backward looking" orientation in the United States was an initiative to record language folkways before they vanished: thus, the rise of dialectology, with its passion for recording the words of older, rural speakers, and the start of the massive Linguistic Atlas of the United States and Canada, a project that is still underway (see Linguistic Atlas Projects, http://us.english.uga.edu/).

A study conducted in 1952 of the language of African Americans in the Alabama Black Belt illustrates such an approach to preserving relics (annotation from McMillan/Montgomery 1989, 1:140):

> **Cobbs, Hamner.** 1952. "Negro Colloquialisms in the Black Belt." *Alabama Review* 5.203–12. Some unreported folk etymologies. [South Alabama]. Characteristic archaisms, colorful vocabulary, malapropisms of rural blacks whose "vivid imaginations, together with their highly developed genius for imita-

tion, have conspired to produce for them a rich and often baffling language."
[Note: I assume the *richness* is for the speakers and the *bafflement* is for the author!]

In a project to compile a bibliography of linguistic studies concerning Alabama, I found that the majority reflected trends of older linguistic interests. Many presented research into place-names in Alabama (culminating in Foscue 1989). Many others presented preliminary research into lexical variation, for example, where Alabamians say "red bug" and where they say "chigger," to prepare groundwork for the Linguistic Atlas mapping of dialects of the Gulf States (however, the Linguistic Atlas of the Gulf States as later reconceived and completed took a very different approach; see Montgomery 1998b).

While these old-school studies retain value, linguistics, born again, as it were, in the 1960s, is also a new science, constantly discovering new areas of language to study and developing new techniques of analysis. To give a few examples, how does each individual's unique use of a language represent social standing, grouping, and ties (sociolinguistics)? How do we put together our thoughts and share them (discourse studies)? How do our nervous systems, seemingly preprogrammed to acquire language from the airwaves around us, perform this amazing feat (psycholinguistics)? Such new subdisciplinary concerns have largely eclipsed preservation and relic finding, though study of language change is still a major concern. However, interest in language change more likely explores how the *current* language is changing and what social forces are driving the change rather than the big, long-range sagas of how Latin gave rise to French.

The essays in this volume have taken advantage of newer linguistic methods and motives to update research on Alabama language. However, linguistics is renewed not only by areas of inquiry but also by the new people who take it up. I am especially pleased that several scholars near the beginning of their careers have contributed to this volume. But before I introduce each of the essays, I want to set up a context for how linguists look at language, sometimes in ways surprisingly different from those of nonlinguists. Then I want to comment on the state of linguistic study of Alabama.

How Linguists and Nonlinguists Look at Language

First, most nonlinguists consider a given language, such as English, to have a basis in reality, to be a real "thing." For example, Britishers might talk about "the King's English" as "real English" and may consider all departures from it (especially by barbaric Americans) to be incorrect, corrupted, improper. But what is language? Since Noam Chomsky's pioneering approach in the 1960s, language has been understood as the unique human *ability* to create and understand utterances that have never been uttered or heard before. Linguists use the term *grammar* not in reference to a list of rules of dos and don'ts but in reference to native speakers' largely unconscious knowledge of the systems of their languages (its sounds, word formations, grammatical relationships, sentence constructions). A little thought shows that language, in the sense of this internalized system for creating communication, can't exist outside the neurons of its speakers. Records of what a language produces, such as texts or recordings, can and do exist independently of speakers, but not language itself, that *ability*. So the concept that there is somehow a perfect English or German or Tagalog that exists platonically is a social (and *very powerful*) construct, an idealization. It turns out that this idealized construct of a language invariably draws its features from the variety of speech and writing of the powerful and the elite. This prestigious variety is nurtured and pedestalized as the norm, the standard of that language, or the Standard, and thus within the consciousness of society the Standard becomes the "real" language.

Linguists, on the other hand, consider the name of a particular language to be a cover term for all the varieties of it. In fact, some linguists go so far as to speak not of English but of Englishes (British English, American English, Singapore English, etc.) to get at the fact of these overlapping varieties. To put it another way, Ciceronian Latin of the Golden Age, a highly refined and artificial form of Latin, was no more "real" Latin than the varieties of Latin spoken in the far-flung ends of the Empire, the varieties that still exist, though today called French, Spanish, Italian, and so on.

Secondly, nonlinguists, working off the concept of a "real-thing," self-existent language, tend to divide everyday varieties of a language into *good* and *bad*. Those perceived as closely approximating the idealized language, the Standard, are *good*, while those departing to significant degrees from the perceived "real thing" language are the *bad* forms, usually called *dialects*, or accents. Someone might comment, "Shirley doesn't have a *dialect* [or accent]; she just speaks regular (or good, or proper, or correct, or standard) English." Rather than categorizing varieties of English as good or bad, however, linguists prefer to study, not condemn, the varieties of a language. Each variety, whether close to the Standard or close to unintelligible in comparison to the Standard, is a dialect. In point of fact, *everyone* speaks a dialect, and it is the dialect of the most powerful and most influential that, as we said, is taken as *the* language. Societies generally value some varieties more highly (those seen as approaching the mythical "real thing," the King's English, again) and value others less highly or even highly disdain them (those seen as most radically diverging from the "real thing").

When linguists speak of dialects, they simply mean varieties of a language associated with a particular group of speakers. Thus dialects can be regional (Southern, Northern), ethnic (African American, Chicano), socially marked (working class, upper class), even gendered ("I do hope you find this shade of ecru lovely" would *more likely* be said by a woman than by a man). Obviously, they can also mix together, as a Northern, African American, middle-class woman will have formed her particular dialect, her idiolect, as a reflection of her relationships to all these groups. Also, linguists pay attention to the way speakers adapt their speech, or "style-shift"; that is, a speaker can draw upon several styles of her or his dialect, often seen as ranging from informal to formal, to meet different circumstances.

Finally, linguists have found that some people can adapt even further than in style only and move from one dialect to another, or "code-switch." Such speakers may be termed bidialectal, just as some people with fluency in two languages are bilingual (see the essay by Johnson and Nunnally in this volume).

While differences in words (e.g., *shopping cart* versus *buggy*) and grammar (e.g., second person plural forms *you-uns* versus *youse guys* versus *y'all*, or alternate verb form usage like "he done" for "he did") certainly help identify dialects, differences in pronunciation stick out more in identification of regional dialects. Sound differences are more easily observed, since every sentence is potentially full of opportunities for occurrences of sounds that vary from the hearer's way of speaking, whereas every sentence will not contain words or grammatical forms that illustrate dialect variation. Thus, sound differences may immediately alert the listener to regional facts about the speaker. Speech sounds associated with regions and groups are so salient as to become stereotypical: Midwestern twang, Yankee accent, Southern drawl. As for grammatical variation, researchers have found that nonstandard grammar forms, with a few exceptions, are more associated with class dialects than with regional dialects (see Murray and Simon 2004; a third type of dialect, ethnic dialects such as African American English, will be discussed below). Both Northern and Southern members of the working class are likely to say, "I seen him pen the dog up after he come in here." The Southern speaker's regional identity will be evident, however, probably by the way he says "I" and by the way he says "pen," since the majority of Southerners say "pen" and "pin" alike. (That's why we Southerners have to stipulate "straight pin" or "ink pen.")

Of course, with all the regional and social varieties that, in a sense, separate us, it's a good thing for society to have a standard variety, the one that we are all familiar with in the press, in most nonfiction books, and in broadcasting and that is the basis of education and commerce. It allows people across the United States and the world to transmit their thoughts, hold a dialogue, and share knowledge in a common format. Though, as I have said, such a standard variety does not have an actual, physical reality within any native speaker, its construct is real enough to be studied and emulated ("You should write 'neither of the boys *is* going,' rather than 'neither of the boys *are* going'"), and anyone wishing to "move up" in life ignores the written standard at his or her peril. As a teacher of college composition for more than thirty years, assigning and evaluating a type of writing that assumes competence in the standard variety, I certainly enforced Standard Edited American English ("Those continued sentence fragments are jeopardizing your grade, Mr. Jones!").

But most of us in the profession object to using the standard as a whip or a brickbat, that is, claiming that those coming from backgrounds that did not afford them the opportunity to acquire a variety close to the standard are obviously stupid and incompetent. This language prejudice is, unfortunately, so strong as to be unquestioned. Someone who speaks a variety close to the Standard (seen as a real thing) usually feels entirely justified in looking down on those who speak differently. As an educated (some would say overeducated) Deep South PhD myself, during a summer at Western Michigan University I became aware of linguistic bigotry toward my Southern dialect emanating from Michigan blue-collar workers (for more on the prejudices against Southern English and other varieties, see Lippi-Green 1997).

But nonspeakers of a devalued variety aren't the only ones to disdain it. As we'll see in the essay by J. Daniel Hasty, speakers of less-standard varieties, such as Southern English, often buy into what has been termed Standard Language Ideology and develop attitudes of disdain toward their own dialects, a sense of "linguistic inferiority." Even these attitudes toward language are an important area of linguistic research, as understanding them throws light on our concepts of regional and ethnic identity, power relations, and gatekeeping mechanisms that control an individual's entry into greater areas of opportunities in life.

To summarize my first two points, linguists understand that there is no such thing as, for example, English in the commonly held sense, and linguists research language varieties not to condemn them but to understand their various origins, structures, uses, and social meanings (and even to find better ways of teaching the standard variety). It's a fair question, however, to wonder why all people *do not* choose to use the same variety, to try to all sound alike. One reason is that none of us has just one variety of our language but several, as mentioned above, which we mostly unconsciously trot out in relation to the group/person we are around at a given moment. We need these varieties because we present ourselves to the world with a multitude of faces, what Catherine Evans Davies (2007, 87) calls "a fluid presentation of self." I, for example, am a Southerner and proud of it, but I sound more Southern talking to some people than to others, and there have been times (I'm thinking of a job interview at a non-Southern university) when I have tried *not* to sound overly Southern. But since we acquire our dialect(s) from the airwaves around us and not from books, I was not entirely successful, of course. (I was asked by an associate dean during my job interview, "Do you think you can teach here with a Southern accent?") I have never been in enough constant and direct communication with non-Southerners to gradually add a functional non-Southern-sounding dialect to my repertoire, y'all.

Basically, how we talk says who we are, and no matter how much attention I try to pay to my speaking self, my heritage raises its flag. Even more, if I become emotionally involved in what I am saying, I become distracted from self-monitoring my speech, resulting in a higher occurrence of Southern dialect features (see the essays by Spence and Feagin for their methods of eliciting "unmonitored speech"). But even if I could remove all traces of Southern dialect, would I *want* to? What would it cost me in terms of my sense of self to lose my linguistic projections of Southern identity? Others agree with Davies on the nature of fluidity in identity. Schiffrin states that "identity is neither categorical nor fixed: we may act more or less middle-class, more or less female, and so on, depending on what we are doing and with whom" (1996, 199). And, as Coulmas summarizes, a person's "identities are not mutually exclusive but form a complex fabric of intersecting affiliations, commitments, convictions, and emotional bonds such that each individual is a member of various overlapping groups with varying degrees of incorporation. Each individual's memberships and identities are variable, changing in intensity by context and over time" (2005, 179). It seems obvious that a single form of speech cannot give voice to the crowd within us. (For more on our modulations of our dialects, see the essays by Feagin, Doxsey, and Johnson and Nunnally in this volume.)

A final difference to explore here between linguists' and nonlinguists' basic beliefs about language concerns language change. Nonlinguists, again working off the ingrained belief in a reified language, hold that it once had or now has a perfect form, and deviation is therefore decay. Language change, from this common viewpoint, equates to language destruction and must not be tolerated. But linguists, looking at the actual history of languages (and taking English as the example here), accept the fact that from *Beowulf* to Brexit there has never been one form of English and certainly never a time when English was not undergoing change. As one may paradoxically put it, language exists only in a state of change.

In the area of sound change, long-term changes in the vowel system of English explain why our vowel sounds are spelled differently from the vowels of other languages like French, German, and Spanish. We say that our vowels are "a, e, i, o, u" (forgetting "y" for a moment), but speakers of those other languages would read the first three letters "a, e, i" as something like "ah, ay, ee" instead of our "ay, ee, eye." For example, compare the sound of the letter <a> in English **rage** and the borrowed French word *garage* and the sound of the letter in English **lice** and the borrowed French word *police*. Before AD 1500 and the basic completion of a major change called the Great Vowel Shift, an English sentence like "Mouse food was made with leeks and cooked fine" would have sounded something like "Moose fode was mahd with lakes ahnd coke-ed feen." (Phonetically [mus fod wɑs mɑd wɪθ leks ɑnd kok-ɛd fin]; see appendix A for more on the International Phonetic Alphabet that allows linguists to use a standard set of symbols to represent sounds.)

Looking at grammar change instead of sound change, consider, for example, the -s verb ending for third-person singular present tense (as in "She swims"). The examples below of two varieties of English, African American Vernacular English (sentence A) and Standard Edited American English (sentence B), exhibit the absence and presence of this grammatical ending:

A. *He go to school.*
B. *He goes to school.*

Which is correct? Obviously, B, the standard English form, contains the verb to employ when using what scholars have aptly named "the language of wider communication." The verb *go* in sentence A, besides being the nonstandard form, also raises a host of negative reactions from many who believe such an innovative form is destroying "pure English."

But turn the clock back six hundred years, and the verdict changes: in relation to the standard English of around 1400, sentence B is incorrect and sentence A is the correct one in special circumstances. The prestige English of Chaucer's day would require "He goeth to school." Sentence B with the verb form *He goes* was around but was a nonstandard, countrified form. In the *Canterbury Tales*, in fact, Chaucer used just that -s verb ending to depict non-Londoners. The poet evidently drew a chuckle from his listeners at the speech of Northern bumpkins who didn't use the refined speech of the court. As for sentence A, "He go to school," that was another correct form of the third-person singular present tense called the subjunctive and meaning "May he go to school" just as "God bless you," a frozen expression from long ago that we have retained, means "May God bless you."

So, we see that the standard itself has shifted as to what is acceptable. But shouldn't we step up to the challenge and draw the line to stop change? If everyone went around saying, "He go to school," wouldn't the loss of third-person singular present tense (indicative) -s be a catastrophic loss of meaning since *goes* is singular and *go* (They *go* to school) is plural?

It is difficult to take this argument seriously when we notice that in the past tense no such -s ending is ever deemed necessary in current standard English to "show the difference" between singular and plural:

He went to school, not *He wents to school*.
They went to school.

Could it be that the retention of some grammatical rules is more about power, privilege, and identity than about actual grammatical necessity?

Another problem with the attitude that language change is language decay is its inconsistency. Changes to the perceived Standard regularly slip in under most people's radar, though not within major systems such as the verb endings explored above. For example, forty years ago, language purists spewed invective over the seemingly gross impropriety of using *hopefully* in a sentence to mean "it is to be hoped" when more and more people started using *hopefully* in this way. They insisted that one must employ *hopefully* only to modify a verb and mean "in a hopeful manner." If a hiker was lost in the woods, one could write, "He looked hopefully [in a hopeful manner] for trail markers," but you *must not*, they would warn, write, "Hopefully [meaning 'it is to be hoped'], he is looking for trail markers." A quick internet search of the *New York Times* editorials shows, however, that the pernicious sentence-modifying *hopefully* is a mainstay today in that august newspaper.

Even the purists, however, probably don't raise an eyebrow today over the use of *contact* as a verb ("I contacted him"), though this usage was a bugbear of the early to mid-twentieth century. (Ironically, my own inner grammar grumbled over the parallel innovative use of *impact* as a verb. It took about a decade before this change of noun *impact* to verb *impact* impacted my grammar to the point that I was surprised one day to hear it coming out of my own mouth.) It is human to prefer the familiar and, I believe, an important trait to help preserve and hand down culture (including language) for the survival of humanity. The important point is to perceive whether change from the familiar and comfortable is just that and only that or is a harbinger of the end of the world.

So, if language can and does change, why don't folks just decide to speak the more prestigious varieties? Surely that would make more sense than sticking with a dialect that contributes to social and economic marginalization and distrust of, or even outright discrimination toward, its users. Here is where the interplay of social forces creates a dilemma. Is it better to be thought well of by one's superiors but considered "uppity" by one's peers or to speak the same as one's peers in order to fit in with them?

To bring these views of nonlinguists and linguists into relief, we will consider for a moment the controversy surrounding African American Vernacular English, especially when this variety came to be called Ebonics.

The term *Ebonics*, catapulted into controversy in the 1990s, is a relatively old term, coined in the 1970s by Afrocentrist scholars. Based on the words *ebony* (a word denoting darkness but with positive associations) and *phonics* (sounds), the term was more political than linguistic in purpose, originally put forward to stress a language unity among all diasporic Africans in the Western Hemisphere. The claim was that a layer of linguistic commonality existed at a level above the various languages spoken by those of African descent who emerged from slavery. As originally used, Ebonics had more to do with ethnicity of user than the language used. But during this same period, linguists began systemic study of African American English (AAE), especially the vernacular variety (AAVE) spoken by young African Americans in Northern inner cities. Linguistic findings demonstrated that AAVE was a dialect of English having its own logic, rules, and systems. This field of study then accelerated and hasn't stopped yet.

In contrast to the Afrocentrists, linguistic researchers analyzing the facts of AAVE recognized it as a form of English—not as a separate language—yet their research clearly showed that AAVE contained some crucial differences from standard written English. The educational effect of these differences is that native speakers of AAVE (that is, those for whom AAVE was their home language and therefore their first dialect) would face greater challenges in the study of standard written English and on tests keyed to standard English than would speakers whose dialects of spoken English are closer to the standard.

Recent use of the term *Ebonics* as a synonym for AAVE is connected with the original 1996 Oakland School Board controversy. The board's point in using the term *Ebonics* was to stress that the home language of most African American schoolchildren differed from standard written English, in the board's view, enough even to allow AAVE to be called a different language from English, that is, Ebonics. The board's strategy was also a political move, since California students whose first language is not English were to be taught in their own language *as a bridge to obtaining English*, not as an end in itself. However, this "other language" argument was not linguistically informed. In the revised statement by the board (1997), Ebonics was more sensibly defined as a dialect of English. For an excellent and moving analysis of that controversy, see Baugh (2000) (for web sources, see appendix C).

While America was stewing over Ebonics and state legislatures were trying to outlaw the use of AAVE in pedagogy, linguists were continuing to study this important dialect of a large minority of citizens in general and of one-quarter of Alabamians. Walt Wolfram summarizes the state of research in regard to African American (Vernacular) English: "No variety of English has been more closely scrutinized over the past half-century than African American English. We have learned much about its historical development and structural description, and its status as a legitimate variety of English is unquestioned. At the same time, it remains embedded in enduring controversy, due no doubt to the sensitivity of race and ethnicity in American society" (2007a).

John Baugh poignantly explains how the level of regard for the speech of African Americans ties in with the majority's level of regard for the speakers: "But even after slavery was abolished in the U.S., a recurrent combination of racial segregation and inferior educational opportunities prevented many African Americans from adopting speech patterns associated with Americans of European ancestry. As a result, generations of white citizens maligned or mocked speakers of AAVE, casting doubt on their intelligence and making their distinctive speaking patterns the object of racist ridicule" (2005).

But as a Southerner and a linguist, I also aver that the English varieties of my region have suffered from similar linguistic prejudice, certainly less tragic and less severely limiting, but a reality just the same. As an Alabamian, I reluctantly must admit that the national reputation of the state sets the tone for the national repudiation of those who speak the English of the state (see Hasty's essay in this volume).

Alabama: A Linguistic Wilderness?

Just as AAVE has received the most study of any ethnic dialect, the Southern dialects of American English have received greater scholarly scrutiny than any other regional varieties. That level of research reflects the nature of the South as a special (though, for a while, unwilling) part of the union. One scholar calls the South the linguistic "touchstone" of the country (Preston 1997). As I said above, how we talk says who we are. In the case of the South, the secession that the Southern states could not accomplish politically or militarily they did accomplish linguistically. This assertion is amply supported by recent research (summarized in Schneider 2003) that demonstrates a surprising fact: some of the linguistic features that most strongly identify Southern English today did not become widespread until *after* the Civil War.

The Southern dialects of Alabama, the putative Heart of Dixie, are generally well documented, therefore, in the sense that the whole region is documented. But what of the specifics of Alabama English? My own linguistic specialty is language change in English for the last twelve centuries or so, especially the period from *Beowulf* to Shakespeare. Over the decades since graduate school, I've enlarged this historical study to include understandings of modern dialect study (dialectology) and language use by social groups (sociolinguistics). Still, I had never specifically set out to discover what was known about the languages of my own native state of Alabama. I assumed that the work had been done at a level similar to that for other states. This illusion was destroyed when *Birmingham News* reporter Thomas Spencer approached me for assistance in writing a feature article on the dialects of different politicians in Alabama (see Spencer 2006). In helping Spencer characterize and categorize the speech of Bob Riley, Lucy Baxley, Jim Folsom, and others, I had to rely on descriptions of the South as a whole to discuss the two main Southern dialects spoken in our state, Inland Southern and Coastal Southern (see essays by

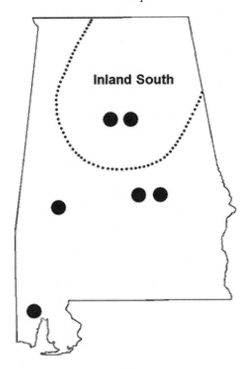

Map 1.1. Alabama dialect division according to the TELSUR Project and *Atlas of North American English*, University of Pennsylvania Linguistics Laboratory (see Labov, Ash, and Boberg 2005)

Davies and by Nunnally and Bailey in this volume), and on general studies of African American Vernacular English. Though a few studies had been carried out, it appeared to me that Alabama is still a wilderness in terms of linguistic research.

To illustrate, consider the three maps below. Map 1.1, based on sound production alone (phonetics), divides Alabama into two dialects, one associated with the Appalachian chain and the other with the South in general. Maps 1.2 and 1.3 are not based on sounds but on differences in word usage (for example, whether one calls spider-mite larvae "red bugs" or "chiggers"). Even so, map 1.2 divides the state at a considerably lower point than map 1.3. Maps 1.2 and 1.3, however, agree in placing all of North Alabama in one region, rather than gouging out just a part of it, as map 1.1 does. Finally, map 1.1 does not posit a dialect boundary running down the state borders of Alabama and Georgia as map 1.3 does. What these differences mean is not that some are right and some wrong but that insufficient data were available to form a detailed picture of the state. For example, the six dots within Alabama on map 1.1 indicate that speech samples of only six individuals form the basis of the map.

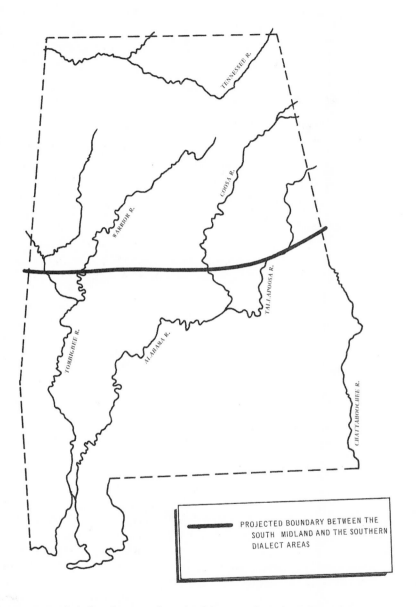

Map 1.2. Foscue's dialect division of North Alabama and South Alabama (Foscue 1971; copyright 1971, the American Dialect Society. All rights reserved. Republished by permission of the copyright holder and the present publisher, Duke University Press)

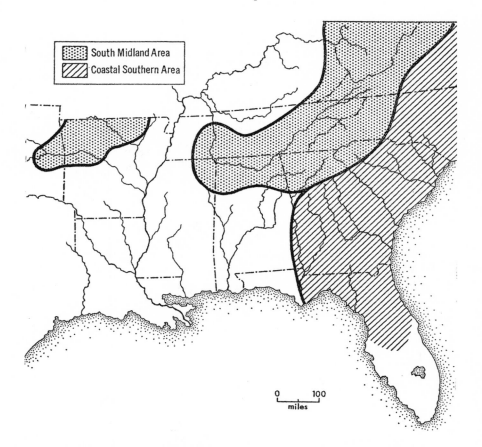

Map 1.3. Detail from Wood's map of dialect contours in the Southern states (Wood 1963, reprinted from Harold B. Allen, "Minor Dialect Areas of the Upper Midwest (map 1)," in Publication of the American Dialect Society, Volume 30 [copyright 1958, the American Dialect Society. All rights reserved. Used by permission of the publisher, Duke University Press])

All three maps reflect white Southern English. As for state varieties of African American English (AAE), no statewide study has occurred to my knowledge, in spite of Wolfram's description above of the robust study of AAE in general.[1] Perhaps this lack is more excusable than the paucity of careful study of the majority dialects. The fall of segregation and the beginning of the slow climb toward equality, not in statute only but in deed, for Alabama's African Americans required energy expenditure in many areas, particularly in the struggle for parity in basic education and voter participation. Against such needs, linguistic investigation of Alabama's AAE(s) paled in comparison.

At least there is still plenty of work to go around. As this volume will show, pioneering work such as these essays is making headway in mapping the lay of the land, but it is just a beginning.[2] Earlier research pertinent to language in Alabama has also been done (see Bernstein 2006; essays by Fitts, Rich, and Schneider in Montgomery and Nunnally 1998; essays by Labov and Ash and by Taylor in Bernstein, Nunnally, and Sabino 1997; and Rich and Montgomery 1993), but here I turn to introducing the other essays in this volume.

Our Studies of Language in Alabama

The eleven other essays in the body of this volume are organized into the following content areas: two essays presenting the larger picture of language in Alabama, one multipart essay exploring language history and change mainly in North Alabama, four studies of speech sounds centered at various Alabama locales, two essays examining attitudes toward and perceptions of dialects, and two essays returning to the larger picture.

We start with a look at non-English languages of Alabama, past and present. Michael D. Picone presents a linguistic tapestry that both sobers by tales of loss and also amazes by outlining the plethora of non-English languages formerly or currently spoken in the state. After tracing the history of various groups of non-English speakers, he focuses our attention on the inexorable change coming to language in Alabama as the demographics of the state change through immigration.

Next, Catherine Evans Davies is our guide in looking at characteristics of Alabama and general Southern English. The core of this essay is a lecture that Davies presents around the state for the Alabama Humanities Foundation. The purpose of the lecture, expanded and elaborated in the essay, is to give a nontechnical, accessible overview of the history, current state, and future of Southern American English in Alabama. Davies ends her essay with an annotated list of suggested works for further study and an invitation to participate in sociolinguistic research.

Above I touched on the role of sound differences between dialects. Pronunciation differences are indeed one of the most important processes studied in linguistics. Of great importance to the fabric of American life is the question of whether dialects are becoming more alike (converging) or less alike (diverging), and much has been done and published on this question. Appendix C lists some websites for further study. Several of the essays in this volume, not surprisingly, touch on this issue and help us understand a little about the linguistic landscape of Alabama.

Appendix A: The Sounds of English and Southern English, mentioned above, will aid you in reading the next five essays.

The fourth essay, by Thomas E. Nunnally and Guy Bailey, plays off Picone's and Davies's essays to blend additional exploration of the state's historical saga with a detailed investigation of socially driven language differences over time. Drawing from history, geography, agronomy, and linguistic research, the findings demonstrate that in the earliest decades of extreme North Alabama's settlement, cultural conflict produced linguistic consequences and that speech differences marking old antagonisms linger for a surprisingly long time both in North Alabama and, expanding the investigation, throughout the state.

Internationally recognized linguist Crawford ("Corky") Feagin, from Anniston, is one of the pioneers of sociolinguistic study of Alabama English. Her 1979 study of the speech of white Annistonians and subsequent research continue to guide researchers. Her essay on the Southern feature called "drawling" is based on data from Anniston as well but has implications for drawling across the South. As is often the case after reading linguistic research, you may suddenly start to hear and understand the significance of a language feature that you have been around all your life but never consciously considered.

The next three articles continue to explore major sounds that define the Southern dialect of present-day Alabama. Like Feagin, Rachael Allbritten, Anna Head Spence, and Jocelyn Doxsey are Alabamians who researched their own home areas. Just as University of Alabama English professor James B. McMillan, founder of the University of Alabama Press and the "Dean of Southern Linguistics," brought his heritage to bear on his scholarship, so we see residents once again taking a linguistic interest in the state. And just as McMillan's scholarship solidly reflected the linguistics of his day, so their research projects, reported on here, reflect cutting-edge approaches to the study of language at the community level.

When the waitress at the Huddle House in Tallassee asks me if I want more "swuheet tuhee," she is demonstrating a dialect that has undergone a language change called the Southern Vowel Shift. This well-documented major change in vowel placement is the focus of Huntsvillian Allbritten's essay. But she presents a tale of caution to those who overgeneralize the extent of language change. Her analysis of the vowel qualities of speakers from the Huntsville area offers compelling evidence that while some speakers use the shifted system of vowel sounds to various degrees, others in the same area have stuck with the less-changed system. Allbritten also presages some of the ways that Huntsville's continuing urban development and the influx of "outsiders" could change the Rocket City linguistically.

Elba native Spence studies phonological variation in Southeast Alabama's Wiregrass region. Her essay summarizes research into the prevalence of [aɪ] pronounced as [aː] (e.g., ride pronounced something like "rahd" rather than "rah-eed." See Davies's essay and appendix A for more explanation). To increase the nonspecialist's understanding of research (by my request), Spence accompanies her findings with explanations of her use of area residents' stories about flooding by the Pea River for linguistic data and of the range of social and linguistic influences that scholars must take into account to adequately understand variation of even this single pronunciation feature.

Last in this group, Doxsey explores the linguistic uniqueness of the Gulf Coast, also looking into the prevalence of the monophthongized [aɪ]. Doxsey provides evidence of important differences between the Southern Englishes of the Gulf Coast and the Southern English of Elba, communities less than two hundred miles apart. Using some methodology similar to Spence's study of Elba, Doxsey also explores the effect of different levels of formality on variation. Finally, her essay gives a glimpse of the gap between speakers' *perceptions* of their own dialects and their *beliefs* about their own dialects.

The next two essays take us from measuring sounds to measuring attitudes—analyzing perceptions associated with dialects in Alabama and the actions these perceptions precipitate.

Doxsey's data touch on how an informant's attitude interacts with his perception. J. Daniel Hasty takes us further into the study of language attitudes, how untrained people (common folk) perceive and judge speakers on the basis of their dialects (or perhaps judge dialects on the basis of their speakers). Hasty played recorded examples of texts read by individuals from the South, North, and Midwest to college students at Auburn University, asking them to rate the speakers as to their personal attributes in areas of Personal Integrity, Competence, and Social Attractiveness. Perhaps the results will not surprise you, but they may be a stinging reminder of what linguistic bigotry does to its targets' attitudes toward their own cultures.

If Hasty's college students—themselves white Southerners—judge Southern dialects so differently and so harshly from non-Southern dialects, how much greater are the tensions for people whose original dialect is African American English? To gain better socioeconomic conditions for themselves and their families, they may adopt a second, more standard dialect but at the risk of alienating themselves or their children from a rich and nurturing culture. Award-winning eighth-grade teacher Kimberly Johnson and I explore her modulation between two style levels of African American English and her "white" English—practices called style-shifting and code-switching. Johnson helps nonspeakers of AAE to enter the psyche of a professional but somewhat conflicted African American by educating readers about the perils and profit of bidialectalism. We learn of the challenges that bidialectal speakers face as they negotiate between different worlds and of their concerns over the effect of this strategy on their children.

The last two essays in the body of the volume return to the larger picture, Charlotte Brammer by looking at Alabama English in terms of its function in narrative and Robin Sabino by discussing one long-silenced Alabama Native American language that refuses to stay dead.

Brammer explores Southern storytelling in general as well as its influence on college students' academic writing. As she explains, for Alabamians and Southerners in general, telling stories does much more than just entertain. It creates and reinforces cultural connections between the teller, the listener, and shared Southern life. However, while features of Southern speech are important for effective storytelling, these same features may work to the disadvantage of a college student when they influence academic writing.

Sabino, project administrator for the Tsalagi Language Revitalization Project in conjunction with the Echota (Cherokee) Tribe of Alabama and Auburn University, reports on the Echota Tribe's project to revitalize, or in the case of Alabama, resurrect their language, Tsalagi (Cherokee). Her essay includes explanations and examples of the exciting technology that makes such a project possible. But as Picone illustrates, language shrinkage is more normal in our era than is language proliferation. Language revitalization, as Fennell explains, requires great commitment: "A shrinking language minority cannot be saved by the actions of well-wishers who do not belong to the minority in question. . . . It can be saved only by itself; and then only if its members acquire the will to stop it shrinking, acquire the institutions and financial means to take appropriate measures, and take them" (quoted in Jones and Singh 2005, 122). Will the Echota Tribe be successful? They have made a good start, but only time will tell, especially after Auburn University's institutional support is no longer available.

Finally, I wish to stress the integral connection of Walt Wolfram's and Michael B. Montgomery's essays to the overall book. As is to be expected of a foreword and an afterword, both function partially as commentary on the main body of this volume, but they go much further. Wolfram and Montgomery, major contributors to the study of Southern English varieties (including African American English), are not only eminent scholars but also consummate educators. Both have expended enormous time and energy mentoring new generations of linguists, as often outside the classroom as in it. Not surprisingly, their essays point the way to needed work. Wolfram provides a prolegomenon for scholars who desire to enhance understanding and appreciation of their own states' linguistic heritage and diversity. Montgomery outlines a major program of historical research, raising important questions and surveying abundant but untapped materials available to scholars who would seek to answer them. I can think of no better outcome than for this book to inspire new knowledge as well as share what has been learned.

CONCLUSION

I close with two comments on my home state. First, Alabama is noted as one of the nation's most biologically diverse states. The research presented in this volume has begun to uncover its concomitant linguistic diversity. As I have said elsewhere, "Alabamians' linguistic differences are not local diseases that need to be cured, but exotic plants that need to be studied" (quoted in Spencer 2006). The other authors and I hope that research into the language of all the folk of this state will continue: of those marched out of Alabama by force long ago, those brought over the seas and to Alabama against their will, those who scratched out a living on the scrabble of North Alabama hillsides, those who luxuriated in the largesse of the Black Belt, those who mined the coal, lime, and iron ore and those who worked the foundries and mills, those adopting "Sweet Home, Alabama," those who shrimp the coast, and those who touch the stars.

Second, it has been a joy to work with scholars connected in different ways to the state's institutions. Considering the level of animus that develops in our state over football loyalties, a work like this serves as a reminder of something the other authors and I know very well: that the teachers and scholars of Alabama are all on the same team.

NOTES

1. Research into African American English as it was spoken across Alabama in the 1970s is possible to scholars who avail themselves of data for the numerous African American Alabamians who were interviewed for the Linguistic Atlas of the Gulf States (LAGS or *LAGS* for LAGS publications), references given under Pederson et al. 1981–1992). See the essay by Nunnally and Bailey in this volume for a preliminary study of AAE in extreme North Alabama using some of these data and for more on the untapped research potential of LAGS.

2. A model program for linguistically oriented study of a single state is the Language and Life Project (LLP), under the auspices of North Carolina State University. As the LLP website describes it, "The project was established at North Carolina State University in 1993 to focus on research, graduate and undergraduate education, and outreach programs related to language in the American South. The goals of the [project] are: 1. to gather basic research information about language varieties in order to understand the nature of language variation and change; 2. to document language varieties in North Carolina and beyond as they reflect varied cultural traditions; 3. to provide information about language differences for public and educational interests; 4. to use research material for the improvement of educational programs about language and culture" (http://www.ncsu.edu/linguistics/ncllp/index.php).

The full incorporation of folklife into this project gives it a balance and public accessibility worthy of emulation by any state desiring to meld serious academic study and public outreach. See Wolfram's foreword in this volume for additional information on the project and its activities.

2

Multilingual Alabama

Michael D. Picone

Language diversity in the United States has asserted itself in recent years as a topic of public concern, and Alabama is no exception, even though compared to many other states the population of non-English-speaking households in Alabama is still relatively small (4.4 percent in 2008, according to the US Census Bureau). In particular, the growing presence of Spanish speakers has led to the adoption of a defensive posture. In 1990, by a nine-to-one margin, Alabama voters amended the state constitution to include the following:

Amendment 509

English is the official language of the state of Alabama. The legislature shall enforce this amendment by appropriate legislation. The legislature and officials of the state of Alabama shall take all steps necessary to insure that the role of English as the common language of the state of Alabama is preserved and enhanced. The legislature shall make no law which diminishes or ignores the role of English as the common language of the state of Alabama.

Any person who is a resident of or doing business in the state of Alabama shall have standing to sue the state of Alabama to enforce this amendment, and the courts of record of the state of Alabama shall have jurisdiction to hear cases brought to enforce this provision. The legislature may provide reasonable and appropriate limitations on the time and manner of suits brought under this amendment.

This amendment was interpreted by the Alabama Department of Public Safety to be in conflict with its prior practice of offering the state driver's license test in languages other than English for those not proficient in English. When non-English testing was suspended, a class action suit against the Department of Public Safety was filed, on the claim that English-only testing was discriminatory and resulted in disproportionate economic hardship for populations of certain national origins, which conflicted with Title VI of the federal Civil Rights Act of 1964. The Eleventh US Circuit Court of Appeals agreed, but the case went all the way to the

US Supreme Court (*Sandoval v. Alexander*, April 24, 2001) where the prior decision was overturned. The court's 5-4 decision, however, did not put the matter to rest, because the discriminatory aspect of the complaint was not addressed by the court, which ruled that the plaintiff, a private party, lacked the grounds to sue the state, since the purported discrimination was an unintentional effect and therefore did not meet the criteria relevant to Title VI. While the US Supreme Court's decision seemed to represent a victory for the state, it did nothing to offset the idea that the challenged practice was in fact discriminatory, intentional or not, and multilingual driver's license testing was reinstated in Alabama. This resulted in yet another legal challenge—this time on the part of ProEnglish, a Virginia-based group of English-only advocates, claiming that multilingual testing violates Amendment 509—which made its way to the Alabama Supreme Court in June 2007. On October 19, the Alabama Supreme Court handed down a 5-4 decision that allows for the continuation of multilingual testing. The majority opinion stated that the plaintiff failed to present sufficient evidence that the administration of the driver's license examination in multiple languages diminishes the status of English as Alabama's common language.

The issue did not go away, however. State Senator Scott Beason (R-Gardendale, Jefferson County), in his capacity as vice chairman of a panel examining immigration issues, proposed a constitutional amendment stipulating that English alone be used for administering the driver's license exam. According to Beason: "People realize the best thing for our state and our country is to remain a one-language country. It's also a safety issue. Road signs are in English" (*Tuscaloosa News*, 1-26-2008, 2B). State legislators were divided in their support for the proposed measure, which never came to a vote. The proposal was opposed by State Senator Roger Bedford (D-Russellville, Franklin County), who saw an impediment to business recruitment: "How can we recruit people from China and Japan to come to Alabama and not let them get a driver's license?" (*Tuscaloosa News*, 1-26-08, 2B). Interestingly, Bedford's stated objection did not mention the fact that his own county has the highest per capita percentage of Hispanics of any county in the state (see below), providing essential labor for the poultry industry there. No doubt this was politically astute on his part, since the momentum of opinion in Alabama favors attracting more Japanese automakers to the state and forging profitable connections to the Chinese economic juggernaut, but the general electorate is insecure about the growing presence of Hispanic laborers. Nevertheless, Bedford's objection, as worded, proved to be prescient. Mindful of successful recruitment efforts that resulted in the German steel giant thyssenrupp's selection of Calvert (just north of Mobile) as the site for a new multibillion-dollar mill (see below) and the European aeronautic conglomerate EADS Airbus's selection of Mobile for a new multimillion-dollar assembly plant, the Mobile Area Chamber of Commerce went on record in official opposition to the proposed bill. In April 2008, the bill was killed in committee. The issue resurfaced in 2010, when Tim James ran for the gubernatorial nomination of the Republican Party. Featured prominently in his televised ad campaign was his promise to do away with the multilingual driver's license exam. However, his bid for the nomination was unsuccessful. For the time being, the controversy has been laid to rest, and the Department of Public Safety continues to offer the driver's license exam in Arabic, Chinese, Farsi, French, German, Greek, Japanese, Korean, Russian, Spanish, Thai, Vietnamese, and American Sign Language, as well as in English.

Nevertheless, given the strong English-only sentiment demonstrated by the crushing margin of victory for Amendment 509 and the still-small size of any potentially countervailing non-English electorate, there was little to dissuade Alabama's senior US senator, Richard C. Shelby, from introducing the Language of Government Act (1995) in an attempt—unsuccessful so far—to designate English as the sole language of the federal government as well. An excerpt citing the justification for the proposed legislation follows: "In order to preserve unity in diversity, and to prevent division along linguistic lines, the United States should maintain a language common to all people; . . . The purpose of this Act is to help immigrants better assimilate and take full advantage of economic and occupational opportunities in the United States; . . . By learning the English language, immigrants will be empowered with the language skills and literacy necessary to become responsible citizens and productive workers in the United States."

It is not the purpose of this essay to take a stance regarding English as an official language. Strong arguments can be marshaled on both sides of this debate. Indeed, some of those arguments can be exemplified from the pages of Alabama's history, as demonstrated below. Nevertheless, an Anglo-centric bias in the selective recounting of the cultural and linguistic history of our nation and our state arguably deprives us of a more objective benchmark for assessing the present nature of linguistic diversity. This is especially true for Alabama, which was a theater of immense rivalry between three great European powers in constant interaction with each other as well as with indigenous peoples and with peoples of African descent. This sociopolitical and ethnic diversity was accompanied by an enormous amount of language diversity. The story of that linguistic diversity, though fascinating in all of its aspects, is not well-known and is rarely told. This essay offers a précis of some of the salient chapters of the earlier phases of Alabama's sociolinguistic history, with brief additional commentary on modern developments. The emphasis is on languages other than English. With the exception of Sabino's essay on the revitalization of Tsalagi (Cherokee), the other contributions to this volume treat historical and contemporary profiles of English in Alabama.

Alabama's First Languages

The story begins long before any European ever set foot on southeastern shores, but the most ancient voices—arguably the most interesting—are unfortunately muted. The stone spear points and scrapers found throughout the territory that is now Alabama are tangible evidence of the hunting practices of its earliest nomadic inhabitants, the Paleo-Indians (10,000–7000 BC), but even the faintest echoes of the tongues spoken by those early residents are impossible to ascertain. With the demise of the megafauna and the introduction of the atlatl, a hunter-and-gatherer profile emerged (7000–1000 BC): the Archaic Indians lived in semipermanent camps and subsisted on small game, fish, nuts, berries, and roots. This was followed by the Woodland period (1000 BC–AD 850), when cultivation of the soil began, leading to a more dependable food supply for a more sedentary existence and leaving time for other endeavors such as pottery-making, stone-carving, and the elaboration of socioreligious ritual. These unfolding changes in social organization certainly exerted pressures on language and had a profound impact on the circumstances of its use and, quite probably, on its form. This would have been true not only in the area of vocabulary and the likely grammaticalization of new features but also in the type and structure of discourse, to provide the appropriate linguistic infrastructure as societies became more hierarchical and more culturally and politically complex.

Indeed, one of the largest and most complex societies north of Mexico emerged in future Alabama during the Mississippian period (AD 850–1500), well before first contact with Europeans. A constellation of villages and secondary hubs had as their primary hub a palisade-protected town of about three thousand residents surrounding twenty artificial mounds—supporting temples, council houses, and elite homes—on the bluffs overlooking the Black Warrior River, about sixteen miles south of present-day Tuscaloosa (Walthall 1980, 211–27). Similar configurations existed elsewhere in Alabama (especially along the Middle Tennessee Valley in northern Alabama), in the Southeast, and along the Lower Mississippi, but none were quite so large. While language must have played a role in the organization and maintenance of these small empires, there is no precise knowledge of the forms and functions of the languages involved.

Nevertheless, a Proto-Muskogean language, with its branches differently hypothesized by different researchers (for a summary see Galloway 1995, 316–20), has been reasonably posited, extrapolating backward from the diversity of Muskogean languages predominating later in the Southeast. And if Emanuel Drechsel (1996, 1997) is correct in his speculations, a prevalent aspect of linguistic usage dating back to the Mississippian period is preserved in the form of Mobilian Jargon, a trade language whose last speakers survived into the middle of the twentieth century. Though some scholars see Mobilian Jargon as the outgrowth of trade relations established after the arrival of Europeans (Crawford 1978), Drechsel counters that only the presence of a lingua franca such as Mobilian Jargon could have accounted for the development of extensive trade and the concomitant widespread diffusion of cultural traits, leading to the subsequent sociocultural uniformity among all the various tribes encountered in the Southeast, despite the linguistic diversity reported by the first Europeans. For Drechsel, Mobilian Jargon underpins the entire pre-Columbian Mississippian complex (1997, 350).

Most closely resembling Choctaw, Mobilian Jargon has a simplified morphology, a reduced inventory of sounds, and an unusual syntactic configuration (object-subject-verb). Other designations for the pidgin include Mobilian Trade Language, Chickasaw Trade Jargon, Chickasaw-Choctaw Trade Language, and Yamà ("yes" in Mobilian Jargon). The fact that the pidgin subsisted among a small number of speakers into the twentieth century is surprising. The slower-than-expected demise, despite stiff competition from French and then English as common media

D a	**R** e	**T** i	**Ꮭ** o	**Oᴼ** u	**i** v
S ga **ꮒ** ka	**Ꮀ** ge	**Ꭹ** gi	**A** go	**J** gu	**E** gv
Ꮂ ha	**Ꮅ** he	**Ꮵ** hi	**Ꮂ** ho	**Г** hu	**Ꮕ** hv
W la	**Ꮧ** le	**Ꮅ** li	**Ꮐ** lo	**M** lu	**Ꮑ** lv
Ꮤ ma	**Ꮁ** me	**H** mi	**Ꮙ** mo	**Ꭹ** mu	
Ꮎ na **Ꮏ** hna **Ꮐ** nah	**Ꮑ** ne	**Ꮒ** ni	**Z** no	**Ꮕ** nu	**Ꮕ** nv
Ꮖ qua	**Ꮝ** que	**Ꮗ** qui	**Ꮯ** quo	**Ꮜ** quu	**Ꮛ** quv
Ꮜ s **Ꮞ** sa	**4** se	**Ꮀ** si	**Ꮚ** so	**Ꮨ** su	**R** sv
Ꮣ da **W** ta	**Ꮝ** de **Ꮖ** te	**Ꭰ** di **Ꮧ** ti	**V** do	**S** du	**Ꮪ** dv
Ꮫ dla **Ꮪ** tla	**L** tle	**C** tli	**Ꮴ** tlo	**Ꮏ** tlu	**P** tlv
Ꮳ tsa	**V** tse	**Ꮲ** tsi	**K** tso	**Ꮥ** tsu	**Ꮯ** tsv
Ꮤ wa	**Ꮽ** we	**Ꮰ** wi	**Ꮼ** wo	**Ꮗ** wu	**6** wv
Ꮿ ya	**ꞵ** ye	**Ꭵ** yi	**Ꮷ** yo	**G** yu	**B** yv

Figure 2.1. Cherokee syllabary (public domain image found on multiple sites; retrieved from http://www.omniglot.com/writing/cherokee.htm)

of communication, may be attributable to the fact that Mobilian Jargon remained expedient as a way of asserting Indian identity while avoiding the improper use of a tribal language with outsiders (Drechsel 1997).

In an essay devoted to language in Alabama, a lingua franca that came to be known as "Mobilian Jargon" would seem to denote a geographical connection to the region and is of obvious interest. How that name was acquired is part of the larger story of language contact stemming from European exploration and colonization, which will be the subject of the next section. First, however, a brief inventory of the region's languages at the time of European arrival will complete this sketch of the indigenous languages of Alabama.

Cherokee (or Tsalagi). The populous Cherokee Nation extended its domain to the Appalachian foothills of northeastern Alabama. Indeed, the most famous Cherokee, Sequoyah (d. 1843), would invent his celebrated Cherokee syllabary (see figure 2.1) while residing in Willstown, now Fort Payne, Alabama, in 1821. Sequoyah's achievement is all the more remarkable given that he was illiterate in English, such that written English served only as an inspiration and not as a direct model for his system of symbols to codify Cherokee. This also helps explain his decision to use syllabic representation rather than individual sound segments, as found in English and all other European languages. In his system, eighty-six symbols capture all the possible syllables of Cherokee. After the removal of the majority of the Cherokee, including Sequoyah, from their homeland, tribe members remaining in the East and those who had been removed were able to communicate with each other in writing by virtue of Sequoyah's syllabary. The first person who learned to read and write in Cherokee, other than Sequoyah himself, was his daughter Ahyokah who, at six years of age, astonished other Cherokee—and won over many skeptics who had thought that Cherokee could not be put to writing—with her demonstrations of literacy in the Cherokee language.

In 1838, of approximately twenty-two thousand Cherokee in the Southeast, all but about a thousand were removed to present-day Oklahoma (many did not survive the Trail of Tears), and the Cherokee language (or *Tsalagi*), a member of the Iroquoian family, underwent dramatic decline in Alabama. According to the 2000 US Census, 270 individuals reportedly speak Cherokee at home in Alabama (the same census lists 1,415 Cherokee speakers in North Carolina). Nevertheless, a linguistic revival effort is now underway among the reconstituted Echota Cherokee Tribe of Alabama (see Sabino's essay in this volume). According to the 2000 US Census, there remain about 7,280 speakers of Cherokee in Oklahoma.

With the exception of Cherokee and the possible exception of Tawasa, which was reclassified as a Timucuan language (compare Swanton 1911, 9; Munro 2015) and which was spoken near the Gulf of Mexico along the banks of the Chattahoochee River on Alabama's eastern border, virtually all the other indigenous languages of Alabama either belong to the Muskogean family or fall into the undocumented category (Munro 2015; Hardy and Scancarelli 2005). Historically, most speakers of these languages relocated to other parts of the Southeast and to Texas and Oklahoma, either voluntarily during the colonial period (notably, some groups migrated west to be closer to their French allies as colonization began to center on the Lower Mississippi) or involuntarily due to flight from enemies or to forced removal during the 1830s.

Creek (or Muskogee). Among the Lower Creeks near the Gulf, the Poarch Band of Creek Indians escaped removal to Oklahoma in 1836, gained federal recognition in 1984, and now reside in southwestern Alabama, constituting a small remnant of the former Creek Confederacy that once encompassed most of Alabama and Georgia, as well as part of eastern Tennessee, at the beginning of the eighteenth century. There are no known fluent speakers of Creek remaining among the Poarch Band (according to Paredes 1992, 121; however, according to the 2000 US Census, 145 individuals speak Muskogee at home in Alabama). However, in 1814, many Upper Creeks from the vicinity of the Coosa and Tallapoosa Rivers relocated to Florida, where Creek or Muskogee (traditionally *Mvskoke*, v = [ə]) is still spoken. This migration gave rise to the Seminole tribe in Florida, and hence the language is sometimes referred to as Seminole as well. Some Seminole were subsequently removed to Oklahoma (1835–42), such that Seminole speakers reside there also. In Florida today, a third of the tribe speaks Seminole, out of a total Seminole population of ap-

Figure 2.2. Paddy Carr, Creek interpreter, 1826 (from McKenney and Hall, courtesy of Alabama Department of Archives and History)

proximately 1,600. The forcible removal from Alabama and Georgia to Oklahoma in the 1830s resulted in the relocation of approximately twenty thousand Creeks, with a few thousand succumbing to cholera during the process. According to the 2000 US Census, there are approximately 4,145 Muskogee speakers in Oklahoma. Creek formerly served as a lingua franca within the sprawling Creek Confederacy, which included non-Creek tribes (see below). A lithograph of Paddy Carr, a Creek interpreter, appears in figure 2.2. He was born in 1807, at Fort Mitchell, Alabama, and bears the name given to him by his Irish father, Erin Carr. His mother was a Creek woman. Due in part to the lack of white women in frontier settings, marriages and cohabitations between white men and Indian women were common in areas of English settlement (Sequoyah's father was also a white man) and, even earlier, in areas of French settlement (see below).

The lithograph is based on a portrait made in Washington, DC, in 1826, when Paddy Carr served as interpreter for a delegation of Creeks (McKenney and Hall 1854). It should be noted that protocol sometimes demanded the presence of an interpreter, even when Indians knew English or French, as the case may be, so that Indians would not dishonor themselves by being forced to speak a different language when acting in an official capacity to represent the tribe. Also present at the 1826 meeting in Washington was Yoholo Micco (see figure 2.3), principal chief of the Creek villages between Tallassee and Oakfuskee, along the Tallapoosa River. Despite his faithful service to the US Army against Indians allied with the British during the Creek Wars, Yoholo Micco (whose name means "royal chief") was removed from his homeland along with his people. He died during the removal.

Hitchiti, Mikasuki. In what is now Southeast Alabama, the Hitchiti became associated with the Lower Creeks of the Creek Confederacy, but their language was distinct from Creek. The language is now extinct, but about five hundred speakers

Figure 2.3. Yoholo Micco, Upper Creek chief, 1826 (W. S. Hoole Special Collections Library, University of Alabama)

of Mikasuki, very closely related to and mutually intelligible with Hitchiti, now reside in southern Florida, where the spelling Miccosukee is usually preferred as a tribal name and where the language itself is referred to as *Ilaponki* (Kersey 1992). Two-thirds of the Florida Seminole are also speakers of Mikasuki.

Alabama, Koasati. Originally living in association with the Upper Creeks of the Creek Confederacy, the Alabama (in the earliest records, usually rendered Alibamou or Alibamon) were located in the center and the Koasati in the northeast of what is today the state of Alabama. They migrated westward to Louisiana and Texas, where the two tribes maintained close links and where their descendants now have tribal lands and still speak both languages. These languages can still be heard spoken by about one hundred speakers of Alabama among the Alabama-Coushatta in Livingston, Texas, and by about four hundred speakers of Koasati (Coushatta is the tribal preference for spelling) among tribesmen divided between Elton, Louisiana, and Livingston, Texas (see Kniffen, Gregory, and Stokes 1987, 122–36).

Choctaw, Chickasaw. Usually thought of as two distinct languages, Choctaw and Chickasaw are closely related, though their speakers were habitually at odds. In addition to most of the middle of present-day Louisiana and the southern half of present-day Mississippi, the Choctaw formerly occupied part of what is presently western Alabama. A powerful rival to the Creek Confederacy to the east, the Choctaw pulled many bordering tribes into their sphere of influence, including many tribes in the vicinity of the Mobile Bay and the Lower Alabama River, such as the Pascagoula, Tohomé, Naniaba, and Mabila (or Mobilien), most of whom, according to early accounts, appear to have been speakers of Muskogean languages

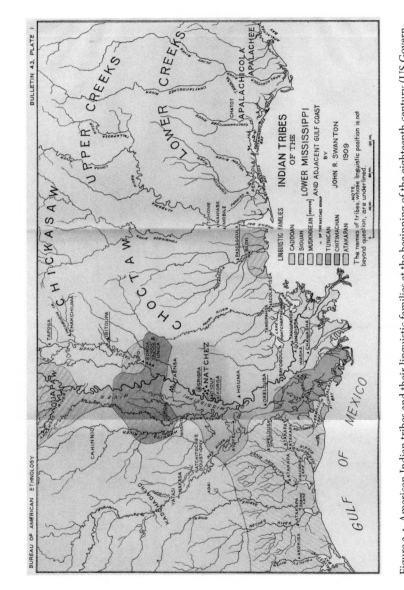

Figure 2.4. American Indian tribes and their linguistic families at the beginning of the eighteenth century (US Government Printing Office)

as well. The rival Chickasaw had dominion over what are presently northern Mississippi and a small part of northwestern Alabama. Many Choctaw migrated westward to be closer to their French allies. Those who ended up in Louisiana escaped removal to Oklahoma in the 1830s, though some migrated to Oklahoma later. In 1831, out of approximately twenty thousand Choctaw in Mississippi and Alabama, all but six thousand were removed to Oklahoma. Choctaw is still spoken in Mississippi (by about 5,420 speakers, according to the 2000 US Census), where tribal lands were eventually reestablished in the vicinity of Philadelphia, Mississippi, in Louisiana, among the small Jena Band of Choctaw (Kniffen, Gregory, and Stokes 1987), and in Oklahoma, where approximately 3,375 speakers remain, according to the 2000 US Census. The MOWA Band of Choctaw Indians in Alabama (the name is derived from Mobile and Washington Counties, in the area where most of the members reside), now numbering about 3,500, is composed of the descendants of a remnant who did not comply with the 1830s removal (Cormier et al. 2006). Though no fluent speakers of Choctaw remain among the MOWA, a language revitalization program has resulted in conversational ability for approximately 360 individuals so far (see MOWA website at www.mowachoctaw.org). According to the 2000 US Census, sixty-five individuals speak Choctaw at home in Alabama. The Chickasaw were also removed to Oklahoma in the 1830s, where approximately six hundred speakers remain today.

The map drawn by Swanton in 1909 (figure 2.4, US Government Printing Office) depicts Indian populations at the beginning of the eighteenth century, when European colonization began in earnest (Swanton 1911).

EARLY LANGUAGE CONTACT WITH THE EUROPEANS

The pre-Columbian Mississippian complex referred to above, whether its main communication network was dependent on the early presence of Mobilian Jargon or not, was already well past its apex when the first Europeans, the Spanish, arrived in the Southeast in the sixteenth century. (There is an unproven claim that a pre-Columbian incursion of Welshmen took place via Mobile Bay in 1170; see Montgomery 1993 for a critique.) In 1540 the Spaniard Hernando de Soto encountered independent chiefdoms composed of palisaded villages and temple mounds. These chiefdoms were sometimes loosely confederated, as in the cases of the Creek and the Choctaw (Galloway 1995), but there was no overarching political unity comparable to the Mississippian complex. The independent chiefdoms were characterized by considerable linguistic diversity. When de Soto set out across the Southeast, including Alabama, his initial interpreter was Juan Ortiz, who could communicate with some Florida Indians (presumably Timucuan or Calusa speakers, who predominated in northern and southern Florida, respectively) by virtue of being a survivor of the prior expedition into Florida by Pánfilo de Narváez in 1528. As de Soto moved across the region, other Indian interpreters were pressed into service in sequential fashion, each added interpreter being able to communicate with a neighboring tribe, such that, in some cases, as many as fourteen interpreters were needed, with Juan Ortiz last in line, to successfully transmit a message (Crawford 1978, 16–17). But de Soto's intentions were unfriendly and provoked resistance—

Chief Tuscaloosa's ill-fated encounter with de Soto at the Battle of Mauvilla provid-ing salient evidence—and the Spaniard's linguistic contact with indigenous peoples was therefore transient. Though de Soto's expeditionary contract stipulated that he establish coastal settlements, he apparently made no attempt to do so, prefer-ring instead to conduct a generally hostile search for plunder, as he had done pre-viously in Peru, and successfully, in the company of Pizarro. But a three-year pe-riod of wandering in the Southeast proved vain and was capped by his death near the Mississippi River in 1542. His surviving soldiers abandoned the expedition and made their way to Mexico (a province of New Spain). Other than occasional raids by Caribbean-based or Atlantic shore-based slavers who would make momentary forays to capture Indians and would then retreat, there would be no further op-portunity for linguistic contact between indigenous peoples in Alabama and Eu-ropeans until the very end of the seventeenth century, at which time that contact would become permanent and, eventually, pervasive.

In 1682, with New France (that is, Canada) as his point of departure, French-man René-Robert Cavelier de La Salle was the first European to travel the length of the Mississippi to its opening at the Gulf of Mexico. For France he claimed the entire Mississippi Valley and all its tributaries, naming the territory *la Louisiane*, in honor of the reigning Louis XIV. Most of what is presently Alabama became a part of that territory. In 1699, the best location for a harbor and fort having already been taken by the Spanish a few months prior at Pensacola, the French sought the next-best site to protect their claim to the Mississippi Valley. A short stint at Fort Maurepas in the vicinity of the Biloxi Indians (near present-day Biloxi, Mississippi) was superseded by the first serious attempt at colonization and settlement on the Gulf Coast by any European power. This took place just upriver from Baie de la Mobile (Mobile Bay), where Fort Louis de la Mobile was erected in 1702 (Higgin-botham 1977). In 1711, the fort was moved southward to a point directly on the bay (see figure 2.5). The name Mobile was incorporated in deference to the closest In-dian group upriver, the Mabila Tribe (sometimes *Mauvilla*, in French *Mobilien*, in English *Mobilian*). Because the French became acquainted with and used the re-gional trade jargon in association with this nearby tribe, the pidgin was referred to as *le mobilien* (Mobilian Jargon). Use of the pidgin, however, was not confined to interaction with the Mabila. Indeed, the heterogeneity of the Indian population in the greater region around Fort Louis as well as within the early settlement itself (wherein the Indians were slaves, for the most part) makes obvious the utility of a common pidgin. The French missionary to the Taensa Indians, Jean François Du-mont de Montigny, declared the utility of Mobilian Jargon in the following terms: "When one knows it, one can travel through all this province without needing an interpreter" (from his *Mémoires historiques sur la Louisiane*, cited in translation by Usner 1992, 258).

Fort Louis was more than a military outpost. Surrounding lands were distrib-uted to an initial cohort of colonists who included craftsmen, their French wives, and also slaves, mostly Indian but also African. Three priests were present as well; they are the authors of the earliest records extant for the Louisiana Territory, in French, now housed at the Cathedral of the Immaculate Conception in Mobile.

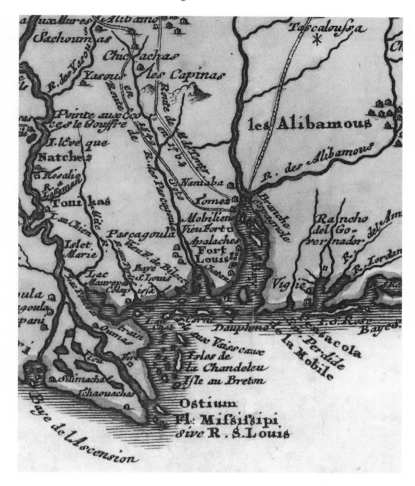

Figure 2.5. Detail of map by Guillaume de l'Isle, published in 1730, showing Fort Louis on Mobile Bay (1711), the nearby Mobilien village, Alibamous villages, and other Indian villages and sites including Vieu F. de Bilocci ("old fort at Biloxi," 1699) and Vieu Fort ("old Fort Louis," 1702) (Warner Map Collection, W. S. Hoole Special Collections Library, University of Alabama)

These records give a fascinating glimpse of colonial life and the ethnic diversity characterizing the settlement effort from its inception, and they allow us to draw inferences about linguistic realities. From the *registre de baptêmes* we learn that the first recorded baptisms in the Louisiana Territory occurred in 1704 (see figure 2.6).

Transcriptions with translations and additional information:

Le sixième du mois de septembre mil sept cent quatre a Eté baptisé un petit anfant femelle apalache par moy miss. apost. sousigné   davion

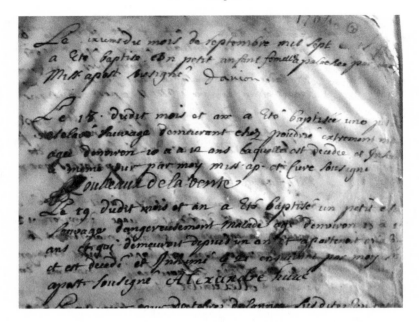

Figure 2.6. The first three entries of the *Registre de baptêmes* of *Fort Louis de la Mobile*, each signed by one of three different officiating clergymen assigned to the fledgling colony (courtesy of the Archives of the Archdiocese of Mobile)

(The sixteenth of September, 1704, was baptized a young Apalachee girl, by me the undersigned, apostolic missionary, [Albert] Davion)

Le 18 dudit mois et an a Eté baptisée une petitte esclave sauvage demeurant chez poudrié extremement malade agee denviron 10 a a 12 ans laquelle est decedee et Inhumee le meme jour par moy miss. ap. et cure sousigné HRoulleaux dela vente

(The eighteenth of the same month and year, was baptized a young Indian slave girl residing at the household of Poudrié [François-Xavier Lemay, aka Poudrier 'powder maker'], extremely sick, approximately 10 to 12 years of age, who died and was buried the same day, by me, the undersigned, apostolic missionary
H[enri] Roulleaux dela Vente)

Le 19 dudit mois et an a Eté baptize un petit esclave sauvage dangereusement malade age d'environ 13 a 14 ans et qui demeuroit depuis un an et appartenoit a la Vigne et est decedé et Inhumé le 21 ensuivant par moy miss. apost. sousigné   Alexandre huué

(The nineteenth of the same month and year, was baptized a young Indian slave boy, dangerously ill, approximately 13 to 14 years of age, residing for the

last year [at the household of] his owner [Antoine Rivard de] La Vigne, who
died and was buried on the twenty-first of the same month, by me, the undersigned, apostolic missionary   Alexandre Huvé)

For the first entry, unlike the second and third entries given here and many others in the *registre* there is no indication that this young Indian girl was ill and on
her deathbed, or that she was a slave. Her Apalachee tribal affiliation is appropriate to the vicinity just east of Mobile Bay (today's Florida panhandle), where the
French and nearby Spanish were vying for influence among the tribes comprising
the lower territory of the Creek Confederacy. The English on the Atlantic coast
were also competitors for the allegiance of the Creek tribes farther upriver. In the
first few years, records show that other Creek-affiliated Indians, both lower and upper, were baptized, including some Chatot tribal members (all free) bearing Hispanic names, indicating an obvious prior contact of some duration with the Spanish to the east—indeed, the colonist André Pénicaut described their language as "a
mixture of Spanish and Alabama" (Higginbotham 1977, 194). The fact that in some
cases the same Indians were having contact with both the Spanish and the French
underlines again the probable utility of Mobilian Jargon. The Apalachee and Chatot figured among the Lower Creeks; their languages, members of the Muskogean
family, are now extinct. The early records also attest to the baptism of Alibamou-
speaking Indians (mentioned above) affiliated with the Upper Creeks.

Interestingly, however, Indians from more distant tribal affiliations and language
families were also present at Fort Louis. These were all listed as slaves, which was
typical of the prevalent configuration: Indian slaves captured (or bought from another tribe) who originated in some distant location, rather than nearby, were preferred, because their enslavement was much less likely to lead to disharmonious
relations with the local population. Furthermore, the practice of enslaving rival
tribespeople was current before the arrival of Europeans. Hence, the same practice at Fort Louis fit with the prevailing regional convention. At Fort Louis, for example, Taensa slaves, whose language was a member of the Natchesan family, were
baptized, and so were Chitimacha slaves, whose language was the main member of
the small Chitimachan family, and at least one Natchitoches Indian slave, whose
language belonged to the Caddoan family. The Taensa were located along the Mississippi River in what is today northern Louisiana, and the Chitimacha and Natchitoches were located west of the Mississippi. Given that the French at Fort Louis
continued to have contact with Biloxi Indians directly to the west (whose language
belonged to the Siouan family), as well as with the Choctaw Confederacy to the
northwest and with the Chickasaw further north (both their languages belonging
in the western branch of the Muskogean family), as evidenced as well by the baptismal records, it is clear that a tremendous early linguistic diversity prevailed. That
diversity may have been even greater than what can be discerned from the records:
most of the other entries concerning baptized Indians gave no indication of a tribal
affiliation but simply listed the baptized as *sauvage* or *sauvagesse*.

In this environment, high value was placed on the acquisition of indigenous languages, and some Europeans in the colony who were not willing or able to make

any such investment were derided, as evidenced by correspondence between the Jesuit Father Jacques Gravier and Le Moyne de Bienville, governor of the colony beginning in 1706: "Monsieur Huvé knows not a single word in the savage tongue, although he has been here several years. He has . . . served for some time in the village of the Apalachee . . . but he knows nothing of their language, and he hears confessions, baptizes, marries and administers communion and extreme unction, without understanding the savages at all" (Letter from Père Gravier, dated February 23, 1708; cited in translation by Higginbotham 1977, 255).

By way of contrast, carpenter and chronicler André Pénicaut was of great value to the settlement partly because, having spent many years among the Biloxi and other nearby Indians, he had by his own account "learned their languages tolerably well . . . especially Mobilian [Jargon], the principal one, which is understood in all the nations" (McWilliams 1953, 81). Indeed, it was fairly common for young French boys to be placed among neighboring Indian tribes as a token of trust for cementing alliances and for the purpose of acquiring linguistic skills along with intimate knowledge of Indian lifeways.

European Languages in the Colonial and Antebellum Periods

The baptismal records also contain tantalizing hints about the linguistic profile of the Europeans during the initial undertaking at Fort Louis. It is often assumed, somewhat anachronistically, that colonists from France (and from New France) must have been speakers of French. However, there is an ongoing debate about the actual linguistic profiles of the early French colonists in the New World. One camp of scholars (e.g., Barbaud 1984) maintains that the earliest colonists to Canada (at the beginning of the seventeenth century) brought with them regional romance varieties (i.e., patois) that were not mutually intelligible, leading inevitably and necessarily to the relatively rapid development of lingua franca in the form of the common brands of French that subsequently emerged in Québec and in Acadia. In the opposing camp, scholars maintain that strongly divergent patois in the motherland simply no longer existed (e.g., Asselin and McLaughlin 1994) or, if they did exist, that the early colonists also spoke some brand of widespread "popular French" before embarking for the New World (e.g., Poirier 1994). Though it is certainly possible to infer too much from a signature, on the face of it, the fact that forty-two different signatures of attesting witnesses (thirty *parrains* "godfathers" and twelve *marraines* "godmothers") appear on the first 108 birth records (1704–1710) would lead one to believe that a certain level of literacy prevailed among a significant portion of the founding population of French inhabitants at Fort Louis (the total population stood at about 250). Any level of literacy would seem to lend credence to the proposition that popular French did have currency among those inhabitants, whether or not they also spoke any patois. Furthermore, even if the theory that patois were still prevalent in Canada at the moment of its initial colonization is accurate, since the colonization of *la Louisiane* began exactly a century later, the Canadian officers and soldiers present would likely already be speakers of the popular Canadian French that would have subsequently emerged.

In the earliest years then, even if spoken with a variety of accents, it is likely that French was a linguistic common denominator among the colonists at Fort Louis de la Mobile, whether or not patois speakers were also among them, to the probable exclusion of any other major European language, except for some limited use of Spanish (particularly by colonist Châteaugué, see Higginbotham 1977, 194). It is less clear that this would remain the case in *la Louisiane*, however, in the next phase of colonization (see below). Regarding Spanish, first, it should be noted that, in a pattern that would be repeated on the western frontier of *la Louisiane* in the vicinity of the Cane River (in present-day northwestern Louisiana near the Texas border), relations with Spanish rivals on the eastern frontier, though sometimes officially hostile (and occasionally overtly so), were generally cordial. Indeed, the French at Fort Louis de la Mobile and the Spanish at Fuerte de San Carlos located at nearby Pensacola Bay were often mutually dependent for trade and for protection against the English and their Indian allies. In 1710, for example, the baptismal records indicate that the *commandante* of the Spanish fort was the godfather of the newborn son of a French merchant at Fort Louis. In subsequent years, when hostility did break out, sovereignty over the area between Mobile Bay and Pensacola Bay would sometimes pass back and forth between the French and the Spanish. Later, according to the Treaty of Paris in 1763, the area was ceded by the French to the British, only to be retaken in 1780 by the Spanish, who would retain control until the Mobile Bay area was seized by the United States in 1814 (Thomason 2001). Documentary evidence shows that Spanish was used by administrators and by some residents of the Mobile area at least up until the 1860s. For example the legal notes and papers of the Mobilian judge John Test (1771–1849), housed at the Alabama Department of Archives and History, in Montgomery, include correspondence and documents in both French and Spanish, though the majority are in English. A highly interesting eyewitness testimony can be gleaned from the remarks of a British journalist visiting the South on assignment for the London *Times*. His observations about his visit to Mobile in the spring of 1861 include: "After dinner we walked through the city. . . . The market was well worthy of a visit—something like St. John's at Liverpool on a Saturday night, crowded with Negroes, mulattoes, quadroons, mestizos of all sort, Spanish, Italian, and French, speaking their own tongues, or a quaint lingua franca" (Russell 1863, 275). Clearly, based on this testimony, French and Spanish were commonly heard on the streets of Mobile at the time of the Civil War. The reference to a "quaint lingua franca" may be an allusion to the continued use of Mobilian Jargon, to plantation creole (see below), or to some other unidentified pidgin. The reference to the Italian language marks the beginning of an extended history of Italian immigration to Alabama, which would become prominent in the late nineteenth and early twentieth centuries (see below).

To back up, however, to complete the account of the French colonization of the area and the concomitant linguistic implications, it must be noted that the prospect of voluntary relocation and resettlement in *la Louisiane* proved a hard sell in France, causing la Compagnie générale d'Occident, the entity to which a royal franchise was granted in 1717 for the development of the colony, to resort to other measures. A significant number of colonists speaking Germanic dialects were recruited from central Europe (today's Germany and Switzerland). Jails and brothels in some French cities were emptied of their unskilled and uneducated occupants, who were then sent to the Louisiana territory (their regional origins and linguistic profiles are not easily determined; among their ranks, the early novelist l'abbé Prévost placed the fictionalized femme fatale Manon Lescaut). The importation of African slaves increased significantly. All told, between 1717 and 1721, la Compagnie générale d'Occident brought seven thousand Europeans and two thousand African slaves to *la Louisiane* (Usner 1992, 31–33). By 1731, an additional five thousand African slaves had been imported.

The class, ethnic, and linguistic disparity of the resulting mix of Europeans, Africans, and Indians could not have readily led to social cohesion in the expanding colony, and it can be asserted with some degree of certainty that linguistic diversity was the norm, even as the status of French progressively solidified (Picone and Valdman 2005; Picone 2015). However, during this second phase of the colonization, the center of gravity for the colony as the gateway to the lower Mississippi shifted rapidly from la Mobile to la Nouvelle Orléans, founded in 1718 by la Compagnie. In 1723, la Nouvelle Orléans became the new seat of administration for the colony, and though la Mobile was not abandoned, its status waned. Mobile later became more prominent as a port and center of development under British, Spanish, and American administrations (as mentioned above), but the use of French there, followed by Spanish, suffered inevitable decline as English asserted itself as the new linguistic norm.

A probable exception to the semichaotic linguistic conditions described above merits mention, because it involves a location in Alabama. The Upper Creek tribes were mostly allied with the British, but a breakdown in relations opened the door for the Alabama (Alibamou) Indians to form a trade alliance with the French. The Alabama approved the building of a fort by the French to show solidarity, to afford protection, and to generate competition for British traders, in an effort to rectify the previous trade abuses. In 1717, Fort Toulouse was erected at the juncture of the Coosa and Tallapoosa Rivers (D. Thomas 1989), near present-day Wetumpka. Some years later, a French sergeant from Poitiers (in west central France), Jean-Louis Fonteneau (born 1686), was assigned to the fort. He had arrived in Mobile in 1720 and had married a local French widow. Together they reportedly had a dozen children, including many sons who became soldiers and who constituted the core personnel manning the fort. The Fonteneau sons married the daughters of other soldiers at the fort, and the Fonteneau daughters also married soldiers *in situ*, leading to the formation of a rather tight-knit community—virtually an extended family—at Fort Toulouse. In this context, it is likely that French (and/or some common patois such as Poitevin from west central France) would become the linguistic norm. For external purposes, Lingua Franca Creek and Mobilian Jargon would have certainly been important in dealings with surrounding Indians, all the more so given that the fort was never attacked and became more of a trading post than a site for military engagement. In 1763, when the British took control of the area, in accordance with the Treaty of Paris, there was an exodus of the Fonteneau clan to what would become the state of Louisiana (Jean-Louis, the patriarch, remains buried at Fort Toulouse, where he died in 1755). Usually rendered with a slightly different orthography, the Fontenot name in Louisiana is now one of the most widespread.

Though it is generally associated with Cajun ethnicity, the Fontenot family line, as just shown, did not in fact originate as part of the 1765–85 Acadian migration to Louisiana but came instead from France via a forty-year sojourn in Alabama.

The ethnic term *Cajun*, which is a derivation of the earlier term *Acadian*, is sometimes misapplied to the MOWA Choctaw community described above. Though there are many individual French speakers from Louisiana living in Alabama, such as the former longtime mayor of Tuscaloosa, Al DuPont, there are no known Cajun communities in the state. However, the popularity of Cajun music led to the formation of at least two "back-door Cajun" music groups in Alabama whose repertoires include French songs: the Birmingham-based Steel City Ramblers and Nuit Blanche (for an overview of French in Louisiana, including Cajun, see Picone 1997).

Under a similar set of circumstances, another French fort was established within the boundaries of present-day Alabama. Fort Tombecbé was erected in 1735, at a point on the banks of the Tombigbee River between the territory of the Choctaw (French allies) and the Chickasaw (allied with the British). A linguistic profile similar to the one at Fort Toulouse probably characterized the interactions at Fort Tombecbé, with the difference that Mobilian Jargon would have played a more important role among surrounding tribes than Lingua Franca Creek.

Though French would rapidly wane in importance once the British took control of Alabama in 1763 (followed by the Spanish and the Americans, in the chronology already mentioned), at least one new cohort of French speakers subsequently made their way to Alabama in the earlier portion of the nineteenth century. After Napoleon's defeat, there was a short-lived attempt at restoration of the French monarchy. Hence, the former *Bonapartistes*, as they were referred to, became *persona non grata* in France, and many went into exile. In 1818, one such group of exiles, along with French refugees from St. Domingue (now Haiti) fleeing the slave revolt there and other French from France (Blaufarb 2005, 2006), founded a community at the confluence of the Tombigbee and Black Warrior Rivers. The correspondence of this well-educated group (some of which, the Lajonie letters, was recently discovered by French historian and author Eric Saugera; see Wolfe 2006) shows that French was certainly current in the colony, even as English was being acquired. Their attempts to raise grapes and olives at the sites they founded (first at Demopolis, then Aigleville and Arcola) met with little success, however, and virtually all 108 original French members of the settlement subsequently dispersed. But the surrounding county bears the name Marengo, commemorating one of Napoleon's great victories, in which the prominent colonist Count Lefebvre Desnouettes had distinguished himself.

AFRICANS AND LANGUAGE ISSUES

It was under American sovereignty in the nineteenth century that the plantation system would fully develop in Alabama (see Davies's essay in this volume). Because the international slave trade was experiencing restriction at that time, most of the Alabama slaves of African descent did not come directly from West Africa but were born in the New World, either in the South or in the Caribbean. Some slaves did come directly from Africa (either as contraband or during brief periods when restrictions were relaxed), but relatively little is known about their tribal affiliations and specific languages. It can be assumed that those who shared a common language would have used it, where circumstances allowed. Among them may have been literate Arabic speakers, as attested elsewhere in the South (Diouf 1998). The best-known exception to the prevailing anonymity of origin involved the clandestine shipment of 110 slaves to Mobile in 1860 on the *Clotilda*, purportedly the last shipment of African slaves to the United States (Lockett 1998; Diouf 2007). This contraband shipment became known to federal authorities almost immediately, and arrests were made, with the result that ensuing events unfolded in the public eye and were followed closely by the press. Hence, more is known about this last cohort of African slaves than virtually any previous group in Alabama (or anywhere in the South). They came from various tribal affiliations around the Bight of Benin. After the Civil War, some were able to reunite on land that they purchased, forming a community known as "African Town" (now Africatown) north of Mobile on Magazine Point. Their native West African languages (especially Yoruba, but probably Dendi, Hausa, and Ewe as well, and possibly West African Pidgin English) remained in use and in some cases were passed on to their children (who were simultaneously acquiring English) and to their grandchildren, such that West African languages were still spoken by a few as late as the 1950s (Diouf 2007, 190–91). A prominent member of African Town, Cudjo Lewis (originally Kossolo), a Yoruba speaker, was the last surviving member among those arriving on the *Clotilda* and, by virtue of this, the last surviving African brought to the United States on a slaver (figure 2.7). He died in 1935, having never realized his dream of being repatriated to his native land.

There is no generally accepted evidence suggesting that African slaves or their descendants in Alabama systematically spoke an English-based creole, with the possible exception of transplanted Gullah speakers (see below) on some plantations. However, a French-based creole primarily associated with the plantations of Louisiana had spillover into neighboring coastal regions, including Mobile. The plantation system developed earlier in Louisiana (especially during the Spanish administration) than in Alabama, and most of the slaves brought to Louisiana before American sovereignty came directly from Africa. Hence, conditions were appropriate for French-based creole to manifest itself in Louisiana and contiguous sites such as Mobile, but not for English-based creole to manifest itself later in Alabama. The *Language* volume of the *New Encyclopedia of Southern Culture* is a useful resource for succinct commentary on all matters of language in the South. Creole formation is summarized below (see also the entry on Gullah [Weldon 2007] for a description of an English-based creole that formed along the South Atlantic coastline; some Gullah speakers most certainly ended up in Alabama, due to the westward migration that accompanied the development of the plantation system):

Theories vary as to the genesis of Louisiana Creole, as it is usually referred to by scholars. The debate surrounding the origin of creole languages is complex, but, at the risk of oversimplifying, the two poles of opposition can be posited in the following terms. Some scholars contend that creole languages were spontaneously generated on (large) plantations where slaves were lin-

Figure 2.7. Cudjo Lewis and his twin great-granddaughters, Mary and Martha, in African Town, circa 1927 (Erik Overbey Collection, The Doy Leale McCall Rare Book and Manuscript Library, University of South Alabama)

guistically heterogeneous and did not share a common tongue and that the structural parallels among creole languages are due to either linguistic universals or the interaction of a particular set of African and European languages. Others contend that most creole languages are simply daughter dialects of a pidgin associated with the slave trade, and though the lexicon can vary from one site to another due to different vocabulary replacement, their basic structure remains the same. Regardless, Louisiana Creole became the native mode of communication within the slave population of Louisiana, and very frequently it was also the first language of the slave-masters' children, who were typically raised by domestic bondservants. (Picone and LaFleur 2007, 61–62)

For the purposes of this present study, it is noteworthy that the last speakers of an earlier nineteenth-century French-based creole were found in Alabama and were interviewed on Mon Louis Island (situated below Mobile; bearing the name of the former Monlouis plantation) in the early 1980s (Marshall 1991). Because the Mon Louis Islanders were deprived of continued contact with French, which did not persist in the Mobile area to the same extent as it did in Louisiana, the creole spoken on Mon Louis Island contained features that differ from the creole spoken in Louisiana, and it is probably representative of an earlier stage of the language.

LATE-NINETEENTH AND TWENTIETH-CENTURY IMMIGRATION

As in the rest of the United States, foreign immigration played an important role in Alabama during the latter half of the nineteenth century and in the twentieth century, especially as new industries and urban centers arose. Among non-Anglophone immigrant groups, Italians and Germans in particular have been prominent in Alabama, followed by Greeks (of special note is the Greek colony founded in Baldwin County in 1906 by Jason Malbis), Welsh, and Eastern Europeans, as well as Armenians, Turks, and Sephardic Jews (possibly speakers of Ladino). Space limitations preclude a detailed accounting of the contributions of the many nationalities represented and the languages they spoke. The stories of many immigrants remain obscure, moreover, due to the increasing value placed on assimilation (see Sabino's essay in this volume). Access to public schools in the latter half of the nineteenth century (beginning in 1850 in Mobile, for example) became a critical factor leading to assimilation and language loss among the descendants of the various immigrant groups. Indeed, the urgency to assimilate became paramount in the South, first as a natural consequence of the aftermath of the Civil War during Reconstruction and then as a shared imperative characterizing the entire nation up until the end of the twentieth century. Assimilation resulted in enhanced economic opportunity, to be sure, and it was also a way to escape the hostility directed toward immigrants. Hostility to all "outsiders" was particularly prevalent during Reconstruction, in large part due to the oppressive and impoverished conditions facing a ruined South. Nevertheless, for a period in the early twentieth century, walking down the streets of some coal towns and some districts of Birmingham, for example, Ensley, one was as likely to hear Italian spoken as English.

Though the French vine and olive colony founded in 1818 in the vicinity of Demopolis failed, an Austro-Italian named Serafino Brock proved that successful grape farming and winemaking were possible in Lambert (Mobile County), where he and his wife, Constanza, landed in 1893. Brock was attracted to Lambert's Italian agricultural colony established earlier by Mastro Valerio. Brock, who became prominent in Lambert, was born in 1864 in the Trentino region of northern Italy (part of the Austrian Empire at the time) and spoke a number of languages, including Italian (information compiled by Russell M. Magnaghi, Italian American historian at Northern Michigan University). Brock and other members of the colony most certainly spoke, as their maternal languages, the *dialetti* of their respective regions (the equivalent of the regional patois of France, but the *dialetti* have survived much longer in Italy). It appears that most of the colonists, including Brock, were from the greater Tyrol area and would have been speakers of a Rhaeto-Romance language. To the extent that they did not share a mutually intelligible dialect, Italian would have served as their lingua franca, as it continues to today in many parts of modern Italy. Cesar Bartina, another member of the Italian agricultural colony in Lambert, is pictured with his fiancée, Sadie Hattenstein, in figure 2.8. Born in Italy in 1881, Bartina arrived at the United States in 1903. The photograph was taken sometime before 1907, when Hattenstein (b. 1889) died suddenly.

Though other Italians farmed at various locations in Alabama, far more Italians came to work as laborers, steel mill workers, miners, and small-business entrepreneurs, especially in the newly booming Birmingham vicinity. Indeed, in 1911, there were about 2,500 Italian immigrants in Jefferson County (Moroni 1913). The highest concentrations were at Bessemer (600), Ensley (500) (the Italian District

Figure 2.8. Cesar Bartina, member of the Italian agricultural community at Lambert, and his fiancée, Sadie Hattenstein, circa 1905 (W. S. Hoole Special Collections Library, University of Alabama)

in Ensley gained notoriety as the site of the Ensley Community House, a settlement house modeled after the famous Hull House of Chicago to serve the immigrant community; see Hubbs 2005), Pratt City (450), and Thomas (450). Among their ranks were many Sicilians (including Vincent and Maria Bruno, arriving in 1909, whose family went on to found the Bruno supermarket empire) but also immigrants from the Piedmont (northeastern Italy), Romagna (north central Italy), Venetia (northwestern Italy), and from elsewhere, whose respective *dialetti* would likely have been members of the following language groups: Sicilianu, Piedmontese, Emiliano-Romagnolo, and Vèneto. Given this diversity, Italian (and eventually English) likely filled the role of lingua franca to facilitate many of their interactions. Another fairly large concentration of Italians, about 500 in 1911 (Moroni 1913), were attracted to the coal mines of Bibb County. In Blocton, they encountered much xenophobia and were obliged to live, die, and be buried in segregation: confined to "Little Italy" in life, their final repose was in the Italian Catholic Cemetery (Adams 2001), where the majority of the tombstones tell their stories in the Italian language. These Italians came primarily from northern and north central regions of Italy: Emilia-Romagna (including Bologna), Liguria, Lombardy, Tuscany, and Modena. Once again, given the associated dialectal diversity, Italian likely served as a lingua franca, even as the speakers were acquiring English. (For a study of the linguistic interaction of immigrants and African Americans as mine coworkers in Alabama, see Harris 2003.) Of all Southern states, only Alabama has Italians ranking near the top of the list of origins for new European immigrants at this time (Bayley 2007, 75).

Cullman County and the city of Cullman are named after John Gottfried Cullmann (born in Bavaria in 1823), who founded the city in 1873 and succeeded in attracting many other German immigrants in the early years (despite serious hostility from local anti-immigrationists). In Baldwin County, circa 1904, Elberta was founded by German immigrants, as commemorated every fall and spring by the Elberta German Sausage Festival. However, the two world wars waged against Germany accentuated the pressure to assimilate and led to the suppression of German language and identity in Alabama as elsewhere. Nevertheless, a variety of noteworthy connections continue between Alabama and Germany. Alabama was the site chosen for a constellation of prisoner-of-war camps for Germans during World War II (the largest was at Aliceville, but there were four others: Camp Opelika, Camp Rucker, Camp Sibert, and Fort McClellan; see Cook 2006). World War II was followed by the arrival of another group of Germans, in this case destined to become new Alabamians, as German rocket scientists and others came to live and work in Huntsville at the outset of the Cold War. Instead of hostility, these German immigrants appear to have been met with local acceptance and even appreciation. Figure 2.9 captures a unique moment. A special swearing-in ceremony was held at Huntsville High School, on April 14, 1955, when 103 German-born scientists, technicians, and their family members took oaths of American citizenship, the most notable among them being Wernher von Braun (see also Allbritten's essay in this volume).

More recently, new industry has increased the population of German speakers in Alabama. One can point to the arrival of many Germans in Tuscaloosa County when Mercedes-Benz opened its first North American automotive assembly plant in 1997. Today, about three hundred Germans live in and around Tuscaloosa, one of the few small cities in America where it is not surprising to hear German being spoken on a regular basis in restaurants and shops and also in the schoolyard (most of the German families send their children to the Capitol School, a private institution bordering the preserved ruins of the old state capitol building). The city boasts a German bakery catering to the tastes of this special clientele, and since 2008 the First Presbyterian Church of Tuscaloosa has offered worship services entirely in German, including a *Christvesper* on Christmas Eve, an *Osternacht* on the Saturday before Easter, and a morning worship service the first Sunday of each month. Similarly, in Calvert, twenty-five miles north of Mobile, the 2010 opening by thyssenkrupp AG of a $3.7 billion steel plant has forged a new German connection of importance. As was the case for French settlers during the colonial period and for Italian immigrants in the late eighteenth and early twentieth centuries, it must be remembered that most Germans speak regional dialects (not always mutually intelligible) and rely on Standard German for crosscommunication.

The story of another German immigrant—emblematic of countless other for-

Figure 2.9. One hundred and three German-born individuals become American citizens at swearing-in ceremony, Huntsville High School, April 14, 1955 (Courtesy of the US Army)

gotten and invisible immigrants in Alabama—remains to be told: Thomas Dauser, from Schömberg in the Württemberg region of Germany, came to Tuscaloosa sometime before 1882 and set up shop as a shoemaker and bookbinder. Why he came and what he experienced are secrets to be unlocked by someone willing to take the time to study his correspondence, all in German, housed at the Special Collections Library at the University of Alabama.

Entering the Twenty-First Century

The opening remarks on the state of linguistic legislation in Alabama are a testimony to the continued value placed on linguistic assimilation aimed at securing conformity to an Anglo-centric norm. As we enter the twenty-first century, however, there is public debate, which was largely missing in previous eras, about the tension between the necessity for intercomprehension fostering social cohesion and the value of preserving cultural and linguistic diversity—and, in the case of indigenous languages, the value of preserving ancient linguistic heritage. In other words, the urgency placed on assimilation is still the dominant sentiment but is somewhat tempered compared to the recent past. In a "smaller" highly interconnected world, multilingualism has taken on new value, including commercial and strategic. However, the fast-growing Hispanic presence in Alabama, as in the rest of the nation, brings with it a set of linguistic challenges that have given assimilation renewed prominence, resulting in legislative initiatives such as those mentioned earlier in this essay.

In Alabama, the Spanish-speaking population (which is not coterminous with the self-identifying Hispanic population in the US Census, though the two populations do overlap greatly) has increased dramatically, despite a recession-induced deceleration in the projected rate of growth and despite recent legislation aimed at discouraging undocumented immigration. Progressing from 42,653 to 89,730, there was an increase of 110 percent in the Spanish-speaking population between 1990 and 2000, according to figures provided by the US Census. According to figures available from the American Community Survey, the count of Spanish speakers in Alabama in 2008 was approximately 107,842, which, due to the recession, was down from a prior projection of 135,000 for that same year but which still represented another robust increase of 20 percent. Language use figures are not derivable from the 2010 US Census, which was taken just before the immigration crackdown, because the monitoring of language use has been delegated henceforth to the American Community Survey. However, an estimate established by the American Community Survey for 2011 sets the number of Spanish speakers in Alabama at 153,845, representing an increase of 71 percent over the preceding eleven years. The rebound in the rate of increase is a natural consequence of an improving economy, which is attracting more migrant laborers. Indeed, the overall Hispanic population in Alabama has increased to 185,602, according to the 2010 US Census. Over the last two decades, the increase has been especially dramatic in the northern part of the state, where immigrant Hispanics have been responding to the need for intensive labor in poultry plants. While the largest concentration of Hispanic residents is found in the greater Birmingham area in Jefferson County (approximately 20,500 in 2008), the highest per capita Hispanic populations are found in northern counties such as Franklin (12.5 percent in 2008) and Marshall (9 percent in 2008). In Russellville (Franklin County), for example, more than 3,500 Hispanics (mostly from southern Mexico and Guatemala) constitute more than one-third of the population (Mohl 2002, 243); Mexican and Guatemalan cultures, and the Spanish language, are well implanted, for the time being at least—the children, many of whom were born in Alabama, are being schooled in and are acquiring English. Decatur, in the north central part of the state, also has a high concentration of Hispanics. In fact, in all urban locations in the state, the Hispanic population is on the rise, and Spanish can be heard with increasing frequency (on Mexicans in Birmingham and Hoover, see Kelley 2005).

Churches in Alabama are now regularly ministering in Spanish to this burgeoning population. The Holy Spirit Catholic Church in Tuscaloosa conducts mass in Spanish every Sunday, drawing an attendance of about four hundred, and celebrates the Roman Catholic feast day dedicated to *Nuestra Señora de Guadalupe* (Our Lady of Guadalupe) with a procession and bilingual Spanish-English mass (see figure 2.10). In addition to adding mass in Spanish, a growing number of other Catholic churches in Alabama are likewise joining countless churches throughout the Americas to commemorate the reported visitation of *La Virgen Morena* (the brown-skinned Virgin) to Juan Diego in Mexico in December 1531, an event that has become an important religious and cultural touchstone for Hispanic populations everywhere. Spanish language services and day care centers are also sprouting up in various Evangelical and Pentecostal churches, such as Harvest International Ministry and *Mis Amigos* day care, located in Saks (Calhoun County).

Figure 2.10. Celebrants of *Nuestra Señora de Guadalupe* observances, Holy Spirit Catholic Church, Tuscaloosa, December 9, 2007

Some Hispanics are in fact using Spanish as a lingua franca because they are maternal speakers of various Indian languages, particularly Mayan dialects from Guatemala (especially K'iche' and Huastec). And in a few cases, they are virtually monolingual speakers of an Indian language. Typically, such individuals remain under the radar but are discovered when there is a medical emergency or delivery requiring hospitalization, and when the Spanish-speaking interpreter or medical staffer is brought in, it is quickly determined that the patient does not, in fact, speak Spanish.

In addition to the question of the English-only policies mentioned at the outset, Alabama Hispanics also feel threatened by federal initiatives aimed at expelling illegal immigrants, and they are flexing their muscle to show that they are a growing economic force that contributes to financial health and profitability in the state. There were well-attended protests and boycotts at various locations in the northern part of the state and in Birmingham, on May 1, 2006, timed with a national day of protest. These actions temporarily shut down some businesses and caused profits to dip in areas with high concentrations of Hispanics. However, the enactment in Alabama, in June 2011, of the nation's strictest anti-illegal immigration law (HB 56, sponsored by State Representative Micky Hammon and State Senator Scott Beason) has had a chilling effect on many of Alabama's Hispanic residents, including those who are properly documented, and will likely be a decelerating factor even as the economy becomes more vibrant. Though popular with conservative constituencies when enacted, the law raised concerns for businesses dependent on immigrant labor, school officials required to monitor documentation, churches fearing criminal-ization of outreach activities to undocumented immigrants, and civil rights groups. Challenged in court, some key provisions of the law were struck down by the US Court of Appeals for the Eleventh Circuit in August 2012. In April 2013, the US Supreme Court refused to entertain an appeal. This essay is concerned, of course, with language in Alabama, not with immigration policies and practices *per se*. The two are linked, however, in the following way: any brake on immigration, legal or otherwise (it is estimated that there are far more illegal than legal Hispanic immi-grants in the United States), will inevitably affect the rate of maintenance of Span-ish in the United States. The dynamic of Spanish language maintenance, whether one is for it or against it, is fostered partly by the constant influx of new mono-lingual Spanish speakers into the existent Hispanic communities. This, coupled with the growing numbers overall and with the relatively easy access to nearby Spanish-speaking countries and to the Spanish media, sets Spanish apart and puts it on a footing that was not available to other immigrant languages in years past. Of course, given today's extensive transportation infrastructure and electronic me-dia, almost any immigrant language can now enjoy some of the same kind of sup-port that Spanish does, but the big difference is the larger number and continual influx of Hispanic immigrants. While the Hispanic portion of the total population in Alabama is presently only about 3.9 percent, the Hispanic presence in the state grew by 144.8 percent between 2000 and 2010; only one other state had a higher rate of growth over that same period (South Carolina had a growth rate of 147.9 percent, and six of the eight next highest growth rates are also located in the South-east: Arkansas, 114.2 percent; Georgia, 96.1 percent; Kentucky, 121 percent; Missis-sippi 105.9 percent, North Carolina 111.1 percent, Tennessee 134.2 percent.) Hence, barring a prolonged economic lull, and despite a fairly dramatic change in pres-ent immigration practices aimed at a crackdown on illegal immigration, it is likely that the Spanish language will continue to make headway in Alabama and in the rest of the nation, even though this will be offset somewhat by many younger His-panics, who will be raised in a predominantly English environment and will be-come semispeakers of Spanish or lose it entirely (for an overview of trends in the South, see Bailey 2015). It is also noteworthy that Spanish instruction in Alabama is on the rise, as elsewhere in the nation, in recognition of the prominent role that Spanish will likely play in the future of the United States (as well as among trad-ing partners abroad).

Spanish seems destined to play a special role, but there are many other lan-guages spoken in Alabama as we enter the twenty-first century. In Alabama, as elsewhere in the United States, there has been a significant upswing over the last twenty years in immigration from Eastern Europe, the Near East, the Far East, and South Asia (of special note is the significant influx of Korean speakers into the Au-burn area due to new Kia and Hyundai plants: of the 250 students identified as hav-ing ESL needs in the Auburn City Schools system in 2008, more than 75 percent were Korean), in addition to Latin America. Table 2.1 (see below) gives the com-plete breakdown of populations (five years of age and older) who speak close to one hundred different languages at home in Alabama, as reported by the US Census

Bureau. Although it is probable that some of the changes between 2000 and 2008 derive from differences in survey methodology, table 2.1 clearly shows that multilingualism is both vibrant and constantly evolving in the state.

CONCLUSION

The social fabric of Alabama, from the beginning of human habitation right up to the present, has always been characterized by multilingualism, even if that multilingualism has been more overtly recognizable (or less suppressed) during some periods than others. Visible or not, as the foregoing demonstrates, there has always been a complicated interweaving of diverse linguistic threads in the region that we now think of as our state. The prevalent notion, bred through popular ignorance of our own rich history, that Alabama's linguistic past can be reduced to two phases, namely the distant presence of Indian languages followed by the advent of English, is a bleached, threadbare version of the truth. The pattern of this thick and colorful fabric, if one can be discerned, is attributable to the warp and weft of great linguistic diversity and the need for common communication. The need for intercomprehension among various social groups and subgroups has been illustrated repeatedly in the history of Alabama, and that need has always been addressed, whether via Mobilian Jargon, Lingua Franca Creek, Popular French, Plantation Creole, Italian, German, Spanish, or English. Simultaneously, Alabama is clearly much richer and its history more compelling because of the striking linguistic diversity and complexity that have been the region's constant hallmark.

Table 2.1. Languages in Alabama: Speakers five years and older in 2000, 2008, and 2011

Language grouping	Language name	Number of speakers in 2000	Number of speakers in 2008	Number of speakers in 2011
Muskogean	Alabama	45	4	
	Choctaw	65	18	
	Muskogee	145	128	
Other North American Indian	Cherokee	270	269	
	Dakota (Northern)	85	59	
	Cheyenne (Northern)	—	19	
	Navaho (Southwestern)	55	33	
	Keres (Southwestern)	15	—	
	Amer. Indian (unspecified)	85	72	
Mexican, Central American and South American Indian	Mayan languages	250	509	
	Aztecan	—	18	
	Quechua		15	
English related	English	3,989,795	4,139,666	4,234,018
	Jamaican Creole	80	503	
	Pidgin	25	—	
Other Germanic	German	14,890	10,019	
	Pennsylvania Dutch	25	94	
	Yiddish	205	30	
	Dutch	690	230	
	Afrikaans	95	138	
	Swedish	220	155	
	Danish	110	90	
	Norwegian	90	275	
	Icelandic	45	—	
	Frisian	—	116	
Celtic	Irish Gaelic	65	56	
	Welsh	—	18	
French related	French	13,410	7,324	
	Patois	90	170	
	French Creole	240	714	
	Cajun	155	49	
Other Romance	Italian	2,160	1,502	
	Spanish	89,730	107,842	153,845

Language grouping	Language name	Number of speakers in 2000	Number of speakers in 2008	Number of speakers in 2011
	Portuguese	775	1,117	
	Romanian	325	617	
Hellenic	Greek	1,395	857	
Balto-Slavic	Russian	1,220	1,593	
(Eastern Europe)	Ukrainian	145	162	
	Polish	650	381	
	Czech	430	242	
	Slovak	80	85	
	Bulgarian	25	43	
	Serbo-Croatian	155	149	
	Croatian	95	258	
	Serbian	35	56	
	Macedonian	—	4	
	Lithuanian	65	18	
	Lettish (= Latvian)	50	51	
Other Eastern	Finnish	110	26	
European	Hungarian	185	163	
	Albanian	40	—	
Turkic	Turkish	420	929	
	Uyghur	—	23	
Central Asian	Armenian	135	—	
	Caucasian (unspecified)	—	333	
Indo-Iranian (Iran,	Farsi (= Persian)	965	1,147	
Pakistan, and North	Hindi	1,535	3,283	
and Central India)	Bengali	390	789	
	Panjabi	220	340	
	Marathi	55	239	
	Guajarati	1,055	767	
	Urdu	630	766	
	Nepali	115	85	
	Sindhi	35	—	
	Sinhalese	85	33	
	Oriya	—	45	
	Pashto	—	58	
	from India (unspecified)	330	586	

Continued on the next page

Table 2.1. *Continued*

Language grouping	Language name	Number of speakers in 2000	Number of speakers in 2008	Number of speakers in 2011
	from Pakistan (unspecified)	—	271	
	Romany (Gypsy)	20	28	
Dravidian (South India)	Telugu	725	1,112	
	Kannada	85	229	
	Tamil	310	486	
	Malayalam	150	124	
Chinese	Cantonese	175	305	
	Mandarin	230	1,089	
	Formosan	215	313	
	Chinese (unspecified)	4,655	5,264	
Other Far Eastern	Thai	815	970	
	Laotian	635	1,441	
	Hmong	—	28	
	Mon-Khmer, Cambodian	495	424	
	Burmese	—	43	
	Vietnamese	4,560	5,484	
	Japanese	2,200	3,043	
	Korean	4,030	4,546	
	Mongolian	—	3	
	Tungusic	—	40	
Polynesian	Somoan	95	232	
	Hawaiian	25	19	
Other Pacific Oceanic	Indonesian	190	83	
	Javanese	—	43	
	Malay	45	25	
	Tagalog	1,700	2,107	
	Bisayan	35	46	
	Cebuano	30	19	
	Ilocanao	—	22	
	Chamorro	115	130	
	Palauan	50	14	
	Melanesian	—	4	
Semitic	Arabic	2,620	3,930	
	Hebrew	410	422	
	Amharic	135	141	

Language grouping	Language name	Number of speakers in 2000	Number of speakers in 2008	Number of speakers in 2011
Other Afroasiatic	Berber	—	49	
	Chadic	—	13	
Bantu (Africa)	Swahili	700	632	
	Bantu (unspecified)	792	588	
Other African (Sub-Saharan)	Mande	95	21	
	Nilotic	—	13	
	Nubian	—	44	
	Sudanic (unspecified)	—	87	
	Fulani	35	70	
	Kru, Ibo, Yoruba	955	915	
	Efik	—	25	
	African (unspecified)	65	89	
Not specified		35	173	
All Indo-European languages combined other than English				35,826
All Asian and Pacific Island languages combined				37,389
All other languages combined				8,770

NOTES

1. Figures for 2000 come from the US Census. Figures for state language use are not derivable from the 2010 U.S. Census. Henceforth, the task of tracking language use has been delegated to the American Community Survey, which is the source for the 2008 and 2011 figures.

2. Language group labels do not appear in the original census tables and have been added here. Some of the language names used in the US Census are inexact and based on popular nomenclature rather than on accurate linguistic classifications. Labels for the combined language groups appearing at the end of the table were established by the American Community Survey.

3. The French Creole figure includes Haitians as well as transplants from Louisiana.

Sources: 2000 US Census and American Community Survey of the US Census Bureau

3

Southern American English in Alabama

Catherine Evans Davies

Almost everyone in the United States, Southerner or non-Southerner, knows that there is a Southern dialect and can probably mention a few hallmarks. But what exactly makes the variety we call Southern American English stand out from other varieties of American English? This article, intended for a nonspecialist audience, is designed to give a basic understanding of this variety, especially as it is spoken by Alabamians. As I hope to show, the range of features is much broader than just a few pronunciation differences and "funny words." The variety has a fascinating history, forged along with the nation and shaped by each epoch of national development. In fact, that history has left Alabama not with one Southern American English but with two subvarieties, one for North Alabama and another for South Alabama.

Our overview of the specific characteristics of Alabama's English looks at four key elements of language (vocabulary, accent, grammar, and discourse patterns and pragmatics). Also, we'll briefly consider how non-Southerners and Southerners alike feel about this variety and conclude with an overview of dialect and social changes in progress—how is Southern American English changing?

This essay also serves broader interests. Because it prepares you for the more detailed studies of Alabama English in this volume, you will be referred to those other articles at appropriate points. To conclude this essay, I offer a brief annotated list of works for further study, and I provide information on how you can participate in ongoing linguistic research; we need to document much more of the current state of Alabama English.

The core of this expanded and elaborated essay is a lecture that I have given about a dozen times around the state of Alabama since 2004, as part of the Road Scholars program of the Alabama Humanities Foundation. I have spoken in public libraries, at community colleges, at meetings of civic organizations in restaurants, and at club meetings in private homes. The purpose has been to foster an appreciative perspective on the history, current state, and future prospects of Southern American English in Alabama. I have included some discussion of differences between black and white speakers but have emphasized commonalities rather than differences.

Terminology

Ironically, linguists often confuse people through their use of language. Here are some key terms. *Linguistics* is the study of language as a phenomenon in itself. *Language* is a form of symbolic communication that is characteristic of human beings as a species. The term *linguist* in an everyday sense means someone who speaks more than one language, but as a technical term it means a scholar who studies language and languages. Academic linguists have traditionally analyzed language as a complex system with the following interrelated elements: the sounds of a language (*phonology*), the words or vocabulary of language and their meaning (*lexicon* and *semantics*), the grammatical and derivational endings and ordering of words (*morphology* and *syntax*, often lumped together as *grammar*), and the way people use language to accomplish their purposes (*pragmatics* and *discourse patterns*). An *individual language* (e.g., English) is a way of communicating used by a particular group; in many cases individual languages have become standardized over time with their own official grammar books and dictionaries. (Such grammar books normally do not explain all the workings of the standard language but tell the reader what NOT to do instead, weeding out features and structures of "nonstandard" varieties of the same language.) Every individual language includes a range of *dialects* or *varieties*; these include ways of speaking associated with particular social categories (e.g., gender, ethnicity), as well as with particular geographical regions (e.g., the American Southeast, New York City). In addition, all languages include *styles* of speaking associated with different levels of formality, from the most informal spoken context (chatting with close friends) to the most formal written context. Each person has, of course, a unique way of using language (sometimes referred to as an *idiolect*), incorporating elements associated with social categories, regionality, and formality. Most people modify their way of speaking to some extent, usually in relation to the level of formality in a particular context. Relatively few people (many of whom become actors) are able to shift varieties (i.e., to sound British rather than American, to shift in and out of a Southern accent, to sound like a man rather than a woman, etc.).

A Thumbnail Geography and History Lesson

Because we can't understand where we are without understanding where we've come from, let's begin with some historical context in terms of the early linguistic history of Alabama, including how geography shaped immigration patterns in Alabama. We will link contemporary linguistic traces in Southern American English in Alabama to the earliest known languages of the indigenous people in Alabama and to the earliest colonial empires. Then we will move forward in time to the formation of the United States to consider the linguistic effects of immigration patterns in Alabama.

Geography. Looking at the topographical map of Alabama in map 3.1, you can see that the northern half of the state is the end of the Appalachian mountain range, and the southern half of the state is generally an alluvial plain including the Black Belt, famous for its dark, rich soil. An important Native American settlement was

Map 3.1. Topographical map of Alabama (compiled by the Cartographic Research Lab, University of Alabama)

located just below Tuscaloosa on the Black Warrior River at present-day Mound-ville. The river system and the topography in general affected how Alabama was settled, with linguistic implications.

Indigenous People. The Native American civilization at Moundville flourished between 800 and 1200, representing ancestors of the present-day Choctaw. Other Native American languages spoken within Alabama were Creek and Cherokee. Even though most of the indigenous people were removed from the land, their words remain—ironically—as important place-names. The name of the state itself is a Native American word: Alabama, an Upper Creek tribe known to the French in 1702 as "Alibamons." The name is derived from Choctaw *alba*, "plants," "weeds," plus *amo*, "to trim," "to gather"—that is, "those who clear the land," or "thicket clearers" (Read 1937/1984). Other examples include the names of important cities like Tuscaloosa, from the Choctaw *tashka*, "warrior," and *lusa*, "black" (Read 1937/1984). In English we usually place the adjective in front of the noun (as in "black warrior"); notice that in Choctaw the adjective follows the noun, as in many other languages in the world.

Colonial Empires in Alabama. The territory of Alabama was first claimed as part of a colonial empire by Spain, when de Soto explored the area in 1540. We find no linguistic traces of that empire, because the Spanish were looking for gold rather than attempting to establish settlements. (The Spanish names of the towns of Gordo and Chula Vista are from a much later era.) The French, on the other hand, were interested in settlement and trade when they arrived in the early 1700s. They founded a settlement on the large bay in South Alabama, naming it for a nearby Native American tribe. Our local pronunciation of that name, Mobile, with the stress on the final syllable, represents a trace of French linguistic influence in contrast with typical English word stress patterns. I'm sure you've noticed that Americans from outside Alabama, when they first see that name, try to pronounce it with a stress on the first syllable. In 1763, at the conclusion of the French and Indian War, the territory passed to the British, where it stayed until the American Revolution.

American Settlement. Returning to the geography of Alabama, with the advent of American migration into the area, the northern and southern parts of the state were settled by different groups. The northern, more mountainous part of the state was settled mostly by Scots-Irish small farmers. They had originally migrated from Scotland to northern parts of Ireland in the early 1600s, and then migrated further to North America beginning in the 1700s. They came typically through the port of Philadelphia, and then southwest into the Appalachian Mountains of Tennessee and northern Alabama. The defeat of the Creeks at the Battle of Horseshoe Bend in 1814 opened up this land still further to settlement by European Americans. Southern Alabama, on the other hand, was settled by people who were in a position to buy land for cotton plantations on the rich alluvial plain. Many came from Tidewater Virginia or South Carolina and imported slave labor from West Africa through the Caribbean to work the plantations. As will be discussed in more detail below under *accent*, the pronunciation of the written letter *r* was different in northern and southern Alabama, based on these settlement patterns.

The presence in Alabama of a large number of African slaves—originally speakers of West African languages who encountered English as part of their servitude—has naturally led linguists to try to determine the possible impact of those native languages on the English of the slaves as part of the heritage of African American English. Another question, since groups of people tend to differentiate themselves by language, has been whether black and white Alabamians actually speak differently, and if so, how.

There has been substantial research on the language of African Americans, but virtually all of it has been conducted outside of Alabama. See Nunnally's introduction for a discussion of this research, and Johnson and Nunnally's essay for examples of features that are part of the repertoire of African American speakers and may be characteristic of Alabama (e.g., contractions that are not typical for white Southern speakers, a wider intonation range, auxiliary verb deletion). In some cases, however, the perception of difference between black and white speech may often be simply a question of greater frequency of the same feature (e.g., "g-dropping," or consonant cluster deletion). The classic construction that is given as characteristic of African American Vernacular English is the "invariant habitual BE," which according to Rickford and Rickford (2000, 113–14) "describes only an event that is performed regularly or habitually, as in 'He BE talkin' with his lady every day' in contrast with [the zero auxiliary in] 'He talkin' to her right now,'" which is used to describe an event taking place at the moment of speech. You can see the difference between "Mama sick" (right now) and "Mama be sick" (with a chronic condition). Wolfram (2007), however, convincingly shows that earlier sociolinguists' conceptions of African American English as a uniform variety lacking significant regional differences is inconsistent with research findings from rural African American communities. While the features discussed here are no doubt common in the speech varieties of many Alabama African Americans, we must be careful not to overgeneralize. An accurate description of Alabama's African American English varieties including their disparate and common features awaits a major research initiative (see the essay by Nunnally and Bailey for a pilot study of differences between speech features of African Americans in extreme North Alabama).

Interestingly, some features of African American Vernacular (informal) English that we often assume to be unique to that variety can also be found in British dialects (e.g., "habitual" BE, as in He be late = He's habitually late). Some dialectologists assumed, for this reason, that the Africans learned English from English speakers they had contact with, namely, speakers of vernacular British dialects who were the plantation overseers, and so on. Other linguists, looking at evidence from Gullah (the language of slaves and ex-slaves on islands off the coasts of South Carolina and Georgia), became convinced that the native West African languages of the slaves had influenced the first English of the slaves, in the same way that virtually all adults who learn a new language carry their native language over into the second language. An example of this is the simplification of the consonant clusters that are a characteristic of English, as in the pronunciation of "past" as "pass" and "cold" as "cole." It was assumed that these patterns had then been perpetuated within the slave communities, particularly since slaves were denied opportunities for education. Current thinking favors a combination of these two influences.

In terms of the relationship between the speech of black and white Alabamians, British travelers in the South during the antebellum period commented that the white women spoke like the black slaves. If there was any truth to this, it could be understood in terms of the upper-class women having been raised by black nannies, and then kept at home, whereas the young men were sent away to be educated. Currently, the thinking is that black and white Southerners share virtually all of the features of Southern American English, with just a few features unique to either group. For example, "remote time stressed *béen* [that is, BIN] to mark a state or action that began a long time ago and is still relevant" as in "You *béen* paid your dues a long time ago," may be unique to African American English (Wolfram/Schilling-Estes 2006, 214). What differentiates the two groups linguistically is actually the frequency of occurrence of features and the particular combination of features.

The migration of Southern blacks to Northern American cities at several points in the twentieth century brought Southern speech into other areas of the United States. In the minds of non-Southern Americans, this has led to the association of the way African Americans speak with ethnicity, that is, that it is "African American Vernacular English," whereas in fact it started out as a regional dialect, namely Southern American English.

Other groups have also settled in Alabama at different times during the past two centuries. Germans settled in Cullman in the nineteenth century and in Vance in the twentieth century in connection with the Mercedes plant. A group of French people settled in Demopolis in the nineteenth century. The Welsh came to the Birmingham area to mine coal. More recently Vietnamese fishermen settled on the Gulf, and Japanese and Koreans came to set up plants for Honda and Hyundai. In the late twentieth and early twenty-first centuries, many Spanish speakers came to Alabama to work in the chicken processing plants, the timber industry, and so on. There seems to be little in terms of linguistic influence from these groups, apart from the occasional place-name, like "Abernant" (just south of Birmingham on I-20/59), a Welsh word that means "mouth of the brook" (for a more in-depth look at the linguistic history of Alabama, see Picone's essay).

Now we turn to a point-by-point overview of the features that give Southern American English its own identity: its vocabulary, accent (pronunciation), grammar, and discourse patterns. Interestingly, recent scholarship has found it helpful to divide the development of Southern American English into two phases: the hundred years before the Civil War (i.e., approximately 1750 to 1850), and the post–Civil War Reconstruction period, significant for the development of a greater sense of regional identity within the United States. Each phase gave rise to distinguishing features of the variety, some older and some more recent (see Schneider 2003 and Nunnally and Bailey in this volume).

VOCABULARY (THE FORMS AND MEANINGS OF WORDS)

Inspired by an interest in settlement patterns in the United States, linguists ("dialectologists") tried to study the words that people used in different parts of the country. These "linguistic atlas" projects were initiated in the early part of the twentieth century. Linguists would conduct structured interviews (e.g., what do you call this item?) and plot their results on maps, showing where people used different words for the same item (like "pail" versus "bucket"). The typical interviewee for the first atlases was an older white male speaker who had lived in the same location since birth. Alabamians were interviewed for the Linguistic Atlas of the Gulf States (LAGS) between 1968 and 1983. The director of LAGS, Lee Pederson, expanded the linguistic value of this atlas by including interviews of nearly an equal number of women, a wider range of ages, people of color, and even urban dwellers (Pederson et al. 1981; Pederson, McDaniel, and Basset 1986; Pederson et al. 1986–1992). The LAGS data from the oldest interviewees provide a snapshot of language use at an earlier era and thus allow us to track language change. For example, a person eighty years old in 1970 in Tuscaloosa would have been born in 1890 and thus would have established patterns of speaking in the late nineteenth century.

The settlement pattern for European Americans in Alabama that we discussed earlier showed a clear difference in terms of vocabulary based on this data. A former colleague of mine at Alabama, Dr. Virginia Foscue, used pre-LAGS preliminary surveys to establish the boundary that follows the edge of the Appalachian plateau (see map 1.2 in Nunnally, "Exploring Language in Alabama"). Fifty years later there are still faint traces, as in the result when I ask middle-aged Alabama audiences how they refer to a tiny red insect that burrows into the skin and causes itching: members of the audience who grew up in North Alabama (N AL) say "chigger," whereas those who grew up in South Alabama (S AL) say "red bug." On the other hand, many differences found in Foscue's data seem to have faded with changes in technology and with the homogenization of culture. For example, bread that is baked with yeast is no longer called "loaf bread" (N AL) or "light bread" (S AL) but simply "bread." An invertebrate that lives in the soil and that you put on a hook for fishing is not called a "red worm" (N AL) or a "wiggler" (S AL) but simply a "worm" (unless you're a fisherman, for whom these words have taken on specialized meanings). The insect with a long straight tail and long straight double wings that hovers over water is called a "dragon fly" by almost everyone, with little trace of the earlier differentiation Foscue discovered between "snake doctor" (a name based on a folk belief that dragonflies take care of snakes) in North Alabama and "mosquito hawk" in South Alabama.

These words were from interviews with white Alabamians. Turning now to the influence of the African slaves on the vocabulary of both black and white Alabamians, I have selected three common words that are very poignant in terms of representing the lives of the slaves—they worked hard, they brought seeds of their own familiar vegetables and grew them to eat, and they created music as a way of coping with the difficult context of their lives. *Tote* is "probably from an English-based creole; akin to Gullah and Krio *tot* to carry, of Bantu origin; akin to Kikongo *-tota* to pick up, Kimbundu *-tuta* to carry," with "First Known Use: 1677" (http://www.merriam-webster.com). *Okra* derives from "a West African language, probably Igbo ọ́kụ̀rụ̀. Compare Akan ŋkrūmā, Twi ŋkrakra broth. In U.S. regional form *okry* with ending remodeled" (*Oxford English Dictionary*). *Banjo* is "probably akin to Kimbundu and Tshiluba *mbanza*, a plucked stringed instrument" (*American Heritage Dictionary*). Notice how all these words have become part of the vocabulary of American English. In particular, the "tote bag" has moved the word into the usage of the upper socioeconomic levels.

ACCENT

When people speak of a Southern accent, they are probably referring to some of the pronunciation variations discussed below. These phonological (sound-system) differences between Southern English and other varieties have been widely studied and continue to be a hot topic for linguistics.

"Rhoticity" (the pronunciation of an -r where it is written). In the classic old-style Southern accent that we hear in our Alabama storyteller Kathryn Tucker Windham, a written -r is turned into a vowel except when it occurs at the beginning of a syllable or after a consonant in a syllable. In the following list of words,

for example, the written -r in (1) *red* and (2) *grow* and (3) *around* is pronounced as -r while in (4) *far*, (5) *farm*, and (6) *ladder* it is pronounced as an "uh"-like vowel. (The name of this vowel sound is schwa, with the symbol [ə], and it is formed by the tongue in the middle of the mouth.)

A form of this accent is used to represent film versions of classic Southern characters in literature such as Scarlett O'Hara in *Gone with the Wind* and Blanche DuBois in *A Streetcar Named Desire*. This pronunciation of written -r is believed to come partly from the contact of the Southern plantation owner families with England after the American Revolution, as the r-less prestige accent in Britain developed. We saw a similar r-lessness in the upper-class accent of Northern American cities before World War II (e.g., Boston, New York), and it can still be heard in today's Boston accent.

At the same time that this nonrhotic (r-less) accent was influential in the southern part of Alabama, associated with plantation culture, the Scots-Irish in North Alabama were bringing their form of English with a strong rhoticity to that part of the state. This pronunciation of -r, which has become the typical American pronunciation, involves the following manipulations of the mouth and tongue: curl the tip of your tongue back, round your lips, and raise the back of your tongue. An even stronger form of this pronunciation, classic "pirate" pronunciation as in "ahoy, me hearrrties!" is associated with the Westcountry of England, and some dialectologists link it to the old Anglo-Saxon r pronunciation.

"Monophthongized [aɪ]" (turning a two-sounds vowel into a single-sound vowel). A pronunciation that has become a stereotype of a Southern speaker is what we call the monophthongization of [aɪ], with [aɪ] representing the sound for non-Southerners of the word "I." A non-Southerner begins this diphthong (two-part sound) with the tongue lying in the bottom of the mouth and the mouth slightly open, as when you say "ah." The tongue then moves forward and up to produce a sound like "ee," with the mouth closing a bit and the lips spreading. Thus the result is the combination of two sounds making one vowel (a diphthong). For the Southerner who "monophthongizes" this diphthong, the tongue does not glide up to the front into the "ee" sound, with the result that the pronunciation sounds like a single vowel (symbolized as [a:], with the colon showing the lengthening of the sound as compensation for the omitted "ee" where the non-Southerner would produce a diphthong. Thus "I" sounds more like "ah" (see Spence's essay for a short history of this monophthongization). Tom Nunnally, a native Alabamian and linguist, points out (personal communication) that the Southerner actually starts to say "I" and "ah" with the mouth and tongue in slightly different positions: for "I" (the [a:] sound) the jaw is not as far open, the lips are spread a bit, and the tongue is actually a bit farther forward in the mouth than for "ah" (symbolized by [ɑ], not [a:]). Thus monophthongizing Southerners easily distinguish between the words *sod* and *side* even with no tongue movement at all in *side*, as in "Put the sod [sɑd] on the other side [sa:d]." He also notes that it's unfortunate that our English spelling system has no accurate way to spell the [a:], aptly named the "Confederate a." English speakers have been aware of this characteristic of Southern speech for quite some time and have made negative judgments about it; Michael B. Montgomery documents lessons in schools in the South in the late nineteenth century when teachers tried to make students pronounce the phrase "fine white rice" with diphthongs (personal communication). Many Alabamians seem to make negative judgments about extreme forms of this pronunciation, which is associated with North Alabama and also with a "country" accent (see the essays by Doxsey and by Nunnally and Bailey).

Merger of Pen and Pin as "Pin". Almost as noticeable to non-Southerners as the [a:] pronunciation of [aɪ] is the pronunciation of –en to sound just like –in, so that *pen* and *pin* become homophones pronounced "pin." As Nunnally explains (personal communication), "This 'pin/pen merger' affects basically all words with an 'eh' [ɛ] before the nasal consonants -m and -n, producing homophonic pairs for *ten/tin*, *hem/him*, *Ben/bin*, and similar words. Although Southerners are oblivious to the sound distinction, Northerners who come South would be puzzled when told to pick up highway 'tin' or that a dress has a new 'him.' It took a few years of attention, but I now fairly consistently address my non-Southern students named *Jen* as 'jehn' instead of, to their ears, an alcoholic drink, a card game, or a machine for removing seeds from cotton bolls *(gin)*." Because of the stereotype, both Southerners and Northerners may mistakenly believe that Southerners merge these two vowels wherever they occur, but this is not true; Southerners pronounce the vowels in "non-nasal" words (e.g., led/lid) as distinct, the same way that non-Southern Americans would.

The Southern Vowel Shift. One of the most prominent sociolinguists, William Labov, has documented the Southern Vowel Shift using data from Birmingham and elsewhere in the South (Labov and Ash 1997). The following chart, using phonetic symbols, theme words, and the common reading-book names for the sounds, shows the key shifts, as these pairs of sounds are swapping places in their vocal production:

/i/ vowel in "field" (called "long e") ↔ /ɪ/ vowel in "filled" (called "short i")
/e/ vowel in "sale" (called "long a") ↔ /ɛ/ vowel in "sell" (called "short e")

To clarify what this would sound like, the switch between /i/ and /ɪ/ means that the word "field" as in "They were on the field" sounds like "filled." Conversely, the word "filled" in "They filled it to the top" sounds like "field." Moving down to the next pair of vowels that are switching places, /e/ and /ɛ/, the word "sale" in "There's a sale at the mall" sounds like "sell," and the word "sell" in "I can sell it to you for less" sounds like "sale." (Several essays in this volume add to this discussion of the Southern Vowel Shift. For a study of the inroads of this shift into the Huntsville area, see Allbritten; for the relationship of this shift to the Southern drawl, see Feagin; and for a more detailed look at the vowel changes, see appendix A.) If the idea of a vowel shift worries you, you should know that the vowel system of English has made significant movements in the past, in particular between the English of Chaucer in 1400 and the English of Shakespeare in 1600 (see Nunnally, "Exploring").

Other Alabama Sounds. I will briefly mention just two other distinctive pronunciations, both of which are dying out in the South. One is the pronunciation of words that begin with an alveolar stop (t, d, n) followed by a back vowel /u/ (the "long u" often spelled "oo") as if they had the sound of "y" at the beginning of "yard" inserted after the consonant and before the vowel. Examples are words such as *tune, duke,* and *news* being pronounced something like teeYOON, deeYOOK, and neeYOOZ.

The other is a special case of -r in words such as *term, first, word,* and *church.* The receding Southern (and Alabama) pronunciation is not the equivalent of the Brooklyn stereotype "boid" and "thoidy-thoid" but pronounced uh-ee, not oh-ee. This pronunciation, once associated with high social class and cultured speech in the South, is still retained by some generally older African American and white Alabamians, including former Lieutenant Governor Jim Folsom Jr., who pronounced *church* as "chuh-eech" in his political ads (Nunnally, personal communication).

GRAMMAR

In linguistic study, grammar does not refer to rules of correctness in writing ("don't use *ain't*") but to the internalized system of language processes that every speaker of every language has formed in acquiring that language. Grammar is the set of "traffic rules" of a language, such internal knowledge as how words fit together to form clauses and phrases, how grammatical meanings such as "plural" are added to words, and many other processes. We will consider a few Southern American English grammatical features that set it apart from some but not all other varieties. (For more on how linguists look at language, see Nunnally, "Exploring.")

A Southern Improvement to the Pronoun System. Just as the vowel system of English has changed over time, so has the pronoun system. In Shakespeare's time, what we refer to as "Early Modern English" had the following pronoun system:

	Singular	Plural
First person	I/me	we/us
Second person	thou/thee	ye/you
Third person	he/him; she/her; it	they/them

The *thou/thee* form was the second person form used in the singular, as in contemporary French *(tu),* Spanish *(tu),* and German *(du),* showing intimacy. For mysterious reasons, the *thou/thee* form was eliminated from the standard language; many of us know it now only through texts like the King James Bible, which was translated in the early 1600s. The subject pronoun *ye* was also dropped, leaving just one pronoun to express the second person, *you.* Thus in contemporary standard English we have the following pronoun system:

	Singular	Plural
First person	I/me	we/us
Second person	you	you
Third person	he/him; she/her; it	they/them

Responding to the problem of the lack of distinction between singular and plural, Southern English has produced a plural form, "y'all," which is a contraction of "you" + "all." Southerners use this form as a part of their speaking style even in relatively formal contexts but not in formal writing. Contemporary Southern English thus provides the following pronoun system:

	Singular	Plural
First person	I/me	we/us
Second person	you	y'all
Third person	he/him; she/her; it	they/them

Double Modals for Subtlety. The contemporary standard grammar of English allows only one "modal" verb, the "helping verbs" that indicate ability, possibility, or probability. Thus to add the idea of possibility or ability to a basic sentence such as "I go there Friday," a speaker would add one of the following verbs:

I can go there Friday.
I could go there Friday.
I may go there Friday.
I might go there Friday.

To add both possibility *and* ability to the sentence, the speaker must say, "I might be able to go there Friday."

Southern English, however, allows two modals to be stacked up for just such complex meanings. The most common are the following combinations, which typically occur in an informal speaking style:

I might could go there Friday.
I may can go there Friday.

At a recent Weight Watchers meeting in Tuscaloosa, the leader posed the following question: "What's something that you might can do to take your mind off of eating?" Again, this is a form that would not be used in formal writing, although Southern speakers may not be aware of this restriction until they encounter a teacher with a red pen.

Creative Use of Negation. Even though multiple negation is found in Shakespeare and other authors of classic works of English literature, the standardization movement that began in the eighteenth century outlawed double negation and tried to claim a mathematical basis for the ban ("two negatives make a positive"). Thus in contemporary standard English we find the following allowable patterns:

Positive sentence:
    I saw it.
Negative sentence:
    Early Modern English: I saw it not (now rare and archaic).

Modern English: I did not see it.
Single negation with polarity item:
I saw nothing like them/I didn't see anything like them.

Moving now outside the realm of the standard grammar books, and from the realm of written English into the domain of informal spoken English, we find the following patterns of negation:

Double negation:
I didn't see nothin' like them. (But formal standard English allows:
I saw something not unlike them.)
Triple negation:
I didn't see nothin' like them nowhere.
Pre-posed negation with "ain't":
I ain't seen nothin' like 'em nowhere.
Ain't seen nothin' like 'em nowhere.
Dreamland Barbeque:
"Ain't nothin' like 'em nowhere."

This last line is the slogan of the famous Tuscaloosa barbeque joint. As one of my Southern students commented, "Would you want to eat barbeque cooked by somebody who said, 'There is nothing like them anywhere'?" This use of multiple negation is not only emphatic, increasing its power with each additional layer, but also expressive in other complex ways. A famous quotation by Paul "Bear" Bryant, a University of Alabama football coach of legendary importance, is rendered in writing as, "I ain't never been nothin' but a winner." The University of Alabama has an official T-shirt with this slogan printed on it.

PRAGMATICS AND DISCOURSE PATTERNS

Now we have looked at vocabulary, accent, and grammar, but how do Alabamians bring these features together to go about the daily business of communicating? To answer this question, we turn to "discourse" and "pragmatics," newer areas of research that have to do with things like politeness, indirectness, and traditional storytelling. In other words, does Southern American English differ from other regional varieties of English in its pragmatic and discourse strategies?

Use of "Ma'am" and "Sir". A distinctively Southern language trait is the use of the address terms *Ma'am* and *Sir* to show respect. Alabamians may not feel as strongly about this as citizens of another Southern state (Louisiana), who passed a law requiring children to address their teachers in this way, but many Alabamians are raised to believe that they are not being polite if they do not use these terms. The usage is particularly prevalent in yes/no answers, which feel incomplete and impolite without a following *Ma'am* or *Sir*. Such beliefs may cause problems when Alabamians interact with speakers from other areas (non-Southern Americans, Canadians, British speakers) who have ways of showing politeness without using these terms, and who may in fact object to the terms as marking hierarchy too overtly.

Indirectness. Whereas politeness is signaled overtly and directly with an address term like *Sir* that shows deference, another way that Southerners express politeness is through indirectness. Such a strategy avoids confrontation and can be manifested in various ways. One way is to avoid getting directly to the point, talking around it to allow your interlocutor to figure out what you're getting at. Another is manifested in the grammatical system in the double modals discussed above: telling someone "You could do it this way" is somewhat tentative and not rude, but "You might could do it this way" is much more indirect and polite.

Storytelling Traditions. Research on oral storytelling in the United States outside of the South has identified a linear pattern in which the speaker is supposedly trying to make sure that the audience never feels compelled to ask, "What's the point?" In contrast, suggesting that there may be a different Southern aesthetic, Alabama's own professional storyteller the late Kathryn Tucker Windham proclaimed at a performance: "I'm a Southern storyteller; we digress." In such an aesthetic, which may be related to the idea of indirectness noted above, digression adds to the richness of the listener's experience, as the speaker feels free to provide elaboration in the absence of the imperative to move quickly to come to the point. (See Davies 2015 for more on these differing traditions, and see Brammer's essay for examples of how Alabama college students use their Southern dialect features rhetorically.)

THE PARADOX OF ATTITUDES TOWARD SOUTHERN ENGLISH IN ALABAMA

I am always struck in my classes at the University of Alabama by the range of attitudes about Southern American English and particularly by the complex ambivalence of my Alabamian students. On the one hand, they may be fiercely proud of Southern American English as spoken in Alabama, representing region, locality, family, heritage, and tradition. At the same time they make judgments about accents and grammar within Alabama, in particular judging negatively the extreme monophthongization of [aɪ] discussed above that is associated with North Alabama. Thus a "country" accent has less prestige than an urban accent. Some maintain their Alabama accents while grammatically adapting both their spoken and their written language to the formal prescriptive requirements of the university. Others become "bidialectal," speaking one way at the university and then realizing that when they go home they shift into the local accent and grammar. Still others, aware of the prejudice against Southern accents in the rest of the United States (where, unfortunately, because of the history of our nation and the lack of educational opportunities in the South, the accent may still be associated with ignorance and even racism) reject Southern English very vehemently. These are the students who strive to eradicate any evidence of Southern English in their speech and writing and whose career aspirations typically involve moving to another part of the country. (See Hasty, for a study of how students at Auburn University similarly view Southern English versus other regional US dialects; and Johnson and

Nunnally, for the account of how a young African American schoolteacher shifts her dialect according to her social and work roles.)

Linguistic Changes and Regional Identity

All language changes over time, including Southern American English, as we saw in regard to the Southern Vowel Shift above. Another change is an increase in "r-fullness" among younger speakers. Whereas the old-style Southern accent, particularly in the southern part of the state, was nonrhotic, as discussed above, it is clear that the pronunciation of r is changing in the younger generations. Interestingly, African American Vernacular English is the dialect that seems to maintain r-lessness. It is unclear why the increase in rhoticity among Southern speakers is happening, and some suggest the influence of the mass media that brings the general American r-pronunciation into every home with radio and television. My students at the University of Alabama, both white and black, representing an elite of educated young people from within the state, are almost uniformly rhotic. This may reflect their orientation to a national rather than a regional norm with respect to this aspect of language.

Shifting Populations within the United States and Patterns of Immigration

A significant demographic phenomenon of the early twentieth century was the migration of African Americans from the South to Northern cities, where their dialect became associated in the minds of non-Southerners with ethnicity, as noted above. Later in the twentieth century, and continuing into the twenty-first, we see the migration of African Americans back to the South. I have a colleague whose parents left Alabama for jobs in upstate New York in the mid-twentieth century, where they raised their family. Now they have retired back to the South as one of their sons has taken a professional job at a Southern university, where he will raise his family back in Alabama. He is, in fact, part of another trend, that of the movement of non-Southerners into the South as the economic center of gravity of the United States has shifted into the Sunbelt. Whereas these non-Southerners will adapt to Southern American English in some ways, for example adopting "y'all" as an improvement over the deficient standard pronoun paradigm, they will also have an impact on Southern English, in the natural process of dialect contact that is part of language change. We can also expect to see some influence from Spanish, as the number of people in Alabama who chose "Hispanic or Latino" on the census increased more than sevenfold between 1990 and 2010, from 24,629 to 185,602 (or 3.9 percent of the total population), and was projected for 2016 to reach 4.2 percent of the population (figures from the US Census Bureau). This is a very large increase compared to states outside of the South, although other Southern states have seen similar increases. Unlike the Spanish speakers of the early colonial empire, these speakers may stay and have an impact, even if it is not on the form of Southern American English as spoken in Alabama but rather on the number of

Alabamians who can also speak some Spanish (see Picone's essay for information on Spanish and other languages spoken in the state).

Opportunities to Participate in Linguistic Research

As you can see from this survey of features and will see from the other essays in this volume, Southern American English in Alabama is a complex and dynamic phenomenon that linguists and dialectologists need to document and study. With the development of technology in the form of digital recordings, we now have the possibility of capturing wonderful data and storing it in easily accessible forms. If you are interested in contributing to this developing database and being part of our ongoing research on Southern American English in Alabama, please contact us in the English Department at the University of Alabama.

Suggested Works for Further Study, with Annotations

In addition to the other essays in this volume, the following works will allow you to pursue this subject further on your own. (Also see appendix C for pertinent online sites.)

Algeo, John, ed. 2001. *The Cambridge History of the English Language, Vol. 6: English in North America*. Cambridge: Cambridge University Press. An authoritative treatment with information related to Alabama as part of the American South.

Bernstein, Cynthia, Thomas Nunnally, and Robin Sabino, eds. 1997. *Language Variety in the South Revisited*. Tuscaloosa: University of Alabama Press. (LAVIS II). A collection of articles by scholars in the field representing the state of the art in the 1990s.

Cassidy, Frederic G., and Joan Houston Hall, eds. 1985–2013. *Dictionary of American Regional English*. Cambridge, MA: Belknap. A fascinating resource in six large volumes that is the recognized authority on the subject. The DARE project is now expanding into digital form as well. See Montgomery's afterword in this volume for a list of words that are concentrated in Alabama.

Feagin, Crawford. 1979. *Variation and Change in Alabama English: A Sociolinguistic Study of the White Community*. Washington, DC: Georgetown University Press. A study of Anniston, Alabama, within a variationist sociolinguistic framework. A general reader would probably find this study too technical, but reading the introduction and conclusion would give a good sense of the findings and significance of the work.

Fischer, David Hackett. 1989. *Albion's Seed: Four British Folkways in America*. Oxford: Oxford University Press. A massive attempt to look at "cultural origins" by tracing four waves of migration from the British Isles to North America in the settlement of the United States. This volume is not recommended for linguistic information but rather for general cultural information. It has, however, been criticized for a too-simplistic view of culture.

Flanders, Stephen A. 1998. *Atlas of American Migration*. New York: Facts on File. A useful history of migration to North America using maps as illustrations.

Foscue, Virginia. 1971. *A Preliminary Survey of the Vocabulary of White Alabamians*. Publication of the American Dialect Society Number 56. Tuscaloosa: University of

Alabama Press. Results of a preliminary linguistic atlas approach to mapping the speech of Alabama, before the *Linguistic Atlas of the Gulf States*, that details major vocabulary differences between the northern and southern parts of the state.

———. 1989. *Place Names in Alabama*. Tuscaloosa: University of Alabama Press. The classic work that explains the origins of names and gives their pronunciation.

Lippi-Green, Rosina. 1997. *English with an Accent: Language, Ideology and Discrimination in the United States*. New York: Routledge. A book with a definite point of view about accent as a focus of discrimination, discussing prejudice toward the Southern accent.

McMillan, James B., and Michael B. Montgomery. 1989. *Annotated Bibliography of Southern American English*. Annotated listings of more than three thousand scholarly and popular treatments of Southern English covering the full range of linguistic areas from the earliest writings through works of the late 1980s. Updated and expanded ed. Tuscaloosa: University of Alabama Press.

Montgomery, Michael B., and Guy Bailey, eds. 1986. *Language Variety in The South: Perspectives in Black and White*. Tuscaloosa: University of Alabama Press. (LAVIS I) A collection of articles by scholars in the field representing the state of the art in the 1980s.

Montgomery, Michael B., and Ellen Johnson, eds. 2007. *Language*. Vol. 5 of *The New Encyclopedia of Southern Culture*. Chapel Hill: University of North Carolina Press. More than sixty wide-ranging entries on languages, language study, and language issues across the South, including indigenous languages. (Although the other volumes in *The New Encyclopedia of Southern Culture* do not address language specifically, all provide helpful context for language in Alabama and the South in general.)

Montgomery, Michael B., and Joseph S. Hall. 2004. *Dictionary of Smoky Mountain English*. Knoxville: University of Tennessee Press. A recent publication that applies to North Alabama as part of Appalachia.

Montgomery, Michael B., and Thomas E. Nunnally, eds. 1998. *From the Gulf States and Beyond: The Legacy of Lee Pederson and LAGS*. Tuscaloosa: University of Alabama Press. A collection of articles on the *Linguistic Atlas of the Gulf States*.

Nagle, Stephen J., and Sara L. Sanders, eds. 2003. *English in the Southern United States*. Cambridge: Cambridge University Press. A collection of essays by important scholars in the field, oriented to the general reader.

Picone, Michael B., and Catherine Evans Davies, eds. 2015. *Language Variety in the South: Historical and Contemporary Perspectives*. Tuscaloosa: University of Alabama Press. (LAVIS III) A collection of articles by scholars in the field representing the state of the art in the first decade of the twenty-first century.

Read, William A. 1937. *Indian Place Names in Alabama*. Tuscaloosa: University of Alabama Press. Repr. 1984. The classic work that demonstrates the influence of Alabama's aboriginal culture on many of the state's place-names.

Wolfram, Walt, and Natalie Schilling-Estes. 2006. *American English*. 2nd ed. New York: Blackwell. A popular textbook that I use in my dialectology class at the University of Alabama and that students describe as accessible and substantive. Chapter 7, "African American English," is not concerned with Alabama specifically but will greatly aid readers interested in learning more about the variety, especially the list of "some distinguishing features of vernacular African American English" (214–15).

4

Extreme North Alabama

CULTURAL COLLISIONS AND LINGUISTIC FALLOUT

Thomas E. Nunnally and Guy Bailey

PART 1

Other than Alabama's port city of Mobile, with its long and varied history and gradual growth since 1702, most of the rest of Alabama was settled by European-derived peoples in an extraordinarily short time, from the territorial period, starting in 1805, through the early decades of statehood before the Civil War (1861–1865). Also, two basically different kinds of new residents set the tone. Both the speed of the settlement and its prime participants sowed the seeds for a divided state culture. Alabama's history reveals a deep and enduring animosity between population segments of North Alabama and South Alabama that predates the Civil War and continues into modern times. This "sectional bitterness, this struggle between northern Alabama and southern Alabama for the control of the State" (Jack 1919, 85) is often cast as the yeoman farmer of North Alabama against the big planter of South Alabama (for an overview, see, for example, Hagood 2008).

While the north versus south sectionalism of Alabama is well-known, an examination of the earliest history of the territory and state also highlights a bitter struggle of the same competing cultures in the northern tiers of Alabama's current counties (see, for example, Jack 1919; Rogers et al. 1994; and Thornton 1978, 2007; for more on the settlement of the Southeast in general and Alabama, also see, e.g., Flynt 1989; Meinig 1993; Pillsbury 2006; and Pederson et al. 1986, 1:41–79). The earlier top-of-the-state battle for political and cultural supremacy involved the same four factors that fueled the more familiar sectionalism of North Alabama versus South Alabama: 1) the state's physical geography and land-use capabilities, 2) the "white gold" rush occasioned by King Cotton, 3) patterns of migration into newly opened territory, and 4) the cultural differences between groups of settlers. But unlike the statewide conflict, the struggle within North Alabama produced a victor, subsuming a once ascendant Lowland South culture of power and prestige within a second-wave Upland South, common-man culture. So complete was this victory that maps of the cultural geography of the South divide Alabama into distinct regions of Upland South and Lowland (Deep) South, as in map 4.1 (also see Wine-

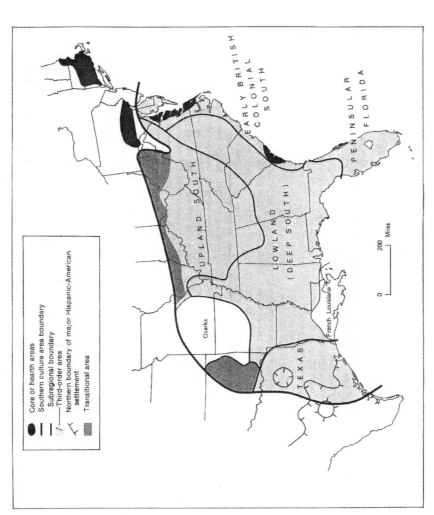

Map 4.1. LAGS map dividing Alabama into Upland and Lowland cultural areas (Pederson et al. 1986, 69, figure 23; used by permission of the University of Georgia Press)

miller 2008 and compare maps 1.1, 1.2, and 1.3 in Nunnally's essay in this volume for three slightly different demarcations based on various linguistic studies but still dividing the state into Upland South and Lowland South areas). The standard Upland versus Lowland cartographic division of the state, a tribute to the victory of Upland South culture, tends to obliterate the more complex history of North Alabama and its lasting effects that are our concern.

In addition to the work of historians noted above, language research reveals not only the general division of the state into North Alabama and South Alabama but also the early top-of-the-state conflict in the form of pronunciation and vocabulary differences. Documentation of the speech of North Alabamians undertaken between 1970 and 1980 and published between 1981 and 1992 by the Linguistic Atlas of the Gulf States (LAGS) shows that linguistic traces of the cultural conflict more than one hundred years earlier lingered in the ten northernmost Alabama counties, shock waves, as it were, that had rippled down through the generations.[1]

The genesis of this article, therefore, was not Alabama's larger and commonly noted north-versus-south history but dialect differences that seemed anomalous to it, suggesting the need for a closer look at regional history. A map published by LAGS in 1986 plots just a single difference in pronunciation that by itself complicates the division of Alabama into Upland South and Lowland South. The map in question shows the distribution of r-less speech and r-full speech across the whole eight-state area investigated by the LAGS project (Pederson et al. 1986: figure 24). (Map 4.2 below reproduces only a section of that map, to focus on Alabama.) Plotting of the LAGS data for pronunciation of *(y)ear(s)* (that is, the words *ear, ears, year,* or *years*) pictured an extremely important sound variation in the linguistic history of the South, perhaps the first accent feature used to distinguish Southerners, according to Stephenson (1977, 85): pronunciation of the -r sound as "uh" in certain sound environments, that is, *ears* pronounced as "ee-uhz."[2] Because the sound environment for this variation occurs when -r follows a vowel, the feature in question is called the postvocalic -r. Those who pronounce the postvocalic -r as "uh" (e.g., *ear* as "ee-uh") or delete it (farm as "fahm") are called r-less speakers (though of course they have -r in other locations, as in *red, hairy,* and *drab*), and those who give the full -r sound following a vocalic sound are called r-full speakers.[3]

An important subclass of r-lessness concerns nuclear -r, also called syllabic -r. It occurs when the "er" sound alone functions as the vowel of a stressed syllable and is followed by another consonant, as in *bird, learn, first,* and *perch.* Most postvocalically r-less speakers use the same "er" sound in these words as r-full speakers, that is, all say "brd," "lrn," "frst," and "prch." However, other r-less speakers, more so in the past, have pronounced nuclear -r as a diphthong (two-sound vowel), to produce "buh-eed," "luh-een," "fuh-eest" and "puh-eech" (see E. Thomas 2001, 49).[4]

One may say that ethnographically Alabama's settlement history from the early nineteenth century to at least the mid-twentieth century is written in its Rs. That is, whether a native Alabamian called the grower of crops a far-mer or a fah-muh told the tale of origin, regionally, socially, or both. That being the case, the Alabama data within the LAGS region-wide map of -r pronunciation called for a closer look at the

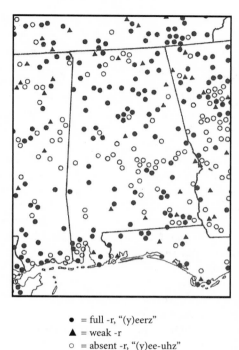

● = full -r, "(y)eerz"
▲ = weak -r
○ = absent -r, "(y)ee-uhz"

Map 4.2. Pronunciation of -r in *(y)ear(s)* by Alabama LAGS informants (detail from Pederson et al. 1986: 71, figure 24; used by permission of the University of Georgia Press)

LAGS findings. Map 4.2, an excerpt from the larger map, records the r-lessness or r-fullness of 131 LAGS informants from a pool of 176 interviewed throughout Alabama. In general, among the informants who were mapped, r-lessness was strong in South Alabama (clear circles and black triangles), especially in the physiographic area called the Black Belt. The feature's association with this fertile band of soil is to be expected, since it was largely r-less settlers from the Coastal South (Virginia, the Carolinas, Georgia) who possessed the capital and power to develop the antebellum "cotton kingdom." Along with their sophisticated culture and their slaves, they brought their version of English, the ancestor of Alabama's Lower South (or Plantation or Coastal or Deep South) variety of English, and as is usually the case, the dialect of the people with power and prestige became established as the region's vernacular standard (that is, the everyday speech variety as opposed to the written Standard).

In contrast, r-fullness was strong among the North Alabama informants (the black circles in map 4.2), also to be expected. The majority of North Alabama settlers hailed from the Upland or Inland South, especially middle and eastern Tennessee, and brought their own r-full version of English, the ancestor of Alabama's Inland or Upland Southern (also thought of as South Midland, Hills, or even Hillbilly English). We mention in passing that LAGS data amassed for Alabama as a whole confirm the north-south linguistic division, reflected in this instance by r-lessness and r-fullness in map 4.2 (see Fitts 1998 for a LAGS-based study of North Alabama versus South Alabama vocabulary, and see the essay by Davies in this volume for a summary of other main dialect features of Alabama, some state-wide and some regional). The question remains, however, why do people in various geographic regions tend to stick together linguistically to form clear dialect areas? For explanation, linguists propound a theory called the founder principle. As Mufwene explains:

> One cannot disregard the effect of the founder principle, according to which features of the variety developed by the founder population tend to become deeply entrenched in the speech of a community, subject to stochastic [i.e., random] events that have affected the community's evolution. The reason for this is what Wimsatt has named "generative entrenchment," according to which what came earlier has a better chance of establishing deeper roots in a system than what was adopted later. In the case of language, speakers are very accommodating. Dispersing individuals in a metapopulation find it easier to accommodate the locals in adopting their speech habits than to maintain their own traits. . . . In the vast majority of cases . . . colonial populations grew by moderate increments, so that immigrants' children born in a colony became native speakers of the local (emergent) vernacular and increased the number of its transmitters to later learners. As their parents died, while the population increased both by birth and immigration (and there were children among immigrants) the founder population's features became more and more deeply entrenched, even if overall the original system was gradually being restructured under the influence of newcomers. This scenario lends plausibility to Kurath's observation that the boundaries of American regional dialects, i.e., their regional distributions (consistent with Kretzschmar's observation that dialect areas lack clear boundaries), reflect the settlement patterns of the earliest successful colonists, although the dialects were no longer the same. (2003, 77; note that in this quotation and elsewhere in this essay, when research is cited within a quotation, we omit internal citation dates but not authors; see the quoted original for full bibliographical information)

The founder principle is explanatorily accurate for the state as a whole for whites, with the dominant settlers establishing Lowland Southern r-lessness to the south and Upland Southern r-fullness to the north. However, -r distribution in North Alabama in map 4.2 also discloses a pattern of variation within the northernmost ten counties: a distinct pocket of r-lessness within the r-full countryside.[5] More than 150 years after North Alabama's first white settlements, LAGS discovered and recorded culturally differentiating speech features such as r-lessness and others to be discussed below. Elite Coastal Southern settlers brought the seeds of these same dialect features to South Alabama, where they became part of the widespread vernacular standard. In North Alabama, however, r-lessness and the other features formed an isolated pocket highlighting a sectionalism within extreme North Alabama that predated the statewide divide.

Mufwene also explains the antithetical processes by which, we believe, North Alabama in general did not follow the founder principle to end up with the same dialect as the Black Belt: the overwhelming of the founders' culture by a competing culture, as discussed below. The usual scenario of entrenched founder population features will prevail "unless [new arrivals of a different speech variety] are numerous enough to overwhelm the current local population or are not (sufficiently) integrated in it. An overwhelming influx of colonists from backgrounds that are different from those of the founder population may account [for example] for the development of New England's English as different from the largely homogeneous East Anglian background of its founder population" (2003, 77).

While statewide pronunciation of postvocalic -r in general reflects linguistically the historically documented cultural and political sectionalism of the state (see map 4.2), an initial presence in North Alabama of a founding group of power-wielding, wealthy, wealth-developing, educated, class-conscious slave owners typifying Colonial Coastal South values would be expected to have created the linguistic scenario across North Alabama predicted by the founder principle, just as the same kind of settlers did, in fact, in South Alabama. An overwhelming influx of culturally distinct settlers who could prevent the usual operation of the founder principle is exactly what happened in the tumultuous early history of northern Alabama, circa 1802–1840, changing it into *North Alabama*, a region distinct from the southern counties. What the Upland settlers lacked in power and prestige, compared to the Coastal South white settlers, they made up for in sheer numbers, so that their variety of Southern English became North Alabama's vernacular standard. Even so, as we shall see below, the dialect of the original but outnumbered elite founders in North Alabama did persist within the distinct area of North Alabama r-lessness projected on map 4.2, suggesting the continued existence of more than one founder dialect.[6] (For the similar idea of competing, coexisting "prestige norms" within a community, see Dorian 1994.)

Our explication below of the LAGS findings demonstrates how cultural conflict has lingering linguistic consequences. This essay also looks beyond the LAGS research period to suggest how certain speech features are functioning in the twenty-first century to define and redefine social allegiances in Alabama.

The Context of Cultural Collision in Early North Alabama

Before we discuss linguistic findings, it will help to review the history of North Alabama in context. We start by considering a single technological advance of around 1800 that made the physiography of North Alabama (and of the South Alabama Black Belt a few decades later) vastly important and that largely created competing settlement patterns essential to understanding the state's speechways.

Eli Whitney: Inventor of the "Cotton Kingdom"

As often happens, technology initiated a new era, this time creating the social and historical context that brought large numbers of speakers of English to Alabama and other newly opening areas in the South (or "the old Southwest," as it was known at the time). When Eli Whitney invented the cotton gin in 1793, this simple mechanism made short-staple cotton a productive cash crop by allowing efficient removal of the fuzzy seeds trapped within the cotton fibers. Despite Whitney's efforts to retain production rights to his invention through patents, the cotton gin was soon fabricated and marketed at will throughout the South (see Phillips 2004 for a history of the invention and its spread).

As summarized from Bailey (1981, 2001), the emergence of short-staple cotton as a viable cash crop produced the following results:

- made plantation agriculture a viable economic system for much of the area south of a line marking the two-hundred-day growing season, extending from the South Carolina Piedmont to the Brazos Valley in Texas, and thus radically altered the geographic limits of slavery,
- created an insatiable desire for cotton-suitable land and thus became a driving force in the removal of Native Americans from those areas,
- ensured a rapid influx of English-speaking settlers into the Lower Mississippi Valley after 1803 (when the area was purchased from the French) and a revitalization of plantation agriculture and slavery there,
- provided the impetus, especially since the foreign slave trade was slated to become illegal in 1808, for a dramatic increase in the importation of slaves, something that would "re-Africanize" slavery in the Lower South, especially in the interior cotton lands, and
- led to the development of a massive domestic slave trade that exceeded even the foreign slave trade in the number of African-derived persons involved.

The magnitude of these developments and their impact on American culture (and more specifically on African American culture) is hard to overestimate. In the half century after 1790, plantation agriculture, with cotton as its cash crop, became solidly established throughout the Lower South from the South Carolina Piedmont to the Brazos River in Texas and as far north as west Tennessee in the Mississippi Valley (Bailey 1981, 2001). Cotton production in the South, which totaled only three thousand bales in 1790, increased to nearly 4 million bales in 1860 (Gray 1958, 1026), and slavery became the dominant mechanism for expanding the labor force throughout the Lower South. As summarized by "The Spread of Cotton and of Slavery 1790–1860," "Never before or since has a single commodity so dominated the American economy, and the vast majority of that commodity was being produced with slave labor" (1997). As for the impact on Alabama, of those 4 million bales in 1860, almost 1 million were produced in Alabama ("Alabama History Timeline," n.d.), and of the thirty-three states of the Union in 1860, Alabama ranked among the wealthiest top ten (Phillips and Roberts 2008), with the wealth concentrated in the hands of the plantation owners.

Instant Alabama

Once the wealth-producing potential of cotton was clear and the Native American lands of the Southeast had been taken over by the federal government and opened to settlement west of the first colonies (see essays by Picone, Davies, and Sabino in

Table 4.1. Alabama population growth by race, 1800–1860

Year	Total population	White (% of total population)	Black (% slaves versus free blacks)
1800	1,250	733 (59)	517 (95.6)
1810	9,046	6,422 (71)	2,624 (97.8)
1820	127,901	85,451 (67)	42,450 (98.7)
1830	309,527	190,406 (62)	119,121 (98.7)
1840	590,756	335,185 (57)	255,571 (99.2)
1850	771,623	426,514 (55)	345,109 (99.3)
1860	964,201	526,271 (55)	437,770 (99.4)

Source: US Census Bureau, internet release date: September 13, 2002

this volume), the desire to buy land for cotton cultivation created an "epidemic" called at the time "Alabama Fever" (see Keith 2011 and Meinig below). Between 1800 and 1860, a period of only sixty years, Alabama grew from a population of 1,250 non–Native Americans to almost a million, and in the most feverish decades, 1820 to 1840, the population doubled twice (see table 4.1).

For our investigation, it is crucial to note that before 1830 would-be cotton barons moving to Alabama headed not for the Black Belt but for the extremely fertile bottomlands of North Alabama's Tennessee River watershed, or Tennessee Valley. It was not until 1830 that methods were mastered for farming the sticky soil of the Black Belt to unleash its tremendous potential for cotton production (Abernethy 1922, 74). But wealthy plantation planters, who bought up the high-priced, best land in North Alabama, and their numerous enslaved workers were not the only ones flooding into the new territory and state. Historians tell us that "ownership of slaves was spread among a remarkably broad proportion of the white population" in the South (Olsen 2004, 417), that "numerous plantations [throughout Alabama] had fewer than 20 slaves working the land" (Vejnar 2008), and that "the typical Alabama slaveholder owned fewer than five slaves" (Hébert 2009); nevertheless, it may be inferred from table 4.1 that massive numbers of non-slave-holding white Alabamians were part of the mix. For example, using the populations of 1830 (309,527), if we concentrate the slave population (around 118,000 of the total black population) into groupings of the "typical" five owned slaves to provide 23,600 slave groups and the white population (190,406) into average family units of four to provide 47,600 white families, fewer than half the white families could have owned slaves. So, who were the non-slaving-owning settlers?

"Squires" and "Squatters"

For the first migrations to newly opened settlement areas (including Alabama, first as part of the Mississippi Territory from 1798, then as the Alabama Territory from 1817, and then as the twenty-second state from 1819) in the early nineteenth century, the impetus differed decisively for two important types of settlers. Those with little money, power, or social status were searching for cheap or squatter's rights land upon which to build a self-sufficient life. Those of wealth and prestigious backgrounds, as we have seen, were seeking to buy and develop plantations to create riches with the new wonder crop, short-staple cotton, using slaves to provide the intense labor. Meinig's sweeping description of the settlement of the Gulf captures the desire and energy driving both the wealthy Southeast coastal planters and the opportunity-starved Inland and Upland South poor from out of their "hearth areas" and transient holding areas (see map 4.1) and into new lands for new opportunities:

> As for expansions in the Old Southwest, there was a steady extension and thickening of settlement in Kentucky and Tennessee, states that grew by 342,000 in the first decade of the [nineteenth] century. There were no federal lands in these two states (and western Tennessee was not open to colonists until 1818), and the first new thrust of the advancing frontier in this general area was southward out of Middle Tennessee into what was to become Alabama Territory, where the federal government had opened a land office in Huntsville to peddle the tract lying north of the great southerly swing of the Tennessee River. . . .
>
> . . . A broad belt of land reaching from the Tennessee River on the north to Mobile Bay was wrested from the [Native American tribes]. In March 1817, the Territory of Alabama was created; in August the first lands of the Creek Cession were put up for sale at Milledgeville[, Georgia]; by November a North Carolina planter reported that "the Alabama Feaver [*sic*] rages here with great violence and has *carried off* vast numbers of our citizens."
>
> . . . All the while, however, many kinds of country less attractive to commercial speculation [for cotton production, etc.]—the sandy and gravelly soils of the flatwoods and piney hills, the heaviest canebrakes and swamplands, the rougher hills and districts remote from the main roads and waterways—were being occupied in common Southern backwoods fashion by stockmen-hunters. Drifting out of all the older settlement regions, such people infiltrated every district and spread restlessly and relentlessly across the entire Gulf South from the Carolinas deep into Texas. Creating loose clusters of kith and kin, such pioneers supported themselves on their cattle and hogs, patch farming and kitchen gardens, hunting, fishing, and trading, with only occasional connection with the rapidly extending commercial world. (1993, 231–32, 234)

Flynt picks up the settlement story as it relates specifically to Alabama and the politics of its divided citizenry:

> The acquisition of land, which dominated the thoughts of most early settlers, also established the broad contours of Alabama politics. From the first settlement patterns in the Tennessee Valley, divisions arose between planters with mainly Georgia connections and small farmers generally of Tennessee ori-

gins. The key to election was at first mainly rhetorical: to convince the plain folk of one's genuine claim to be a common man in a state with universal [white male] suffrage. But as politicians sought substantive issues on which to launch careers, they early fixed on the issue of land. Their position on land—the extinction of [Native American tribes'] claims, preemption rights for squatters, reduction of land prices and minimum acres per purchase, the graduation of land prices according to the quality of soil—became the litmus test of their Jacksonian rhetoric.

Expressed in class terms, resentment of the rich and fear of corporate wealth became important themes in antebellum Alabama history. Democrats sought to identify Whigs with "commercial elements" who warred against farmers. The public issue became "the supremacy of the rich over the poor," despite the fact that Alabama Whiggery seldom espoused elitist views. Within the legislature this ideological class dispute took the form of poorer elements favoring reduced taxes and biennial sessions of the legislature while opposing aid for internal improvements or state charters for banks or railroads. Common whites also opposed expansion of women's rights, prohibition, or increased expenditures for education and mental health. Their tax policy was to levy the highest rates on slaves [i.e., taxing the owner of the slave on the slave as property], with land a lesser source of tax revenue. Secondary taxes should be levied on the ostentatious symbols of wealth: gold watches, private libraries, race horses, and the like. Thanks to the legislative successes of common whites, the wealthiest one-third of Alabama's population paid two-thirds of the taxes. Despite their influence on tax legislation, the single consistent thread running through the tapestry of common white ideology was opposition to laws that would concentrate more power in government. They justifiably believed that strong government was more likely to respond to the special interests of planters.

Insofar as land and public policy were debated, poor whites and yeomen shared a common outlook. The economic mobility of the Alabama frontier was so great, the social structure so fluid, that this year's squatter could easily become next year's landowning yeoman. Yeomen and poor whites worshiped in the same churches, crafted the same white-oak baskets, told the same tales, plucked the same dulcimer or banjo tunes, danced the same jigs, and fought the same politicians.

However limited their formal educations might be, poor whites had a profound understanding of their own self-interest. They also had a fierce class consciousness that even casual observers noticed. Antebellum travelers commented on the frequency with which they observed ostracism based on a reversal of social status: most Alabamians disdained wealth and education. (1989, 6–7)

As for the settlement of North Alabama specifically, it may be true that the predominant origin for settlers (1815–1828) to upper Alabama counties was Tennessee while South Carolina, North Carolina, Virginia, and Georgia immigrants predominated as settlers for the rest of the state (Abernethy 1922, 27–32; Rogers et al. 1994, 67). But the explanation for the linguistic island of Lowland Southern r-lessness (see map 4.2 above) and other speech features documented for North Alabama informants by LAGS lies in a more detailed history of the area.

In strong contrast to North Alabama's mainly Tennessean "squatters" were the "squires," wealthy planters or their sons of the Colonial South who bought up the best lands, sometimes at surprisingly high prices, and established plantations. Most prominent were a group of Virginian relatives and associates, many being veterans of the Revolutionary War, who moved first to the Broad River area in Georgia (thus they are called the Broad River Group, Thornton 2007) and afterward bought lands and started plantations in the Tennessee Valley. These prosperous, well-connected planters turned the squatter's would-be land of promise into a land of privilege. Into the most fertile bottomlands of North Alabama marched the social order of the original southern colonies' plantations, re-energized by now easily ginned short-staple cotton to feed the textile industry both in the United States and abroad. The squires' dreams of wealth brought a two-fold doom to the aspirations of Upland South pioneers: political shenanigans, such as in 1817 having the office for land auctions in the Tennessee Valley placed in Milledgeville, Georgia, out of reach of North Alabama's Tennessean homesteaders (Rogers et al. 1994, 61); and land speculation itself, raising prices to the extent that squatters could not afford their own homesteads.

From Hunt's Spring to Twickenham to Huntsville

In the thick of things during the earliest period of expansion into what would later become North Alabama was Madison County. Created in 1808 as a county in the Mississippi Territory, it thus preceded Alabama's territorial status by a decade. Between 1802 and 1808, before the county's creation, white squatters from Tennessee were illegally homesteading the lands still recognized federally as belonging to Native American tribes (Lewis 2007), but by 1809, Native American lands were ceded, settlement was legitimate, and as Meinig stated above, Huntsville was available for a federal land office to oversee initial sales of lands in the Tennessee Valley.

Ironically, one squatter who had "his" land bought out from under him was John Hunt, after whom Huntsville is named. Hunt, coming down from Tennessee in 1805, was the first white person to settle at the Big Spring (a lagoon now part of Huntsville) and founded the village of Hunt's Spring. When in 1808 Hunt left his homestead and returned to Tennessee to bring his family to Alabama, another settler bought his Alabama squatter holdings, including for $1000 the village of Hunt's Spring. In 1809, the one thousand acres of Hunt's Spring were resold for $23,000, twenty-three times the original purchase price, to wealthy LeRoy Pope, a Revolutionary War veteran from Virginia and member of the Broad River Group. Pope laid out a town and had it named Twickenham after the home of English poet Alexander Pope, with whom he claimed ancestral links. The name did not sit well with most settlers and was legislatively changed to Huntsville in 1811 in honor of the dispossessed Hunt (Owen 1921: Vol. 1, Schmidt 2009). But Pope continued to exert great control as a judge, as founder and president of the Huntsville Bank, and as owner of a large plantation with many slaves (Owen 1921: Vol. 4).

In Madison County, Pope and his compatriots created an Alabama outpost of the aristocratic South with deep roots in the culture of George Washington and Thomas Jefferson but built on slave labor to an even greater degree (see Anne Royall's letters, 1830, depicting a contemporary view of Huntsville in 1817–18 and 1821–22). Though sneeringly identified as the "Royal Party" by political foes who claimed to be "champions of the common [white] man," these planters were still able to hold political sway from 1810 to 1820 in the Tennessee Valley (Rogers et al. 1994, 54–66). Aristocratic Southern cultures also developed in surrounding cotton-sustaining counties, especially Limestone, where Athens, the county seat founded in 1818, "quickly became a prosperous antebellum agricultural center," created the state's first institute of higher education, and produced three early governors of Alabama (Schmidt 2010). No areas, however, were as powerful as Huntsville and Madison County. Even so, as Rogers et al. explain, though wealthy "planters dominated the social and financial life of the area, . . . the vast majority of landowners in Madison County were small farmers from Tennessee. The ingredients for class conflict were in place from the beginning" (1994, 66).

Although the successful production of cotton certainly gave North Alabama statewide political clout during the first decades of the 1800s, by 1840 Alabama's Black Belt counties were approaching parity with those of North Alabama. By 1850 the Black Belt had surpassed the Tennessee Valley in both product and density of production. By 1860, on the eve of secession, Alabama's Black Belt production was overwhelming. The Black Belt counties maintained their unadulterated plantation system and political power until secession, but as the decades wore on in North Alabama, its cotton-rich counties—Lauderdale, Limestone, Madison, upper Franklin (now Colbert), Lawrence, and Morgan—faced political realities of Jacksonian democracy and a populous white yeoman citizenry that forced compromise.[7] The original "Old South" power base of North Alabama was overwhelmed by Upland Southern encroachment.

As the Black Belt plantations from the 1830s onward began to outstrip North Alabama's cotton frontier, class conflict became less ferocious across the northern counties, while the state evolved its enduring pattern of North Alabama versus South Alabama. In response to the growing power of South Alabama, self-preservation of North Alabama autonomy became more important than a divisive preservation of the Deep South enclave in the cotton counties. A detente, as it were, developed across upper North Alabama and Madison County. According to Jack, "To a very marked extent, the owners of slaves in the few 'cotton counties' in the Tennessee Valley gradually aligned themselves with the predominant element, politically speaking, in the northern section, despite their differences in economic and social position" (1919, 32). When Alabama experienced an economic depression in 1837, the detente held. Dupre explains,

Madison County may have participated in the larger national stories of politics and war in 1836, but it was a bit removed from the tumult and excitement sparked by the prosperity of that period. Its citizens, of course, enjoyed the rising cotton prices during the flush times of the mid-1830s, but the bustling scenes being played out daily in Alabama's Black Belt of land offices crowded with eager farmers and speculators anxious to stake their claims lay far in their past. That detachment from the speculative fevers of the boom proved a blessing when the flush times came to an end, destroyed by the plummeting cotton prices and specie suspension of the Panic of 1837. Almost twenty years earlier, the collapse of the first cotton boom had plunged Madison County into economic and political crisis, polarizing the community. In contrast, the citizens of the county responded to the Panic of 1837 with relative equanimity. Distance from the traumas of settlement and connections to the institutions and identities of the larger society muted conflict in 1837, preventing a replay of the divisiveness of the 1820s. (1997, 239)

However, the detente did not lead to class homogeneity nor, as LAGS discovered, one predominating set of dialect features such as r-fullness or r-lessness across the whole region. A deeper look at the land itself and its later history is necessary to understand why.

North Alabama's Three Enduring Population Groups in Geographical and Social Context

Concerning the influence of physiography on Alabama's culture, one may say without serious overstatement that the land itself recruited the two main types of immigrants discussed above (although the third major group, people of African descent, were brought not of their own volition). Flynt remarks, "The configuration of the culture . . . is determined, some would even say deterministically determined, by the soil zones, the geology, the natural resources of Alabama" (2005). Alabama's terrain, the ground under one's feet, influenced the where and the who of settlement and thus the original zones of conflicting cultures.

A physiographic formation named the Highland Rim covers much of the seven western counties within the ten-county Tennessee Valley area of Alabama.[8] To understand its relationship to antebellum settlement by Uplanders and Lowlanders (and the numerous African-derived slaves brought by force), we must turn to agronomy. The Highland Rim, besides serving as a physiographic name for a section of Alabama, is also a term in agronomy. For agronomists, the term *highland rim* designates a soil type, a grayish, rather infertile topsoil (grayland) starting in Tennessee and running down into Alabama's Tennessee Valley. Rather confusingly because of the terminology, it was not grayland highland rim topsoil in Alabama's Highland Rim section that attracted the wealthy or would-be wealthy cotton plantation founders but another soil predominating in the area, a reddish topsoil (redland), that reached amazing depths of twenty to thirty feet. The high fertility of redland topsoil and its depth as a stay against the effects of monoculture and erosion created Alabama's first cotton kingdom decades before the fertile riches of the Black Belt and its easier transport of cotton through the state's river systems were

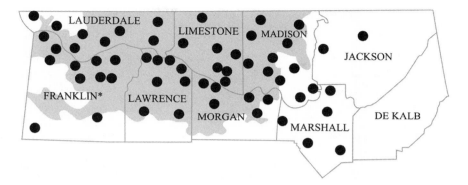

Map 4.3. Alabama's ten northernmost counties, the Highland Rim physiographic region (shaded), and cotton production in 1840 (2,000 bales per dot). Map created by University of Alabama Cartography Laboratory from a state map of counties; from "General Physiography" produced by the Department of Geography, University of Alabama; and from Hilliard 1984, 67
*Franklin County included Colbert County until 1867, when the original county's cotton-rich north was separated into Colbert County

mastered and exploited (details of agronomy courtesy of Charles Mitchell, Extension Specialist and Professor of Agronomy and Soils, Auburn University, personal communication).[9]

Map 4.3 is a composite of three types of information: Alabama's northern tier of counties before the Civil War, the Highland Rim physiographical section containing the redland topsoil, and antebellum cotton production of 1840 (based on Hilliard 1984, 67). The counties we examine are, from west to east, Lauderdale, Limestone, Madison, and Jackson, across the top, and the next row down, Franklin (divided into Colbert and Franklin in 1867), Lawrence, Morgan, Marshall, and DeKalb. The shaded area within these counties is the Highland Rim physiographic section consisting of rivers and creeks and the tremendously fertile redland soil. The sections outside the shaded area are, for the most part, much less fertile, more prone to topsoil erosion, and rocky and mountainous, the kind of land Meinig, in the quotation above, associated with settlement by stockmen-hunters. Finally, the dots represent cotton production for the year 1840, each dot representing two thousand bales of cotton.

What we refer to as the *cotton corridor* for this essay is essentially the physiographic Highland Rim, where cotton production was concentrated. It includes six of the ten counties we are investigating: Lauderdale, Limestone, Madison, Colbert (the upper half of Franklin in map 4.3), Lawrence, and Morgan. Three other counties, Jackson, DeKalb, and Marshall, are part of the Cumberland Plateau physiographic section of Alabama, while the tenth county, Franklin (of which Colbert was part until Reconstruction politics split off the new county), is a mixture of the Highland Rim, the Cumberland Plateau, and the very top of the East Gulf Coastal

Lauderdale 1850: 35% 1970: 11%		Limestone 1850: 49% 1970: 17%	Madison 1850: 55% 1970: 15%	Jackson 1850: 16.6% 1970: 5%	
Colbert (Franklin divided in 1867) 1880: 43% 1970: 17%	Lawrence 1850: 45% 1970: 19%	Morgan 1850: 35% 1970: 9%	Marshall 1850: 10% 1970: 2%	DeKalb 1850: 6% 1970: 2%	
Franklin 1850: 42% 1880: 12% 1970: 5%					
Marion 1850: 12% 1970: 3%	Winston 1850: 4% 1970: 1%	Cullman (created in 1877) 1880: 1% 1970: 1%	Blount 1850: 6% 1970: 2%	Etowah (created in 1866) 1880: 16% 1970: 14%	Cherokee 1850: 12% 1970: 9%

Map 4.4. African American percentage of total population for ten uppermost Alabama counties (Tennessee Valley) and six counties to the south (source of census numbers from Pederson et al. 1986, 161–68)

Plain. But all the ten counties are part of the Tennessee Valley. Except for a fertile spot or two between ranges of hills in Jackson and other counties, the dots on map 4.3 closely follow both the Tennessee River and its feeders and the contours of the redland soil.

The 1840 cotton production within the Highland Rim (dots on map 4.3) outlines the distinct cotton corridor barely twenty years after Alabama's statehood (1819) and less than thirty years after LeRoy Pope and other wealthy Broad River Group members imported the plantation system to the newly opened eastern part of the Mississippi Territory. The dots also correlate strongly, as would be expected, with the distribution of slaves bought and brought in to produce the cotton. Map 4.4, placing the counties into block form for ease of presentation, provides percentages of African Americans in the populations of our ten counties and, for comparison, of the six counties in the next row down (also see maps 33 and 34 in Hilliard [1984, 32] and the module "The Spread of Cotton and of Slavery, 1790–1860" [1997]). The map provides ethnic ratios from early census years and from 1970 (the decade of the LAGS research). The early census percentages of African-derived slaves in the cotton-rich counties (Lauderdale, Limestone, Madison, Franklin-Colbert, Lawrence, and Morgan) approach the ratio of 50 percent or more found in the Black Belt counties in South Alabama. But the Upper Alabama and Lower Alabama African American populations were separated not only by the oppression of slavery but also by a row of counties where slavery was far from the norm (including Franklin, after Colbert was created).

Of particular interest is Franklin County; map 4.3 includes both Franklin

County to the south and Colbert County (created in 1867) to the north and map 4.4 is divided into these two counties. The great difference in cotton production between the northern and southern portions of the original Franklin County marks out its Highland Rim (redland) land area from other physiographic types of land (a finger of the Cumberland Plateau and small intrusions of the East Gulf Coastal Plain). This north-south difference betokens the same settlement patterns, land usability, ethnic ratios, and cultural differences that differentiated Jackson and Madison Counties from the beginning. When the county divided into Franklin and Colbert in 1867, the division merely codified clear physiographic and demographic divisions and the resulting culture clash from settlement by Upland South and Lowland South populations (see map 4.5 below). It also left the newly carved-out county, Colbert, with a much larger percentage of now-freed but hardly free African Americans in the population, 43 percent versus Franklin's 12 percent, as reflected in the 1880 census.

Where the redland topsoil ran deep (map 4.3), so would a Lowland Southern English spoken by whites and their multitudes of African-derived slaves. Conversely, the Upland South settlers with dialect features distinct from Lowland Southern dialect features generally resided outside the cotton corridor. Furthermore, as the white planters of one culture and the white yeoman and poor whites of another grew their crops and created their different worlds across North Alabama, they also embossed their Lowland versus Upland cultural differences upon the countryside. Jordan-Bychkov's study (2003) of Upland South cultural artifacts illuminates the impact of the Deep South cotton corridor within a largely Upland South settlement area by showing how Upland-Southern culture-artifact creation was stymied in the cotton-corridor counties. Map 4.5 (mapping the counties in block form) excerpts data from Jordan-Bychkov's larger map of the Southeast. It depicts degrees of Upland Southernness based on what he terms "five greater artifacts in the cultural landscape" (2003, 84). In map 4.5 the counties containing the cotton corridor (in map 4.3, the greater density of dots), especially Limestone, again stand out as different from the more Upland South counties, especially Jackson, with their greater density of these artifacts. Jordan-Bychkov cautions readers "not to take [his] cartographic synthesis too literally" because of variables in the size of counties from state to state and "spotty" fieldwork; he presents his map as only suggestive. In the context of our study, however, his findings become compelling, added to the cotton corridor, African American population, and, of course, the linguistic variation documented in the discussion to follow (for another view of the area, see Dunaway 2003, but note that Dunaway concentrates only on Appalachia as an area, without differentiating between the cultures of settlement).

The Conserving Power of Mythos: the "Lost Cause"

An intriguing question is why the Deep South culture implanted in North Alabama survived after the political consolidation and cultural detente from the 1830s on. Such survival seems even less probable considering the fact that North Alabama was largely against secession. For example, Winston County, just south of

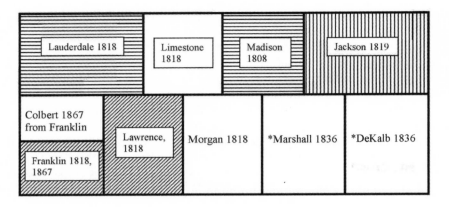

Map grid pattern	Score for presence of the five Upland South artifacts	North Alabama counties by artifact rates
	0 to 1 artifact	Colbert, Limestone, Morgan
	2 artifacts	Lauderdale, Madison
	3 artifacts	Franklin, Lawrence
	4 artifacts	Jackson
N/A	5 artifacts	N/A to counties in the area

*It is unclear from the source whether Marshall and DeKalb were examined for Upland-South artifacts. As part of the Cumberland Plateau region extending from Tennessee through Jackson County into Alabama, settlement by Upland South Tennesseans would be probable but could not have occurred in the early period of settlement, as was the case for the other counties. Both Marshall and DeKalb were founded in 1836 from lands ceded by the Cherokee, 95 percent of whom were forcefully removed to Oklahoma in 1838 by President Andrew Jackson (see essays by Picone and Sabino in this volume).

Map 4.5. Block format map of Upland-South artifact rates in Alabama counties of the Tennessee Valley (adapted from Jordan-Bychkov 2003). Presence of "five greater artifacts in the cultural landscape: [1] half-dovetail log notching, [2] the dogtrot log dwelling and open-runway double-crib barn, [3] the transverse-crib barn, [4] the 'Shelbyville' courthouse square, and [5] the graveshed" (Jordan-Bychkov 2003, 84)

our ten-county area (see map 4.4), proclaimed itself the "Free State of Winston" in 1861 and threatened to secede from Alabama. The state's overall north-south sectionalism and hostility that steadily developed in the early decades of Alabama's existence hardened even further after the fall of the Confederacy, in 1865. As Rogers et al. explain:

> [Most of] . . . the planter and professional classes who supported secession and war . . . had lost heavily, not simply in money and property but in the status of leadership. They were the authors of misery, the leaders who had

failed. . . . Another group from the old ruling class whose material fortunes suffered just as much faced a different future. They were the conservatives of 1860, men of wealth and position who opposed secession but supported the Confederacy with varying degrees of loyalty and drive. They had a better claim to preferment on the relative scale of loyalty to the Union. Yet few of them could have taken the "iron-clad" oath required of federal officeholders.

Like their leaders, the rank and file of white Alabamians split along the lines of ideology and interest. The majority [had been] swept up in the course of events and willingly or under coercion supported the Confederacy. Many, particularly from the hill counties of North Alabama, opposed the war, evaded conscription, or deserted from the army. . . . If there were Confederates bitter in defeat, the Alabama Unionists were a group bitter in victory—and hopeful of righting the wrongs they had suffered during the fighting. (227)

State sectionalism was further strengthened after Reconstruction when the Black Belt planter class and allied business leaders of South Alabama were able to reassert political hegemony (resulting in the state's repressive constitution of 1901— see Rogers et al. 1994, 343–54), largely disenfranchising poor whites and African Americans. Such a return to power was not the case for the once supreme cotton kings of North Alabama, whose preeminence had eroded long before the war. Instead, though subsumed in the Upland South culture politically, North Alabama's Old South aristocracy created a psychological reality to live within, in concert with other originally plantation-based communities across the Deep South: the ideology of the Lost Cause. As summarized by Cox (2008), the Lost Cause refers to

a conservative movement in the postwar South that was steeped in the agrarian traditions of the Old South and that complicated efforts to create a "New South." For diehard believers in the Lost Cause, the term *New South* was repugnant and implied that there was something wrong with the values and traditions of the antebellum past. For individuals devoted to the idea of the Lost Cause, the Old South still served as a model for race relations (blacks should be deferential to whites as under slavery), gender roles (women should be deferential to their fathers, brothers, and husbands), and class interactions (poor whites should defer to wealthier whites). Moreover, individuals believed that the Confederacy, which sought to preserve the southern way of life, should be respected and its heroes, as well as its heroines, should be revered.

This ideology was key to the development of a distinct white Southern identity for the defeated Confederates. Robert Penn Warren, Pulitzer Prize–winning author and cofounder of the Southern Agrarian writers group, famously wrote, "We may say that only at the moment when Lee handed Grant his sword was the Confederacy born; or to state matters another way, in the moment of death the Confederacy entered upon its immortality" (1961, 15). As is the case when honoring any immortalized dead thing, it required looking backward, not forward, and the

devotees repudiated change, especially change that would align them with the kill-
ers, in this case, the victorious Northern states. As Cobb explains, "Traditionally,
'identity' has been defined as the condition of being simultaneously both 'one's
self . . . *and not another.*' Typically, the creation of any sort of group identity . . . has
required . . . a 'negative reference point,' against which it may be defined in stark
and favorable contrast" (2005, 3).

For white North Alabamians with Deep South roots, antebellum pride of place
and assumption of status remained, creating what may be termed a psychological
enclave that would preserve Deep South culture. In North Alabama, Huntsville
again led the way. As Stephens explains in her history of the city, "Like Southerners
in general, Huntsvillians found defeat galling and Reconstruction repulsive. . . . The
pain of it all lent to thoughts of a happier past a greater comfort than they perhaps
warranted. Within a year, nostalgia had taken the form of mass hypnosis. The major social event of 1866 was a jousting spectacle" (1984, 60). We might ask, what better celebration of Deep South chivalry, defeated by Northern savagery, than for the
white upper classes to identify it with the glories of mythic Celtic Camelot before
it fell to the barbarous onslaughts of the Anglo-Saxons? Stephens continues, "Like
the kudzu plant, this romanticization of the past was to spread rapidly, smother-
ing out fresh air, light, and new growth, wrapping the South in a protective man-
tle of folklore" (1984, 60–61; for an account of how Huntsville transformed into the
vibrant "Rocket City" of today and linguistic consequences of that change, see the
essay by Allbritten in this volume).

As we have seen, Stephen's "the South" means only the upper-class whites identifying with the Deep South, not North Alabama's yeoman and poor-white contin-
gencies of Upland South origin, and especially not the now-freed African Americans. It may seem puzzling that African Americans were not welcomed as allies by
the excluded lower classes of white populations. The historical reality is that while
much of North Alabama yeomanry was indeed against secession, it was decid-
edly not antislavery. According to Thornton (1978, especially 204–27), the antebellum yeoman farmer strongly favored slavery for self-interest just as firmly as the
self-interested capitalistic cotton planters did for the cheap labor enabling profitable cotton monoculture. Along with the yeomanry, the so-called poor whites also
supported slavery (for a complete history, see Flynt 1989). The nonplanters considered slavery their hedge against peonage to the wealthy. Without slaves to produce cotton, the nonwealthy whites could easily become enthralled as workers to
the wealthy (the sharecropping system, often called "virtual slavery," that developed
after the Civil War fulfilled this prophetic fear). Suspicion of and hostility toward
freed African Americans by whites after the Civil War was an unfortunate reality
in non-cotton-corridor counties—witness the infamous Scottsboro Boys trial in
Jackson County (for a history of Alabama's regrettable but undeniable white su-
premacist past, see Novkov 2007).

To summarize, when North Alabama's Tennessee Valley was opened to settlement in the early 1800s, a blend of fertile and nonfertile soil resulted in land-pricing
policies that created settlement patterns responsible for cultural and ethnic demographics unique to the state. Geographical and social influences—the North

Alabama conflict of white Upland South and Lowland South settlers during the earliest territorial and state periods—worked against the development of a homogeneous culture and toward the retention of internalized codes of separate identities. Even after a necèssary, politically expedient detente developed between the culturally separated white populations in response to the challenge of South Alabama's Black Belt power base, separate Upland and Lowland Southern cultural affinities continued to strengthen because of the patterns of land ownership, the accompanying traditional cultural differences of the two settlement groups, and, after the Civil War, the mythos of the Lost Cause. Freed African Americans and their descendants, living under the strictures of legal segregation, also continued a separate cultural existence, experiencing only tangential contact with the other groups. Evidencing these early, conflicting patterns are footprints of cultural artifacts and linguistic vestiges. The language of these three groups, as usually prevails, reflected these exclusionary categories. The general language principle at work here, aptly summarized by Downes, is that "linguistic traits are the result of real face-to-face contact, not the standard norms experienced in school or the mass media" (1998, 173–74). Furthermore, as linguistic research has constantly affirmed, differences in language patterns function to denote solidarity with some and dissociation from others. In our ten-county area, such linguistic badges of membership were passed down from three groups, two white and one African American, to each new generation of language learners, so that more than one hundred years later LAGS research of the 1970s through the early 1980s detected the linguistic effects of the settlement history.

PART 2

The Linguistic Landscape

Commenting on the cultural meaning of language differences, Wolfram and Schilling-Estes highlight two interconnected areas, namely, linguistic features themselves and their contexts: "We can only ascribe social meaning to the patterns of covariance between dialect variables and social variables as we understand the sociohistorical background, the interactions, the ideologies, and the identities that define the local social context of dialect" (1996, 107). In the earlier part of this essay, we added another dimension in that we have also considered the geography underlying, literally lying under, the "local social context." Now that we have surveyed upper-North Alabama's sociohistory and physiography, we move on to reviewing major dialect features that play out against this historical and cultural background in terms of "interactions," "ideologies," and "identities." We begin by considering salient features of Lowland (Deep South, Coastal, or Plantation) Southern English within a framework of language change to better understand that dialect's evolution across the South. Next we present LAGS findings for features that reflect vestiges of Lowland Southern English stranded within North Alabama's Upland Southern boundaries: four pronunciations and two combined vocabulary choices. A generation has passed since the LAGS surveys recorded these findings, so we conclude this study by branching out to examine current linguistic momentum in the area and in the state.

Two Lowland Southern Dialects: Traditional and New

Though it is tempting to think of Lowland Southern English as having been static since its importation to Alabama during settlement two hundred years ago, research into language history and variation suggests that Lowland South speech has changed quite a bit since the Civil War. Based on his and others' research, Schneider proposes two forms of Lowland Southern English: Traditional and New (2003, 17–35). As defined by Schneider, Traditional Lowland Southern is "associated with the antebellum, rural plantation culture of the Old South and its related value system."[10] New Lowland Southern, on the other hand, is "the product of late nineteenth-century and early twentieth-century developments which are also embodied in the sociocultural catch phrase of the 'New South,' associated, amongst other things, with urbanization, industrialization, in-migration, and a characterization of the region as the 'sunbelt' of the United States. . . . New [Lowland] Southern is found predominantly among the young and among urban dwellers" (34).

As native baby boomers who grew up in relatively urban environments (Bailey in Montgomery and Nunnally in Tuscaloosa), both authors acquired speech that exhibits the New South features while lacking the Traditional features except Traditional [ju] "eeOO" in some words like *Duke* and *tune*. But other Traditional Lowland Southern features are not far distant from Nunnally or Bailey. On his mother's side, Nunnally is just two generations removed from overwhelming r-lessness. His maternal grandparents were rural Black Belt farmers in Sumter County and fully r-less, including pronouncing "nuclear -r," the stand-alone "er" in words like *term, learn, first, bird,* and so on, as an "uh-ee" diphthong ("buh-eed" for *bird*). Nunnally vividly remembers his maw-maw's glowering "Don't dispute my wuh-eed [*word*]" when as a child he questioned her authority. Nunnally's mother, when a young woman, had moved to more urban-oriented Tuscaloosa and worked in a doctor's office, a far cry from the cotton fields of Kinterbish near the Mississippi border. She acquired r-fullness in accommodating to her new environment and friends and married a North Alabama r-full speaker. She replaced r-less productions with -r's in most postvocalic -r words, but remained r-less in "plah-uhz" for *pliers*, "begguh lice" for *beggar lice* (tick-trefoil), "pahluh" (the formal sitting room) for *parlor*, and "bobbed wire" for *barbed wire*. She acquired the nuclear -r (stand-alone "er" sound) in *church* and *first* but retained the diphthong "uh-ee" in "puh-eech" for *perch*. In each case the lexical items (words) that stayed r-less were terms of lower frequency in everyday speech (the "parlor," for example, being replaced by the "living room" in most home schemes) and therefore not as subject to pressure to conform to an r-full pronunciation. These seldom-used words passed under the radar, so to speak, of Mrs. Nunnally's socially motivated self-monitoring as her dialect gradually changed, mostly unconsciously, to reflect a more urban and urbane Tuscaloosa identity within her new professional and social networks. Of her six siblings, two others also became r-full: her brother who joined the Air Force and a sister who also moved to Tuscaloosa and became a registered nurse. Her four other siblings, who remained in the West Alabama Black Belt, retained their r-less speech.

Table 4.2. Features of Traditional and New Lowland Southern English, based on Schneider (2003, 34)

Lowland-Southern English feature (features in **bold** examined in LAGS data for this essay)	Traditional (antebellum, recessive in postbellum period)	New (postbellum diffusion)
Postvocalic R-lessness (e.g., *farmer* as "fahmuh")	YES	NO
/j/ retention (e.g., *tune* as "tee-OON" [tjun])	YES	NO
Intrusive R (e.g., "warsh" for *wash*)	YES	NO
-s ending for 3rd person PLURAL present tense (e.g., "some folks says")	YES	NO
a- onset before verbal –ing (e.g., "a-walking")	YES	NO
Loss of /j/ before /u/ (e.g., *tune* as "toon" [tun])	NO	YES
Merger of /ɛ/ and /ɪ/ to [ɪ] before nasals (e.g., *ten* and *tin* both pronounced as "tihn" [tɪn])	NO	YES
Monophthongization of [aɪ] in certain phonetic environments (e.g., *ride* pronounced as "rahd" [ra:d] but *right* NOT pronounced as "raht" [rat])	NO	YES
Southern drawl (vowel breaking, e.g., kit as "keeyuht" [kiət])	NO	YES
Pronoun *yall*	NO	YES
Verbal aspectual *fixin to* (e.g., "I'm fixin to [about to] take a walk.")	NO	YES

Nunnally himself pronounced *perch* with a nuclear -r and *pliers* with a postvocalic -r like his fully r-full father, but acquired the words "pahluh," "begguh lice," and "bobbed wire" with the r-less pronunciations of his mother. He pronounced these words r-lessly well into adulthood, unaware of these Black Belt vestiges before they were pointed out to him. Similarly, Bailey's parents and grandparents were partially r-less, especially when /r/ followed back vowels and occurred in unstressed syllables (*farmer* as "fahmuh"). Bailey is also just two generations removed from his grandparents' use of third person plural, present tense verbal -s and of a-prefixing of verbs (see table 4.2). Thus the authors' personal linguistic histories show the progression of Traditional Lowland Southern English to New Lowland Southern English features within their own families.

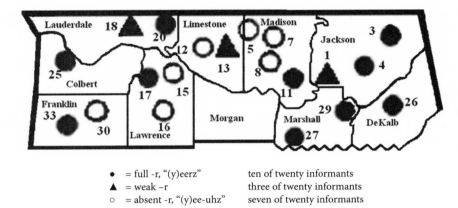

• = full -r, "(y)eerz"   ten of twenty informants
▲ = weak –r   three of twenty informants
○ = absent -r, "(y)ee-uhz"   seven of twenty informants

Map 4.6. Magnified detail from map 4.2, late-twentieth-century r-fullness and r-lessness in *(y)ears*, LAGS North Alabama Primary informants, overlaid with informant numbers and counties (N = 20)

Probing Deeper with LAGS Publications

Returning to our starting point of -r pronunciation, map 4.6 (an enlarged excerpt adapted from map 4.2 above) presents the northernmost ten-county area of Alabama from the LAGS map of r-lessness or r-fullness in *(y)ear(s)* marked with the r-full or r-less status of twenty LAGS informants. We have overlaid the LAGS map of informant responses with the counties and included informant numbers assigned for this investigation. A comparison of map 4.6 with map 4.3 above associates r-lessness (the clear circles) with the cotton corridor of North Alabama's history and physiography. At the most general level, map 4.6 clearly implies that the early settlers whose histories we surveyed above implanted two main varieties of Southern English into upper North Alabama and that reflexes of these Englishes continued side by side for well over one hundred years. The postvocalic r-lessness (i.e., pronouncing *year* as "yee-uh") documented by LAGS is a major hallmark of Lowland Southern English and is especially associated with the old plantation culture of Alabama's Black Belt. In other words, the Upland South Tennessee settlers, numerically dominant in settling the area, did not bring this highly salient non–Upland Southern English linguistic feature with them, but neither could their r-full Upland Southern dialect erase its presence by the 1980s, presumably because of the influences of solidarity and social distancing among the r-less minority as discussed above. R-less speakers apparently felt no compulsion to accommodate to the r-fullness of the majority.

LAGS Data: Stage Two

Though provocative, map 4.6 (adapted from *LAGS* vol. 1, 1986) presents only a fraction of what *LAGS* volumes four through seven reveal about North Alabama's competing Englishes. Explaining their quest to make the gigantic LAGS database usable, Pederson and Leas remark, "Failure to bring the facts of an investigation to the surface prevents a reader from understanding the implications of the data base and the substance of the materials from which the generalizations are drawn" (1981, 20). To present a major portion of the facts to readers, LAGS took advantage of then-current computer technology in the 1980s to create a program named the graphic plotter grid for automated map production. The grid situates each of the 914 Primary LAGS informants by his or her unique alphanumeric location, and each "matrix" map in *LAGS* volume 4 (regional matrix maps, 1990) and volume 6 (social matrix maps, 1991) reports the responses of the Primary informants for linguistic features selected for their revelatory power. Through the unambiguous plotting of each Primary informant's responses, each dot on each map ultimately leads the researcher directly back to a particular informant's taped interview and the transcriber's notes (Pederson et al. 1989: ix–xxiii; Pederson 1993).

Map 4.7 presents the 914 Primary informants plotted on the graphic plotter grid. Though topographical dimensions of the grid are not precisely accurate, they generally approximate the shape of the LAGS eight-state area. For ease of reference, we have outlined the areas of the LAGS grid corresponding to Upper Alabama (letter *F*s), Lower Alabama (letter *G*s), and Gulf Alabama (a portion of letter *H*s). The Upper Alabama sector (letter *F*s) comprises fifty-three Primary informants, with thirty-nine of these informants located within LAGS Land Region A4, the Highland Ridge and Cumberland Plateau regions of Alabama. Of these thirty-nine, twenty informants lie within the ten-county area of our investigation, as shown on maps 4.3 and 4.6.

To illustrate the LAGS graphic plotter grid's efficiency in projecting information, we plot the responses from map 4.6 for r-lessness or r-fullness in *(y)ear(s)* into a grid of the Upper Alabama sector (letter *F*s) outlined in map 4.7.[11] Thereby, map 4.8 reproduces the symbols and locations of map 4.6 within the grid-coordinate squares of map 4.7, along with each informant's county, the number we assigned each informant for this study, and his or her LAGS identifying number. The equidistant spacing and linear placement of informants necessary to create the graphic plotter grid for the LAGS matrix maps, as explained above, allowed an approximation of the upper Alabama counties but led to minor distortions in their actual topography within the fertile cotton corridor (see map 4.3). Thus, the clustering of r-lessness/weak -r diluted somewhat from its projection on map 4.6. (We present a more accurate topography in block-format maps later in this study.) However, the clustering is still robust. Map 4.8 clarifies one basis of the clustering by revealing the role of ethnicity in creating the island of r-lessness in Upland Alabama. Five of the seven r-less speakers are African Americans.

But the pattern also raises questions. Why is a sixth African American, in Jackson County, not fully r-less like the African Americans in the other counties? Why are two white r-less informants in the cluster, if the feature appears to be predominately an African American feature? Each layer of LAGS data presented below helps answer these questions, as we add more Lowland Southern English features to r-lessness and then increase the pool of informants by including fourteen LAGS Secondary informants from our ten-county area.

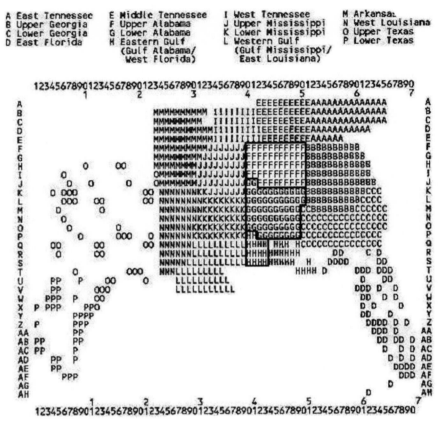

Map 4.7. The LAGS "graphic plotter grid" placing 914 Primary informants on a Gulf States approximation, with Upper, Lower, and Gulf Alabama outlined (Pederson et al. 1990: xix, with Alabama boundaries overlaid; used by permission of the University of Georgia Press)

LAGS Micro-Mosaics of Extreme North Alabama

In general, the linguistic features recorded in LAGS materials indicate that Upland Southern English prevails in the Upper Alabama sector (the sector of outlined *F*s in map 4.7), but as in the pronunciation of -r in *(y)ear(s)* in map 4.2, the twenty Primary informants in the ten northernmost counties complicate the Upland Southern English pattern. The speech data of some of them reveal Lowland Southern English traces presumably left over from North Alabama's settlement history. Maps 4.9a through 4.9f draw from *LAGS* volumes 4–7 to plot five such features on the graphic plotter grid for the ten counties: four pronunciations from Schneider's list in table 4.2 above (with -r pronunciation subdivided into postvocalic -r and nuclear -r) and one combination of vocabulary items that LAGS determined to be regional markers of the Interior (Upland) South versus the Coastal (Lowland) South.[12] Map 4.9f summarizes the five findings. We have placed maps 4.9a through 4.9e in descending order of responses that reveal Lowland Southern English influence, as follows:

40	41	42	43	44	45	46	47	48	49	50	
Colbert Inf 25 IS 351 •	Lauderdale Inf 18 IS 349 ▲	Lauderdale Inf 20 IS 350 •	Limestone Inf 12* IS 344 ○	Limestone Inf 13 IS 345 ▲	Madison Inf 7 IS 341 ○	Madison Inf 5* IS 340 ○	Madison Inf 8 IS 342 •	Jackson Inf 1* IS 337 ▲	Jackson Inf 4 IS 339 •	Jackson Inf 3 IS 338 •	F
N/A* [Marion]	Franklin Inf 33 IS 365 •	Franklin Inf 30* IS 364 ○	Lawrence Inf 17 IS 348 •	Lawrence Inf 15* IS 346 ○	Lawrence Inf 16* IS 347 ○	N/A [Winston]	Madison Inf 11 IS 343 •	N/A [Cullman]	Marshall Inf 29 IS 354 •	DeKalb Inf 26 IS 352 •	G
N/A [Marion]	N/A [Winston]	N/A [Winston]	N/A [Walker]	N/A [Jefferson]	N/A [Jefferson]	N/A* [Jefferson]	N/A [Blount]	N/A [Blount]	Marshall Inf 27 IS 353 •	N/A [Cherokee]	H
n/a B2 [Fayette]	n/a D2 [Pickens]	n/a B2 [Tuscaloosa]	n/a B2 [Tuscaloosa]	N/A* [Jefferson]	N/A [Jefferson]	N/A [Jefferson]	N/A [St. Clair]	N/A [Etowah]	N/A [Etowah]	n/a* B2 [Calhoun]	I
	n/a* B2 [Tuscaloosa]	n/a B2 [Tuscaloosa]	n/a B2 [Shelby]	n/a B2 [Shelby]	n/a B2 [Talladega]	n/a B2 [Talladega]	n/a B2 [Talladega]	n/a* B2 [Calhoun]	n/a B2 [Calhoun]		J

Map Legend

• = full -r, "(y)eer(z)"   ten of twenty informants, zero of six AA, ten of fourteen white

▲ = weak –r   three of twenty informants, one of six AA, two of fourteen white

○ = absent -r, "(y)ee-uh(z)"   seven of twenty informants, five of six AA, two of fourteen white

F–J = north to south coordinates

40–50 = west to east coordinates, e.g., F/50 is informant #3, located in Jackson County

Inf = our renumbered designation of informants included in this study

IS = Idiolect Synopsis (discussed below) and Protocol number of LAGS informants included in this study

N/A = Coordinate square for LAGS Upper-Alabama Primary informant in Land Region A4 not included in this study (squares are located in Land Region A4 unless otherwise noted)

n/a B2 or n/a D2 = Coordinate square for LAGS Upper-Alabama Primary informant in Land Regions B2 or D2 not analyzed for this study

[] = county of location for informants not included in this study

* within shaded block = African American Primary informant included in this study

* within unshaded block = African American Primary informant in Upper Alabama LAGS sector among informants not included in this study

Note: LAGS Upper Alabama–sector counties Morgan (one of the ten counties of our investigation, see map 4.6), Lamar, and Cleburne, having no LAGS primary informants, are not represented on this LAGS grid map. LAGS Secondary informants for Morgan County and the other counties in our ten-county area are included in our analysis farther on.

Map 4.8. R-fullness or r-lessness in *(y)ear(s)* of the twenty Primary LAGS informants in Alabama's ten northernmost counties (LAGS Land Region A4 unless otherwise noted), a recasting of map 4.6 into the LAGS matrix map grid coordinates (outlined section of letter Fs in map 4.7) with additional information

Map 4.9a, Terms for *earthworm* and *green beans*, fifteen of twenty are Lowland responses.

Map 4.9b, Merger of [ε] in *ten* and [ɪ] in *tin*, fourteen of twenty are Lowland responses (**applicable to this region of Alabama only**).[13]

Map 4.9c, R-fullness and r-lessness in *ear*, eleven of twenty are Lowland responses.

Map 4.9d, Non-smoothing of [aɪ] in *right*, ten of twenty are Lowland responses.

Map 4.9e, Nuclear -r in *church* pronounced as "uh-ee," five of twenty are Lowland responses.

Maps 4.9a–4.9f share the following legend identifiers in common:

F–H = north to south coordinates

40–50 = west to east coordinates, e.g., F/50 is informant #3, located in Jackson County

Inf = our renumbered designation of LAGS informants included in this study

* within shaded block = African American Primary LAGS informant

L = Lowland Southern English feature (with modifications explained as needed in the maps below)

U = Upland Southern English feature (with modifications explained as needed in the maps below)

(Note: Morgan County, with no Primary informant, is not represented on these grid maps)

40	41	42	43	44	45	46	47	48	49	50	
Colbert Inf 25 U	Lauderdale Inf 18 L	Lauderdale Inf 20 U	Limestone Inf 12* L+	Limestone Inf 13 L	Madison Inf 7 L+	Madison Inf 5* L+	Madison Inf 8 L	Jackson Inf 1* U	Jackson Inf 4 U	Jackson Inf 3 U	F
	Franklin Inf 33 L	Franklin Inf 30* L	Lawrence Inf 17 L	Lawrence Inf 15* L	Lawrence Inf 16* L+		Madison Inf 11 L+		Marshall Inf 29 L	DeKalb Inf 26 L	G
									Marshall Inf 27 L		H

U = Upland Southern influence, lack of Lowland Southern lexical influence, Upland term *red worm* and term other than Lowland term *snap beans*, five of twenty, one of six AA

L = Weak Lowland Southern influence, evidence of Lowland Southern lexical influence, Lowland term *snap beans* OR term other than Upland term *red worm*, ten of twenty, two of six AA, eight of twenty white

L+ = Strong Lowland Southern influence, Lowland term *snap beans* AND term other than Upland term *red worm*, five of twenty, three of six AA, two of twenty white

L and L+ Total: Fifteen of twenty, five of six AA, ten of twenty white

Note: The importance of vocabulary items as a marker of influence in our ten-county area is supported by the strongly Upland responses of the eleven Primary informants in the row of six counties to the south, Marion, Winston, Cullman, Blount, Etowah, and Cherokee: eight Us, three Ls, and no L+.

Map 4.9a. Upland Southern and non–Upland Southern terms for *earthworm* and *green beans*.

Each map exhibits a pattern similar to map 4.8 above, with clustering of "L" (Lowland Southern English) forms mainly within the cotton corridor and of "U" (Upland Southern English) forms mainly outside it (see map 4.3). The concentration is certainly strengthened by the five African American informants in the old Plantation South counties, yet as in map 4.8, non-African Americans also reflect strong Lowland Southern influence. In the summary map 4.9f, while no white informant matches the five Ls scored by four out of five African Americans in the cotton corridor, two white informants accumulate scores of four features, informant #13 (F/44) in Limestone and informant #8 (F/47) in Madison Counties. For these two white speakers in the most important counties of the cotton-corridor plantation era, linguistic influence from Alabama's first cotton kingdom appears to have

40	41	42	43	44	45	46	47	48	49	50	
Colbert Inf 25 L	Lauderdale Inf 18 U	Lauderdale Inf 20 L	Limestone Inf 12* L	Limestone Inf 13 L	Madison Inf 7 U	Madison Inf 5* L	Madison Inf 8 L	Jackson Inf 1* L	Jackson Inf 4 U	Jackson Inf 3 L	F
	Franklin Inf 33 U	Franklin Inf 30* L	Lawrence Inf 17 U	Lawrence Inf 15* L	Lawrence Inf 16* L		Madison Inf 11 L		Marshall Inf 29 U	DeKalb Inf 26 L	G
									Marshall Inf 27 L		H

U = *ten* and *tin* distinct, "eh" [ɛ] and "ih" [ɪ] not merged, six of twenty, zero of six AA, six of fourteen white

L = *ten* and *tin* sound alike, "eh" [ɛ] and "ih" [ɪ] merged, fourteen of twenty, six of six AA, eight of fourteen white

Note: Across the LAGS eight-state area *in general*, the symbols U for Upland Southern (unmerged [ɛ] and [ɪ] before nasals) and L for Lowland Southern in this map would mischaracterize the merger as a marker of Lowland-Southern English, because merger of [ɛ] and [ɪ] before nasals occurs frequently in both Upland and Lowland Southern English in the LAGS data. Nevertheless, it developed local significance as a group marker in these counties. (See data to support this conclusion in endnote 13.)

Map 4.9b. Merger of [ɛ] in *ten* and [ɪ] in *tin* before nasal (*ten* as "tihn").

40	41	42	43	44	45	46	47	48	49	50	
Colbert Inf 25 L	Lauderdale Inf 18 L	Lauderdale Inf 20 U	Limestone Inf 12* L	Limestone Inf 13 U	Madison Inf 7 L	Madison Inf 5* L	Madison Inf 8 L	Jackson Inf 1* L	Jackson Inf 4 U	Jackson Inf 3 U	F
	Franklin Inf 33 U	Franklin Inf 30* L	Lawrence Inf 17 U	Lawrence Inf 15* L	Lawrence Inf 16* L		Madison Inf 11 U		Marshall Inf 29 L	DeKalb Inf 26 U	G
									Marshall Inf 27 U		H

U = -r pronounced in *ear*, nine of twenty, zero of six, nine of fourteen white

L = -r vocalized in *ear* ("eeyuh"), eleven of twenty, six of six AA, five of fourteen white

Note: R-fullness/r-lessness in this map reflects a later stage of LAGS publication than map 4.2 and, following LAGS's further analysis, differs for a few informants in assignment of response. For example, LAGS later designated informant #1 (F/48) as being r-less rather than as having the "weak -r" shown in map 4.2.

Map 4.9c. R-fullness (Upland) and r-lessness (Lowland) in *ear*.

remained strong. The scoring of other residents will be considered in the larger context of both Primary and Secondary informants discussed below.

PART 3

LAGS Data: Stage Three

We trust that maps 4.9a–f, our own adaptation of LAGS survey results published in the *LAGS* volumes, have shown how the settlement history's resulting cultural turmoil and social and ethnic partition help explain extreme North Alabama's mixture of Upland and Lowland Southern English, but another source of LAGS data strengthens our explication, leading to refined understanding. The additional data also tap into the greater usefulness of LAGS in line with its ultimate purpose. The aim of the project was "to provide a general reference for sociolinguistic study in the Gulf States, not a definitive projection of dialect areas. Authoritative descrip-

40	41	42	43	44	45	46	47	48	49	50	
Colbert Inf 25 L	Lauderdale Inf 18 U	Lauderdale Inf 20 U	Limestone Inf 12* L	Limestone Inf 13 L	Madison Inf 7 L	Madison Inf 5* L	Madison Inf 8 L	Jackson Inf 1* U	Jackson Inf 4 U	Jackson Inf 3 U	F
	Franklin Inf 33 U	Franklin Inf 30* L	Lawrence Inf 17 U	Lawrence Inf 15* U	Lawrence Inf 16* L		Madison Inf 11 L		Marshall Inf 29 U	DeKalb Inf 26 L	G
									Marshall Inf 27 U		H

U = *right* as monophthong [rat] "raht" or with short central glide [raət], ten of twenty, two of six AA, eight of fourteen white

L = *right* as full diphthong [raɪt] "raheet" or with short high glide [raɨt], ten of twenty, four of six AA, six of fourteen white

Notes: The LAGS matrix maps occasionally reported split results for informants' pronunciations of [aɪ] in *right* or *rice*. In these few cases, the idiolect synopses (discussed below) served as tiebreakers. Several informants whom we mark L are diphthongal in both *right* and *ride*, numbers 5*, 12*, 13, and 25. We believe, however, that [rat] "raht," that is, the presence of monophthongal [a] in *right/rice*, is the social marker for Upland South identification, not the presence of [aɪ] in *ride*: those who said [raɪd] invariably monophthongized [aɪ] in another sound environment (e.g., *miles* as [maːlz] or *nine* as [naːn]) except before the voiceless obstruents (*right/rice*), thus retaining the Lowland Southern English distinction.

Map 4.9d. Non-smoothing (no monophthongization) of [aɪ] "ayee" in *right* and *rice*.

40	41	42	43	44	45	46	47	48	49	50	
Colbert Inf 25 U	Lauderdale Inf 18 U	Lauderdale Inf 20 U	Limestone Inf 12* L	Limestone Inf 13 L	Madison Inf 7 U	Madison Inf 5* L	Madison Inf 8 U	Jackson Inf 1* U	Jackson Inf 4 U	Jackson Inf 3 U	F
	Franklin Inf 33 U	Franklin Inf 30* L	Lawrence Inf 17 U	Lawrence Inf 15* U	Lawrence Inf 16* L		Madison Inf 11 U		Marshall Inf 29 U	DeKalb Inf 26 U	G
									Marshall Inf 27 U		H

U = nuclear -r ("er") in *church*, fifteen of twenty, two of six AA, thirteen of fourteen white

L = no nuclear -r ("er") in *church*, (e.g., "chuh-eech" or "chuh-uhch"), five of twenty, four of six AA, one of fourteen white

Note: Although we categorize informant responses as U or L for illustration of the clustering, r-full (nondiphthongal) nuclear -r does not automatically imply Upland Southern, since it had become the overwhelmingly favored variant within Upland- and Lowland-Southern white dialects. However, the presence of the highly recessive nonrhotic pronunciation of nuclear -r is strongly indicative of Traditional Lowland Southern and especially of older African American English.

Map 4.9e. Nuclear -r in *church* as constricted ("er") or r-less diphthong.

tion of that kind must follow an exhaustive inventory of evidence because such description gains acceptance only through comprehensive explanation" (Pederson, McDaniel, and Adams 1991: ix, xi). It is obvious, therefore, that by design the seven published *LAGS* volumes would render only part of what could be learned, and, indeed, we found that the greater pool of LAGS data held other surprises: fourteen additional voices from our ten-county area, all of them Secondary informants, whose speech was analyzed just like the twenty Primary informants but whose data were not reported in the books. A more detailed picture of the linguis-

40	41	42	43	44	45	46	47	48	49	50	
Colbert Inf 25 3	Lauderdale Inf 18 2	Lauderdale Inf 20 1	Limestone Inf 12* 5	Limestone Inf 13 4	Madison Inf 7 3	Madison Inf 5* 5	Madison Inf 8 4	Jackson Inf 1* 2	Jackson Inf 4 0	Jackson Inf 3 1	F
	Franklin Inf 33 1	Franklin Inf 30* 5	Lawrence Inf 17 1	Lawrence Inf 15* 3	Lawrence Inf 16* 5		Madison Inf 11 3		Marshall Inf 29 2	DeKalb Inf 26 3	G
									Marshall Inf 27 2		H

Cumulative scores for production of five features implying Lowland Southern English influence in each of the twenty informants' speech: non-Upland terms for *earthworm* and/or *green beans* (map 4.9a), "ih" pronunciation of both *ten* and *tin* (distinctive to this LAGS area only) (map 4.9b), postvocalic r-lessness (*ear* as "eeyuh") (map 4.9c), NON-smoothing of diphthong in *right* (map 4.9d), and diphthongization of vowel in *church* as "uh-ee" (4.9e).

Note: The equidistance and linear configuration of the LAGS plotter grid distorts the topography of the counties and thus the contouring of the Lowland area of influence. For example, Colbert County (informant #25, F/40) actually lies south of the Tennessee River between Franklin and Lauderdale Counties and borders Lawrence County on the east. See maps 4.3, 4.6, and 4.10.

Map 4.9f. Cumulative number of "L" features in maps 4.9a–4.9e per Primary informant.

tic landscape emerges by repeopling the ten counties with these additional two African American and twelve white Secondary informants, bringing the total number of speakers to thirty-four.

Although Secondary informants are not plotted on the *LAGS* maps (or on our maps 4.9a–4.9e, which are based upon the *LAGS* maps), their complete materials are contained in the LAGS microform *Basic Materials* (Pederson et al. 1981) just like those of the Primary informants, and their responses are included in the LAGS *Concordance* (Pederson, McDaniel, and Bassett 1986). Admittedly, adding the Secondary informants may distort the careful balance of LAGS architecture in its final choice of Primary informants and therefore weaken the comparable ratios between age groupings, class membership, gender, and so on, as well as dilute the attempt by LAGS to reflect ethnic population ratios (for detailed discussion of the guiding principles for LAGS Primary informant selection, see Pederson et al. 1986). But we believe that loss in these respects is compensated for by gains in local understanding. Our microanalysis above (maps 4.9a–e) suggests that settlement history and its lasting legacy of cultural and racial division weigh in more heavily than informant categorizations. In fact, *only* the early history presented above explains the anomalous r-lessness of North Alabama in map 4.2, as it is the reason for the pocket of r-less African Americans and whites in the cotton-corridor counties within generally Upland North Alabama (see map 4.9c). Inclusion of the Secondary informants furthers our examination in four ways. It 1) adds data from Morgan County, a cotton-corridor county not otherwise represented since it had no Primary informant; 2) reflects more industrialized areas of Franklin and Lauderdale Counties; 3) reinforces our understanding of strongly Upland South Jackson County by adding an additional African American informant (#2); and 4) increases the number of informants from socially supreme Huntsville in Madison County, including informant #9. She is especially important because of her "aristocratic" social class and comparative youth.

Table 4.3 lists all thirty-four Primary and Secondary informants. Along with county locations and a sampling of information that LAGS provides, we include our own cotton-corridor classification for each informant based on the Highland Ridge physiographic area and pre–Civil War cotton production maps (see map 4.3 above). Since the LAGS interviews occurred over a ten-year span, we list both the birth date and the date of interview for each informant to ensure a more accurate understanding of the research data and time frame of collection.

Map 4.10 is drawn in a block format that better approximates the topography of the counties than LAGS grid maps do. It locates the thirty-four informants within the ten North Alabama counties, denoting their LAGS Target Communities, their ethnicity, and their residence inside or outside the cotton corridor, according to our classification given in table 4.3 (for an explanation of the choice of Target Communities and for conventional topographical maps of the LAGS Target Communities in Alabama and the other LAGS states, see Pederson et al. 1986).[14]

It is important to keep in mind that, just as in every *LAGS* and *LAGS*-based map encountered so far, each number on map 4.10 represents a single, real person who brought to the LAGS interview up to eight decades of hard-fought survival. That person's utterance of r-full *years* or of r-less "yee-uhz" and the other features recorded in the interview brings with it a lifetime of using language not just to communicate facts, opinion, and feelings but also to declare in the same instance of speaking who the person is: his or her regional, social, and ethnic identities. Plotted features in *LAGS* are never disembodied data, homogenized into insipidity. On the one hand, the responses reveal the informant's "social dialect," the "variety of language that unites speakers according to shared factors, as for example, racial caste, sex, age, and formal education" (Pederson and McDaniel 1992: ix); on the other hand, as Lanehart explains, one's idiolect (unique dialect) manifests "the language that person identifies with and is therefore very important to the individual." Language then is dualistically "a part of one's culture and [one's] identity" (1999, 212). The language patterns of these thirty-four North Alabamians document the sociohistorical trends and physiographic realities that have interacted with their personal histories and personalities to mold each idiolect. Each voice is individually distinct yet projects multiple identities by necessity and by choice.

The Souths in Their Mouths

In the microform records (Pederson et al. 1981), LAGS provides social and historical information about each of the thirty-four informants as well as a crucial one-page chart (called an "idiolect synopsis") summarizing the speaker's personal dialect, that is, his or her idiolect. Although the transcribed protocols for each informant make possible an exhaustive account of each idiolect, we content ourselves for this study with the streamlined data from the thirty-four idiolect synopses, as these outline the vowel pronunciations and vocabulary items of the informants that we found to function as markers of regional differences.

Tables 4.4 and 4.5 draw from the idiolect synopses to score the informants on whether their use of the five features detailed in maps 4.9a–f above identifies them with Upland or Lowland Southern English.[15] Along with the informants' linguis-

Table 4.3. Informants of North Alabama's ten northernmost counties by cotton-corridor location, with LAGS identifiers and selected LAGS information (N = thirty-four, twenty-six white, eight African American)

Informant number and LAGS protocol number (letter suffix = secondary informant) * = African American	LAGS grid coordinates for maps in LAGS vol. 4 (1990) and vol. 6 (1991)	Cotton corridor categorization based on map 3	Alabama county	Sex	Year of birth	Age at interview	Social class	Atlas speaker type	A = farmer B = parent was a farmer C = No farmer for two generations
1*	F/48	NO	Jackson	F	1931	41	middle	common	C
2*	n/a	NO	Jackson	M	1884	88	lower	folk	A
3	F/50	NO	Jackson	F	1916	64	middle	common	B
4	F/49	NO	Jackson	M	1944	28	middle	cultured	C
5*	F/46	YES	Madison	M	1907	69	lower	folk	B
6	n/a	YES	Madison	F	1899	74	lower	folk	A
7	F/45	YES	Madison	M	1894	78	lower	folk	A
8	F/47	YES	Madison	F	1912	61	middle	common	C
9	n/a	YES	Madison	F	1926	47	aristocrat	cultured	C
10	n/a	YES	Madison	F	1953	25	middle	cultured	C
11	G/47	YES	Madison	F	1951	27	upper	cultured	C
12*	F/43	YES	Limestone	M	1889	84	lower	folk	A

Continued on the next page

Table 4.3. *Continued*

Informant number and LAGS protocol number (letter suffix = secondary informant) * = African American	LAGS grid coordinates for maps in LAGS vol. 4 (1990) and vol. 6 (1991)	Cotton corridor categorization based on map 3	Additional LAGS information about informants						
			Alabama county	Sex	Year of birth	Age at interview	Social class	Atlas speaker type	A = farmer B = parent was a farmer C = No farmer for two generations
13 345	F/44	YES	Limestone	F	1901	69	lower	folk	B
14 345A	n/a	YES	Morgan	M	1882	89	lower	folk	A
15* 346	G/44	YES	Lawrence	F	1901	73	lower	folk	A
16* 347	G/45	YES	Lawrence	F	1909	66	lower	folk	B
17 348	G/43	YES	Lawrence	F	1925	50	middle	common	B
18 349	F/41	YES	Lauderdale	M	1892	81	lower	folk	B
19 349A	n/a	YES	Lauderdale	F	1905	65	middle	folk	C
20 350	F/42	YES	Lauderdale	M	1907	64	lower	common	A
21* 350A	n/a	YES	Lauderdale	M	1909	63	middle	folk	B
22 350B	n/a	YES	Lauderdale	M	1908	65	lower	common	A
23 350C	n/a	YES	Lauderdale	F	1917	55	middle	common	B
24 350D	n/a	YES	Lauderdale	M	1935	38	upper	cultured	B

25	351	F/40	YES	Colbert	F	1894	80	middle	common	B
26	352	G/50	NO	DeKalb	F	1960	19	middle	cultured	C
27	353	H/49	NO	Marshal	M	1891	87	lower	folk	A
28	353A	n/a	NO	Marshal	M	1903	70	middle	folk	A
29	354	G/49	NO	Marshal	M	1910	63	middle	common	A
30*	364	G/42	YES	Franklin	M	1892	81	lower	folk	A
31	364A	n/a	NO	Franklin	F	1906	72	lower	folk	A
32	364B	n/a	YES	Franklin	M	1924	50	middle	common	A
33	365	G/41	YES	Franklin	F	1928	45	middle	common	B
34	365A	n/a	YES	Franklin	M	1896	77	upper	cultured	C

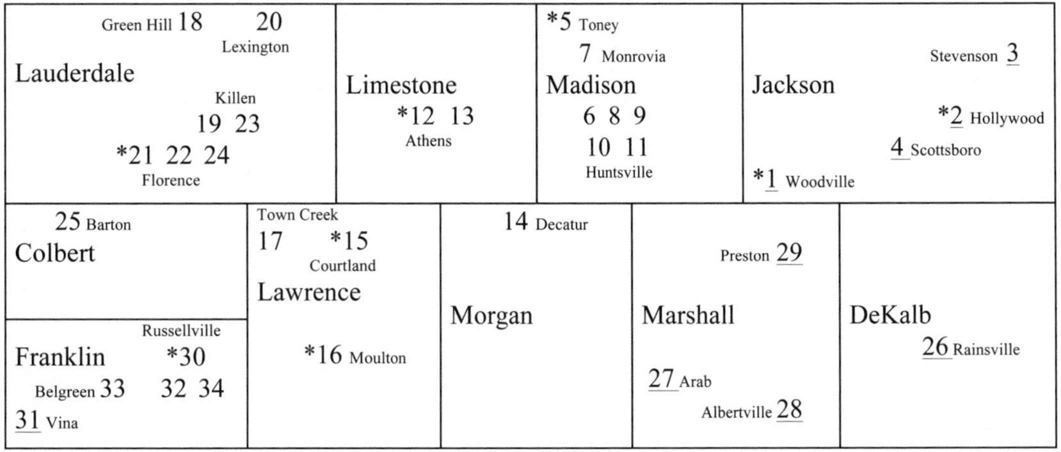

Lauderdale

Green Hill 18   20 Lexington

Killen 19 23

*21 22 24 Florence

Limestone

*12 13 Athens

*5 Toney

7 Monrovia

Madison

6 8 9

10 11 Huntsville

Jackson

Stevenson 3

*2 Hollywood

4 Scottsboro

*1 Woodville

Colbert

25 Barton

Town Creek 17   *15 Courtland

Lawrence

*16 Moulton

14 Decatur

Morgan

Marshall

Preston 29

27 Arab

Albertville 28

DeKalb

26 Rainsville

Franklin

Russellville *30

Belgreen 33   32 34

31 Vina

KEY

Plain numeral = cotton-corridor location, N = 25
Underlined numeral = non-cotton-corridor location, N = 9
* = African American, N = 8 (six classified as located in cotton corridor)
Large font = County
Small font = LAGS Target Community

Map 4.10. Block format map locating all thirty-four LAGS informants (Primary and Secondary) within the ten uppermost Alabama counties

tic scores, we provide each county's "Degree of Upland Southernness," that is, its score for Upland-South artifacts (see map 4.4 above). We present white and African American informants separately, because combining them in a single table obscures the mixed showing of features for the white informants and the more uniform and generally higher scores of the African American informants. (We concluded that for proper understanding the findings for the African American informants required separate analysis, which we present later in this essay.)

Table 4.4 presents twenty-four of the twenty-six white informants, with informants #24 and #34 omitted because the lack of vocabulary answers in their idiolect synopses prevents a full range of comparable scores. Table 4.5 presents the eight African American informants and repeats the data for the two highest-scoring white informants, Madison County informants #7 and #9, for comparative purposes later on. Both table 4.4 and table 4.5 divide the informants within them into two groups.

Table 4.4 separates those white informants exhibiting zero to one feature (in our view, indexing Upland Southern orientation) from those exhibiting two, three, or four features (indexing Lowland Southern orientation); no white informant scored five features. Had any informant in table 4.4 scored only the single feature of postvocalic r-lessness (*ear* as "ee-uh"), our division based on two or more features would not have been reasonable because of the *social loading* of r-lessness as a marker of the Lowland South. In actuality, all four r-less white informants exhibited at least two Lowland Southern English features. Other Lowland markers accompanying r-lessness hint at the transition from Traditional to New Lowland Southern (see table 4.2 above). That fewer Lowland Southern–oriented informants exhibit postvocalic r-lessness and diphthongal nuclear -r (*bird* as "buh-eed"), compared to the considerably higher numbers for the other Lowland features, reveals the clear recessive nature of r-less forms: by the time of the LAGS interviews in the 1970s, r-lessness had lost its status as the main differentiator of Lowland Southern English for many informants. In fact, dialectal differentiation could be accomplished without r-lessness through combinations of three other features we trace: pronunciations of *right* and of *ten* and choice of terms for *earthworm* and/or *green beans*.

For the African American informants in table 4.5, however, the profile of scoring suggests that different forces are at work. Although all eight informants, six in the cotton corridor and two in Jackson County, exhibit postvocalic r-lessness, the two Jackson County informants exhibit *only* the single Lowland Southern feature of postvocalic r-lessness. For the other four features, the Jackson County African American informants scored zero, a remarkable difference from the non–Jackson County informants, none of whom scored lower than four features. Since, in addition to ethnicity, r-lessness is the only common feature, we assume this feature must be functioning differently for this group of informants than for the white informants of table 4.4, as we will discuss below.

The "Degree of Upland Southernness" for each informant's county often suggests a pattern in relation to the informant's score on features. For the white informants, in table 4.4, the two score-values (features and "Degree") do not form a perfect inversion, but lower linguistic scores in general are accompanied by higher scores for "Degree," and the converse also generally holds true. Upland South Jackson County (informants #3 and #4) and cotton-corridor Madison County (informants # 9 and #7) show the strongest inverse relationships. For the African American informants, in table 4.5, the inverse relationships for the two values are apparent for the two Jackson County informants (low number of features and high "Degree" score) and for the Limestone County informant (high number of features and low "Degree" score). These relationships in table 4.5 are not surprising, given how starkly the physiography, the pre–Civil War cotton production, and the historic ethnic ratios contrast for Upland Jackson County versus cotton-corridor Limestone County (see maps 4.3 and 4.5). However, the inverse relationship is not as robust for African Americans located in other counties, which suggests an interesting mixture of strong cultural and ethnic influences, to be discussed below.

Finally, our designation of informants as cotton-corridor or non-cotton-corridor appears to have been useful if not perfectly predictive. Although we classified all informants as cotton-corridor or non-cotton-corridor before our analysis of their scores on the five features and based solely upon their location within the ten-county area, four of the seven white informants in table 4.4 whom we placed outside the cotton corridor are in the low-scoring group on Lowland Southern features. Six of the seventeen other informants whom we placed inside the cotton corridor also scored a 0 or 1, indicating Upland orientation by our scale, but only one of these six informants hailed from Madison or Limestone, the most cottony of the cotton-corridor counties, while the other six Madison/Limestone informants scored 2, 3, or 4 to indicate Lowland orientation. For the African American informants in table 4.5, cotton-corridor or non-cotton-corridor designation was a very good fit regarding scores on the Lowland English features. We conclude, therefore, that settlement history and the cultural conflict between Upland and Lowland pedigrees continued to exert linguistic consequences that were discernible more than a century later in these counties.

Mapping the scores presented in tables 4.4 and 4.5 for the five features provides a final, visual summary of the enduring linguistic impact of settlement history on the ten counties, as reflected in LAGS data. In map 4.11, we place the informants' scores against the backdrop of "Degree of Upland Southernness" for the counties and convert those scores into symbols, with upward-pointing tokens indicating Upland Southern orientation and downward-pointing tokens indicating Lowland Southern orientation. A comparison of Madison and Limestone Counties with Jackson County presents the cultural divide occasioned by the early history particularly starkly. As the symbols with asterisks show, the divide extends even to African American informants, raising interesting questions about the nature of African American English in the ten-county area.

North Alabama's African American Englishes?

In preparing table 4.4 (all the white informants), we were not surprised to see linguistic patterns that implied cultural divisions between the cotton-corridor and non-cotton-corridor white informants, because of the two historically combative white Southern settlement cultures and the linguistic effect of competing speech varieties. As we discussed above, an early Lowland Southern English established a linguistic outpost in Alabama's first cotton kingdom, when the fertile riches of the Tennessee valley were discovered and eastern planters bought up the best lands and imported cotton monoculture and the slaves whose labor made it pay. This elite population's founder dialect gave rise to a vernacular standard in the immediate area (see map 4.11 for a reflection of that influence) but failed to flourish throughout wider North Alabama, where the overwhelming number of Upland settlers had no social impetus to adapt to the speech of the elite. We argue that for early white settlers, two founder dialects of English were established: a Lowland Southern one in the cotton-corridor areas and an Upland Southern one in the other areas. Sometime later, as the power of Alabama's second cotton kingdom, the Black Belt, expanded, the antagonistic north-south political sectionalism of the state developed and intensified. The Upland Southern culture and accompanying dialect prevailed and set the tone for North Alabama. Even so, it appears straightforward to find Lowland vestiges among the white informants of the cotton corridor (see table 4.4). The occurrences of non-Upland linguistic features across the ten northernmost Alabama counties represent the skeletal remains of a once powerful culture.

We were intrigued, however, by the demarcation of African Americans at the Jackson County line. As shown in table 4.5 and on map 4.11, the scores of the eight African American informants divide unequivocally between the two informants inside Jackson County and the six informants outside Jackson County. For the five speech elements tallied, the similar incidence of usage confined to each group and the strong disagreement in usage between the two groups require careful analysis. Basically, we find that the founder principle once again has explanatory power, though in this instance the founders are not the elite and powerful but the oppressed. Nevertheless, to understand table 4.5 we posit a third founder dialect imported during extreme North Alabama's settlement: the Lowland Southern English–based language of the slaves.

When LAGS interviewed African Americans in extreme North Alabama more than one hundred years after emancipation, the pool of informants recruited from across the ten-county area did not include members of a relatively recent diaspora (the Great Migration, see Yaeger-Dror and Thomas 2010, 6–7), like African American populations studied in urban areas of Northern states for the first wave of research into African American English. Rather, these LAGS informants had deep historic roots in the area. The African American English (AAE) planted in the cotton-corridor locations by the first slaves established an ethnically separated standard variety. We find it reasonable to argue that within a rigid, caste-based society that forbade movement into another caste, different founder language varieties would arise and persist side by side. Such an AAE could neither be overwhelmed by Upland Southern English nor evolve consistently with Lowland Southern English, because of its users' social segregation. While there was obviously interaction between the races, the cultural chasm between the African Americans and the white members of both competing white cultures was too broad for the operation of true "social networks," that is, the interracial formulation of "strong social network ties" that are so important to language maintenance or of "weak social network ties" that promote language change (see Milroy 1991). Instead, effectual "social networks" would have been limited to within the African American community. As Eckert explains, "interacting with the same people in a variety of contexts—work, neighborhood, church, leisure activities, family, etc.—would have a strong vernacular norm-

Table 4.4. Features in common for white informants having scores for all five features
(N = 24, informants #24 and #34 omitted as incomplete)

Informant	Total score	Degree of Upland Southernness for the county (map 4.4)	County	Year of birth	Age at interview	Sex	Speaker type	Class[a]
33	0	3	Franklin	1928	45	F	common	M
3	0	4	Jackson	1916	64	F	common	M
4	0	4	Jackson	1944	28	M	cultured	M
17	0	3	Lawrence	1925	50	F	common	M
29	0	?	Marshall	1910	63	M	common	M
19	1	2	Lauderdale	1905	65	F	folk	M
20	1	2	Lauderdale	1907	64	M	common	L
10	1	2	Madison	1953	25	F	cultured	M
14	1	0-1	Morgan	1882	89	M	folk	L
28	1	?	Marshall	1903	70	M	folk	M
32	2	3	Franklin	1924	50	M	common	M
18	2	2	Lauderdale	1892	81	M	folk	L
22	2	2	Lauderdale	1908	65	M	common	L
13	2	0-1	Limestone	1901	69	F	folk	L
8	2	2	Madison	1912	61	F	common	M
6	2	2	Madison	1899	74	F	folk	L
27	2	?	Marshall	1891	87	M	folk	L
25	3	0-1	Colbert	1894	80	F	common	M
26	3	?	DeKalb	1960	19	F	cultured	M
31	3	3	Franklin	1906	72	F	folk	L
23	3	2	Lauderdale	1917	55	F	common	M
11	3	2	Madison	1951	27	F	cultured	U
9	4	2	Madison	1926	47	F	cultured	UA
7	4	2	Madison	1894	78	M	folk	L

[a]Class abbreviations: (I) Indigent, (L) Lower, (M) Middle, (U) Upper, (A) Aristocrat.

Table 4.4. *Continued*

A = farmer B = parent was a farmer C = no farmer for two generations	Cotton corridor	Five Lowland Southern English features, scored as 1 (Lowland) or 0 (non-Lowland)				
		right as "rah-eet" ([raɪt]) NOT "raht" ([rat]) 1 = full or reduced high glide AH-ee or AH-ih 0 = reduced mid glide AH-eh or smooth [a]	*ten* ([tɛn]) as "tihn" ([tɪn]) ([ɛ]/[ɪ] prenasal merger) 1 = *ten* as "tihn" 0 = *ten* as "tehn" [ɛ]	-r as "uh" in *(y)ear(s)* (post-vocalic -r-lessness) 1 = -r-less "EE-uh" 0 = -r-full "eer"	no "er" in words like *bird* (diphthong replacing a nuclear -r) 1 = "UH-ee" or "UH-uh" for "er" 0 = "er"	non-Upland term for *red worm* and/or *green beans* 1 = non-Upland term for either or both terms 0 = Upland terms
B	Y	0	0	0	0	0
B	N	0	0	0	0	0
C	N	0	0	0	0	0
B	Y	0	0	0	0	0
A	N	0	0	0	0	0
C	Y	1	0	0	0	0
A	Y	0	1	0	0	0
C	Y	1	0	0	0	0
A	Y	0	0	0	0	1
A	N	0	0	0	0	1
	no.	2 of 10	1 of 10	0 of 10	0 of 10	2 of 10
	%	20	10	0	0	20
A	Y	1	1	0	0	0
B	Y	0	0	1	0	1
A	Y	1	0	0	0	1
B	Y	1	0	0	0	1
C	Y	1	1	0	0	0
A	Y	0	1	1	0	0
A	N	0	1	0	0	1
B	Y	1	1	0	0	1
C	N	1	1	0	0	1
A	N	1	1	0	1	0
B	Y	1	1	0	0	1
C	Y	1	1	0	0	1
C	Y	1	1	1	1	0
A	Y	1	0	1	1	1
	no.	11 of 14	10 of 14	4 of 14	3 of 14	9 of 14
	%	79	71	29	21	64

Table 4.5. Lowland Southern English features in common among two African American non-cotton-corridor informants, six African American cotton-corridor informants, and two white cotton-corridor informants

Informant	Total score	Degree of Upland Southernness for the county (map 4.4)	County	Year of birth	Age at interview	Sex	Speaker type	Class[a]
1*	1	4	Jackson	1931	41	F	common	M
2*	1	4	Jackson	1884	88	M	folk	L
21*	4	2	Lauderdale	1909	63	M	folk	M
12*	4	0-1	Limestone	1889	84	M	folk	LI
15*	4	3	Lawrence	1901	73	F	folk	L
16*	4	3	Lawrence	1909	66	F	folk	L
30*	5	3	Franklin	1892	81	M	folk	L
5*	5	2	Madison	1907	69	M	folk	L
7	4	2	Madison	1894	78	M	folk	L
9	4	2	Madison	1926	47	F	cultured	UA

[a]Class abbreviations: (I) Indigent, (L) Lower, (M) Middle, (U) Upper, (A) Aristocrat.

enforcing power" (n.d., 10). Therefore, the language that LAGS recorded more than a century and a half after the first slaves were brought to the area is much more uniform for the six Alabama-born African American speakers located in the cotton corridor than is the English of the analogous white informants, which mixes Upland South and Lowland South features in various concentrations and exhibits a dramatic fading of the white founder population's Traditional Lowland Southern r-lessness (more on this below).

Table 4.5. *Continued*

		Five Lowland Southern English features, scored as 1 (Lowland) or 0 (non-Lowland)				
A = farmer B = parent was a farmer C = no farmer for two generations	Cotton corridor	*right* as "rah-eet" ([raɪt]) NOT "raht" ([rat]) 1 = full or reduced high glide AH-ee or AH-ih 0 = reduced mid glide AH-eh or smooth [a]	*ten* ([tɛn]) as "tihn" ([tɪn]) ([ɛ]/ [ɪ] pre-nasal merger) 1 = *ten* as "tihn" 0 = *ten* as "tehn" [ɛ]	-r as "uh" in *(y)ear(s)* (postvocalic r-lessness) 1 = r-less "EE-uh" 0 = r-full "eer"	no "er" in words like *bird* (diphthong replacing a nuclear -r) 1 = "UH-ee" or "UH-uh" for "er" 0 = "er"	non-Upland term for *red worm* and/or *green beans* 1 = non-Upland term for either or both terms 0 = Upland terms
C	N	0	0	1	0	0
A	N	0	0	1	0	0
	no.	0 of 2	0 of 2	2 of 2	0 of 2	0 of 2
	%	0	0	100	0	0
B	Y	0	1	1	1	1
A	Y	1	0	1	1	1
A	Y	0	1	1	1	1
B	Y	1	1	1	0	1
A	Y	1	1	1	1	1
B	Y	1	1	1	1	1
	no.	4 of 6	5 of 6	6 of 6	5 of 6	6 of 6
	%	66	83	100	83	100
A	Y	1	0	1	1	1
C	Y	1	1	1	1	0
	no.	2 of 2	1 of 2	2 of 2	2 of 2	1 of 2
	%	100	50	100	100	50

In contrast to their high population ratio in cotton-corridor areas, African Americans historically have formed a much smaller population segment in Jackson County (under 17 percent even in the cotton-boom year of 1850, when Madison County was 55 percent; see map 4.4) and presented much lower actual numbers. Considering the tiny minority of free African Americans in Alabama who could have owned land (see table 4.1), it is reasonable that African Americans in Jackson County were part of the pre–Civil War forced immigration of slaves into the area

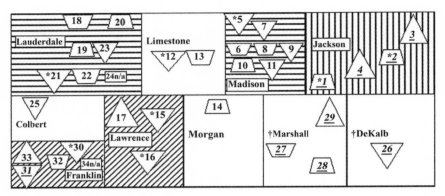

KEY

Plain numeral = cotton-corridor location, N = 25

Italicized, underlined numeral = non-cotton-corridor location, N = 9

* = African American, N = 8 (six classified as located in cotton corridor)

▽ = Strong Lowland South influence: informant score of 3, 4, or 5 on five features of Lowland Southern English, thirteen of thirty-two, six of eight AA, seven of twenty-four white (see tables 4.4 and 4.5)

▽ = Medium Lowland South influence: informant score of 2 on five features of Lowland Southern English, seven of thirty-two, zero of eight AA, seven of twenty-four white (see tables 4.4 and 5.5)

△ = Medium Upland South influence: informant score of 1 on five features of Lowland Southern English, seven of thirty-two, two of eight AA, five of twenty-six white (see tables 4.4 and 4.5)

△ = Strong Upland South influence: informant score of 0 on five features of Lowland Southern English, five of thirty-two, zero of eight AA, five of twenty-six white (see tables 4.4 and 4.5)

n/a = Informant not applicable for lack of vocabulary data to score

Fill patterns designating degree of Upland Southernness by presence of "five greater artifacts in the cultural landscape" (Jordan-Bychkov 2003: 84; see map 4.5 above)		
Pattern	Score for presence of the five Upland South artifacts	North Alabama counties by artifact rates
	0 to 1 artifact	Colbert, Limestone, Morgan
	2 artifacts	Lauderdale, Madison
	3 artifacts	Franklin, Lawrence
	4 artifacts	Jackson
N/A	5 artifacts	No counties found in the area
†Source unclear on whether Marshall and DeKalb were examined for Upland-South artifacts.		

Map 4.11. Block format map of Alabama's ten uppermost counties showing Upland-South artifact rates plus informants' score ranges indicating Lowland Southern English or Upland Southern English features

and would have been concentrated in the few plantation areas of the county (see map 4.3), with dispersal after emancipation limited to whatever their economic means allowed. If, as we believe, the English of enslaved African Americans in Jackson County was basically like that of enslaved African Americans in general who came to North Alabama, then a significant degree of postemancipation "overwhelming" of the presumed AAE founder variety by Upland Southern English occurred within Jackson County (see table 4.5), even within an African American population that was caste-bound and legally segregated until the civil rights legislation of the 1960s. Although true interracial "social networks" were no doubt improbable, changes to AAE in Jackson County took place not only because of much lower African American population densities outside the cotton corridor but also because of physical isolation. A dearth of convenient transportation cut off Jackson County's African Americans from regular interaction with large populations of African Americans in the cotton-corridor counties. Any current map of Jackson County's major roads and towns shows that few significant roadways enter Madison County from Jackson even today, and these are only in the extreme southwest corner of Jackson County, bordering Madison. Lack of continual interaction between African Americans in Jackson County and those in the cotton corridor would greatly reduce strong social network ties required to maintain the kind of linguistic status quo seen in the cotton-corridor AAE.

As seen in table 4.5, the comparatively low percentage of African Americans in Jackson County and their isolation from neighboring cotton-corridor African American populations allowed both lexical and phonological changes to shape Jackson County's AAE dialect. Although r-less like the six cotton-corridor African American informants, the two Jackson County African American informants do not otherwise follow the prevailing AAE pattern of the other six, as the list below illustrates:

Single Point of Agreement (see table 4.5):
1. All are postvocalically r-less ("ee-uh" for *ear*).
   Four Points of Disagreement (see table 4.5):
   1. For nuclear -r, (the stressed "er" sound of *church, third, worm*, etc.), five of the six cotton-corridor informants used the old Lowland Southern diphthong, high-vowel glide "uh-ee" as in "chuh-eech" or central-vowel glide as in "chuh-uhch" (according to the LAGS transcription, informant #16 used a weak -r plus "uh," as in "thuhr-uhd" for *third*, a pronunciation that appears to be transitional). Both Jackson County African American informants (#1 and #2) produced nuclear -r in *church*, like the white Jackson County informants (#3 and #4).
   2. For *right*, four of the six cotton-corridor informants used the high or reduced high glide ("rah-eet"). Both Jackson County informants smoothed to [a] or a mid-front glide ("raht"), like the white Jackson County informants.
   3. As we have shown above, nonmerger of *ten* with *tin* appears to have functioned as a local marker of Upland Southern English in the ten-county area, though not generally across the Gulf States. For the *ten/tin* merger, five of the six cotton-corridor informants showed the merger (*ten* pronounced as "tihn"). Both Jackson County informants pronounced *ten* contrastively with *tin* (*ten* as "tehn"), like the white Jackson County informants.
   4. For terms for *red worm* and/or *green beans*, all six cotton-corridor

informants used a non-Upland term. Both Jackson County informants used an Upland term, again, like the white Jackson County
informants.

Although our conclusion is based on only the two Jackson County African
American informants (#1 and #2) and thus calls for further research, we tenta-
tively conclude that their speech reflects a variety of AAE for Jackson County that
differs substantially from the cotton-corridor variety of AAE, both in vocabulary
and in certain vowels. It is doubtful that influences besides Upland cultural context and shared ethnicity could have resulted in complete agreement on features
for the two Jackson County African Americans: informant #2 is a male, lower-class
farmer and the oldest of the eight African Americans interviewed; informant #1
is a female, middle-class medical professional and the youngest of the eight African Americans interviewed. The two informants are separated spatially by half of
large Jackson County and across time by almost two generations. Also, the persuasive facts remain that the two African American Jackson County informants
agreed with the two white Jackson County informants for four out of five features
and disagreed with the six cotton-corridor African Americans for four out of five
features, agreeing on only one AAE feature, postvocalic r-lessness.

The question remains, if the Jackson County and non–Jackson County African Americans disagreed on all other features, why should r-lessness persist, even
for the youngest African American informant, the Jackson Countian? (Below, we
look at change in r-lessness through time.) Some African Americans are, of course,
r-full in the United States, depending on the linguistic necessities of the worlds they
were reared in and/or later moved in professionally, as for example, career milita-
rist and former secretary of state Colin Powell, former secretary of state and Birmingham native Condoleezza Rice, media announcers, and many others. But the
eight native-born African American LAGS informants in North Alabama, ranging
in age from forty-one to eighty-eight, were interviewed in an Alabama that was at
the time embroiled in the battle for equal rights (see Jeffries 2008) and only four
to eight years after the assassination of Martin Luther King Jr., in 1968. It would
hardly be credible that the informants held a motivating belief that social bene-
fits would accrue to them by adapting r-less "white" speech. Even though LAGS
assigned middle-class status to two of the eight informants, it is doubtful that any
symbols of class membership, including dialect, could have breached a century of
legally sanctioned melanin barrier.

We surmise, therefore, that within the African American population in Jack-
son County there had been a slow and unconscious linguistic accommodation to
Upland Southern English, obliterating many AAE features common for cotton-
corridor African Americans but not as yet having overthrown the heartbeat of
AAE, r-lessness (note the ripe opportunity for research among current African
American Jackson Countians on the prevalence of AAE r-lessness today). As
E. Thomas states, African American English is "probably the most R-less variety
of American English" (2001, 178), and North Alabama's posited two forms of AAVE
are no exceptions. Although by the 1970s many features of the presumed founder-
derived version of AAE had been "overwhelmed" by Upland Southern in Jackson

County, a largely white and Upland Southern locale, r-lessness remained as the main ethnic marker. For all eight North Alabama African American informants, postvocalic r-lessness functioned as a "socially loaded" feature that proclaimed ethnicity, but for the two Jackson County informants we believe that it did even more. Their unique blend of Upland Southern English features and ethnic-marking r-lessness carved out an identity separate from Lowland South–oriented African Americans, separate from Lowland South–oriented whites, and separate from Upland South–oriented whites. They were Jackson Countians *and* they were African Americans.[16]

If we likewise were to claim for the cotton-corridor African American informants (non–Jackon Countians) that the constellation of Lowland Southern English features signaled an AAE variety proclaiming unique ethnoregional identity, a return to table 4.2 immediately pulls us up short. Madison County white informants #7 and #9 both exhibited four out of five Lowland Southern English features, just like four of the African American informants (the other two scoring five out of five features). Did these speech similarities between Madison County whites and African Americans signal close cultural connection and social solidarity? It is difficult to believe that, since, as Novkov explains, comprehensive social and legal segregation had its roots back in post-Reconstruction and was fully institutionalized in 1901, when the new Alabama state constitution "rested upon white supremacy as a basic element of governance" (2007). To understand the actual situation of dialect similarity without cultural solidarity, we must reorder our LAGS material once again, this time through time.

LAGS as a Linguistic Time Machine

Map 4.11 above projects a linguistic landscape using the decade of LAGS interviews around the 1970s as a temporal reference point, that is, offering a synchronic perspective, but a perspective through time, a diachronic perspective, is also possible. The LAGS record of each informant's year of birth allows his or her linguistic data to be considered through *apparent time*. The apparent-time construct assumes that for most people, their language remains relatively stable once they become adults. As a result, comparing language features of different generations of adults should suggest how features of a language change over time—in "apparent time." Comparing speech patterns from informants born at different times should therefore reveal how the features we have surveyed have changed. A reshuffling of our data by informants' year-of-birth permits the incidence of Upland versus Lowland features to be examined across almost eight decades (earliest date of birth, 1882, versus latest date of birth, 1960). Upland and Lowland identities persist throughout the full span, as the overall scores on features support (tables 4.4 and 4.5), but certain linguistic differentiators of Lowland allegiance, the two forms of r-lessness and vocabulary items, become much rarer through time. Pederson has remarked that incidence of r-lessness is especially illustrative of diachronic change, because across the whole LAGS area its presence relates to the age of informants (Pederson et al. 1991: xii). Table 4.6 supports Pederson's assertion on r-lessness for our small area of inquiry and also throws into relief several interrelated issues.

From the diachronic perspective of table 4.6, the non-Upland features yield

Table 4.6. All informants sorted by year of birth (N = 34, * = African American)

Informant	Total score	County	Year of birth	Age at interview	Sex	Speaker type	Class[a]
14	1	Morgan	1882	89	M	folk	L
2*	1	Jackson	1884	88	M	folk	L
12*	4	Limestone	1889	84	M	folk	LI
27	2	Marshall	1891	87	M	folk	L
30*	5	Franklin	1892	81	M	folk	L
18	2	Lauderdale	1892	81	M	folk	L
7	4	Madison	1894	78	M	folk	L
25	3	Colbert	1894	80	F	common	M
34	1 of 4	Franklin	1896	77	M	cultured	U
6	2	Madison	1899	74	F	folk	L
15*	4	Lawrence	1901	73	F	folk	L
13	2	Limestone	1901	69	F	folk	L
28	1	Marshall	1903	70	M	folk	M
19	1	Lauderdale	1905	65	F	folk	M
31	3	Franklin	1906	72	F	folk	L
5*	5	Madison	1907	69	M	folk	L
20	1	Lauderdale	1907	64	M	common	L
22	2	Lauderdale	1908	65	M	common	L
21*	4	Lauderdale	1909	63	M	folk	M
16*	4	Lawrence	1909	66	F	folk	L
29	0	Marshall	1910	63	M	common	M
8	2	Madison	1912	61	F	common	M
3	0	Jackson	1916	64	F	common	M
23	3	Lauderdale	1917	55	F	common	M
32	2	Franklin	1924	50	M	common	M
17	0	Lawrence	1925	50	F	common	M
9*	4	Madison	1926	47	F	cultured	UA
33	0	Franklin	1928	45	F	common	M
1*	1	Jackson	1931	41	F	common	M
24	1 of 4	Lauderdale	1935	38	M	cultured	U
4	0	Jackson	1944	28	M	cultured	M
11	3	Madison	1951	27	F	cultured	U
10	1	Madison	1953	25	F	cultured	M
26	3	DeKalb	1960	19	F	cultured	M

NOTES
Shaded columns denote the recession of features for informants born after 1910. Since for this table scoring for all five features is not necessary for comparability, informants #24 and #34, omitted from table 4.4, are included here, along with their scores on the

Table 4.6. *Continued*

A, farmer B, parent was a farmer C, no farmer for two generations	Cotton corridor	Five Lowland-Southern-English features, scored 1 if present				
		right as "rah-eet" ([raɪt]) NOT "raht" ([rat])	*ten* as "tihn" ([ɛ]/[ɪ]) pre-nasal merger, local feature)	-r as "uh" in (y)ear(s) (post-vocalic R-lessness)	no "er" for nuclear -r, e.g., *bird* as "buh-eed"	non-Upland term for *red worm* and/or *green beans*
A	Y	0	0	0	0	1
A	N	0	0	1	0	0
A	Y	1	0	1	1	1
A	N	0	1	0	0	1
A	Y	1	1	1	1	1
B	Y	0	0	1	0	1
A	Y	1	0	1	1	1
B	Y	1	1	0	0	1
C	Y	0	0	1	0	n/a
A	Y	0	1	1	0	0
A	Y	0	1	1	1	1
B	Y	1	0	0	0	1
A	N	0	0	0	0	1
C	Y	1	0	0	0	0
A	N	1	1	0	1	0
B	Y	1	1	1	1	1
A	Y	0	1	0	0	0
A	Y	1	0	0	0	1
B	Y	0	1	1	1	1
B	Y	1	1	1	0	1
A	N	0	0	0	0	0
C	Y	1	1	0	0	0
B	N	0	0	0	0	0
B	Y	1	1	0	0	1
A	Y	1	1	0	0	0
B	Y	0	0	0	0	0
C	Y	1	1	1	1	0
B	Y	0	0	0	0	0
C	N	0	0	1	0	0
B	Y	1	0	0	0	n/a
C	N	0	0	0	0	0
C	Y	1	1	0	0	1
C	Y	1	0	0	0	0
C	N	1	1	0	0	1
		18/34	16/34	13/34	8/34	17/32
		53%	47%	38%	24%	53%

four features for which their idiolect synopses included responses. The column for non-Upland terms thus has only thirty-two responses.

[a]Class abbreviations: (I) Indigent, (L) Lower, (M) Middle, (U) Upper, (A) Aristocrat.

different histories. Competition with respect to two features is stable through the seventy-eight-year stretch of birth dates (1882–1960): pronunciation of *right* and of *ten*. High-glided *right* versus unglided/mid-glided *right* continues to occur (and as we shall see below, strong social forces retained the two competing forms but with different social loading). But surprisingly, the competition between *ten* pronounced as "tehn" and *ten* pronounced as "tihn" (*ten/tin* merger) also remains strong throughout the time span. The fact that more than half of the informants born after 1910 (eight of fourteen, 57 percent) pronounce *ten* contrastively with *tin* rather than both as "tihn" supports our view that the otherwise relentless merger of *ten* and *tin* both to "*tihn*" throughout the South in general was stymied by local development. Evidently, *ten* pronounced as "tehn" rather than as "tihn" was serving as a social-dialect marker.

For informants born after 1910, these two features (high-glided versus mid-/unglided *right* and merged versus unmerged *ten/tin*) appear to do the lion's share of Lowland/Upland differentiation in relation to cotton-corridor status: four of five non-cotton-corridor informants born after 1910 have neither of these Lowland features, while seven of nine cotton-corridor informants have both or one of the features. The other three features (i.e., postvocalic -r, nuclear -r, and vocabulary) pattern regularly with pronunciation of *right* and *ten* for informants born before 1910 to denote Lowland orientation but recede severely for informants born after 1910. Only two of eight cotton-corridor informants born after 1910 exhibit non-Upland vocabulary; only one of nine cotton-corridor informants exhibits r-lessness. Of the fourteen combined cotton-corridor and non-cotton-corridor informants born after 1910, only African American non-cotton-corridor informant #1 (b. 1931) and white cotton-corridor informant #9 (b. 1926) retain any r-lessness.

Complicating a straightforward diachronic interpretation based on year of birth, however, are differences in the profile characteristics of the informants born after 1910 whom LAGS interviewed. First, no informants designated as lower class appear after the 1910 birth cutoff. This loss of class comparison raises the question of whether the seeming reduction in r-less forms and non-Upland vocabulary is merely a reflection of the types of informants interviewed. When only the middle- and upper-class informants born before 1910 are examined (sorting not shown) to test for this bias, postvocalic r-lessness, diphthongal nuclear -r, and non-Upland vocabulary all occur at higher rates. Social-class membership does not seem to be what is being measured.

Besides class membership, a second characteristic of informants also shifts after 1910: the number who are farmers or nonfarmers (noted as A, B, or C in the ninth column from the left in table 4.6). More than half the informants born before 1910 worked as farmers, whereas only two of fourteen informants born after 1910 did so; furthermore, half of these younger informants (seven of fourteen) are at least two generations removed from farming, according to their *LAGS* biographies (marked by C in the column in table 4.6). But as was the case with social class, the pre-1910 nonfarmers also display the recessive features more often than the post-1910 nonfarmers (sorting not shown).

Finally, a third issue of informant makeup that may muddle diachronic clarity concerns the ethnic ratio. Seven of the twenty pre-1910-born informants are African American, whereas just one of the fourteen post-1910-born informants is. Would a higher ratio of post-1910-born African Americans, especially from the cotton-corridor counties, have presented a different view of change through time? As table 4.5 depicts, all African American informants have postvocalic r-lessness, and the African Americans outside Jackson County almost all merged *ten* and *tin*, diphthongized nuclear -r ("buh-eed" for *bird*), and used non-Upland vocabulary terms. We assume in this case that a similar mix of informants would have changed the incidence of some Lowland features: that more African American informants from any county who were born after 1910 would have increased postvocalic r-lessness and that more cotton-corridor African Americans born after 1910 would have increased merged *ten/tin* and non-Upland vocabulary, and possibly would have increased diphthongal nuclear -r. For the other feature, pronunciation of *right*, since the African American informants' mixture of glided versus unglided responses in table 4.6 is not much different from that of the pre-1910 white informants, we assume that additional younger African American informants would have yielded similar results. We conclude that other than for gliding/ungliding of *right*, a greater concentration of African American informants might have buffered the "apparent-time" change seen in table 4.6 but not overthrown it. Therefore, we believe the recession of the r-less features and of non-Upland vocabulary is authentic for the white informants.

The dramatic diachronic erosion of three of the five Lowland-marking features rivets attention on the only two informants born after 1910 who were still r-less, informant #1, who exhibited postvocalic r-lessness, and informant #9, who exhibited both postvocalic r-lessness and diphthongal nuclear-r. We have already presented above our view that postvocalic r-lessness occurred in the speech of informant #1 for purposes of ethnic identification within Jackson County. But the late-dated postvocalic r-lessness and especially the diphthongal nuclear -r exhibited by white informant #9 makes her usage unique.

"Old Times There Are Not Forgotten"

Around 1970, while Nunnally was a young man living in Tuscaloosa, Alabama, he was friends with a young man whose mother was descended from a venerable, white, aristocratic family. Her married name, Birch (fictitious but similar to her actual name), contained a nuclear -r. When Nunnally telephoned his friend's house and a woman answered, she always said, "Buh-eech residence," and he was never able to determine in the first interchange whether the answerer was his friend's aristocratic mother or their African American housekeeper of many years, because of the similarity in their speech.

As table 4.5 records, a similar sharing of features is the case for the six African American informants of the cotton corridor and the two highest-scoring white informants, #7 and #9 from cotton-corridor Madison County, all of whom exhibited at least four of the five features. No doubt, the dialects of Madison County white informants #7 and #9 and of the six cotton-corridor African American informants (#5, #12, #15, #16, #21, and #30) differ to varying degrees in grammar, vocabulary, pronunciation, and the performance aspects of language, differences that the idiolect synopses reveal somewhat and that interview notes (the LAGS protocols) and the LAGS audio recordings would make abundantly clear. But according to the idiolect synopses that we used to investigate five culturally differentiating features, the cotton-corridor African American informants had more in common with these two Madison County white informants than they did with the two Jackson County, non-cotton-corridor African American informants (#1 and #2); and white informants #7 and #9 had more in common with the African American cotton-corridor informants than they did with 70 percent of the other white informants, for 70 percent of white informants scored no more than 2 on the features (see table 4.4).

In considering the score of informant #7, born in 1894, the diachronic perspective of table 4.6 reveals that of seven white informants born before 1900, four (57 percent), including #7, were r-less, all born between 1892 and 1899. These four white informants and the three African American informants born before 1900 hold r-lessness in common, but, as we contend above, with a different sociolinguistic meaning attached to r-lessness (see Downes 1998, 175, for a discussion of various meanings of rhoticity across cultures). It is, we suggest, an ethnic marker in one case and a vestigial marker differentiating white groups in the other, both descended from separate though historically connected founder dialects. Similarly, informant #7 shares diphthongal nuclear -r not only with five of seven African Americans born before 1910 but also with white informant #31. This feature, though superficially sounding the same in white and African American usage, is described by E. Thomas as occurring in old-fashioned Lowland Southern English and in African American English (2001, 49), two different speech-community bases.

Informant #7 grew up while r-lessness was still viable for language acquisition in Madison County for African Americans and for whites; however, the diachrony of table 4.6 situates informant #9 very differently. For the other LAGS white informants, birth around 1900 begins the period when r-lessness would not normally be acquired in Madison County.[17] Yet informant #9, born in 1926 within an area that had strongly moved toward r-fullness from its earlier r-lessness, exhibits postvocalic r-lessness, harkening back a whole generation. Britain has shown how the nonconforming linguistic features of the "outlier," an individual whose speech differs significantly from others in the speech community, can be explained by careful analysis of his or her personal history (2003). Such may be the case with informant #9. A special linkage with Madison County and Huntsville's plantation past most likely explains her throwback r-lessness. She is the only informant in our ten counties whom LAGS placed in the social class "aristocrat," which LAGS defined as follows: "*Aristocrat* includes a very small number of LAGS informants whose families have dominated the community for several generations. They have great socioeconomic influence, inherited wealth, and superior education. This type also idealizes the past and recognizes the primacy of lineage" (Pederson et al. 1986, 287). *LAGS*, Vol. 1, provides a biographical summary for each of the 1,121 informants (Pederson et al. 1986, 81–280). Our informant #9 (LAGS 342a), the Huntsville aristocrat, is described as follows (with abbreviations silently expanded and additional information added for clarity):

Female, aristocratic, white, 47 years old, Atlas informant type III, modern and worldly [as opposed to old-fashioned and insular]. She was born in Huntsville and is a landowner and Presbyterian, active in her church [one of only two Presbyterians among our thirty-four informants; the other is also from Huntsville and upper class]. She finished about one year of college in Virginia, and has travelled to New York. Her mother was born in Huntsville and was a housewife with some high school education. Her maternal grandparents were from Madison County. Her father was born in Huntsville, had a tenth-grade education, and was a carpenter. Her paternal grandparents were from Tennessee. She is unmarried, is extremely cooperative and intelligent, and is candid in matters of usage. Her interview lasted three hours. (162)

Of course, we have no way of knowing the size of her social group, which may have included others sharing her r-less dialect. However, we can state that her label as an aristocrat and her biographical summary both suggest that her dialect was scarcely the result of backwoods isolation and insulation and a lack of contemporary social ties with r-full speakers. When she spoke, in our opinion, she was performing her chosen and perceived identity as a Southern lady, and that persona especially projected r-lessness in her idiolect synopsis. Out of twenty-one opportunities recorded in her synopsis for postvocalic -r in stressed and unstressed syllables, she was r-less or, rarely, weakly constricted 100 percent of the time. A sample of terms includes "ee-uh," "shoo-uh," "poo-uh," "haw-uhs" (hoarse), "hammuh," "goobuh" (goober, i.e., peanut), and "wood peckuh." Out of five opportunities for nuclear -r, she pronounced nuclear -r "er" in *heard* but produced a mid vowel plus -r in three other target terms (e.g., "guh-ruhl" for *girl*) and exhibited the full diphthongal sound in *church*, that is, "chuh-eech."

Comparing the idiolect synopses of informant #9 with that of informant #12, an African American man located in Athens, Limestone County, and born in 1889, we find their r-lessness essentially the same. Although #12 more consistently diphthongized nuclear -r, both pronounce *church* almost exactly the same, "chuh-eech" (for the specialist wanting to investigate the narrow transcriptions of the LAGS scribes, we have included both informants' idiolect synopses in a note[18]). In stark contrast to informant #9's aristocracy, however, informant #12 is the only informant of our group given the social-class label of *indigent*, used to designate "a small number of LAGS informants whose families live at the poverty level. Their social position is the lowest in the community" (Pederson et al. 1986, 287). Thus, it is reasonable to conclude that the near identical r-lessness for informants #12 and #9 held vastly different meanings at the social poles of indigence and aristocracy. It is socially loaded for caste, on the one hand, and class, on the other; it is an enduring product of earlier involuntary oppression and racial segregation for one and of voluntary social-class exclusivity for the other. While they lived less than thirty miles apart and some of their words sounded "the same" for a preeminently salient feature, their worlds were incalculably far removed. As stated above, the early history of Alabama is written in its -r's, but to what contrasting histories could r-lessness point!

The foregoing analysis of LAGS data for the twenty-six white and eight African

American informants across the northernmost ten counties of North Alabama suggests unique applications of the founder principle. Not one but three varieties of English were introduced as founder dialects into the area, and each developed differently. We suggest that the ensuing century and a half from the period of "Alabama Fever" until the LAGS interviews of the 1970s left four areal dialects in its wake for LAGS to uncover and document: two varieties of Southern white English and two varieties of African American English.

We have also seen that some of the differentiating markers have receded, leading us to consider below what new linguistic resources have come into play as markers of group loyalties and differences and whether the developing contrastive dialects continue to center upon region and its history or shift to other factors.

PART 4

Linguistic Conflict in Present-Day Alabama, or What's Wrong with *Right?*

Our journey began with Alabama's proverbial north-south sectionalism being complicated by a *LAGS* map (see map 4.2) locating Lowland Southern r-lessness in Upland Southern Alabama. Investigating the history of that apparent anomaly led us to discover a cluster of linguistic features that indexed four social dialects in the 1970s, all of which had arisen in response to North Alabama's sudden and turbulent settlement more than a century earlier. However, as that settlement period grows increasingly dim, the linguistic badges of group membership that LAGS collected in the 1970s will not necessarily operate in the same way in the twenty-first century, not only because once-differentiating features like r-lessness and non-Upland vocabulary have receded (see table 4.6) but also because once-importance social groupings have shifted. The preceding investigation has tried to show that North Alabama's original social groupings were not set in stone but set in soil. With the area moving away from that physiographically determined agronomy and toward industry, modern technology, and the service sector, new group identities and new spatial distributions of group members across the old, historically shaped landscape have developed, identities that appear to partake of larger statewide themes. We end our look at the relationship between cultural conflict and its linguistic consequences by expanding our purview to the whole state, wherein north-south sectionalism may be giving way to a different, though subtly connected, alignment.

The Selectivity of Salience

We saw that the r-less Southern lady (informant #9) was part of the 1970s tableau, her speech a throwback to the cotton-corridor glories of the Huntsville of old. Through her speech, the Lowland-imported aristocracy was hanging on by its fingernails. However, r-lessness, once a premier feature for differentiating varieties of white Southern English, had receded by and large, and it continues to do so. Rachael Allbritten, whose essay on the Southern Vowel Shift is included in this volume and who is a native of modern Huntsville (aka Rocket City), tells us that she never remembers hearing r-less speech among white Huntsvillians (personal communication). Her report becomes all the more striking when we consider that her linguistic research focuses on the epicenter of Alabama's first cotton kingdom. We learn from Allbritten's essay that today's linguistic struggle in and around Huntsville is being played out in contrasting vowel pronunciations, as social-group members differ in their degree of adopting the sound changes called the Southern Vowel Shift (see appendix A for more on this change). Her findings reflect cultural struggles other than the ones we have documented. In particular, her informants orient toward rural versus urban values rather than toward the old Upland versus Lowland distinction. Evidently, social change in North Alabama is similar to that in other Southern Regions. In a study of vocabulary change between the 1930s and the 1990s within the same communities in Georgia, South Carolina, and North Carolina, Johnson found that "rurality is now the primary geographical variable with an influence on language variation, with an effect comparable to that of education, race, and age" (1996, 110; for additional research documenting the urban/rural split as a major sociolinguistic variable in the South, see Bailey, Wikle, and Sand 1991; Bailey, Wikle, Tillery, and Sand 1993; Bailey, Wikle, Tillery, and Sand 1996; and E. Thomas 1997).

There is evidence in North Alabama of evolved social significance or social meaning (connotations associated with the way one speaks) for a linguistic feature examined in LAGS data above. The pronunciation of the diphthong [aɪ] in *right* as [rat] "raht" (that is, without a noticeable glide) as opposed to "rah-eet" (with a high glide) continues to function as a social marker, but arguably not with the same social meaning that the data from the 1970s revealed. To establish the earlier context from which the current social significance arose, we present in table 4.7 the [aɪ] "ah-ee" pronunciation in five different phonological contexts of the thirty-four LAGS informants, as recorded on their idiolect synopses. As table 4.7 shows, every informant, whether a non-cotton-corridor resident or a cotton-corridor resident, monophthongizes [aɪ] to [a] (that is, receives a score of zero) in at least one phonological context. The table sorts informants by year of birth to emphasize the rather equal dispersal of the feature throughout the seventy-eight-year span of birth years. This dispersal shows that this feature has not undergone the diachronic recession of, for example, r-lessness shown in table 4.6.[19]

As opposed to the pronunciation of *ride*, *nine*, *mile*, and *wire*, phonological contexts that showed moderate to zero percentage difference between non-cotton-corridor informants and cotton-corridor informants (see table 4.7), the pronunciation of [aɪ] in *right* strongly divided usage according to non-cotton-corridor areas (seven of nine, 78 percent "raht" versus two of nine, 22 percent "rah-eet") and cotton-corridor areas (nine of twenty-five, 36 percent "raht" versus sixteen of twenty-five, 64 percent "rah-eet"). Such a large difference suggests that prevoiceless [aɪ] had therefore taken on great significance or social loading according to how it was pronounced in the ten-county region (thus, our use of it as one of the five differentiating features in tables 4.4, 4.5, and 4.6). But while vestiges of the old Upland-versus-Lowland settlement loyalties may lurk under a more current social meaning, rural versus urban differentiation seems more apropos than the old pattern of rural-with-cotton versus rural-without-cotton as North Alabama develops away from its agrarian past.

For the urban point of view on *right* as [rat] "raht," we present this pronouncement from a male Auburn University sophomore from Huntsville: "Sounds a little country. We don't have an accent in Huntsville." Of course, everyone everywhere

Table 4.7. Monophthongization of [aɪ] in five phonetic contexts, informants sorted by year of birth and cotton-corridor or non-cotton-corridor location, all informants (N = 34, * = African American)

Informant	Total score	Degree Upland Southernness (Map 4.5)	County	Year of birth	Age at interview	Sex	Speaker type	Class[a]
2*	1	4	Jackson	1884	88	M	folk	L
27	2	?	Marshall	1891	87	M	folk	L
28	1	?	Marshall	1903	70	M	folk	M
31	3	3	Franklin	1906	72	F	folk	L
29	1	?	Marshall	1910	63	M	common	M
3	0	4	Jackson	1916	64	F	common	M
1*	1	4	Jackson	1931	41	F	common	M
4	1	4	Jackson	1944	28	M	cultured	M
26	4	?	DeKalb	1960	19	F	cultured	M
14	0	0-1	Morgan	1882	89	M	folk	L
12*	3	0-1	Limestone	1889	84	M	folk	LI
18	1	2	Lauderdale	1892	81	M	folk	L
30*	1	3	Franklin	1892	81	M	folk	L
7	1	2	Madison	1894	78	M	folk	L
25	3	0-1	Colbert	1894	80	F	common	M
34	1	3	Franklin	1896	77	M	cultured	U
6	1	2	Madison	1899	74	F	folk	L
13	3	0-1	Limestone	1901	69	F	folk	L
15*	0	3	Lawrence	1901	73	F	folk	L
19	2	2	Lauderdale	1905	65	F	folk	M
5*	3	2	Madison	1907	69	M	folk	L
20	0	2	Lauderdale	1907	64	M	common	L
22	1	2	Lauderdale	1908	65	M	common	L
16*	1	3	Lawrence	1909	66	F	folk	L
21*	3	2	Lauderdale	1909	63	M	folk	M
8	1	2	Madison	1912	61	F	common	M
23	3	2	Lauderdale	1917	55	F	common	M
32	3	3	Franklin	1924	50	M	common	M
17	4	3	Lawrence	1925	50	F	common	M
9	2	2	Madison	1926	47	F	cultured	UA
33	0	3	Franklin	1928	45	F	common	M
24	1	2	Lauderdale	1935	38	M	cultured	U
11	2	2	Madison	1951	27	F	cultured	U
10	1	2	Madison	1953	25	F	cultured	M

[a]Class abbreviations: (I) Indigent, (L) Lower, (M) Middle, (U) Upper, (A) Aristocrat.

Table 4.7. *Continued*

A, farmer B, parent was a farmer C, no farmer for two generations	Cotton corridor	Diphthong [aɪ] or monophthongization in five phonetic contexts: 1 = full high/reduced high glide; 0 = no glide or mid glide				
		right as "rah-eet" not "raht"	*ride* as "rah-eed" not "rahd"	*nine* as "nah-een" not "nahn"	*mile* as "mah-yeel" not "mahl"	*wire* as "wahee-er" not "wahr"
A	N	0	0	1	0	0
A	N	0	1	1	0	0
A	N	0	0	0	0	1
A	N	1	1	1	0	0
A	N	0	0	1	0	0
B	N	0	0	0	0	0
C	N	0	1	0	0	0
C	N	0	0	0	0	1
C	N	1	1	1	0	1
	no.	2/9	4/9	5/9	0/9	3/9
	%	22	44	56	0	33
A	Y	0	0	0	0	0
A	Y	1	1	0	1	0
B	Y	0	1	0	0	0
A	Y	1	0	0	0	0
A	Y	1	0	0	0	0
B	Y	1	1	1	0	0
C	Y	0	0	1	0	0
A	Y	0	1	0	0	0
B	Y	1	1	1	0	0
A	Y	0	0	0	0	0
C	Y	1	0	0	0	1
B	Y	1	1	1	0	0
A	Y	0	0	0	0	0
A	Y	1	0	0	0	0
B	Y	1	0	0	0	0
B	Y	0	1	0	1	1
C	Y	1	0	0	0	0
B	Y	1	1	1	0	0
A	Y	1	1	1	0	0
B	Y	0	1	1	1	1
C	Y	1	1	0	0	0
B	Y	0	0	0	0	0
B	Y	1	0	0	0	0
C	Y	1	0	1	0	0
C	Y	1	0	0	0	0
	no.	16/25	11/25	8/25	3/25	3/25
	%	64	44	32	12	12

has an accent, that is, language features that denote the social, ethnic, and/or regional underpinnings of one's speech variety. The term *accent* for the Huntsville native means having features not in agreement with the local, standard way of speaking, or, as we saw above, having speech that identified one as an "outlier." Once more it appears that citizens across the state's northern ten-county area are finding linguistic ways to group themselves in the new century, particularly with pronunciation of [aɪ]. Will the old cotton-corridor and non-cotton-corridor areas again present a microcosm of the statewide conflict based on rural stasis versus urban progress? A definitive answer awaits new research similar to the LAGS project of the 1970s to ascertain how and to what extent social distinctions based on speech will continue; nevertheless, we can enlarge our investigation to consider hints from the state as a whole, particularly how the old sectionalism between North Alabama and South Alabama is still reflected by the diphthongal versus monophthongal pronunciation of *right*, but with an added twist of rural versus urban conflict.

Considering that 100 percent of the LAGS informants monophthongized [aɪ] in at least one phonological context (see table 4.7) and considering the status of [aɪ] monophthongization as a major feature of New Lowland Southern (see table 4.2), the selectivity of salience strikes us as amazing in the great "raht/rah-eet" divide— *that only one context of monophthongization, prevoicelessness, would be so powerfully conspicuous to hearers.* In many areas of Alabama's Lowland South, a speaker may monophthongize *my, ride, mine, mile,* and *fire,* with impunity, but woe to him or her who utters *right, nice, knife,* and *hike* as "raht," "nahce," knahf," and "hahk." Terry explains that "there are times when to fully understand the nature of the variation that exists between regional and social groups, . . . we must first confront variation within the individual speaker" (2010, 28). In the account below, we indeed see the confrontation of variation for one speaker and on the most personal level.

The Severity of Censure

Bailey and Tillery, in their description of Southern English, remind us who speak it of a very real linguistic prejudice that many have experienced firsthand, including the authors of this essay. People who speak with a Southern accent "can anticipate at least polite (and often not so polite) condescension to their speech by non-Southerners" (2000, 27). A personal essay written for this publication illustrates, however, that such condescension is not limited to non-Southerners. Even within a Deep South state such as Alabama, linguistic prejudice toward certain kinds of Southern English can be as strong. Chanoah Warren, a rural North Alabamian who moved to Auburn University in South Alabama for college, presents the perspective of one who would be described by the urban Huntsville student above as "having an accent," particularly because of her "country sounding" pronunciation of *right* as [rat] ("raht").

> I grew up near Ranburne, Alabama, a town of under 500 about eighty miles northeast of Auburn in Cleburne County. I lived on seventy-two acres with my mother and my six siblings. We had two neighbors, one on each end of the dirt road where we lived. Ranburne is in a very rural area. There are no traffic lights, and one cop patrols the entire town. My high school, Ranburne

High, consisted of one two-story building with grades 7–12 taking classes. I moved to Auburn in 2002 to start college. I was seventeen at the time. Before I moved to Auburn, I guess I was a hippie farm girl. I really didn't hang out with any particular group; I was nice to everyone. I was all about saving the animals and the earth, peace, love, and happiness. I loved relaxing music like Grateful Dead and Bob Dylan. I rode horses every day and didn't leave the farm except to go to the Carrollton, Georgia, Flea Market on weekends. Where I grew up everybody knew everybody, and everybody was nice.

My daddy is from Texas, and my mom grew up near Auburn in Roanoke, Alabama. My natural accent is a lot like my dad's and my best friend's accent. My best friend grew up in Ranburne, too. She was born in Carrollton, where the closest hospital is located.

When I started college in Auburn, my peers laughed about my North Alabama accent, and I didn't really fit in. They would repeat the word back to me like I said the word and laugh. Sometimes they would say that I talked funny. I remember going into the store with a group of my friends and they made fun of me because I called a "shopping cart" a buggy. They would pick fun at the way I said *like, right, white, nice, ice, rice,* and *might*. I mean, there were people who were nieece (friendly) but not nice, pronounced "nahce," like me (mannerly, happy, and with built-in Southern hospitality), so I joined the punks and goths and watched how I pronounced my words. I especially was made fun of for saying "raht," so I started saying it like "rah-eet." I guess college terrified me, and I felt protected by those "bad" kids. I started wearing big bottomed skater jeans and dying my hair different colors. I changed my taste in music to loud music like Tool and Marilyn Manson. When I visited my daddy back home, he said, "You're losing your Southern accent a little, and what's up with the new look?" I just acted like I didn't know what he was talking about and told him I loved my hair and pants. My best friend would come to Auburn to visit me and would be made fun of for the way she talked, too. So eventually, we grew apart, being that I joined the group that was against her "redneck type."

As I got older, I realized who I truly was and went back to being that calm, peaceful, and happy hippie farm girl. I moved my horses down to Auburn and got back into riding. I started not caring about the way I talk and what people thought about me. I became good friends with my best friend again, and she came to ride horses during my school breaks. Now, when my nephew who lives near Auburn in Salem, Alabama, comes and visits, he sometimes laughs at the way I talk. Most of the time I will change those "ahts" to "ah-eets," but when I don't, he notices, laughs, and says "it's 'rah-eet,' Aunt Noie, not 'raht.'" He even laughed at me the other day because he said I said "beans" funny. I don't know whyeee. —Chanoah Warren

Ms. Warren did face ridicule toward and rejection of the essence of her self-perception. As a freshman in a totally new environment, she was offered no unconditional acceptance but pressured to mold herself into others' preconceptions of the Auburn co-ed. Her reaction was not unlike that described by the theory of oppositional culture for the involuntary minority. Marginalized by the majority who make the rules and who benefit by playing according to them, she rebelled against the oppressive culture to take part in a cultural inversion, in her case, the punks and goths.[20] Over time, she reasserted her truer self, the "happy, hippie farm girl," who knew what "nahceness" was really "lahk," but continued to alter her performance of linguistic identity with her nephew to avoid censure close to home.

Linguistic bigotry against the monophthongal pronunciation of *right* in Lee County, Alabama, is not confined to Ms. Warren's experience. Bernstein's research highlighted similar attitudes held by Auburn University sorority members, where South Alabama prejudice toward the common North Alabama monophthongization of [aɪ] before voiceless sounds (i.e., *right* and *light* as [rat] "raht" and [lat] "laht") is also couched in terms of "country" versus sophisticate. For example, in speaking of *light* pronounced as [lat] "laht," an interviewee commented, "That sounds really hick. In a job interview, you can't say that, or people will think you're ignorant—that you go barefoot and wear overalls." According to Bernstein, such responses "show just how salient" prevoiceless monophthongization of [aɪ] is for forming judgments about those who exhibit it (2006, 227).[21] Other relatively urban-oriented locations in Alabama show the same pattern that we have referenced for Auburn University and Huntsville. In her essay in this volume, Davies points out that for her students at the University of Alabama in Tuscaloosa, "raht" is associated not only with North Alabama but also with "a 'country' accent." Doxsey, in her essay on the Mobile area in this volume, reports that all her informants produced [a] for [aɪ] before voiceless sounds occasionally but were still critical of the pronunciation and saw it as "country" compared to their perception of their own English. Though North Alabama is often referenced in the censures, such evidence suggests a statewide theme that goes beyond historical sectionalism. The repeated connection of monophthongal *right* with rurality ("country," "overalls") leads us to conclude that more than region is involved and that the prejudice is associated with urban versus rural values rather than, strictly speaking, Lowland South culture versus Upland South culture.

E. Thomas reports that in many areas of the South the pronunciation of *right* as [rat] "raht" "is considered less prestigious than the pattern that has strong glides before voiceless consonants" (2001, 37). Since, in general, being rural is considered less prestigious than being urban (consider the characteristics implied when *redneck* is used as a slur), this orientational marking of the pronunciation (its social loading) becomes understandable. But for those who identify rurality as superior to urbanity, as Ms. Warren does, covert prestige comes into play, that is, they will purposefully identify with the nonprestigious in order to revel in a type of counter-prestige.

The Conflict Ahead

Such is the power of language in our lives: the features of our speech can be drawing us toward one group, pushing us away from another, and signaling degrees of membership in various groups, all at the same time (see Johnson and Nunnally's essay in this volume for these forces at work for an African American). Chanoah's return to the North Alabama–flavored dialect of her rearing is little different from her dropping of the "goth" fashion statements and choice of music to once more embrace her more comfortable and genuine identity. She has chosen to gently play out her own oppositional culture: "I went back to being that calm, peaceful, and happy hippie farm girl." Stories such as Chanoah's bear profoundly on the question of dialect maintenance. They should give pause to those who glibly claim that regional and social dialects will certainly die out, as the mass media will eventually have us all sounding alike. As Romaine expresses it, the question is

> whether some features of Southernness may be retreating in the face of pressure from globalization and in-migration of outsiders, or whether they will be exploited to index local identity.
>
> Evidence . . . seems to suggest that the answer to both is yes. Despite the dire predictions made by some pundits of globalization about the death of all that is local and distinctive, sociolinguistic research suggests that pronunciation serves an important identity marking function, perhaps more so than vocabulary or syntax. Thus, we find that the trend in long-term phonological evolution as a whole is towards increasing divergence with respect to British and American English, as well as with respect to other varieties of English around the world in general. Studies of sound change have found that the dialects of Boston, Los Angeles, London, and Sydney are now more different from one another than they were 100 years ago. The limited influence of popular media on actual speech behavior suggests that what is crucial is actual social interaction rather than passive exposure through mass media such as television. (2005, 661)

Or, as Tillery and Bailey express it, "The history of [Southern American Englishes] is largely not one of survivals, but of transformations, of creative and responsive adaptation to new situations. That is why [varieties identified as Southern are] still around" (2003, 171). But since social differences will continue to be considered meaningful not only across major dialect communities but also within them, cultural identities at the local level will influence various groups to mark out their territory by their language, just as rurally oriented North Alabamian Chanoah does while living in South Alabama. In commenting on language differences of high school "jocks" versus "burnouts" in Michigan, Eckert may very well describe the future of "raht" versus "rah-eet" for Alabamians: two groups "are competing for the right to define their community" (1996, 66). Cultural collisions will continue to produce linguistic fallout.

NOTES

1. Between 1968 and 1983 the Linguistic Atlas of the Gulf States (LAGS) collected information on speakers (called informants) from eight Southern states: Florida, Georgia, Tennessee, Alabama, Mississippi, Louisiana, Arkansas, and Texas (the eastern third of Texas, not the whole state). In the planning stage, to divide the states into meaning-

ful segments, meticulous attention was paid to settlement history, physical geography, and migration routes, and because speech is a reflection of cultural identities, the informants were chosen to reflect a predetermined range of educations, ages, and cultural profiles and to include men and women of white, African American, and a few other ethnicities. A sketch of each informant's community and a biographical sketch and short history of each informant are included in the *LAGS* materials so that researchers have access to a remarkable range of information about the responders to accompany their responses. A total of 1,121 informants across the Gulf States were individually interviewed by trained fieldworkers and advanced graduate students, with 914 of the interviews/informants being chosen as Primary and the others labeled as Secondary.

A fieldworker tape-recorded each interview, lasting rarely less than two hours and often more than six. The fieldworkers used a long worksheet designed to elicit predetermined features, that is, target items revealing sounds, words for items, and grammatical features known to correlate with particular regions, as discovered by previous Linguistic Atlas Projects and preparatory research for LAGS. Though fieldworkers could ask sample questions, the method of elicitation was up to them, and they also engaged in free conversation when possible. Fieldworkers did no linguistic transcription in the field, nor did they make written records of data. LAGS was the first project to completely separate the operations of interviewing and of interview transcription. Fieldworkers simply produced the tape-recorded *field records*; from these records, transcribers in Atlanta (called "scribes" by LAGS) compiled *protocols* (transcriptions of the tape-recorded data) and from the protocols created *idiolect synopses* (one-page summaries of protocols, discussed further below).

Thus, the LAGS project maps differences and similarities across the eight-state area, and the information in the protocols and idiolect synopses gives researchers fairly quick access to answers about the characteristics of speech throughout the LAGS states. For example, fieldworkers tried to elicit from each informant the name of the tiny, skin-burrowing creature that plagues Southerners when they have been outdoors, showing thereby that it is called a *chigger* in the upper South and a *red bug* in the lower South. In the case of Alabama, the upper-South term and lower-South term form a horizontal line running roughly through the middle of the state (Pederson and McDaniel 1992, 121).

The massive *Basic Materials* of LAGS (Pederson et al. 1981) are available on microfiche (cards containing reduced copies of pages viewable only on a magnifying reader) at major libraries. Accompanying the *Basic Materials* are a full *Concordance* of the findings (Pederson, McDaniel, and Bassett 1986), also in microform, and seven large printed volumes that explain, document, and map some of the data (Pederson et al. 1986–1992, 7 vols.). In a new development for linguists, the Linguistic Atlas Project, housed at the University of Georgia, has overseen the digitizing of original tape recordings of LAGS interviews. In the first phase, sixty-four interviews were made available for purchase from the Digital Archive of Southern Speech (DASS). These sixty-four interviews were selected by LAGS director Lee Pederson, four from each of the sixteen LAGS sectors, consisting of one African American speaker and three white speakers representing the Atlas types folk (Type I), common (Type II), and cultivated (Type III). Two digitized interviews happen to be with informants used for our study, 342 (our #8) and 364 (our #30). See the Linguistic Atlas Project Data Download Center for further details (*http://www.lap.uga.edu/Site/DDC.html*).

One part of the microfiche-published *LAGS* materials, central to our research, is the idiolect synopsis of each informant, a one-page table summarizing his or her speech, a linguistic sketch, as it were. To create each idiolect synopsis, pertinent transcriptions were copied from each informant's protocol to produce a "snapshot" of his or her speech for pronunciations of vowels and consonant combinations, word choices, and grammatical items (see Pederson et al. 1981, 289–91). Our research on North Alabamians is based on the published *LAGS* volumes and the pronunciation and vocabulary findings available in the idiolect synopses as they relate to Upland Southern versus Lowland Southern dialects. It is important to note what idiolect synopses cannot accomplish: these data cannot give rise to a "variationist" study as the term is normally understood (see the essays by Feagin, Spence, and Doxsey in this volume for such studies). For a particular item of vocabulary, grammar, or pronunciation, the synopsis of each LAGS informant provides only a single sample form rather than a ratio of variability for that item in comparison with other, competing, forms. When the synopsis gives [ra:d] as the pronunciation of key word *ride* for an informant, one cannot conclude that he or she "categorically" produces /aɪ/ as [a:] on every occasion and does not also sometimes produce *ride* as [raɪd]. Such variation of production is the norm in speech and is studied in conjunction with social and linguistic conditioning factors in most sociolinguistic research. With digitized tapes of the LAGS interviews now available, as reported above, variationist studies may be possible in the future. For this study, however, the generalized choice of contrastive feature in the speech of the informants suffices for analysis of linguistic consequences of the Upland Southern versus Lowland Southern cultural competition.

On the other hand, even at the level of abstraction of the idiolect synopses, as used in this study, LAGS data allow researchers to connect, as it were, with real people, not just statistical data, because of the thorough descriptions of communities and informants. For example, our Jackson County informant #2 (LAGS secondary designation 337A), interviewed in 1972, was a very elderly, lower-class, "folk speaker," African American farmer born in 1884. Although the grandson of slaves, he was following generations of his family who had lived in Alabama's highly Upland South–oriented county, where African Americans made up 5 percent of the population, according to the 1970 census (1,980 African Americans out of 39,202 residents). Such background helps contextualize his use of an upper Alabama term, *pole beans*, instead of the lower Alabama term *snap beans* used by five of six African American informants living in counties to the west, with much higher African American population percentages. Nevertheless, our informant #2 participated in African American identity by retaining general r-lessness in extremely r-full Jackson County, like the other six informants to the west. (More on these findings in the text.)

Much of the value of LAGS has yet to be uncovered. Other sociolinguistic methodologies and theoretical interests were taking hold in linguistic programs during its period of compilation and publication, shifting interest from the earlier emphasis on dialectology and historical linguistics that had motivated the Linguistic Atlas projects. Nevertheless, newer projects after LAGS do not present data that offer the density of sample and the scope of findings. For example, although the *Atlas of North American English* or ANAE (Labov, Ash, and Boberg 2005) is valuable and important for its national scale, it does not compare in depth to LAGS for Southern coverage. ANAE analyzes data from a telephone survey (the TELSUR) of 762 respondents for the entire

United States, targeting speakers in around 150 urban areas, termed "Zones of Influence" (Ash n.d.). It also had a very different aim from traditional linguistic atlases: to discover how the sounds of American speech by region were changing. ANAE cannot determine, as LAGS does, baseline Gulf States–region dialect divisions (twenty-nine in number!), myriad social-dialect patterns for the regions, grammatical usages and vocabulary items that have been retained over several generations, and a tapestry of folklife on the wane. In terms of representative speakers, thirteen Alabamians in total were interviewed for ANAE, eleven from urban areas (five from Birmingham, three each from Montgomery and Mobile) and two from rural areas, and only around half of them have their responses plotted on maps (see map 1.1 in Nunnally's essay in this volume). One may compare that thin coverage of Alabama with the density of thirty-four informants just for Alabama's ten northernmost counties (about one-sixth of the state's landmass).

Another reason that LAGS has yet to be fully mined is, to be frank, the considerable time and energy necessary to learn to use the information and to deal with data in microform; furthermore, the 1980s computer-program version of the findings made available for instantly analyzing and creating maps of the data needs updating to current platforms. But most of all, the strength of LAGS is also its weakness: LAGS eschewed the easy generalizations and, to use a figure of speech from display technology, left it to its users to develop their own images from the multitude of data pixels. For example, in Pederson and Leas's discussion of LAGS data on smoothing of [aɪ] "ah-ee" in words like *right*, the authors determine nine varieties of pronouncing [aɪ], not just [raɪt] "rah-eet" versus [rat] "raht" (1981). For our study of the basic Upland-Lowland Alabama divide, we find it necessary to generalize into four productions divided into two categories: 1) the full diphthong as in "rah-eet" ([raɪt]) and the diphthong with reduced but high-vowel off-glide as in "rah-iht" ([raɪt]) and 2) the diphthong completely smoothed into a monophthong as in [rat] "raht" and the diphthong with the reduced but mid-vowel off-glide, [raɛt] "rah-eht."

Finally, we wish to mention the different methodological perspective required by Linguistic Atlas data. The care that LAGS showed in selecting informants makes it highly likely that informants' speech reflected shared features with others from their locations with similar social characteristics, but we would be presumptuous to represent our thirty-four North Alabama informants as a SAMPLE that reflected the majority of speakers across the area, for the 1970s and even more so for the present, and we assume that our findings will not be misinterpreted in that way. As discussed above, research by the Linguistic Atlas Projects including LAGS identified sounds, grammatical features, and terms/phrases (e.g., *pail* in the North versus *bucket* in the South) that were associated with regions, and thus information was developed into questionnaires/worksheets to elicit data for contrastive results. Informants were not chosen randomly. The LAGS sample is a *purposive sample* designed to be representative of the native population of the Gulf States in the 1970s. Because of its historical orientation, it over-represents older, rural people. Nevertheless, in LAGS Pederson pioneered a richer pool of data than the Atlas projects before it by including balanced and/or ratio-reflective numbers of informants according to age, class, education, gender, ethnicity, rural versus urban, and so on. (See Montgomery 1998b for a full description of LAGS.) However, the project data must still be rightly understood as not amenable to the same tests as, say, random-sample telephone surveys.

Similarly, since the "apparent time" trends in our diachronic analysis were not derived from random samples of speakers, it would not be prudent to claim that they indisputably picture language change for the features examined, except perhaps for r-lessness, where the evidence is overwhelming. For less demonstrative findings, however, one may at the least claim that forms stayed current and were passed down generationally in North Alabama as in, for example, the surprising retention of [tɛn] "tehn" for *ten* in opposition to the wide adoption of [tɪn] "tihn" for *ten* across the majority of the LAGS eight-state area. Some of the younger informants whom LAGS recruited in our ten-county area happened to exhibit the recalcitrant form, *ten* retained as *ten*, not merged with *tin*, suggesting resistance to the merger of prenasal /ɪ/ and /ɛ/ across Upland North Alabama for sociolinguistic reasons, but new research must be done to discover the current state of resistance to the merger, if it still exists.

We encourage those wishing to learn more about LAGS than our quick summary and partial explanations provide to start with Montgomery's overview (1998b), then to proceed directly to Pederson et al. 1986–93 for the seven printed volumes (especially the *Handbook*, Vol. 1) that explain and interpret the LAGS materials, and finally to dive into the microform materials. We believe the effort will be richly repaid in linguistic discovery and understanding. Both authors found that their students in linguistics classes gained much from being sent to LAGS for short projects. In LAGS, as Schneider has explained, Pederson "both carried on the tradition of American dialectology and revolutionized the field by introducing innovative techniques and modern technology, and he and his team have amassed enough material for generations of scholars to work on" (1998, 144–45).

2. Phonetically, the sounds are [iɚ] versus [iə]. General readers who want more specialization in their linguistic knowledge can start with appendix A, The Sounds of English and Southern English, in this volume.

3. Note that in some varieties of English, especially African American English, -r sounds may be completely omitted word-finally, as in "foe" for *four*, and word-internally, as in "woh-ee" for *worry*. Though some LAGS African American informants for our area produced such forms, those variants were not an issue in this study; however, further analysis of this greater degree of r-lessness in LAGS data may elucidate its role as a marker differentiating white and African American r-lessness. Note also that some American English dialects outside the South are r-less, especially in New England, but a comparative study is also not an issue here. For study of possible transatlantic links to England for r-lessness and other sounds of Southern English, see Schneider 2004.

4. Readers unfamiliar with the diphthongal nuclear -r (or syllabic -r) may enjoy examples of "uh-ee" for "er" given below produced by white, Mississippi-born-and-reared, Pulitzer- and Nobel Prize–winning author William Faulkner and by African American/Creole, New Orleans-born-and-reared rock-and-roll legend Fats Domino. Though widely separated by social grouping and Jim Crow laws, Southern aristocrat–descended Faulkner and partially slave-descended Domino share Deep South history and tradition.

Diphthong for "er" + consonant in Faulkner's 1957 definition of a fyce: "He is—in our Mississippi jargon, he is any small dog, usually he was a fox or rat terrier at one time that has gotten mixed up with hound, with bird-dog [buh-eed dog], everything else, but any small dog in my country is called a fyce. . . . And he's quite smart. He's quite brave. All's against him is his size. But I never knew a fyce yet that realized that he wasn't as big as anything else he ever saw, even a bear." (http://faulkner.lib.virginia.edu/display/wfaudio03)

Diphthong for "er" + consonant in Domino's performance of 1956 hit "Blue Monday": "Sunday morning my head is bad. / But it's worth [wuh-eeth] it for the time that I had. / But I got to get my rest / Because Monday is a mess." (Many renditions on YouTube, including a remaster of the 1956 release at https://www.youtube.com/watch?v=5qNB3_i46iA)

A widely heard but nonauthentic example of diphthong for nuclear -r occurs in the 1969 Creedence Clearwater Revival recording "Proud Mary." Berkeley, California, native John Fogerty affects the African American "uh-ee" for "er" pronunciation in "tuh-eenin" (turnin') and "buh-eenin" (burnin') evidently as an aspect of his "swamp rock" persona. For acoustic analyses of diphthongal nuclear -r, see E. Thomas 2001, 49.

5. The Alabama counties we examine are the ten northernmost counties of the eighteen counties within the eleven grid units BN–BX comprising LAGS Sector VI, Upper Alabama, in the East Central Zone. See Pederson et al. (1986) for a full description of the LAGS region, grid, and methodology. For a general explanation of another pocket of r-fullness on map 4.2, the one in extreme lower southeast Alabama (in the Wiregrass region), see Pederson 1996. As is mentioned multiple times in this volume, much remains to be done to fully explicate the linguistic landscape of Alabama, its regional, social, and ethnic varieties. The pioneering work of Allbritten, Doxsey, Feagin, and Spence in this volume (and their continued research) points the way for better regional understanding, especially the current waves of change as Alabamians reinvent themselves once again and adopt language features to fit these identities. Equally important is a full accounting of the dialect varieties of African American English in the state (see the essay in this volume by Johnson and Nunnally for dialect variation within just one individual and, later in this essay, the evidence for distinct varieties of AAE in our counties). For an overview of these topics and other needful research, see Montgomery's afterword in this volume.

6. According to Tillery, Bailey, and Wikle (2004), studying and understanding the "fate of the Founder Dialects, which developed following the initial European settlement of the United States," will need to be a major thrust of American dialectology in the twenty-first century. They pose the research question: "Although extensive changes in American English over the last century have eliminated many features of the Founder Dialects, vestiges of them are still extant. What effect will the ongoing demographic changes that are radically reshaping the American population have on the vestiges of the Founder Dialects?" (244). The final part of this essay will consider this question for Alabama as a whole.

7. Despite the eponymous origin of Jacksonian Democracy, Andrew Jackson himself owned a cotton plantation and the sixty slaves who worked it in Lawrence County (Jack 1919, 8).

8. For a map of Alabama's geographical regions, see the online map "General Physiography" at http://alabamamaps.ua.edu/contemporarymaps/alabama/physical /basemap6.jpg.

9. Though first envisioned during Alabama's territorial period (1817–1819) and debated periodically for a century and a half, the controversial project linking the Tennessee River to the Tombigbee for water transport to Mobile was finally begun in 1972 and completed in 1984. See Ress 2009.

10. Schneider (2003) uses the terms *Traditional Southern* and *New Southern* without our added qualifying insertion of *Lowland*. However, his definition linking his presentation of Southern English to "plantation culture" as quoted implies this addition. We do not mean, of course, that New Lowland Southern developed in a vacuum, as speakers of the Lowland Southern dialect since the Civil War have incorporated and continue to incorporate social, cultural, areal, and dialectal influences in the development of New Lowland Southern.

11. Census figures for white and African American populations on map 4.4 imply vast cultural differences between the upper ten counties and the six counties immediately to the south. LAGS data from that band of six counties (from west to east, Marion, Winston, Cullman, Blount, Etowah, and Cherokee) reinforce this assumption, implying greater homogeneity rather than sociolinguistic forces in conflict like those that arose within the northernmost ten counties and left the socially differentiating features of maps 4.9a–f. For example, the incidence of r-lessness for the eleven Primary informants of the lower six counties verifies the importance of treating the ten counties to the north as a significant area of cultural conflict: one r-less compared to ten r-full informants (9 percent), including the r-full African American informant, contrasting with the 55 percent r-lessness within our ten-county area (map 4.9c). The single r-less informant was white and located in Cherokee County, which, compared to the other five counties, is more of an extension upward from the Black Belt of Alabama and Georgia. Cherokee is the only county among the six with significant cotton production in the decade before the Civil War, yet it was separated from the cotton corridor to the north by agriculturally nonproductive areas. It is not surprising that LAGS included only one African American informant from these counties, considering that some have African American populations of less than 1 percent. The r-lessness of the single African American informant (LAGS informant #363), a middle-class farmer from Bexar, in Marion County, born in 1931, reinforces our call later in this essay for research into varieties of African American English across Alabama.

12. Sources for creating maps 4.9a–f from *LAGS* volumes 4–7 are listed below, that is, responses of the 914 Primary informants, thus including responses of the 20 Primary informants from Alabama's northernmost ten counties.

For map 4.9a, vocabulary items for *green beans/snap beans* and *earthworm/red worm* as regional markers:

West Central Gulf Coast/Lower Delta 2A, *snap beans*, LAGS vol. 4 (Pederson et al. 1990, 453)
West Central Gulf Coast/Lower Delta Pattern 2, *snap beans*, LAGS vol. 5 (Pederson, McDaniel, and Adams 1991, 354–55)

Highlands 5A, *green beans*, LAGS vol. 4 (Pederson et al. 1990, 313)

Highlands 4A, *red worm*, LAGS vol. 4 (Pederson et al. 1990, 312)

Social Map 48—White, *red worm*, LAGS vol. 6 (Pederson et al. 1991, 374)

For map 4.9b, merger of /ɛ/ and [ɪ] to [ɪ] before nasals, for example, *ten* and *tin* both pronounced as [tɪn] "tihn":

Gulf States 10B, *ten* and *pen* with [ɪ] "ih," LAGS vol. 4 (Pederson et al. 1990, 286)

For map 4.9c, r-lessness as in "ee-uh" for *ear*:

Texas/West Central Gulf Coast 1B, -r in *ear*, LAGS vol. 4 (Pederson et al. 1990, 445)

Highlands Pattern 1, r-full *beard* and *poor*, LAGS vol. 5 (Pederson, McDaniel, and Adams 1991, 66–67)

For map 4.9d, smoothing (monophthongization) of [aɪ] to [a] before voiceless obstruents, for example, *right* as "raht," presented in our map as non-smoothing, Lowland feature:

Highlands/Piney Woods 10B, for monophthongal or short glide *right*, LAGS vol. 4 (Pederson et al. 1990, 359)

Highlands Pattern 7, for monophthongal or short glide *rice*, LAGS vol. 5 (Pederson, McDaniel, and Adams 1991, 78–79)

Social Map 50—White, for monophthongal or short glide *right*, LAGS vol. 6 (Pederson et al. 1991, 376)

Social Pattern right <{ie}>, for monophthongal or short glide *right*, LAGS vol. 7 (Pederson and McDaniel 1992, 149–51)

For map 4.9e, diphthongal nuclear -r in words like *bird* pronounced with vocalized (nonrestricted) -r:

Regional Matrix 089.2Sa, Upper Alabama versus Lower Alabama, *church* as [ɜɨ ~ əɨ] "uh-ee," LAGS vol. 4 (Pederson et al. 1990, 222)

Lower Delta 4B, *cork* and *church* with vocalized -r, LAGS vol. 4 (Pederson et al. 1990, 470)

Lower Delta 4, *cork* and *church* with vocalized -r, LAGS vol. 5 (Pederson, McDaniel, and Adams 1991, 388–89)

Social Map 16—Black/Age 66+, *church* with vocalized -r, LAGS vol. 6 (Pederson et al. 1991, 342)

13. LAGS does not categorize the pronunciation of both *ten* and *pen* with "ih" instead of "eh" (the merging of phonemes /ɛ/ and /ɪ/ to shared allophone [ɪ] before nasals) as a regional marker or a social marker within its Gulf States area (see lists of such markers in Pederson and McDaniel 1992: xi, xii, xvii), and we realize that within the LAGS eight-state region in general, the symbols U for Upland Southern and L for Lowland Southern used in map 4.9b would mischaracterize the feature as a general marker of Lowland Southern English. Merger of /ɛ/ and /ɪ/ to [ɪ] before nasals occurs frequently in both Upland and Lowland Southern English within the LAGS data. Nevertheless, for a sound change that was already extremely widespread throughout the LAGS area in the 1970s and is now declared to be "all but complete in the Southern area" (Labov 2010, 130), the lower rate of merger depicted in these ten counties less than forty years ago makes it probable that extreme North Alabama's Upland Southern English speakers resisted the merger of /ɛ/ and /ɪ/ to [ɪ] before nasals for purposes of social mark-

ing. Added to the lower incidence of merger, the geographic patterning of evidence in our microanalysis of the *LAGS* matrix maps suggests that nonmerging (i.e., pronouncing *ten* as "tehn," distinct from *tin* "tihn") took on functions of cultural differentiation in our region of inquiry. The results of map 4.9b are thrown into sharp relief by the greater uniformity of the merger for the eleven LAGS Primary informants in the row of six counties to the south (Marion, Winston, Cullman, Blount, Etowah, and Cherokee): nine of ten whites (90 percent) merge both *ten/tin* and *pen/pin*, and eight of fourteen whites (57 percent) merge only *ten/tin* in map 4.9b; a single white merges neither set; and the sole African American Primary informant from the six counties merges *ten/tin* but not *pen/pin*. Unlike the other contrastive features of maps 4.9a, 4.9c, 4.9d, and 4.9e, the merger or nonmerger of *ten* and *tin* suggests that this socially differentiating dialect marker developed locally. An explanation is that the earliest Upland South settlers came to Jackson County and the other hill areas before the merger of /ɛ/ and /ɪ/ to [ɪ] before nasals got underway, and certainly before it entered the phase of rapid movement to completion. Brown documents this time table (1991, 307):

> The Civil War veterans' questionnaires clearly indicate that in mid-nineteenth-century Tennessee, two relatively stable variant forms, /ɪ/ and /ɛ/, were competing in the pronunciation of words like *pen* and *ten*. Over time, however, the raised variant appears to have gained favor, steadily increasing in incidence until the final quarter of the nineteenth century, when it gained dominance, accelerated with sudden rapidity, and went swiftly to completion, replacing the mid front variant almost entirely by 1930.
>
> Evidence derived from the Tennessee veterans' questionnaires establishes the existence of competing variants before nasals as early as the first quarter of the nineteenth century. The similarities in the rate of incidence of the merger among Tennessee veterans born between 1840 and 1851 and North Carolina LAMSAS informants born in the same period are remarkable. These similarities confirm the presence of the merger and also suggest that the unmerged variant was the dominant one. But in the last quarter of the nineteenth century, a dramatic increase in the merger occurs. The merger in North Carolina informants rises 14 percent during the last half of the century, while in Tennessee informants it shows a 35 percent increase over the same period. After 1880, the merged variant appears to have gained dominance in Tennessee, and the sound change, to have proceeded rapidly to completion.

Since our ten-county area's settlement preceded the dates of the trends noted by Brown by decades, we believe the local adoption of unmerged /ɛ/ is explainable: as is often the case, descendants of migrants from an area tend to retain a more conservative form of their speech in the new location even while speech in their original homeland changes (Icelandic versus modern Norwegian being an oft-cited example). Retention of unmerged /ɛ/ before nasals by the Upland Southerners would have been available as another linguistic badge of difference from the planters and their slaves, and as such, the social significance would have countered the regional diffusion of the merger documented by Brown (1991).

14. We do not claim absolute accuracy in our categorizing of informants as inside

or outside the North Alabama cotton corridor, nor did we expect to find (and, indeed, we did not find) perfect correlation between our labeling of "cotton corridor" locations for informants and Lowland Southern English. First, LAGS did not select its Target Communities with the Highland Rim physiography and its fertility in mind but followed its own carefully constructed guidelines for locations from which to select informants. Second, in the period since 1840 (the date of the cotton production areas of map 4.3), the upheavals of the Civil War and the industrialization of Alabama have changed the distribution of population and economic interests. Communities that appealed to LAGS as Targets have assumed new societal profiles since the settlement period and the Civil War. For example, Russellville, founded in 1815, was an early location for cotton ginning and grain milling but experienced an economic surge during Alabama's coal-mining and steel production era after Reconstruction, thus attracting a different mix of residents (see Bergstresser 2008). The three Russellville informants (#30, #32, and #34) provide their own interesting mix of the features we investigate. On the other hand, high scores on Lowland features for some of our non-cotton-corridor designated informants, especially informants #27 and #31 in the counties that had spotty but still rich areas of cotton production, may indicate errors in our classification that possibly weakened our findings.

15. We derived tables, adapted maps, and drew conclusions for sections three and four of this essay from a meticulous analysis of the idiolect synopses of the thirty-four North Alabamians (the LAGS Primary and Secondary informants we used). The original LAGS numbers for our informants (1–34) are the following: 1/337, 2/337A, 3/338, 4/339, 5/340, 6/340A, 7/341, 8/342, 9/342A, 10/342B, 11/343, 12/344, 13/345, 14/345A, 15/346, 16/347, 17/348, 18/349, 19/349A, 20/350, 21/350A, 22/350B, 23/350C, 24/350D, 25/351, 26/352, 27/353, 28/353A, 29/354, 30/364, 31/364A, 32/364B, 33/365, 34/365A.

It is beyond the scope of this already long study to share that full analysis, but some of the conundrums that our look into the different features uncovered and that deserve closer study via a broader use of LAGS data are discussed below.

Six informants (#1, #6, #17, #18, #21, and #27) exhibit "monophthong reversal," that is, smoothing of [aɪ] before voiceless obstruents but exhibiting of the diphthong in other environments normally more predictive of smoothing. Bailey hypothesizes that such speakers in Alabama and elsewhere in the LAGS region demonstrate a phonemic recategorization of /aɪ/ in their vowel systems: the diphthong /aɪ/ has been recategorized as a short vowel /a/, and like the other short vowels it has no off-glide before voiceless obstruents but sometimes does have an off-glide before voiced obstruents (e.g., no off-glides for *bit* and *bet* but off-glides for *bid* and *bed*).

Of the thirty-four informants, twenty-eight are consistently r-full or r-less in both stressed and unstressed environments, but six exhibit r-lessness in unstressed syllables (#10, #19, #20, #23, #25, and #27). Although occasional r-lessness in unstressed syllables by r-full speakers is common (e.g., "govuhner"), the biographies and locations of these informants imply an internalized cultural conflict reflected in their more than occasional production of the recessive r-less form in unstressed syllables.

Finally, the idiolect synopses of two informants pointed to dual allegiance because of the paradoxical nature of findings. Informant #31 was mostly Upland r-full postvocalically but produced the diphthongal nuclear -r for "chuh-eech," an exceptionally strong marker of Lowland Southern English. Likewise, informant #34 was r-less in *years* (Lowland) but monophthongized *right*, allowing for the culturally conflictive collocation "raht eeyuh" (*right ear*).

16. The evidence that LAGS North Alabama African American informants who lived just one county apart in distance (but far apart in historical depth of circumstances) differ in AAE features parallels Pederson's (1972) findings on nonhomogeneous speech of African Americans scattered throughout North Georgia communities. Our findings also give cogency to Wolfram's call for reanalyzes of regional AAE, free from unwarranted assumptions of homogeneity (2007b). The lack of homogeneity between the Jackson County African American informants and the cotton-corridor African American informants supports the conclusions of Childs, Mallinson, and Carpenter (2010) in their study of dialect alignment of African Americans in four rural sites in North Carolina: "In the mountain sites located in western North Carolina . . . we find widespread accommodation to local Appalachian [vowel] patterns, almost across the board. In general, only slight ethnolinguistic differences were found in the phonological systems of speakers . . . , and . . . generally factors related to speaker identity were found to be important in explaining subgroup variation." Like their findings, our findings also, to use their words, "highlight the need to investigate different social, historical, and linguistic factors relevant to each community when examining linguistic patterns and the creation/maintenance of the sociophonetic system" (42). Obviously, there is a need for contemporary research projects to explore the question we raise of divergent varieties of African American English in Jackson County versus the cotton corridor. The full LAGS protocols and the tape recorded interviews along with new interviews of native-born African American Alabamians in, for example, Jackson and Limestone Counties, will allow future researchers 1) to discover whether North Alabama truly developed distinctly different African American English dialects based inside and outside the cotton corridor by the late twentieth century, 2) to establish the baseline features of the two varieties, if they exist, and 3) to ascertain further divergence or convergence since the 1970s (or other outcomes). Also, if a distinct AAE of Jackson County is documented, one that accommodated to Upland Southern English in many respects but still marks ethnicity, it may show, as other recent research has concluded, that African Americans who are interspersed within a less "norm-enforcing" linguistic context can still "index their ethnic identity even after several generations in a community" (Purnell and Yaeger-Dror 2010, 117). Such an AAE may be an exemplar of Winford's description: "Far from being a mere reflection of poverty and lack of privilege, AAVE signals community membership and solidarity across class lines and functions as a badge of resistance to assimilation to the mainstream culture" (2000, 411).

17. Note that in South Alabama r-lessness in white speech continued to be linked with power and prestige much longer: consider the r-lessness of governors George Wallace (Barbour County, three terms between 1963 and 1987), Jim Folsom Jr. (Montgomery County, 1993–1995 and three terms as lieutenant governor), and Fob James (Chambers County, 1979–1983 and 1995–1999). A contemporary study of whether r-lessness is still being acquired in South Alabama among whites and African Americans is needed.

18. For closer study we provide below the target items for phonology, grammar, and vocabulary that LAGS used to construct the idiolect synopses, followed by idiolect synopses (figure 4.1 and figure 4.2) for Informants #9 (LAGS 342A) and #12 (LAGS 344).

PHONOLOGY
Fifteen stressed vowels in five phonological contexts (alternate terms, not listed here, were used when target terms were not elicited). Contexts are A) before a voiceless stop or fricative, B) before a voiced stop or open (+) juncture, C) before a nasal consonant, D) before a lateral consonant, and E) before a retroflex vocalic unit.

	A	B	C	D	E
/ɪ/	whip	cribs	pin	hill	ears
/ɛ/	neck	leg	ten	Nelly	Merry Christmas
/æ/	grasshoppers	bag	hammer	valley	married
/ʊ/	pushed	wood	woman	pull	sure
/ʌ/	shut	husband	sunup	bulb	—
/ɑ/	crop	father	John	college	car
/i/	yeast	three	beans	wheelbarrow	beard
/e/	eight	May	reins	rail	Mary
/u/	tooth	Baton Rouge	wound	mule	poor
/o/	coat	ago	home	cold	hoarse
/ɔ/	daughters	dogs	strong	salt	horses
/ɜ/	church	third	worms	girl	worry
/aɪ/	right	ride	nine	mile	wire
/aʊ/	house	cows	down	owl	flower
/ɔɪ/	oysters	poison	joints	oil	—

GRAMMAR
Plural forms for *posts, pounds, shrimp, wasps,* and *desks*
Function words for expressions *quarter to, toward, ran into, (sick) to the stomach,* and *wait for*
Principal parts for verbs *rise, drive, drag, eat, drink, help, dive,* and *climb*

VOCABULARY
Twenty-eight items indicating region, and so on, by choice of term

andirons	mantel	cow pen	stone wall
paper bag	burlap bag	harmonica	seesaw
flambeau	rowboat	wishbone	pancakes
headcheese	cottage cheese	mush	cling peach
freestone peach	peanuts	cherry tomatoes	green beans
woodpecker (large)	earthworm	terrapin	crawfish
dragonfly	chiggers	serenade/shivaree	lagniappe

FAY 47 3B
CWF/73:PE/78

UA HUNTSVILLE
BN 226.04

/ɪ/	hwɪˀᵊp	krɪ˄ᵊb	t'ɪ˃ˀn	bɪˀʃɛ̄	* ɪˀə
/ɛ/	nɛ˄k	lɛ˄g	* t'ɪ˃n	nɛ̄˃ʃɛ̄	mɛ˃ɾɛgo˄ʋ ra˄ʋn
/æ/	glæ˃ᵋs	bæ˃ᵋg	hæ˅mᵐə̆	p'ǣʃɛ̆t	mæ̆ʋrɛ̆d
/ʊ/	p'ʊ˂ʃ	wʊ˂ᵊd	wʊ̆smǣ	* p'ʊ˄tz (pres.)	* ʃʊ˂ə
/ʌ/	ʃʌ˂kɛ̆n	hʌ̆zbə̆n	* wʌ˂ˀn	bʌ˄˄ɬᵇ	
/ɑ/	* krɑ˃ˀp	* fɑ̄˂ᵊɟ̆ə	p'ɑ˃ˀm	k'ɑ̄lɛ̆d³	k'ɑ˂ᵇ?
/i/	ji˂ist	* θʃɪ˃i˃	* brɪ˃i˃nz	hwɪɛ̄ᵐbæ˄ɾə̆	bɪ˃əd
/e/	eɛ̄ᵋt	he˃ᵌ	stre˃ᵋnɛ̆n	p'e˃ᵋɬ	me̅˃ᵋrɛ̆
/u/	t'yŭθ	* t'ʊu	brʊ˂um	fʊŭɬ	* p'ʊ˂ᵌ
/o/	k'o˂ᵊt	əgŏsʋ	ho˅ᵊm	k'o˃˄ɬ	* fo˃ᵌ
/ɔ/	dɑ˂ɔ˄tə̆	dɒ˄ɔ˄g	gɔ˃ɛɔ˄n	sɑ˂ɔ˄t	* hɑ˅ʋɔ˄ᵊs
/ɜ/	tʃɜ˃ᵌtʃ	hɾd (PP)	k'ɜ˂æ˄ɲ̆	gɜ˂æ˄ɬ	wɜˀrɛ̆d
/aɪ/	ra˄ᵋt	ra˄ɛd	tʃa˄sᵋnə̆	hwa˃ᵊɬ	wa˄˃ᵋə
aʊ	* ha˄ʋs	* k'a˄ʋʋ	gra˄ʋn	æ˃˄ʃz	flæ˄ʋə̆ (=flour)
/ɔɪ/	ʔˀɛstə̆	p'ɔ˃ɛ˄ᵊɲ̆	dʒɔ̆ᵋnts	ɔ˄ˀɬ	ʃɑ˂ɔˀjə̆
PL	p'o˂ʋsᵗ	—		wɑ˂ˀsᵖ	—
FW	—	t'o˅ᵊ̆dz	ʔɪ˄nt'ʋu	—	—

—			dra˄ᵋv / — / —	
— / drʌ˄g / —			ɪ˃i˃t / — / ʔᵋɛt'ɲ̆	
drɛ̆gk (n.) / — / —			hɛ̄˄ʔp~hɛ̄˃ʃp / hɛ̄˄ᵊpt~ hɛ˃ᵊɬp / hɛ˃ᵊpt	

ᵋ̄ndɑ˃ᵊnzᵋ	mǣnə̆ᵊp'i˃s	—	fɪ˄ᵊnts
bɔ˂˃ᵋg	bɑ̄˄ɲlǣ˄ᵊp (bag	hˀ˂ᵊp	sᵋ̄t sɑ˂ɔ˄
—	ro˂ᵊbo˂ᵊt	wɛ˄ɪ˃ʃ bɔ˃ᵊn	p'ᵋ̄˄ᵋn k'e˃ᵋks
sa˄ʋsmɛ̆t	k'ɑ̄dɛ̆dʒtʃɪ˃i˃z	—	—
klɪ˄əsto˂ʋn	gʋ̆ubɔ̆z	—	grɪ̄i˃n brɪ˃i˃nz
wʋ̆dp'ɛ˄kə̆	—	—	krɔ˃ˀfɪ˃ʃ
sne̅˃ᵋᵏdaˀktə̆	—	—	—

Figure 4.1. Idiolect synopsis from LAGS *Basic Materials* (342a)

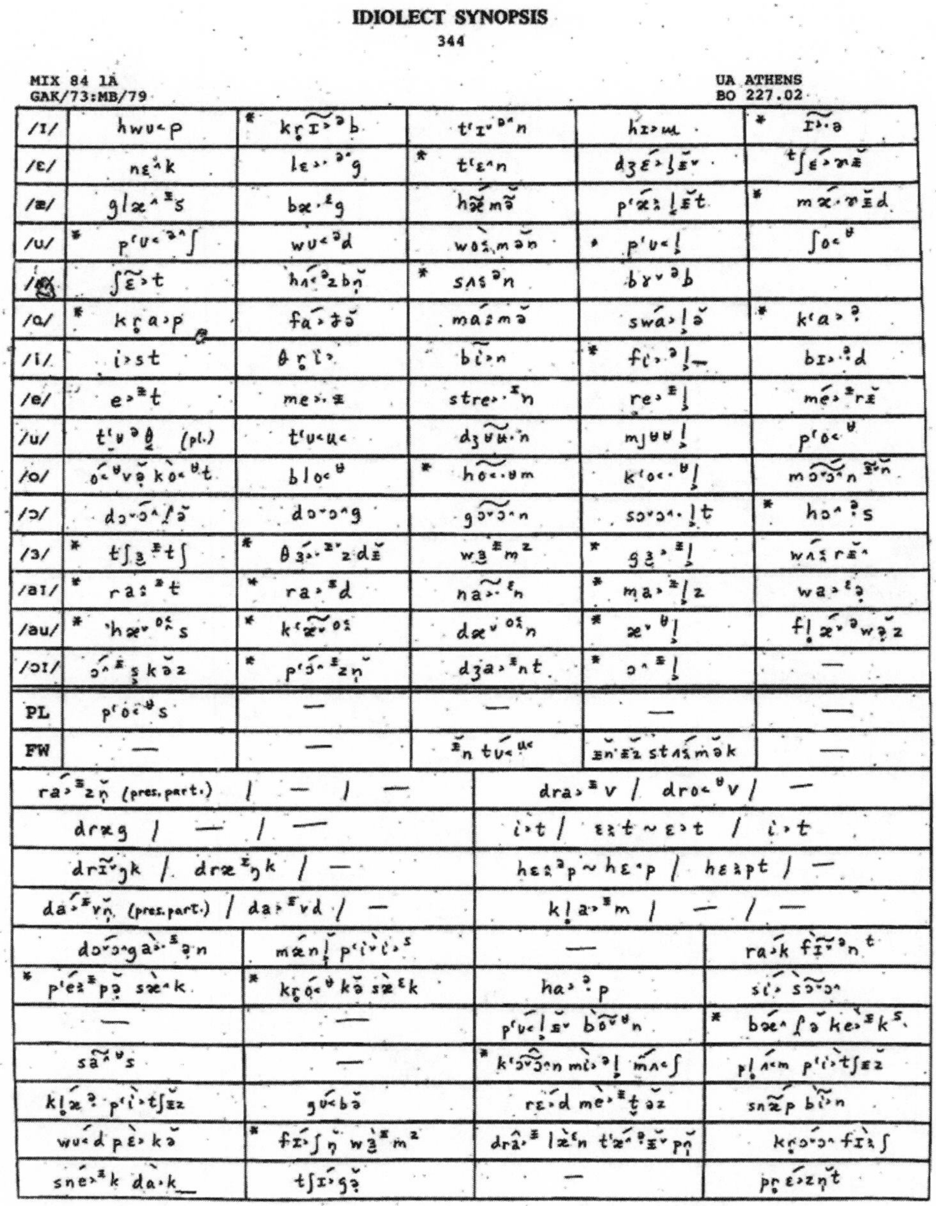

MIX 84 1A
GAK/73:MB/79

UA ATHENS
BO 227.02

/ɪ/	hwuᵉp	kɾɪ̃ᵃb	t'ɪᵛᵃⁿ	hɪ>ʉ	ɪ̃ᵛə
/ɛ/	nɛᵃk	lɛᵛᵃg	t'ɛᵃn	dʒɛᵛʃɛᵛ	tʃɛᵛnɛ̃
/æ/	glæᵛᵛs	bæᵛg	hæ̃mə̃	p'æ̰ʃɛ̰t	mæᵛ·ṽɛ̃d
/u/	p'ʊᵛᵃʃ	wʊᵛᵃd	wɔ̰̃mə̃n	p'ʊᵛl	ʃoᵛᵛ
/ᴀ/	ʃɛ̃ᵛt	hᴀᵛᵃbn̰	sᴀsᵃn	bɾᵛᵛb
/ɑ/	kɾᵃᵛp	faᵛɟə̃	maᵛmã	swaᵛlə̃	k'aᵛ?
/i/	iᵛst	θɾɪ̰ᵛ	bĩᵛn	fɾᵛᵃl̰	bɪ̰ᵛd
/e/	eᵛᵛt	meᵛᵛ	streᵛᵛn	reᵛᵛl	meᵛᵛrɛ̰
/u/	t'ʊᵛᵃθ (pl.)	t'ʊᵛuᵛ	dʒʊ̃ᵛn	mjʉʉl	p'oᵛᵛ
/o/	oᵛᵛvə̰koᵛᵛt	bloᵛᵛ	hõᵛ̃ʉm	k'oᵛᵛl	mõᵛ̃nᵛ̃ⁿ
/ɔ/	dɔᵛɔ̃ᵛlə̃	doᵛɔ̃g	gɔ̃ᵛɔ̃ⁿ	sɔᵛᵛlt	hɔᵛᵛs
/ɜ/	tʃɜᵛtʃ	θɜᵛᵛzdɛ̰	wɜᵛmᵛ	gɜᵛl	wᴀ̰rɛ̰ᵛ
/aɪ/	raᵛᵛt	raᵛd	naᵛ̃ᵛn	maᵛᵛlz	waᵛɟ̰
/au/	'hæᵛᵛs	k'æ̰̃ᵛoᵛ̰	dæᵛᵛn	æᵛᵛl	fl̰æᵛᵛwᵛ̰z
/ɔɪ/	ɔ̰ᵛskɔ̰z	p'ɔ̃ᵛᵛzn̰	dʒaᵛᵛnt	ɔᵛᵛl	—
PL	p'oᵛᵛs	—	—	—	—
FW	—	—	ᵛn tuᵛuᵛ	ɛn̰ɛ̰ stᴀ̰mə̰k	—

raᵛᵛzn̰ (pres.part.)	/ — / —	draᵛᵛv / droᵛᵛv / —	
drɛg / — / —		iᵛt / ɛ̰t~ɛᵛt / iᵛt	
drɪ̃ᵛŋk / drɛᵛ̰ŋk / —		hɛᵛᵃp~hɛᵛp / hɛᵛpt / —	
daᵛᵛvn̰ (pres.part.) / daᵛᵛvd / —		k'l̰aᵛᵛm / — / —	
doᵛɔgaᵛ̰ᵃᵛn	mæn̰ p'iᵛiᵛs	—	raᵛk fɪ̃ᵛᵃnt
p'eᵛᵛpə̃ sæᵛk	kɾɔ̰ᵛkə̃sæᵛᵛk	haᵛᵛp	sɪ̰ᵛsɔ̃ᵛ̰
—	—	p'ʊᵛlɛᵛ bõᵛᵛn	bæᵛʃəᵛkeᵛᵛkˢ
sã̰ᵛˢ	—	k'ɔ̃ᵛnmɪ̃ᵛl̰ mᴀᵛʃ	pl̰ᴀᵛm p'iᵛtʃɛz
kl̰æ̰? p'iᵛtʃɛz	gʊᵛbə̃	rɛᵛd meᵛᵛt̰əz	snæp bĩn
wʊᵛd pɛᵛkə̃	fɪ̰ᵛʃn̰ wᵛᵛmᵛ	drã̰ᵛlæ̰n t'æᵛᵛɛᵛpn̰	kɾɔ̃ᵛfɪ̰ᵛʃ
sneᵛᵛk daᵛk	tʃɪ̰ᵛgᵛ̰	—	pɾɛᵛznt̰

Figure 4.2. Idiolect synopsis from LAGS *Basic Materials* (344)

19. Although in table 4.7 informants #26 and #17 each smooth the [aɪ] diphthong in a single phonological context, the social significance of their patterns is vastly different (like the r-lessness of informant #9 versus informant #12). Informant #26, who smoothed only *mile,* was a nineteen-year-old female of cultured speech, a college student with college-educated parents, and having "some concern for correctness" (Pederson et al. 1986, 165). We suspect that informant #26, perceiving the diphthong as "correct," avoided smoothing it, but still pronounced *mile* as [maːl] "mahl," as do 91 percent of the informants. Informant #17, who smoothed only *right,* was a fifty-year-old female of common speech with "probably some high school" and parents with fifth-grade educations (164). However, informant #17, though her location was cotton corridor, is one of the most strongly Upland Southern English speakers (see table 4.4), probably because her father was from ultra-Upland Winston County. As table 4.7 shows, her production of *monophthongal right "raht" but diphthongal ride identifies* her as one of the Upland Southern monophthong reversers mentioned in note 15.

20. In her work on language differences as they emblemize the oppositional social groups "jocks" and "burnouts" in a Detroit high school, Eckert relates language use and fashion in ways that recall Ms. Warren's joining of the "punks and goths":

Clothing . . . makes jocks and burnouts unmistakable. Every element of their clothing oppositions is based in their ideological oppositions: burnouts wear Detroit and Ford factory jackets while jocks wear school, varsity and cheerleading jackets. Furthermore, burnouts wear these jackets in school, symbolizing and facilitating their fleeting presence in the school, whereas jocks plant their jackets in their lockers. In conscious rejection of the school's in loco parentis role, burnouts do not use their lockers or the cafeteria. Burnouts wear working clothes while jocks wear preppy styles. And the burnouts' clothes are all in dark colors, while jocks wear pastels, in keeping with their opposing orientations to youth, innocence, and mood. This opposition extends to paraphernalia (such as wallet chains), hair styles, makeup, posture, gait, territory, substance use, and food consumption. And all of these differences are highlighted by their concentration in separate school territories—the jocks in prime visible real estate, the burnouts in the outdoor smoking area. Jock and burnout stylistic oppositions, in other words, articulate their ideological opposition across the board. (n.d., 20)

21. Bernstein (2006) also presents LAGS evidence for the entire state, showing the influence of social factors such as region, education, and social class on the incidence of monophthongized prevoiceless [aɪ]. She clarifies Alabama's conflict between [raɪt] and [rat] by comparing it to attitudes in Texas. In contrast to some areas of Alabama, saying [rat] "does not mark a person as uneducated in Texas" (223). Her study demonstrates that a feature has meaning not in and of itself but within the norms of the community in which it is used. The prevoiceless monophthong in Texas does not carry the same social significance as it does in Alabama. Texans are sufficiently aware of the monophthong as a marker of regional speech that they avoid it in their most formal contexts but in all other contexts use it freely in all phonetic environments (230).

5
Just What Is the Southern Drawl?

Crawford Feagin

The mystique of the Old South seems to have reached around the world. When I told some Vietnamese refugees in Washington that I was from the South, they assured me that they knew all about it. They had seen *Gone with the Wind* in Saigon! While *Gone with the Wind* represents the old aristocratic South, another aspect of the South—the white rural working class—has spread its own influence through radio, TV, and recordings. I'm talking about the country and western music industry centered in Nashville and Austin. Possibly because of these phenomena, many people even outside the United States are familiar with Southern speech, especially what is called "the Southern drawl."

Despite popular interest in the drawl, it is surprising that in the explosion of linguistic studies over the past several decades, amazingly little has been written about it. In chasing down scholarly treatments of the drawl, I could come up with only six other linguists who have dealt with it at any length (Wise 1933; C.-J. Bailey 1968, 1969, 1985a, 1985b; Habick 1980; Wells 1982; Schneider 2004; and Allbritten 2011) and only one who devoted a whole article to it (Sledd 1966). That article was written more than fifty years ago, by James Sledd, a native of Atlanta and a linguist on the faculty of the University of Texas at Austin.

One of the first problems with studying the drawl is defining it. I'll return to a more technical and thorough definition later, but for now, we're talking about the pronunciation of a word having some or all these characteristics: the main vowel sound in the word is held longer than usual, the vowel sound changes as it is held, and the pitch of the vowel varies greatly. For example, an extremely drawled *yes* might be written as "YAY-EE-yus," with "YAY-EE" starting on a high pitch and changing its vowel quality from "yay" to "ee" and then dropping from the high pitch to a lower pitch on "-yus."

But an even greater problem is the drawl's tremendous variation in both form and use. What makes the drawl so variable is that it is subject to a wide range of conditioning factors. The linguistic conditioning factors are not only segmental, that is, conditioned by the *segments* or separate units of sound in a word, but also suprasegmental (*supra*—"on top of" segments), that is, conditioned by the intonation (changes in pitch) and stress (pulses) added on top of the segments. In addition, the drawl is subject to several conditioning factors connected with how language use reflects the people who use it, or sociolinguistic constraints. For the drawl these sociolinguistic factors can be seen in five different areas:

1. Geography: both regional variation (north versus south) as well as urban versus rural variation.
2. Demography: age, sex, and social class differences.
3. Language use: the intimacy and solidarity of the interaction versus its formality and distancing.
4. Topic: serious or light.
5. Self-identification: how "Southern" a person wishes to be perceived.

I'll begin by explaining how I go about my research; next I'll define what I mean by the drawl in its linguistic aspects, giving a bit of the technical side. Mostly, I'll discuss the social (sociolinguistic) and psychological aspects of the drawl. Last, I'll make some guesses about the future of the Southern drawl.

METHODOLOGY

Unlike any of the previous studies of the drawl, my work has combined the methodologies of sociolinguistics, of acoustic phonetics assisted by computer analysis, and of more traditional linguistic analysis, such as looking at which vowels can be drawled and at the phonetic context that might promote or inhibit drawling (e.g., Feagin 1987, 1996, 2002). I'll explain how I went about my research at each stage.

Sociolinguistics. In the kind of sociolinguistics I do, you have to take into consideration the location and type of community you're investigating. Then you examine a sample (group of speakers) of that community. One of the main ways to do this is by recording interviews with a selection of people who fit particular categories of age, sex, or social class.

The Speakers. The location of the speech I'm talking about here is Anniston, Alabama, my hometown. Anniston is not a town out of the Old South but an industrial city in northeast Alabama founded in the 1870s. It has a current metropolitan population of about sixty thousand people. The local economy was founded on iron and steel manufacturing and on cotton mills. Two-thirds of the people there are white and one-third are black. This has been the proportion since the town was founded. In this essay, I'll discuss drawling in white speech only.

To get a picture of the range of speech in the white community, I tape-recorded interviews in the late 1960s and early 1970s with urban upper-class and working-class people, both men and women who were over sixty at the time, and with teenaged boys and girls, with an equal number of informants in each category of age/sex/social class. I also interviewed older rural working-class men and women. Altogether, I taped interviews of eighty-two people, including with some middle-

Table 5.1. Sample words analyzed for ±drawl in sentence contexts

Digitized words in CAPITALS in source sentences	±drawl	Clause juncture
1. I said, anything I promise anybody, I'll do THAT, if I can.	drawled	YES
2. Sometimes I poured THAT out.	plain	NO
3. . . . when she DIED.	drawled	YES
4. . . . and she'd take forever at night to go to BED.	drawled	YES
5. I'd go out with younger BOYS.	drawled	YES
6. . . . and sideburns, and long HAIR, just like they got now.	drawled	YES
7. . . . but I couldn't go up and down the STEPS.	drawled	YES
8. . . . if you're not GOOD, Chicken George is gon' getcha!	drawled	YES
9. [sledding account] . . . squatted down and went down the HILL.	drawled	YES
10. . . . 'n they come and pay my BILLS for me.	plain	NO
11. And you'd pick your fresh berries for making jellies and JAMS.	drawled	YES
12. . . . or I didn't wanna do THIS.	drawled	YES
13. Who you gon' do THIS to?	plain	NO

aged and middle-class people. (Later, in 1990–91, I collected more interviews of another cohort of teenagers and re-interviews with some of the previously interviewed teenagers, who were by then approaching midlife.)

For this study of the pronunciation in the town, though, I am limiting myself to a detailed analysis of two people per category of age, sex, and social class.

The Interviews. My interviews with those eighty-two informants were attempts at real conversation. After getting a certain amount of demographic information—for determining their ages, their social classes, and that they were natives of Anniston or of the nearby rural area—I tried to distract them from the artificiality of the interview situation by asking them rules for childhood games and questions such as "Have you ever seen a ghost?" or "Have you ever been in a situation when you thought, 'This is it!', that you might lose your life?" Another good question was to ask how they met their boyfriend or girlfriend or their husband or wife. Or, I'd ask men about hunting or fishing. (The sample sentences in table 5.1 suggest some of my interview questions. See Spence's essay for her similar tactic of asking citizens of Elba to recount their flood experiences.) From these sorts of questions, I'd usually get about an hour's worth of talk. Often, I'd get indications that the informants were relaxed, such as when they laughed or got excited about the story they were telling and started talking faster and louder.

Acoustic Analysis. I analyzed the recordings of the eighty-two people for grammatical variation, which I reported on in *Variation and Change in Alabama English* (1979). Since then, I have reexamined the phonology (i.e., sound systems) of a subset of those people, looking especially at their vowels: first describing them, and then trying to see where change is taking place in the community.

I have now examined the pronunciation of twenty people I interviewed, two each in the ten categories I mentioned: older urban upper-class 1) men and 2) women, older urban working-class 3) men and 4) women, older rural working-class 5) men and 6) women, teenage urban upper-class 7) boys and 8) girls, and teenage urban working-class 9) boys and 10) girls. I have analyzed the speech of these twenty people on computers at the University of Pennsylvania Linguistics Laboratory.[1]

I selected one-second stretches of speech from the taped interviews, which were then recorded digitally into the computer directly from the tape recording—just like digitally recorded music. I recorded into the computer about 180 words from each person. I looked for single-syllable, fully stressed words. I tried to collect from three to five examples of each vowel, so for the sound /ay/,[2] or "long i," I might take *eye, tie, buy, sight, died* (see sentence 3 in table 5.1), depending on what turned up in the conversation. My methodology differs from some older research in that I use conversational speech from various segments of the community for acoustic analysis rather than a person—usually middle class—reading word lists or sentences into a microphone in an acoustics lab. Furthermore, the digital recordings allowed me to listen to the segments repeatedly. That is, the sound of the words or the vowels was recoverable, unlike working with earlier kinds of equipment, such as spectrographs. I also listened and wrote down in phonetic transcription what I heard, a process called "impressionistic phonetics." The advantage of using acoustic analysis on my material, rather than depending exclusively on my own hearing, is that—for most of us—impressionistic phonetics has certain limitations. We tend to screen what we hear through our expectations and through our own system of pronunciation. This type of combined sociolinguistic/acoustic phonetics research (now called sociophonetics) started in the early 1970s at the University of Pennsylvania Linguistics Laboratory, using a spectrograph. Computer analysis of this sort of material started there in the late 1970s.

Once I had the one-second stretches of speech stored in the computer, I could not only listen to each word but also use equipment to analyze it for three types of information: its waveform, its formants (or resonance bands), and its vowel trajectory. Figure 5.1 (images a, b, and c) reproduces printouts of these analyses for the drawled-word *that*, pronounced as "tha-ee-yut" [ðæi ət].

Image a in figure 5.1 is the waveform on a video screen. The various shapes and shadings of the wave indicate the makeup of the sounds of the word. The wave also shows the intensity or loudness of the vowel. The taller the wave, the more intense the sound is at that point.

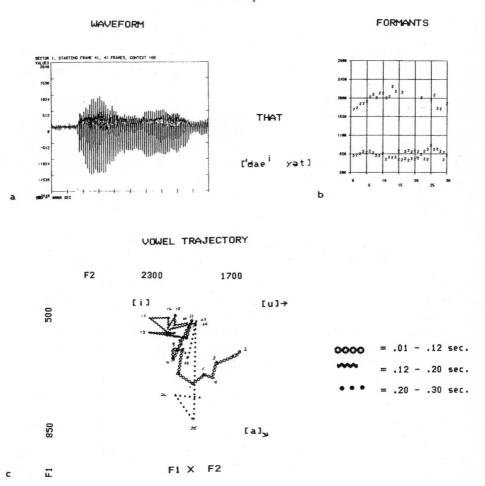

Figure 5.1. Analysis of digitized speech: Wave, formants, trajectory. Word in Context: "I said, anything I promise anybody, I'll do THAT if I can." Speaker: MB, seventy-seven-year-old working-class white woman, native of Anniston, Alabama

The second image, image b in figure 5.1, displays the first two formants across time (in milliseconds). Formants are "resonance bands" that the computer program can highlight. The first two formants tell us about the quality of the sound, whether the vowel is [oooooow] as in "Nooooo!!!" or [iiiiiy] as in "Meeee!!!!!" or [uuuuuuuw] as in "Booooo!!!!" The formants reflect the shape of the vocal tract (inside the mouth), mainly the location of the tongue. They are the two lines you can see in b. The lower one is called the first formant (F1); the higher one is the second formant (F2). I followed these steps for each of the 180 words I worked on for each person.

At this stage I could use the numbers from printouts of F1 and F2 to create a trajectory of the vowel, as illustrated in image c of figure 5.1, which showed me how much and in what direction the tongue is moving, measured in milliseconds. The trajectory display is placed inside the mouth as if you are looking at a cut-away of a left-side profile. It measures the tongue movement of the vowel in *that* over a .30-second interval, numbered. The circles (.01–.12 seconds), zigzag line (.12–.20 seconds), and dots (.20–.30 seconds) show the tongue's movement over time through different spaces in the mouth. As the numbers on the lines indicate, the movement starts in the mid-back of the mouth (number 1, circles), continues across to the front of the mouth (9 and 10), heads up to the high-front part of the mouth (11–18, zigzags), and then rises and plunges to the bottom of the mouth (22–26, dots). Thus, the depicted speaker's pronunciation of *that* is very complex, moving through three vowel spaces in the mouth! We will address such exaggerated "gliding" later.

To try to understand the context of the drawl, I went back to the tape recordings and checked the sentence where each word occurred for stress, intonation, and change of tone on the word or vowel. The interviewee's sentence that accompanies the analysis in figure 5.1 shows that the *that* appeared in the sentence, "I said, anything I promise anybody, I'll do THAT if I can," and that the sentence was spoken by an older, working-class woman.

Observation and Introspection. Since I'm a native of Anniston, I also used observation of other native speakers and introspection to help me think about and analyze the data, as well as careful listening to tapes and checking, say, 150 tokens (or examples) per speaker of a given phenomenon, such as the vowel /æ/, as in *that*.

In my investigation of vowel quality, I did not set out to study drawling specifically, but I ran into the problem of how to deal with the extreme gliding (tongue movement that changes the sound of a vowel as in image c, figure 5.1) for some people on many vowels. At that point, I simply had to account for what turns out to be a uniquely Southern phenomenon: the drawl. The first step was to establish a working definition of the drawl, which in common usage sometimes seems to mean just about anything!

DEFINING THE SOUTHERN DRAWL: A TECHNICAL SURVEY

After running an informal survey of Southern drawlers, Northern nondrawlers, and linguists, as well as reviewing the literature, I found that most people agree that there are three especially noticeable features of the drawl: 1) the lengthening of the vowel (as measured in milliseconds), 2) glides or diphthongized vowels going in every direction, and 3) remarkable changes of pitch during the pronunciation of a single word. Of the linguists who have dealt with the drawl, Tim Habick may have proposed the most useful definition: "In its most basic sense, drawling can be defined simply as a type of tempo, indicating lengthened as opposed to shortened ('clipped') syllables. In its practical realization in Southern dialects, however, drawling has become a complex phonetic and phonological development characterized by a large number of features. . . . [For practical purposes, drawl syllables] can be

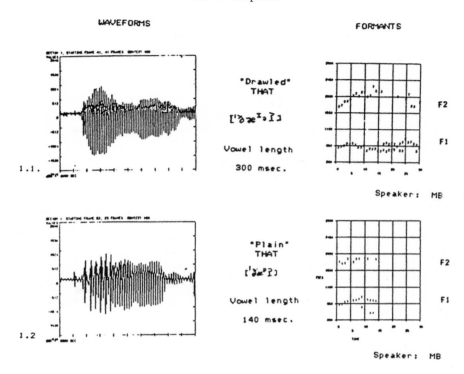

Figure 5.2. Wave, length, and formants of drawled and plain *that*.

described [acoustically] in terms of three major features which may occur singly or in combination: lengthening, [gliding], and amplitude drop" (Habick 1980, 181).

Furthermore, when linguists discuss the drawl, they seem to refer to two different, though interconnected, phenomena: 1) the segmental gliding of diphthongized vowels in words such as *bad* ['bæi ˌyʊd], *ham* ['hæi ˌyʊm], *boy* ['bɑo ˌwi], *horse* ['hɑo ˌwəs] (the marks ' and ˌ indicate primary and secondary stress); and 2) the suprasegmental features of lengthening and change in pitch, as in *John* pronounced with higher pitch on the first part and a drawing out of the words: "JAH-aaan." To keep these two separate, I call the gliding or diphthongized type of drawl the "basic" drawl, while the other type—adding the extra length and changes in pitch—I call the "extended" drawl. I'll explain why further on.

These different aspects of the drawl are illustrated from my data in both waveforms and spectrograph-like displays.

Length. In figure 5.1 we looked at various displays of drawled *that*. Figure 5.2 presents the waveform and formants of the drawled *that* along with displays of an undrawled *that*. Both were pronounced by the same person in conversational speech. The lengthening associated with the drawl is clearly shown, as the drawled vowel at the top of figure 5.2 is more than twice as long, at 300 milliseconds, as the undrawled vowel at the bottom of figure 5.2, at 140 milliseconds.

Drop in Amplitude. The second part of the definition I'm using is that the drawl can involve a drop in amplitude in the middle of a vowel. Look at the waveforms of drawled and undrawled *that* in figure 5.2 again. While 1.2 shows very little change in height in the middle, there is a noticeable dip in the wave of 1.1, making the sound wave look like a tube of toothpaste squeezed in the middle. This is what happens when a single vowel contains rhythmic beats. This dip is what we perceive as—and has variously been described as—a triphthong, a two-syllable vowel, or a vowel on two tones, though these three are not necessarily the same. Some more examples of vowels with two beats:

TRIPHTHONG: BOY [ˈbɑo ˌwi]
                HORSE [ˈhɑo ˌwəs]
TWO TONES: EYE [ˈa ˌa]

Change in Formants (Gliding). Returning to figure 5.2, look at the formant displays for drawled and undrawled *that* to note the greater changes in the formants of the drawled word. When we hear a vowel with a glide in it (a diphthong), as in *white*, with an [a] followed right away by an [i], or as in *boy*, with [ɔ] followed by [i], we are hearing a change in formants. This is caused by the different resonant frequencies that come from the variations in the space in the mouth as the tongue moves from one place to another and as the jaw opens more or opens less. These physical adjustments are what produce different vowel sounds.

In the drawl, there are often glides in places non-Southerners don't expect them. Moreover, Southern glides go in a different direction from glides in other varieties of English. One example is the [i]-glide in *bed* [ˈbɛi ˌyəd]. A New Yorker or Philadelphian might say [ˈbɪ əd]. Another example is the [o]-glide that the drawl produces in words like *dog* and *law*. Northerners have a different glide from Southerners here or no glide at all. While Northerners say [dɔg] or [doəg] or [dʊəg], many Southerners say [ˈdɑ ˌog]. For *law*, Northerners and Westerners pronounce it as [lɑ] or [lɔ] or [lɔə]. Southerners who drawl might instead say [ˈlɑ ˌo]. These differences in direction of glide are very noticeable to non-Southerners—just as non-Southerners' glides (or lack of them) are to a Southerner like me.

Change in Intonation. Last, let's look at stress (the emphasis placed on a syllable) and intonation (the falling or rising pitch accompanying a sentence or a phrase). To understand these concepts, listen to yourself say the word *background*. You'll notice a strong stress on *back-* and a weaker stress on *-ground*. Also you probably pitch *back-* higher than *-ground*, for an intonation that changes from a relatively higher tone to a relatively lower tone. Full or secondary stress contributes to drawling, as does a changing intonation. Often the changing intonation provides two tones for the drawled vowel, one for each pulse, just as in *background*:

Put it *down*! [ˈdæi ˌyown]
Come on *in*! [ˈiː ˌyʊn]
Bring it over *here*! [ˈhi ˌyə]
I thought I'd *die*! [ˈda ˌa]

Notice that in each of these examples the drawled word was a single syllable word (but with the vowel converted into a two- or three-part form by drawling) and occurred in the final position in the sentence. (Note in the sentences in table 5.1 that every drawled word is the last word in a clause, while none of the plain words is clause-final.) While it's not impossible to drawl on longer words in other parts of the sentence, the longer the word, the less likely you are to have drawling. That's why—contrary to imitations of Southern speech—you generally don't get a drawl in the word *Alabama*. It's a four-syllable word, and the stressed syllable is not in final position. Consequently, you don't get a change in intonation on that syllable. It's not that it can't be done, but it's not usual.

As far as I can determine, this use of *tone* in English is unique to the American South.

The drawl can include any one of or all these factors: length (or tempo), drop in amplitude (reflecting saying the vowel on two pulses), glides (change in formants, reflecting the adding of new vowel sounds), or change in intonation. These dimensions just get us started with a definition, so at least we know what we are referring to when we talk about "the drawl."

Inventory of Drawled Vowels. Now let's consider which vowels undergo this phenomenon. Apparently not all vowels are equally subject to drawling. For instance, it is those vowels that have been traditionally called "short front vowels" that are generally discussed in the literature under the topic of the drawl. I'll give some examples in their most extreme form:

"short i" in words like *hill* [hɪl] and *hymn* [hɪm] become [ˈhi ˌyəl] and [ˈhi ˌyəm];
"short e" in words like *help* [hɛlp] and *head* [hɛd] become [ˈhei ˌyəlp] and [ˈhei ˌyəd];
"short a" in words like *had* [hæd] and *ham* [hæm] become [ˈhæi ˌyəd] and [ˈhæi ˌyəm].

The "short vowels" of *could*, *but*, and *hot* don't have such glides but instead exhibit the drawl by simply lengthening and showing a drop in amplitude (displaying two beats) when there is a change of intonation, going either up or down. Again, extreme examples:

[ʊ] in *should, could*, as in "Do you think I *could*?" [ˈkʊ ˌʊd] (with rising intonation);
[ʌ] in *blood, flood*, as in "You shoulda seen that *blood!*" [ˈblʌ ˌʌd] (with falling intonation);
[ɑ] in *hot, not*, as in "It's so *hot!*" [ˈhɑ ˌɑt] (with falling intonation).

The traditional "long vowels" already end in glides, called offglides as in this list of examples:

"long e" /iy/ as in *feed*;
"long a" /ey/ as in *shade*;

Table 5.2. Percent of æ-gliding for ten residents of Anniston, Alabama

I	Birth year	Class/ gender	Categories of æ-gliding				Instances of æ
			% overall	% front	% central	% complex	
HH	1890	uu/f	44	27	3	14	N = 203
CS	1957	uw/f	32	12	4	16	N = 192
MB	1895	uw/f	30	19	5	6	N = 172
MJ	1911	rw/f	26	19	6	2	N = 173
BH	1956	uw/m	19	14	4	0.6	N = 145
SC	1899	uw/m	15	7	7	0.4	N = 223
HB	1906	rw/m	13	9	4	2	N = 164
BK	1953	uu/f	11	4.5	7	0.5	N = 174
HHg	1955	uu/m	8	6	1.5	1	N = 192
RK	1882	uu/m	2	2	0	0	N = 125

Key

I = Informant

Social class abbreviations
uu = urban upper class
uw = urban working class
rw = rural working class

Gliding descriptions
overall = [æi] + [æə] + [æiə]
front = [æi] ("baig" for bag)
central = [æə]("ha-uhv" for have)
complex = [æiə] ("ma- iy-un" for man)

"long i" /ay/ as in *wide;*
"long u" /uw/ as in *food;*
"long o" /ow/ as in *show.*

These vowels lengthen and drop amplitude with rising or falling intonation before moving on to their usual offglides:

"I need some *shade!* [ˈše ˌeid] (falling intonation);
"It's really *wide!*" [ˈwa ˌaid] or [ˈwa ˌa:d] (falling intonation);
"There's no *food?*" [ˈfu ˌuud] (rising intonation).

The vowels that are generally labeled diphthongs, usually pronounced in Southern English as [æo] in *house* and [oi] in *boy,* often add an extra element between the main vowel and the glide, making a triphthong: That is, [æo], as in *house,* becomes [ˈæi ˌyo] to give drawled [ˈhaei ˌyos]; [oi], as in *boy,* becomes [ˈɑo ˌwi] for drawled [ˈbɑo ˌwi].

Finally, the "long open o" [ɔ] as in *law* and *dog* is often pronounced, as mentioned above, as a diphthong [ɑo] ("ah-oh") by Southerners, so that the drawled form becomes two-beat [ˈɑ ˌo], as in [ˈlɑ ˌo] and [ˈdɑ ˌog].

To add to the complexity, gliding is *not* categorical. That is, sometimes it happens and sometimes it doesn't. Look at table 5.2, where I show the results of checking at least 125 tokens (or examples) of /æ/ (the "short a" in *cat)* for ten people—six men and women who were over sixty (in 1972) and four (1972) teenagers. Notice that HH, the most frequent and extreme glider, does it only about half the time, while RK, the one with the least gliding, does it just 2 percent of the time.

Continuing with a close look at /æ/ in table 5.2, I want to point out that most of the glides added to [æ] are front glides, that is, glides that go toward "ee" [i], in the front of the mouth. Only a very small portion are central or schwa glides, that go to "uh" [ə]. A subset of the front glides is made up of what I label "complex" glides in table 5.2. These are multiple glides or triphthongs that start with [æ], then move up and to the front [i], and then go to a central position [ə], as in ['hæi ˌyəm] for *ham*.

Segmental Environment. In some cases, gliding is influenced by the following sound (each sound in a word is called a segment). Let's look at those factors.

Although there is a lot of variation among the people I looked at in terms of the sound environments that promote glides, it is clear that *nasals* have an especially strong influence. *Fricatives* have a rather strong impact for some people (see appendix A for explanations of these consonant types and for phonetic symbols in general, and see my endnote for the additional symbols I use). A few examples will illustrate what I mean:

Everybody eats ham ['hæ ˌyəm]. (Preceding nasal [m])
Yes, ma'am ['mæ ˌyəm]. (Preceding nasal [m])
He really made me laugh ['læi ˌyəf]! (Preceding fricative [f])

To this point, we've dealt with the purely linguistic conditioning factors, all of which have been mentioned before by others in more or less detail, but, so far as I know, no one has presented them all together, as in my account.

From the Technical to the Social (Sociolinguistic) Factors

What have never been addressed before at all, other than in passing, are the sociolinguistic factors involved in drawling. To get into the sociolinguistic factors influencing the drawl, we need to divide the drawl into two categories. One type can vary across individuals, that is, some drawl and some do not drawl. The second type can be varied—deliberately—by the individual, that is, some drawl, but might or might not on a given occasion. From reexamining the data and my own speech and consulting the literature, as I have explained, it seems that what other people call "the drawl" in fact refers to two distinct but overlapping categories—segmental (or gliding vowels) and suprasegmental (extra length and exaggerated intonation).

The segmental drawl, which I call the "basic drawl," is where individual short vowels are converted to diphthongs. The basic drawl of the individual is no more under the control of the speaker than his pronunciation of /æ/ or /ɪ/ but rather reflects his age, sex, social class, and locale. This is not categorical, of course. An individual's "basic drawl," or gliding, is also subject to variation, depending on the linguistic environment—following segment, the syllabic-length of the word, and the position of the word in the sentence, especially in regard to stress. That is clearly demonstrated in table 5.2 for /æ/. Absolutely nobody glides 100 percent of the time; just about everybody uses the three possibilities for drawled /æ/—front glide, central glide, and multiple glide. The proportions vary, but everybody participates.

The "expanded drawl," sometimes called a "heavy" drawl or "extreme" drawl, includes triphthongs (complex glides) on the segmental level and, on the suprasegmental level, the extra lengthening that a vowel can undergo in slow tempo, the drop in amplitude, and the change in tone. These can take place individually or simultaneously. It is this expanded drawl that is under the semiconscious control of the speaker, rather like intonation, and that therefore varies according to the sociolinguistic or pragmatic situation.

This distinction between the "basic" and the "expanded" drawl will help untangle many of the confusions in accounting for the use of the drawl. Now we address the sociolinguistic factors involved in the two kinds of drawling. Here we have five areas of interest, all of which interact with each other: 1) geography, 2) demographics, 3) situation, 4) topic, and 5) self-identification. As we'll see, by the time the discussion reaches *Social Situation* and *Topic*, psychosocial aspects of drawling become apparent as well.

Geography. To begin with, drawling is tied to geography in the South. There is certainly regional variation in the drawl, both basic and expanded, even within the South. Speaking only of the Lower South, the Atlantic Coastal areas around Charleston and Savannah are set off from the rest of the Lower South or Deep South by having a different system of glides, which gives the impression of a more clipped speech. For instance, the pronunciation of the number *eight* has traditionally had an inglided [ɛət] ("eh-yuht") rather than the upglided [ɛit] ("eh-yeet") (O'Cain 1972; Baranowski 2007).

Similarly, Alabama reflects regional variation. Even holding class, sex, and age constant, in Alabama there is more expanded drawling and r-lessness in the old plantation areas, such as Selma, Demopolis, and Montgomery, than in the newer industrial areas of the Piedmont, such as Anniston and Birmingham. Anniston is not in the "heavy drawling" area.

Cutting across such regional distinctions, there is also the contrast between rural versus urban, or maybe rural and small town versus large urban areas. I suspect that for men, at least, expanded drawling is more predominant in rural and smaller urban areas than in large cities such as Birmingham and Atlanta. Young female Atlanta natives have told me that to them, men sound "country" if they drawl. Similarly, a linguist from Atlanta says that he "associates some of the more pronounced versions [of the drawl]—that is, the expanded drawl—with females from the small-town gentry" (Sledd, personal communication, October 5, 1985). This characterization is supported by the report of an eighteen-year-old upper-class native of Atlanta who told me that she and her friends used to enjoy imitating their mothers—all from smaller cities and towns in Georgia and Alabama, such as Columbus, Vidalia, Mobile, and Selma.

Demographics. Let's examine the interaction of the demographic factors of age, sex, and social class.

Most people probably believe that women are the main "expanded" drawlers, but my research finds interesting correlations between age, sex, and the incidence of drawling. From my data, it is clear that working-class men have the expanded drawl, though it is the younger group that drawls more, in this sense. Older upper-class men, on the other hand, don't use the expanded drawl much—certainly not in interviews—and nor do their grandsons, except in special circumstances. Since it is a linguistic given that older upper-class men would have the most conservative speech in the community, perhaps the expanded drawl is a relatively new phenomenon. Older upper-class women certainly have the expanded drawl, as do younger ones. It appears that working-class teenage girls lead the pack in expanded drawling, with the boys somewhat behind them. This female working-class leadership is what most sociolinguistic research in American English and in other Western societies would lead us to expect, if this is a case of "change in progress."

Maybe I need to stop here for a minute and explain the linguistic investigation of "change in progress." This sort of research done in a single community compares the speech of older and younger people of the same sex and social class category and assumes that where the speech differs, permanent language change is going on. I'm not talking about fads in words such as slang. I'm talking about pronunciation and grammar that speakers are not conscious of, that is, the language of informal style. Everybody can cross their "T"s and dot their "I"s when they want to or think it's appropriate. But we all have a relaxed, informal style. However, the assumption is that the doctor, when he relaxes, might talk like a plumber talking formally, so the shift in style is on a continuum. What is informal for one social group might be formal for another. Also, language change can first be seen in informal style, especially in speech of the working class. For this reason, it appears that working-class girls lead in change of pronunciation. This means that the future of the language lies in the hands of working-class girls! Conversely, older upper-class men are good examples of old-fashioned speech.

The obvious question is whether younger people, when they are significantly older, will have kept the same pronunciation that they have today or will talk like today's older people when they reach the same age. (Does aging itself somehow cause people to talk similarly, no matter when they were born?) One way to find out is to return to the locale and interview the same people fifteen years later. Then you can see whether the previous group of teenagers has reversed itself and is now talking like older people did. Another method is to interview current teenagers in the same community fifteen years later and see if the earlier changes noted in teenage speech have continued (along with the addition, one would expect, of new changes). So far, the results of various studies show that basically the original hypothesis was correct—working-class teenage girls are indeed the future of the language!

Look again at table 5.2, especially at the column labeled "complex" /æ/ gliding. The data document that at least for "short a," older upper-class women and working-class teenage girls are the most extreme expanded drawlers, since they have by far the most complex glides, that is, the glides that go first to [i] then to [ə] as in [ˈfæi ˌyəst] for *fast*, or [ˈmæi ˌyən] for *man*. (The vowel trajectory in figure 5.1 for /æ/ in *that* illustrates just that movement). Generalizing from the /æ/ data, the triphthongal variety seems to be more frequent among the younger working class today than among the upper class, though it does exist in the upper class, particularly among older women.

Even limiting ourselves to the basic drawl, which can be seen in table 5.2 in the column labeled "overall gliding" (that is, the combined scores for glides like [fæist] for *fast* or [hæəv] for *have*, as well as the few triphthongs such as ['fæi ˌyəst] and ['hæi ˌyəv]), the ordering is very much by sex. In fact, the "top four" gliders—44 percent to 26 percent—are women. Notice that the second highest score is that of the working-class girl. But look where the upper-class girl is: just above the upper-class men, below all the working-class men. I'll return to that shortly. Even more interesting is the contrast between the upper-class woman, the "top glider," and the upper-class man, at the absolute bottom. For that generation, obviously gliding—or "drawling" in that basic sense—was a marker of feminine speech, something men didn't do much. From the evidence here it is obvious that the basic drawl with glides is more predominant in women than in men, even keeping social class in mind. This leads to a discussion of social class as a factor in itself.

Social class is also reflected in the details of the basic drawl. It appears that having a lot of glided drawling, while never stigmatized, may have become more a feature of working-class speech than of upper-class speech in Alabama, at least for people born after World War II.

Look at that first column of table 5.2, where the social characteristics are noted. Right below the top glider, the older upper-class woman, you will see all the working-class informants, beginning with the teenage girl, followed by the older urban and rural women, the urban working-class boy, and the older working-class men. It is only after all the working-class informants that you find the next upper-class speaker, the teenage girl, followed by the upper-class boy—grandson of the top glider, incidentally—and finally, RK, the older upper-class man, grandfather of BK, the upper-class girl.

What this indicates is that gliding, while certainly not extinct in the upper class, is much less noticeable in the upper classes today, certainly in the younger age groups, while it appears to be gaining ground in the working class!

This trend may explain the difference in local terminology between the "drawl," which is good, and associated with elegant, older, upper-class ladies, and the "twang," which is the supposedly more-nasal gliding associated with the working class in the area. I think everybody has heard of the "hillbilly twang." Well, such working-class drawling may be just what you're looking at—that is, combined with heavy r's (*here* as "hee-yrr" instead of the older upper-class "hee-yuh"). Frankly, I wonder whether nasality is as big a feature as it's thought to be in the twang, but that is a topic that deserves more research.

Return to table 5.2 to see how much ten people from this same town can vary in their gliding of one vowel, /æ/, based on analysis of between 125 and 223 consecutive examples of it. The striking differences you can see here I attribute to the fact that each person was in a different social category, whether age, sex, social class, or urban/rural.

We have witnessed how age, class, and sex interact, with the older upper-class women having the most extreme basic drawl and the working class, especially the younger teenage urban working-class girls, having the most extreme basic and expanded drawls of their generation. These findings will come up again when I discuss the future of the drawl.

Social Situation. Possibly more important than the demographic factor in determining expanded drawling is the social situation, which possibly explains expanded drawling's near absence in my interviews with upper-class men and boys.

Drawling in this sense is very much a marker of intimacy and solidarity, while nondrawling reflects formality and distancing. It is for this reason that women appear to be the bearers of expanded drawling, since in all classes, women use it to make visitors feel welcome, to be solicitous, and to flirt. One linguist friend refers to a typical heavy drawler as a "kittenish female" (Sledd 1966, 33). Expanded drawling is also the vehicle for "gushing"—the exaggerated intonation and gliding that expresses admiration or welcoming. Adult women use this as an expression of solidarity. The expanded drawl is used especially in baby talk—to babies or to pets. It is part of the kindergarten teacher's cajoling repertoire. On the other hand, the expanded drawl is not used, or at least is reduced, when mothers or teachers correct children or when adults express disagreement.

For upper-class men, the expanded drawl is less professional and less businesslike, so it would be less likely to show up in a taped interview. For men, expanded drawling represents being "one of the boys," rather like the masculine use of nonstandard grammar or of "cussin." It is particularly noticeable when men are telling jokes or humorous stories, recounting hunting or fishing exploits, or arguing about football teams. It is also used by professional men to set their clients or patients at ease, especially in unequal power relationships, such as doctors dealing with children or lawyers talking to poor people. They also use the expanded drawl to cajole their wives and to talk to their horses and dogs. That is, expanded drawling is a mark of intimacy for men as well as for women, but for that reason it is less frequently observed in men by outsiders.

Topic. As mentioned above, the topic of conversation seems to influence the presence or absence of expanded drawling, though its influence is perhaps less than that of situation, since certain topics appear more in given settings. However, a sobering change of subject can reduce the drawl considerably, while a lightening of the topic can bring it out.

Self-Identification. The last use of the drawl that I will discuss is in regard to self-identification. It is a fact that in the South some people are known to be "big drawlers." These are people who employ the full range of the expanded drawl—lengthening, amplitude drop, and change in tone often combined with triphthongs. For instance, an older upper-class woman from Anniston remembers that it was said of a sorority sister at the University of Alabama in the early 1930s that "it took her five minutes to say 'Good morning.'" A young woman from Anniston told me that another woman, a friend of her mother's, "takes half an hour to say 'Hello.'" These are judgments of Southerners by Southerners—in these cases, of Southern women by Southern women, all natives of Anniston.

For women, expanded drawling is considered very feminine. Some might say it's sexy. One linguist characterizes the extreme form of the drawl as used largely by what the older generation might have called "a forward hussy" (Sledd personal communication). For that reason, women who grew up as what used to be called tomboys—today's feminists—often reject the extreme languid drawl for a modified one.

For men, expanded drawling is very masculine in the "good ol' country boy" or Huck Finn sense that was popularized by President Jimmy Carter's brother, Billy. Since for Southern men the outdoor life is considered highly masculine, as contrasted with the urban life of reading books and going to art galleries, concerts, and the theater, the projection of a rural persona can be found in all social classes. Regardless of social class, the man or boy who wants to project an image of huntin' and fishin' and other similar rural pursuits will be more likely to have an expanded drawl than the one who is more bookish or urbane. This is exemplified in the difference in drawling between Billy Carter and his brother, Jimmy. I'll remind you that President Carter left the South to be educated at the Naval Academy in Annapolis, spent many years away from the South as a naval officer, and became first governor of Georgia and later president of the United States. Meanwhile Billy was back in Plains, Georgia, running a fillin' station and going fishin'. President Bill Clinton provides another example of an expatriate Southerner who left Arkansas for Georgetown University and Yale Law School and then returned to Arkansas, where he had to sound "local" since he had political ambitions.

A corollary of the urban/rural tension in a man's self-image in the South is that expanded drawling is perhaps more necessary for the self-identification of the truly urban, highly educated, sophisticated man living in the South than for the plain dirt farmer. However, the urban sophisticate will include expanded drawling as only one of his styles—just as he selectively uses "bad" grammar to establish intimacy or his credentials as either "one of the boys" or an "insider." Another aspect of self-identification in regard to the drawl is one's identity as a Southerner. For many complex reasons, some people who leave the South jettison all vestiges of Southern speech—especially the expanded drawl—while others not only maintain it but perfect it, polish it, and exaggerate it to make their identities as Southerners clear to all.

It appears that expatriate Southern women maintain their expanded drawl more than do men in similar circumstances. This is probably because non-Southerners in the United States often perceive men with a "Southern accent" of any sort, much less a "Southern drawl" (which usually means the expanded drawl), as being either effeminate or buffoons—certainly as marking the person who speaks in such a peculiar way as one not to be taken seriously. Even for those not living outside the South, some people identify more closely with being Southern than do others.

To some extent, self-identification and regional loyalty are confounded, so it is appropriate to bring up the topic of attitudes toward Southern speech. Despite the negative evaluations by non-Southerners of Southern speech and of the South in general discussed in several papers by Dennis Preston (e.g., 1986, 1996) and despite the findings in Hasty's essay that Southerners themselves may perceive speakers of Southern English as being less educated and intelligent, many if not most white Southerners find Southern speech the sweetest, most beautiful human sound in the world. "British" may sound more posh, but only the rare white Southerner wants to "sound like a Yankee." To white Southerners, Northern speech can sound harsh, unattractive, and unfriendly. While the configurations of the vowel peaks in phonological space may make a strong contribution, as do the different directions of the glides in the basic drawl, it is the expanded drawl—the many triphthongs on two tones, as well as the great extremes of intonation and tempo—that is probably the main source of what is perceived as Southern speech.

So, now we can see why previous research refers to the drawl as being highly variable. Not only is it variable, but its variability can lie in a multitude of factors, ranging from linguistic inventory and environment—segmental and suprasegmental —to geography; from sex, social class, and age to the dimension of intimacy/ formality; from topic to identification of self as masculine or feminine or as a Southerner, the last category being one that calls up complex strong emotions.

CHANGE IN PROGRESS? PREDICTIONS FOR THE FUTURE OF THE DRAWL

What about the future of the drawl? There is some question as to whether the drawl is increasing, just holding its own, or even dying out. Based on my data from Alabama, it appears that women drawl more than men, at every age and in every social class, rural and urban, and this holds true for both the "basic" drawl and the "extended" drawl. It is possible that this might indicate simply a sex difference or have to do with other stable sociolinguistic matters. However, since the teenage working-class boys and older rural men are rather free in their drawling, while it is almost absent in the older upper- and working-class urban men, it is possible that this is a change coming into Southern speech.

Although I can't yet prove it, I am convinced that the drawl is getting more extreme, partly because of ongoing vowel change—unless it is the case that the drawl is causing the vowel change. Current research is showing that in the South, the vowels are shifting all around, with the short front vowels taking the place of the long vowels and the long vowels going elsewhere (Labov et al. 1972, 2006; Feagin 2003). In this respect, Southern white speech is beginning to resemble Australian speech in words like *rain, wait*. This change, called the Southern Vowel Shift by researchers, is going on in the working and lower-middle classes all across the South, from North Carolina to Texas, and creeping slowly into the middle and upper classes (see Allbritten's essay for a study of this change in Huntsville).

These changes are taking place below the level of consciousness, since the direction of the glides helps to distinguish the vowels from each other. Consequently, this development is not stigmatized. However, the increasing distances between the beginning and the end of the vowel make for yet more extensive gliding, with greater length and more changes of tone. Look again at table 5.2. Notice that after the older upper-class woman, the working-class girl is the most extreme segmental glider. This could indicate an increase in segmental gliding, which would support this hypothesis.

As to precisely why this change in vowels and in drawling is occurring, why, that is, the drawl would be increasing, I would point to the vast social changes in the South. I'll mention only a few, beginning with increasing social pressures for egalitarianism, as symbolized by country music, and by the image of the "good ol' country boy," or "bubba." Up until World War II, the South was an extremely hierarchical society, with strong caste and class barriers that were reinforced throughout the social, political, and economic systems. With prosperity, mobility, education, and racial integration, life is very different in today's South, and more money and power are accruing to the middle and working classes. What may in the past have been a stagnant region of the country is now part of the Sun Belt, with plenty of growth and all the changes that implies. Atlanta, for instance, is unrecognizable to those who knew it in the 1950s. You could say the same for Houston and Dallas, at the other end of the South. Consequently, it should come as no surprise that speech patterns in the South are beginning to reflect this social change, including an increase across society of the more extreme version of the drawl.[3]

Notes

1. Today, such analysis can be done on a personal computer using Praat speech-processing software available at www.fon.hum.uva.nl/praat/. See Allbritten in this volume for an example of its use.

2. The tradition of linguistics that I work out of uses a different set of symbols for and methods of depicting some sounds from the IPA tradition used in the other essays and explained in appendix A. Many of these alternate symbols can be converted to IPA symbols without damage to the evidence, and I have converted them whenever possible for consistency throughout the volume. However, depiction of vowel gliding is essential to understanding the Southern drawl. Most treatments of English vowels include glides for only three diphthongs: /ay/, /aw/ and /oy/. The IPA broad transcription differentiates "short" and "long" vowels by height and tenseness rather than length, so you find /ɪ/, /i/; /ɛ/, /e/; /ʊ/, /u/; and /ɔ/, /o/. Narrow transcription differentiates length by a colon, so you find [ɪ], [ɪː], [i], [iː], and so on. To make clear the sounds of Southern speech, I have used both phonemic designations (sound classes) placed between / / and phonetic transcriptions (exact sounds) placed between [ ], following traditional practice in American linguistics (see appendix A for an explanation of phonemes versus phonetics). In addition, I use the American preference of /y/ for the glide-sound starting *yes* instead of the IPA symbol /j/. (This may conflict with other uses in this collection.) Symbols ['] and [ˌ] denote primary and secondary stress. The following list of words and symbols depicts the "long vowels" of English to show the presence of their glides. They will allow you to compare them to the IPA symbols used in other essays, if necessary:

"long e" /iy/ as in *feed*;

"long a" /ey/ as in *shade*;

"long i" /ay/ as in *wide;*
"long u" /uw/ as in *food;*
"long o" /ow/ as in *show.*

3. See Feagin (2015) for my research into a century of change for five features: (1) historical R (r): syllabic R, as in *hurt* and *mother;* and postvocalic tautosyllabic R, as in *here* and *heart;* (2) historical long I (ay): the vowel of *I, my, sigh, sign,* and *sight;* (3) historical short A (æ): the vowel of *cab, can,* and *cat;* (4) historical long open O (oh): the vowel of *law, dog,* and *caught;* (5) variable (iw): the vowel of *tune, duke,* and *news.*

6

The Heart of Dixie Is in Their Vowels

THE RELATIONSHIP BETWEEN CULTURE AND LANGUAGE IN HUNTSVILLE, ALABAMA

Rachael Allbritten

In a small, locally owned café, a quintessential burger joint in the northeast suburbs a few miles outside of Huntsville, Alabama, I ask a man from the community: "What kinds of things are special about the South and about this area?" "Everything," he says, with a wide grin and small laugh.

I am interviewing a local business owner who has been kind enough to talk to me about the community and about himself. I have traveled back to the community where I grew up to investigate its language and the identity of its people and to gain insight into the language and culture of the Huntsville area. Here, with the café as a jumping-off point, I find people of the area to interview and talk with. "Roger" (all names in this article are pseudonyms) sits with me in the café on his lunch break, wearing a button-down shirt tucked into his blue jeans and a cap advertising the name of his local business. He continues his answer to my question: "It's special to us that live here because this is home. I think Huntsville's a neat city. North Alabama's nice. I mean, the beauty of the mountains and the valleys and the water and everything makes it really ideal." He later tells me, "I'm a redneck because I grew up out in the country. I'm a hillbilly, I guess, too . . . and I say that with pride."

One of the reasons I conduct the interviews is my interest in the area's language "change in progress" (see below). I am particularly interested in a phenomenon called the Southern Vowel Shift (SVS) and its behavior specific to Huntsville and to suburban communities in North Alabama. I have discovered that careful research at the community level is necessary to dispel errors in the thinking of linguists and nonlinguists alike. Much scholarly discussion on vowel shifts such as the SVS assumes that the speech changes are ubiquitous. My research has shown that we should not oversimplify the SVS by assuming, as the literature commonly does, that most if not all Southerners are participating in this shift, particularly with regard to the younger speakers.

My research also has found that many non-Southerners believe that all or most

Southerners speak nearly the same dialect. Somewhat surprisingly, my interviews with Southerners have shown that many also have this perception. Even if Southerners do not believe this for the whole region, many assume that the people within their state have nearly the same accent and certainly that the people within one's community speak a common dialect. From one perspective, there is good reason for this belief: language is a defining part of a people's culture, and sharing culture maintains a bond. Many Southerners feel a kindred spirit with other Southerners, and from the interviews I have gathered, Alabamians are no exception. However, subtle social factors and personal identity play an enormous role in a person's linguistic affiliation, even if it is entirely subconscious, driving linguistic differences. This essay reports on the differences in vowel shifting exhibited by my interviewees and examines the social factors that may be responsible for these differences.

What does it mean to say that vowels are *shifted*? This linguistic term refers to one of the natural processes of sound change in language. There have been many shifts in the English language over the course of its history. Fossils of sound change survive in the spelling of some words. For example, many words spelled like *sea* were at one time pronounced like *say* is today. Now they are pronounced with a vowel sound that is written with the letter *i* in many other languages (for example, *sí, pico,* or *mi* in Spanish). Even though the word *goose* has two of the letter *o*, it is pronounced with the sound written as the letter *u* in many languages. These vowel shifts were due to a change in English known as the Great Vowel Shift, which occurred in England between approximately 1200 and 1600. It is unlikely that during the process of the sound shift the speakers realized that it was becoming more common to say *goose* less like *ghost* and more like we say the word today. Speakers rarely significantly change the way they pronounce vowels over their own lifetimes; the sound changes usually take place from generation to generation.

Because language is forever in a state of change, sounds will always be vulnerable to becoming gradually realized in a different way. Sound shifts are taking place in English today, three just within the United States. One, as mentioned above, is the Southern Vowel Shift (SVS) in the southeastern United States. The pattern of the shift predicts that the pronunciation of *heel* will be realized as *hill* and vice versa. It should make the word *leg* or *head* sound like "laig" or "hay-uhd." The word *laid* could sound like "led" or, most likely, like "lied." Another phase of the SVS involves the changing pronunciation of the "long o" and "long u" vowels. Both vowels are pronounced further forward in the mouth and with the lips unrounded, so that *boat* comes out like "buh-oot" and *goose* (changing yet again!) is realized almost as the word *geese*. (*Geese*, on the other hand, remains separate from *goose* in pronunciation because it sounds more like "guhees.")

Shifts involving a group of sounds are usually caused when a single sound first changes (that is, when a population of speakers starts producing that sound in a different place and/or manner in the mouth). Because sound systems (phonology) in languages crave balance, people will start producing a second vowel differently to fill the place of the first. (See appendix A for a description of vowel production in the mouth and vowel charts.) In turn, the vacated place left by the second sound must be filled and so on, until, over several generations of speakers, the system has achieved balance again. One theory as to the trigger for the SVS is the pronunciation of a word like *time, five,* or *side* ("SAH-eed") as one drawn-out sound without movement to the "ee" sound. When *side* is pronounced without the "ee" sound in the vowel, the resulting sound is called a *monophthong*, and is well-known to anyone who has heard, or heard of, Southern speech (for essays specifically addressing this Southern feature, see Doxsey and Spence in this volume). This sound is sometimes written like "sahd," though any Southerner knows intuitively that it does not sound like *sod* or *sad*; it is somewhere in-between. However, when *side* or *lied* moves out of the "space" for the "ah-ee" sound, it leaves a gap. In the case of the SVS, this space is filled by words containing an "ay" sound, like *laid*, which starts sounding like "luh-ayd," and the shifting process continues (see appendix A for a chart explaining the SVS). It should be strongly emphasized that the vowels can often be shifted more subtly than the examples given here. Pronunciations reflecting the SVS are sometimes difficult to determine conclusively without computer-aided acoustic analysis (I address acoustic analysis further below; also see appendix A and Feagin in this volume).

One way that linguists can research sound change is to have access to recordings made of speakers from the same community over a period of many years: comparing the speech on the recordings would result in what is known as a real-time analysis. However, because recordings from eighty or more years ago are uncommon, especially recordings produced under comparable conditions, and because methods and technology change so often, a more practical solution is often that of an "apparent-time analysis." In 2000, for example, speakers born in 1920, 1950, and 1980 might all have been recorded. The assumption is that the forms of speech they had acquired by adulthood would have remained fairly consistent through the intervening years. Therefore, the researcher is "apparently" analyzing speech features from, say, 1940, 1970, and 2000. This method has been shown to be generally reliable when comparing the speech of older speakers against that of younger speakers, and many researchers have successfully identified gradual sound change (called a "change in progress") as one moves from acoustic analyses of older speakers to those of the younger ones.

Because Huntsville has witnessed great change over the last sixty-five years, it is a rather exciting place to conduct linguistic research. Before the 1950s, Huntsville's nickname was the Watercress Capital of the World (see figure 6.1), an appellation now belonging to New Market, Alabama, very near the café where my interviews were conducted. The population of Huntsville in 1940 was 13,150. In 1950, German rocket scientists came to Huntsville's Redstone Arsenal to work in the early US space program. This development had profound consequences for Huntsville, which is now known as Rocket City (see figure 6.2) and where a large percentage of the population is employed in engineering and information services, especially for defense contractors and the US space program, including NASA. According to the 2010 US Census, the 2010 population of Huntsville was 180,105 and the population of Madison County was 334,811, with a metro area population of 417,593. The

Figure 6.1. Huntsville circa 1930, as "Watercress Capital of the World," loads barrels for shipment to the White House (courtesy of Huntsville Public Library)

Huntsville-Decatur Combined Statistical Area remains one of the fastest-growing areas of Alabama and has a population of 571,422.[1] The participants of my study did not live in Huntsville proper but in Madison County, northeast of, but not far from, the city limits.

Earlier I mentioned that Roger told me "with pride" that he was a redneck and a hillbilly. He is clearly proud to be a Southerner and loves living in North Alabama. So why is it that I detect very little of the shifting of his vowels? To me, he sounds neither like a "redneck" nor like a "hillbilly." One part of the answer is Roger's age: he was born in 1945. When sound change such as SVS is still being realized by the speakers, older speakers may have been born when the change was still nascent. Since the changes are gradual, and since they generally take place generationally, a speaker born in 1945 may be less likely to have significantly shifted vowels. However, another piece of the puzzle is Roger's affiliation with the greater South, since he does business in five different states and travels to them often. Even though he stays within the South, he has subconsciously learned to have a less locally oriented accent or to be able to switch to one that is flexible in more situations—such as an interview by an academic person (albeit a native).

I had had indications before, in my previous research on the progress of the SVS around Huntsville, that the situation regarding the shift was perhaps not a simple

Figure 6.2. Huntsville 1963, as "Rocket City," receives visit from the White House, as President John Kennedy discusses the space program with Wernher von Braun (courtesy of the US Army)

one. I came across a rather more interesting pattern of the SVS than the straight-forward one I had expected. For my investigation, I collected casual interviews (called sociolinguistic interviews) from white adults in Madison County, in the suburbs northeast of Huntsville, between 2004 and 2007. Although I have not yet added interviews with African American north Alabamians, it would be intriguing to see if the pattern among African Americans in the Huntsville area corroborates the current view as summarized by Feagin (2003, 127–28), who points out that African Americans do not necessarily conform to local white norms of pronunciation (also, see Nunnally and Bailey's essay). I selected the data for a pilot study from the pool of interviews conducted between 2004 and 2005, choosing three residents of the northeast suburbs of Huntsville—women from three different generations, born in 1934, 1953, and 1981. Choosing speakers of these different ages allowed me to conduct an apparent-time analysis looking at change in progress.

Although socioeconomic class has repeatedly been shown to have an effect on language features (e.g., Labov 1966), the composition and culture of the northeastern suburbs of Huntsville can make class distinctions unclear, so this demographic proved difficult to assign. Level of income or education may not always be an accurate indicator. The uneducated manager of a construction company may earn more money and live in a bigger house and nicer neighborhood than a college-educated schoolteacher or scientist, who may live in a mobile home. Even the college-educated schoolteacher and the college-educated scientist who have approximately the same income and education level may speak differently depending on their groups of peers, on the church they attend, on their place of employment, on their level of training in academic circles, or on the college where they obtained their degree. The condition and appearance of their dwelling may also be a general indicator of class, as a small but new, well-kept mobile home is generally not held in low regard among community members, whereas a run-down house with, for example, many possessions on the front lawn is generally looked upon with much disdain.

Often, a better indicator of speech patterns for this community is the rural versus urban orientation of speakers, that is, their personal orientation either to the rural part of Madison County or to the city of Huntsville. In some subdivisions (housing developments) in this area, two neighbors may speak completely differently due to orientation. Hypothetically, one can imagine that one neighbor sold his farm and moved into a large suburban house, whereas his next-door neighbor moved from the city to the suburbs to have a bigger lot and still insists that he or she lives "in Huntsville." The former describes a speaker who is rural-oriented and the latter one who is urban-oriented.

A linguistic indicator of orientation is a language feature called deixis ("dike-sis," a Greek word meaning "to point"), referring to the use of words in discourse that provide orientation by "pointing" outside the discourse in reference to person (*You* are a friend of *mine*), time (I went *yesterday*), or space (Put the book *over there*). Therefore, I attempted to note the spatially *deictic*—or perspective dependent— orientation of my interviewees toward Huntsville itself and the more rural area farther outside of the city limits. For example, if a speaker used the phrase "in the city" to refer to being inside the city limits of Huntsville, this would indicate a possible rural orientation. A speaker's uttering "went out to the county" when she was, in fact, already outside of the city limits at our interview location, would indicate a possible urban orientation.

Yet another indicator of orientation can be whether a speaker attended a county school or city school. The periphery around the city of Huntsville is considered "county" and feeds the five high schools in the Madison County School System, while seven high schools within the city limits are part of the Huntsville City School System. The neighborhood where I conduct my fieldwork is an area zoned for a Madison County high school.

Therefore, if I were to place the speakers in probable class categories, much demographic detail would be required. It is necessary to take many things into consideration and, even then, one often cannot be completely sure. In discussing the speakers in the study, I simply present the known demographic details but do not posit a possible class.

The first speaker under investigation, Dolly, was born in 1934 and raised in rural northeast Madison County on a farm that had belonged to her grandmother. Her father was also from the area northeast of Huntsville, but her mother was from just north of the Tennessee-Alabama state line (approximately forty miles north of the area). Dolly owns a custodial business and works both within the city limits and in the northeast suburbs, performing both managerial and cleaning duties. Her highest level of education is high school, and she received her diploma from the local county high school. Her income at the time of the interview was probably about the median for the area. Her peer group, primarily from her church, is a wide range of possible classes. She is the great-aunt of Natasha (below).

Caroline was born in 1953 on a military base outside of the South but to Southern parents from North Carolina. She moved to Huntsville when she "was about eight years old" and was raised there, graduating from a city high school. She also holds two bachelor's degrees from the University of Alabama in Huntsville and works in Huntsville's "Research Park" for a defense contractor. She moved out of the city limits into the northeast suburbs in 1986, at the age of thirty-two, a few years before obtaining her second degree. After spending much of her young adult life far below the median income, she probably earned about twice the median at the time of the interview.

Natasha was born in 1981 on a military base in the South. Her mother is from outside the South, and her father is from the northeast suburbs of Huntsville, as are her paternal grandparents. She moved to the northeast suburbs of Huntsville in "the second grade." Dolly (above) is her great-aunt. Natasha is a military officer/ nurse and her income level is either at or slightly above median. She graduated from the local county high school and holds a BSN in nursing from the University of Alabama in Huntsville.

To get an objective measurement of the speakers' vowels, I digitally recorded the speech from the interviews and measured the acoustic waves of the speakers' vowels with Praat, a computer software program developed for speech analysis (Boersma and Weenink 2007). The vowel in each utterance of a word produces its own pattern. This software takes hertz frequency measures of the patterns in the acoustic signals of each vowel and plots the vowel on a graph. The positions of vowels on the graph approximate the places in the mouth where the vowels are produced (see appendix A in this volume for examples of a vowel-placement chart and of a Praat-type graph). With a sufficient number of a speaker's vowels plotted on the graph, I can compare that speaker's production of the vowels that are influenced by the SVS to see if and how much they differ from unshifted vowel positions. Finally, I can compare the charts of plotted vowels for each of the different speakers to investigate how much evidence of the SVS appears in each interviewee's speech (see Feagin's essay in this volume for similar use of acoustic analysis to plot drawled syllables).

The results from these analyses and comparisons showed that the vowels of Dolly (b. 1934) were slightly shifted and that the vowels of Natasha (b. 1981), Natasha being younger than Dolly, were shifted much more. These findings were not necessarily surprising by themselves. They seemed to indicate that the SVS is progressing slightly from Dolly's generation to Natasha's, though my results showed a much slower progression of the SVS in the suburban Huntsville area than some earlier studies have shown in other parts of the South and of Alabama (Labov, Ash, and Boberg 2005; Feagin 2003). This rate discrepancy alone is intriguing. However, in contrast to both these speakers, the vowels of the middle-aged speaker, Caroline (b. 1953), seemed "stable" and did not show the telltale signs of the SVS (for details, see Allbritten 2008). From the perspective of an apparent-time analysis, this finding leaves a gap in the investigation of sound change and was, at the time, a surprising finding. While Caroline's education and work environment seemed to be the key factors affecting her speech, my own familiarity with the areas and continuing cultural study of it led me to believe that her urban or rural orientation might have a great deal of influence on her personal identity in this suburban community— and therefore on her speech—and that it needed to be considered more closely.

I therefore revisited the transcriptions of the interviews with the three women to look for indications of urban or rural identity in the content. Natasha, for example, explains in example 1 that in high school she was part of the "country crowd":

(1) I had friends in a lot of the different groups like . . . the preppy crowd and the country crowd. . . . I guess because I played ball I knew a lot of different people. . . . As far as going out and stuff, probably the country people that hung out, we hung out, rode four-wheelers on the weekends and stuff like that.

I also found evidence in the interviews of deictic orientation in the speech of Dolly and Natasha. The following two sentences occur in Dolly's interview. In example 2a, Dolly is referring to the tornado of 1989 (an event I ask all my participants about), which destroyed part of the city of Huntsville but left the northeastern suburbs physically untouched.

(2) a. I was **in town** when that one hit.
b. And I remember uh, you know, we didn't get **to town** a lot. So we had movies at the schools.

Here, Dolly says "in town" and "to town," revealing that, from her perspective, we were not currently "in town" while talking in the café, which is approximately seven miles outside the city limits. Like her great-aunt, Natasha also used these phrases to refer to being in Huntsville proper. She is also referring to the tornado of 1989 in example 3a.

(3) a. Mom was **in town** and we didn't know anything about her, so that was pretty scary.
b. She lives close **to town** so it was easier for me to get to work.

Based on the relative perspectives shown in these examples, these two women appear to be rural-oriented. Unfortunately, I did not collect any such deictic references in Caroline's interview. We can speculate that her orientation is urban, since she attended an urban high school.[2] Because I was not able to find any overtly spoken indication of urban-rural orientation in Caroline's interview, I browsed the thirteen other interviews I had collected in the area at that time.

In another interview with a young man I will call Brad, I found the following utterance:

(4) I wanna play soccer with F. and G. and all those guys. They play on a league **here in town**.

Brad's use of "here" along with "in town" reveals that, from his perspective, we are currently "in town," though we are speaking in the same café where Dolly and Natasha uttered examples 2 and 3. I also added an acoustic analysis of Brad's vowel system to find out to what extent it had undergone the SVS.

Brad was born in 1978 to Southern parents and raised from birth in the northeastern suburbs of Huntsville. He attended the local county high school and has a bachelor's degree from Middle Tennessee State University. He works in real estate, in the occupation sometimes called "house flipping," and holds a second job as a bartender. Because Brad appears to be urban-orientated, I conducted an acoustic analysis of his speech to see how it compared with all three women's, but particularly to Caroline's acoustic speech patterns.

The results showed that Brad's speech is not at all advanced with respect to the SVS, even though, as a member of the youngest demographic, like Natasha, his should be the most advanced. Of the three other speakers analyzed in this study, his (lack of) advancement of the SVS most closely patterns to that of Caroline, even though he is only three years older than Natasha and should pattern as she does, if the progress of the SVS is the same for everyone in the area. Given that we have some indication that Brad is urban-oriented, this facet of his identity may be one of the key influencing factors for the general lack of SVS evidence in his vowel production.

While the Southern Vowel Shift has not progressed as clearly in Caroline's speech, her level of education, her urban-orientation, and her work environment should certainly be factored into analysis of the placement of her vowels in acoustic space. However, it is evident from Caroline's speech that she *does* sound like a speaker of Southern American English. What I do *not* want to suggest is that, due to Caroline's demographics, she is not as reflective of general Southern speech as, for example, Dolly and Natasha, and that this makes her a less authentic or representative Alabamian. Rather, I propose that not all speakers in this area are necessarily comparable when it comes to a particular sound shift.

It is entirely possible that Caroline's exposure to the professional world and her need to address wider, nonlocal audiences has diluted some features of her Southern speech. However, through continued interviews in this area, I may also discover that Caroline is merely part of another growing trend. This possibility has already been suggested by the vowel analysis of Brad. We might also predict that a hypothetical middle-aged, rural-oriented speaker would be more comparable to Dolly and/or Natasha.

The takeaway of the research I conducted near Huntsville is that people cannot assume that the speech of all Southerners is undergoing the SVS or that they will adopt every aspect of the shift. In research completed after that which informed this essay, I found that some speakers in the area may only rarely participate in the high front vowel shift. In an investigation of interviews conducted in the area between 2004 and 2007, I used acoustic analysis to look at the mid and high front vowel shifts in seven women born between 1977 and 1987. While the young women did participate to some extent (though variably) in the mid front vowel shift (the vowel sounds in "led" and "laid"), there was little evidence that they shift the high front vowels (the vowel sounds in "leave" and "lid"). We can conclude that there must be a great deal of variability with regard to the SVS among Southerners, based not only on geography within the South but also on social factors within each area (see Allbritten 2011).

It is important to note that there are several contributing factors to realization of the SVS and that there is enormous complexity in the variables that interact to create the manner of speaking of a given member of the community. In my observations, I hear variability in the vowels typical of the SVS even within the speech of one speaker. For example, while our "hillbilly" businessman Roger was relating a recent political event (a mishap in the Alabama senate involving state senator Charles Bishop), his vowels were the most shifted of the entire interview. However, Roger's most-shifted vowels were still hardly shifted when compared with the extremely shifted vowels I overheard in the speech of groups of manual laborers who frequented the café for lunch. For this group, there is possibly a compounding of factors, such as approval of local peers and assignment of a "salt-of-the-earth" meaning to the vowels of the SVS, that cause group members to have a far more advanced SVS: a different path from that of other community members. Perhaps in this community a full realization of the SVS will become increasingly associated with manual laborers, with those who have both low income and low education, and with other factors typically associated with a working class.

I believe as well that the effect of the dichotomy of rural or urban orientation on speech is a byproduct of the changes taking place in this dynamic area of the Southern United States. Huntsville is undergoing extreme demographic and physical change, developments that are very much on the minds of the "native" community members. The Huntsville area in particular may also lend itself to studies of the effects of urbanization (Frazer 2000) and/or globalization (Heller 2003; Meyerhoff and Niedzielski 2003) on the speech of locals, especially the children, whose peers are often the children of non-Southerners who have recently moved to the area for work. These "outsiders" bring with them very different ideas of class relationships as well and have the potential to reshape and redefine existing class boundaries in the area.

It will be interesting to see the future of the SVS in Huntsville. The SVS could turn out to be a shibboleth identifying socioeconomic class membership, if more traditional classes form in Madison County. On the other hand, we could see a more general revival of the SVS in Huntsville over the next decade. Past studies, such as those conducted in Ocracoke Island, North Carolina, (Schilling-Estes 1997; Schilling-Estes and Wolfram 1999) have shown instances in which a dialect's distinctiveness has suffered due to increased exposure to "outside" dialects or due to higher prestige in the ability to speak a "Standard" American English. After World War II, Ocracoke experienced a large upsurge in the tourist industry, exposing locals to other dialects and resulting in a gradual decline of features unique to the island.

By contrast, these same studies show that exposure to outside dialects does not always dissipate dialectal features. Schilling-Estes also studied Smith Island, Maryland, in which the dialectal features are intensifying, as islanders gain contact with the mainland and outside dialects. As more locals move away from Smith Island, the features increasingly hold a sense of pride for those who remain and particularly for those who return with a renewed sense of being an islander (1997). Similarly, in a classic study of Martha's Vineyard, Massachusetts, first published in 1963, William Labov showed that as more new families moved to the island over time, the "old families" of Martha's Vineyard intensified the features of their dialect. They proudly viewed themselves as "true" locals, the authentic residents of Martha's Vineyard and the only ones who had the linguistic right to the traditional features.

All the interviewed residents of the northeastern suburbs of Huntsville commented on the great changes that are molding the city. In particular, a phenomenon called BRAC is on the residents' minds. To the residents, BRAC (Base Relocation and Closure) means that thousands of people are being relocated to Huntsville to work on the Redstone Arsenal Army Base, the Missile Defense Program, and NASA. In 1995, Huntsville had approximately two thousand new residents who had been relocated due to BRAC. The most recent round of BRAC, which began in 2005 and continued through 2011, translated to a much larger influx, *at least* five times that of the 1995 round. Several national defense agencies have also been relocated to Huntsville from Arlington, Virginia. The *Huntsville Times* reported that Huntsville had an almost 10 percent, or 32,947, increase in population between 2000 and 2006 (4-06-2007, 1A). Just as the arrival of the US space program in Huntsville in the 1950s saw a redefinition of the city, the community members I talked to were highly aware of another wave of change on its way. Some of the comments from the interviews I collected in 2007 are included here:

(5) [The area] has grown up so much. It's changed so much since I was growing up. The Redstone Arsenal—obviously, there's tons of people that move into this area because of that. There's tons of people that are government that move to this area. . . . None of this was here, like all these subdivisions. It's crazy. —*Beth, born 1978*

(6) The one thing about Huntsville being so dependent upon the military base [is] there's a lot of different people that move through here. —*Jake, born 1964*

(7) Yeah, it's changed very much. That's been true for many years now—Redstone Arsenal creating that change, I guess. —*Roger, born 1945*

(8) This community has grown so, and so many people are in it. It's just—you wouldn't believe when we were coming up, what wasn't here. It wasn't like it is now. —*Margaret, born 1936*

Some believe that the Huntsville dialect will take a path similar to that which they perceive Atlanta has taken. They believe that a dissipation of the Southern accent is the future, if not already the present. Roger told me, "I'm going to say Georgia—probably from just south of Atlanta north—talk very much like we do. But for a lot of the same reasons. Atlanta has been such a growing city for so many years." In a 2007 interview, I asked Alice (b. 1938), "Do you think [all the growth] is having an effect on the language of the area?" She replied, "Oh, it will eventually, yeah. It's just like anything. If you have a true, clear, pure version of something, once it's intermingled with other versions, you're going to change."

Jake (b. 1964) referred to Huntsville as "a melting pot," as did Roger. When I asked Roger if people in North Alabama speak differently than people in other parts of the South, he replied, "Really, they do. And I think it's our diverse culture. I think it's a melting pot. Huntsville, Alabama, has so few natives."

I noticed that many other community members were sharply aware of the distinction of being native. I asked my interviewees if people in the Huntsville area generally speak the same. Alice responded, "It depends on if they're natives to Huntsville. You find very few natives of this area anymore. Most of them have moved in." Margaret (b. 1936) replied, "Yeah. Unless they've come from up north and come here to live. . . . They're different."

Some lifelong or generations-back residents will inevitably become proud of their "authentic" heritage as Huntsville's population continues to swell with people from all over the United States, and this will surely be reflected linguistically, just as happened with residents of Martha's Vineyard (Labov 1963). As residents increasingly take pride in being "true Huntsvillians," we might see a resurgence and intensification of Southern features such as the SVS. However, if some residents of Huntsville believe it shares commonalities with Atlanta—as Roger did—the opposite effect could take place. Alternatively, North Alabama could witness a dichotomy of its residents' accents: those who want to stress "native" status versus those who want to stress "cosmopolitan" status. (See Nunnally and Bailey in this volume for evidence of social differentiation through accents even among the first settlers to this area.)

A more widespread vowel analysis of the speakers in the Huntsville area would certainly be enlightening for the topic of the Southern Vowel Shift. However, the goal of my preliminary study was not to show how Huntsville is just like everywhere else in the South. Rather, the goal was show how Huntsville actually is. It cannot be assumed that areas in the South—or in any dialect area for that matter—will be linguistically homogenous. Margaret told me, "They say, you know, you can tell the Southerners by the way they speak." While she is almost certainly right, we should not take it to mean that everyone uses the same resources in how they personally construct "sounding Southern."

NOTES

1. The metro area includes part of the population of Morgan County near the city of Decatur, many of whom work and socialize in Huntsville. The Combined Statistical Area includes Huntsville, Madison, Decatur, Athens, Scottsboro, and several other

smaller towns. Sources: http://www.census.gov/; http://blog.al.com/wire/2013/03 /alabamas_fastest-growing_metro.html; http://blog.al.com/spotnews/2011/02/metro _huntsville_population_ex.html

2. All three women spend time working within the Huntsville city limits, and both Natasha and Caroline received their university educations from the same institution. However, this is an oversimplification; there are other considerations, even within these criteria.

7

The Monophthongization of [aɪ] in Elba and the Environs

A COMMUNITY STUDY

Anna Head Spence

Judge Marion Brunson, former probate judge of Coffee County and author of *Pea River Reflections*, wrote, "Practically every generation has had a flood story about the Pea River to pass on" (1984, 7). The passages shown in figure 7.1 are excerpts from narratives about flooding in Elba, Alabama, that I collected in 2002 and 2003.[1] Although the stories bring local history to life, I was not writing a chronicle of disaster. Instead, I was launching a study of Southern English in the Alabama Wiregrass region (Southeast Alabama, especially Coffee, Pike, Dale, Houston, Geneva, and Covington Counties) using the topic of the floods to elicit speech data for linguistic analysis. This study examined linguistic variation within a context of variables, some concerning language itself (internal variables) and some concerning social characteristics of speakers and communities (external variables). This essay reports on the initial stage of my research (Head 2003).

First, I will lay a linguistic and historical foundation for my study, followed by a description of my research community and participants. I then discuss two kinds of variables, social (external) and linguistic (internal), that interact to influence speech variation. My goal in this section is to explain the range of influences that must be considered if research is to be adequate. Finally, I will present my findings and my conclusions regarding the value of the community study.

INTRODUCTION: JUST SAY "AH"

Montgomery points out that "both Southerners and non-Southerners identify the South by its language patterns" (1997, 5), and Metcalf identifies Southern English as "the most notable and talked about style of American speech" (2000, 5). Nagle and Sanders state that "the English of the Southern United States may be the most studied regional variety of any language" (2003, 1). Regarding the specific characteristics of Southern English, Dorrill points to "the salience of phonology [the sound system] as the most distinctive feature of the speech of the 'most distinctive speech region in the Unites States'" (2003, 120). Similarly, E. Thomas states that "discussions of the vowel variants of Southern English have been extensive and have continued without interruption for over a hundred years" and goes on to state that "no other region of the United States has attracted this level of interest in its vowels" (2003, 150). For instance, Clopper reports that nonlinguistically trained Northern listeners (Indiana University undergraduates) categorized talkers as Southerners if they exhibited "a voiced fricative in 'greasy' [that is, a z sound rather than an s sound], a highly diphthongal [o] [*don't* pronounced as *doh-oont*], and highly monophthongal [aɪ] [*my* as *mah*] and [ɔɪ] [*oil* as *awl*]" (2000, 63; see appendix A in this volume for explanations of phonetic symbols).

Of these noticeable vowel variants, E. Thomas calls the Southern pronunciation of the English "long i" a "hallmark of Southern speech" (2003, 150), and Dorrill considers it "the closest thing to a generally identifying feature" of Southern phonology (2003, 123). Sledd refers to this variation of "long i" as "the Confederate vowel" (1966, 25). All are commenting on the fact that throughout the region, most Southerners sometimes pronounce [aɪ] as [aː]; that is, the two-part vowel, or diphthong, in a word like *ride* (Standard English "rah-eed") will sound something like "rahd." To produce this variant, the first sound of [aɪ] is lengthened (written phonetically as [aː]) and the second sound, [ɪ], is weakened or omitted. The diphthong [aɪ] is, therefore, monophthongized into [aː] (changed into a one-part vowel, or monophthong, that does not "glide" to a second sound; see appendix A in this volume for more on the Southern monophthongization of the [aɪ] diphthong). Metcalf observes that "to be recognized as a Southerner, all you have to do is open your mouth and say 'ah'" (2000, 5). This diagnostic monophthongization of [aɪ] is recognizable not only to linguists but also to untrained listeners. In regard to Southerners' own awareness of the variant, Feagin states that "the monophthongal unglided vowel in *I* and *my* symbolizes all Southerners' identification with the South" (2000, 342–43).

Thus, [aː], the monophthongized [aɪ], is held to be a quintessentially Southern variable; however, as Labov tells us, "the more that is known about a language [feature], the more we can find out about it" (1972, 98). In 2003, I completed a study of the frequency as well as the social and linguistic conditioning of [aɪ] monophthongization in South Alabama—specifically, speech in the community of Elba and its environs. However, before discussing this community and presenting some of the findings from Head (2003), I first want to place [aɪ] monophthongization in linguistic history.

THE MONOPHTHONGIZATION OF [aɪ]: A SHORT HISTORY

To understand the present status of [aɪ] in Southern speech, it is necessary to consider its development in the context of a much earlier sound change, the Great Vowel Shift, and a recent and ongoing sound change, the Southern Vowel Shift. The

The 1998 Flood: African American, female, 43
My mom had called and . . . she says, "Get up! You can't even see your front doorsteps!" . . . but when we did get inside the house, my kitchen area was into my living room. I don't know where the living room was. For that water to do that much damage you knew it had to be powerful.

The 1990 Flood: European American, male, 64
We were up all night . . . with the mayor and the city council. Our mayor, when state troopers, the police chief, representatives, myself, we all told him, "Mayor, you need to evacuate at this time," he broke down and cried, "I'm losing my town," and it brings tears now to my eyes to think about it.

The 1929 Flood: European American, female, 78
. . . I had a pet hen and her name was Tootsie, and the next day of course we could just see everything, passing, floating on the water. Furniture just floating, and I looked out there and there was my pet hen Tootsie on a log . . . passing by.

The 1929 Flood: European American, male, 84
I was eleven years old . . . and my brother was just two weeks old, so . . . some men . . . took my mother in a chair holding the baby two doors to the two-story boarding house, and the rest of us followed and went up. And numerous people had to stay there and the water kept coming and kept coming and it was really frightening. . . . There were houses being washed away and during the night it was especially frightening because you could hear cows lowing, and trees and houses and things were hitting this house and shaking it, and you wondered how long we would be there.

4,000 FACE DEATH IN ALABAMA FLOOD, SUBMERGING ELBA

Entire Town Under 3 to 18 Feet of Water With People in Attics and on Housetops.

FRANTIC APPEALS FOR HELP

All Will Perish Unless Aid Is Swift, Says Governor Graves, Speaking to State on Radio.

TROOPS ORDERED TO SCENE

Six Escape From District, Bringing Stories of Terror—350 Children Marooned in Schoolhouse.

Figure 7.1. Front page, *New York Times*, March 15, 1929

Great Vowel Shift, "a systematic change in the articulation of the Middle English long vowels before and during the early Modern English period," is "the most salient of all phonological developments in the history of English" (Pyles and Algeo 1993, 170) and is responsible for the change in which the Middle English sound "ee" (spelled *i* and written phonetically as [iː]) had become a diphthong by 1500. Taking the word *ride*, for example, where Chaucer said "reed," Shakespeare said "ruh-eed" (written phonetically as [rəid]). In most varieties of English, this "uh-ee" diphthong eventually became our modern "ah-ee" [aɪ], as in [raɪd]. From this [aɪ] developed the Southern monophthong [aː], as in [raːd]. Labov and Ash contend that the Southern Vowel Shift, still taking place across the South today, "is essentially a continuation of the Great Vowel Shift, following the general principles of [sound change] that duplicate . . . many of the 16th century movements [in vowel placement]" (1997, 513). The monophthongization of [aɪ] to [aː], they further contend, is part of the Southern Vowel Shift (see Allbritten's essay and appendix A in this volume for more on the Southern Vowel Shift).

Two possible explanations have been offered as to the underlying reasons for the development of the Southern accent as we know it today, including [aɪ] monophthongization. One theory is that settlement history is largely responsible for the development of regional dialects. For example, Bailey acknowledges that it is a "long-standing premise of American dialectology . . . that American regional dialects are largely a consequence of settlement history and were formed by the time of the American Revolution" (1997, 255). Similarly, Mufwene states, "Where the presence of African populations was significant especially during the late seventeenth and the eighteenth centuries, such as in the southeastern parts of the United States, [Africans are likely to have] favored options in English that were more consistent with (some) African languages, such as the monophthongization of [the vowels [aɪ] and [aʊ]]" (2003, 71).

However, Bailey and Tillery (1996), Bailey (1997), and Metcalf (2000) have conjectured that it is after the Civil War that certain fixtures of present-day Southern speech became widely used, including [aɪ] monophthongization. Werner states, "The idea of a 'New South' was perhaps the preeminent intellectual innovation of the post–Civil War era," and proponents of the New South Creed such as Henry Grady "welcomed investment and encouraged business enterprise" (2001, 573). Bailey posits that some of the core features of contemporary Southern English were the product of linguistic activity between 1875 and World War II and cites New South developments, such as the emergence of stores (particularly country stores that held liens on tenant farmers), villages, and towns and the expansion of railroads, as potential "conduits for the diffusion of linguistic changes" (1997, 271). Building upon Bailey's (1997) research, Schneider and Montgomery (2001) have supported and extended Bailey's claims with the Southern Plantation Overseers' Corpus (*corpus* means a body of data for linguistic study); Schneider divides these features into "Traditional Southern" and "New Southern" and following Bailey (1997) classifies monophthongal [aɪ] as a "New Southern" feature (2003, 34; see the essay by Nunnally and Bailey in this volume for more on Traditional Southern and New Southern features).

COMMUNITY AND PARTICIPANT PARAMETERS

Despite the historical and cultural visibility of the region, there is "no monolithic South" (Hitchcock 2000), and subregional differences extend beyond the traditional division of upper and lower South. Fitzgerald explains, for example, that "in large portions of North Alabama [during the Civil War], yeoman disaffection with the Confederacy became a critical political force" (1988, 566); one North Alabama County, Winston, "voted to remain neutral as a 'Free State' during the War" (Dodd 1972, 9). Similarly, the Wiregrass region of Alabama was characterized, though to a lesser extent, by a yeoman Unionism during the war (Fitzgerald 1988, 566). In regard to culture, Southern literature reflects the diversity of the region, and contemporary Southern writers "share a common interest in the stories of those whose voices have long been silenced, whose stories may heretofore have been told only in small, disenfranchised, and often oppressed communities: people of color, members of lower socioeconomic classes, or individuals from subregions whose populations have traditionally been stereotyped by their heritage or the area in which they live, such as the Cajuns in South Louisiana or the poor Whites in the Appalachian Mountains" (Disheroon-Green 2005, 1077). Thus, despite the South's distinctiveness, it is also a diverse region, and scholars of Southern history and literature have been forced to examine the "cultures" of the South.

For this reason, a study of one area of the South cannot characterize Southern English in its entirety. Although it has been established that Southern English is distinctive "among regional varieties in the United States," it contains "rich internal diversity" (Nagle and Sanders 2003, 1). As Montgomery points out, "although the South is the most distinctive speech region in the United States, it is hardly more uniform than the nation as a whole" (1989, 761). No community study can be expected to describe the language of the South as a whole but instead can be understood to contribute to the body of research that exists on Southern English.

For my 2003 study of variation present within Southern English, I chose Elba, Alabama, in the Wiregrass region, as my research community. Elba provides an interesting laboratory, because it is at once a unique part of the South but also highly representative. For example, Linguistic Atlas research designates the Georgia and Alabama Wiregrass region as home to one of eighteen subvarieties of Southern English (Algeo 2003, 7). On the other hand, to untrained listeners the Wiregrass may represent a microcosm of Southern speech. In research into perceptual dialectology, Preston has repeatedly solicited the opinions of lay respondents about where people speak Southern English (1989, 1996, 1997, 1999, 2005). He reports that 96 percent of his Michigan respondents believe that "the heart of the South is to be found in southeastern Alabama" (1997, 317).

Elba, in Coffee County, is a typical small Southern town—almost. Though it is typical in the sense that it celebrates "Friday Night Football Fever" in the fall and that its heart can be found in its "downtown," it is atypical in that the flooding of the Pea River has shaped its history and that among its citizens has been a curious assortment of Alabama historical and political characters. For example, despite the fact that the Wiregrass was largely pro-Union during the Civil War, Alberta Martin (one of the last known Confederate widows, and believed for a time to be the last

Confederate widow) spent most of her life in Elba. Regarding political figures of the Jim Crow era and the civil rights movement, Elba is home to the Folsom clan (including not only Big Jim but also Cornelia Wallace); additionally, Dallas County sheriff Jim Clark, infamous for the "Bloody Sunday" incident in Selma, grew up in Elba and returned there at the end of his life. Recently, the Carsey Institute sponsored research in Elba, resulting in a study titled "Changing Church in the South: Religion and Politics in Elba, Alabama." The Carsey Institute, located at the University of New Hampshire, "sponsors independent, interdisciplinary research that documents trends and conditions in rural America" (Ardery 2006). Elba was chosen based on voting trends; while much of Alabama was overwhelmingly Democratic or overwhelmingly Republican, Elba exhibited a degree of political balance (Julie Ardery, email correspondence, April 23, 2007). Elba's typicality yet simultaneous uniqueness makes it an interesting research community; while it is undoubtedly a prototypical small Southern town in many ways, it is also a meteorological and political anomaly.

Because storytelling produces "styles analogous to how people talk in . . . everyday situations" (Bell 1984, 150), I used Elba's history of flooding as my interview topic. Most people in Elba tell flood narratives, so I asked each of the forty-two research participants to discuss these shared natural disasters. Many of the speakers told performed narratives, that is, stories that they had told time and time again. Others described what they could remember about one or more floods, a format closer in style to the casual interview. In both cases, my goal as the interviewer was to create a comfortable environment to promote speech unmonitored by the speaker. To minimize the observer's paradox—that is, the influence of the interviewer's presence on the interviewee, which changes the language being observed— all interviews were conducted in settings that were comfortable for the individual participants. Additionally, Elba is my hometown, and thus, my prior relationships with the research participants, some extending from childhood, in combination with the interview topic and the locations in which the interviews were carried out, provided a near-optimal environment for natural speech.

All forty-two participants in the 2003 research were residents of Elba at the time of the study, including two males and two females who originally resided in other towns within Southeast Alabama. Two additional male speakers were originally from small communities that are located outside the city limits but are often considered locally to be part of Elba. Half of the participants were male and half were female, and their ages ranged from eleven to eighty-eight. Each participant was either middle class or working class and either European American or African American. (Although I have yet to include Hispanic Alabamians in my research, this large and growing contingent will eventually exert linguistic influence throughout the state. See Picone's essay for an overview of current cultural and linguistic shifts.)

VARIABLES INVESTIGATED

Sociolinguistic research has discovered a range of possible influences on an individual's language use, such as whether and how often a speaker might monophthongize [aɪ] to [aː]. The speaker's incidence and frequency of using the variant may be influenced by (may correlate with) two kinds of variables: social or external factors (e.g., style, urban orientation, ethnicity, socioeconomic status, gender, and age) and linguistic or internal factors (the following sound environment, part of speech, syllable stress, and word frequency). The following survey discusses prior research on each of these correlates of variation and [aɪ] monophthongization.

External Variables

As Bell explains, "style is essentially speakers' response[s] to their audience[s]" (1984, 145). Regarding style, my study addressed two closely related methodological concerns in the sociolinguistic literature: the observer's paradox and audience design. Hay, Jannedy, and Mendoza-Denton (1999) point to audience design as a significant factor in [aɪ] monophthongization in a study that examined the speech of Oprah Winfrey. Their analysis of her popular daytime talk show provided evidence that when Winfrey talked about an African American (usually an upcoming guest) she was more likely to use [aː] in her speech (1999). The implication seems to be that Winfrey manipulates her dialect from a more standard English style using [aɪ] to a less standard form using [aː], and the change is in response to the audience's expectation that her dialect will match the topic. When the topic concerns African Americans, she monophthongizes [aɪ], since [aː] is a pervasive feature of AAVE (see below). Similarly, because my interviewees told their flood stories to me, a fellow Elban Southerner, feelings they might have had that more standard language would be appropriate were reduced.

Regarding the urban/nonurban dimension of [aɪ] variation, Feagin observes that the distinction between urban and nonurban speech in Southern English "has long been noted by [untrained] native speakers and by linguists" (1979, 23). More recently, Thomas, in a study of Texas, has shown a linguistic contrast developing between European Americans living in metropolitan areas and those living in smaller towns and rural areas, with monophthongization as more characteristic of nonurban areas (1997, 144; see also the essays by Doxsey and Nunnally and Bailey in this volume).

Regarding ethnicity, monophthongization has been linked with both African American and European American speech. Edwards (1997) discusses the speech of working-class African Americans in Detroit and notes that they are more likely to use the monophthongized variant; Bailey and Bernstein (1989) also found African Americans in Texas to be more monophthongized than European Americans. Similarly, Hay, Jannedy, and Mendoza-Denton (1999) identify African American ethnicity as a factor in [aɪ] monophthongization. In her study of African American and European American speech in Memphis, Tennessee, Fridland states, "While often considered a feature characteristic of White Southern speech, [aɪ] monophthongization has also been recorded in Black speech, both within and outside the South" (2003, 279). She elaborates by stating that "African Americans in Memphis appear to be moving toward forms which symbolize involvement in the Southern community and its associated heritage" (2003, 296).

Socioeconomic status also plays a role in language variation. With respect to this variable, Crane (1977) found that Tuscaloosa's highest class is most likely to use standard [aɪ]. Similarly, Edwards (1997) finds the highest incidence of monophthongization among Detroit working-class African Americans.

Gender has also been documented as having a significant correlation with monophthongization: researchers have found that, when controlling for age, older men typically use the monophthongized form most. Edwards (1997), examining the speech of working-class African Americans in Detroit, and Bowie (2001), examining the speech of middle-class European Americans in Waldorf, Maryland, report this finding, suggesting that gender may transcend both class and ethnicity.

Regarding age, studies have largely indicated that older speakers of both genders use the monophthongized form [aː] more than younger speakers do. Studies that present evidence to this effect include Crane (1977), Bailey and Bernstein (1989), Edwards (1997), and Bowie (2001). However, Fridland's study of Memphis (2000) found all speaker populations (across ethnicity and age) moving toward monophthongization. This finding was reaffirmed in a 2003 study in which Fridland found [aɪ] monophthongization to be "a feature of Memphis speech generally" (279).

INTERNAL VARIABLES

Researchers have identified four internal variables that affect the incidence of [aɪ] monophthongization: the type of sound that follows [aɪ] in a word (i.e., the following environment), the part of speech, syllable stress, and word frequency. Of these, the following environment is discussed most frequently in the literature (see appendices A and B in this volume for explanation of voiced and voiceless sounds and terms such as *obstruent* below). Several researchers (e.g., Fridland 2000; Anderson 1999, 2002; Labov and Ash 1997) report that monophthongization occurs before voiced obstruents (e.g., in words like *ride* and *prize*). Hazen (2000, 221) reports that the following sound environments that favor [aɪ] monophthongization rank as follows from most to least favorable:

liquids (e.g., [l] as in *mile* and rhotic liquids [i.e., r sounds] as in *tire*),
nasals (e.g., [n] in *mine*),
voiced obstruents (e.g., [d] in *bide*), and
voiceless obstruents (e.g., [t] in *bite*).

Bowie (2001) reports a similar pattern: following liquids strongly favor monophthongization; nasals and voiced obstruents favor monophthongization; and voiceless obstruents disfavor monophthongization. Thomas (2001) also cites following [l] as a favored environment.

Bowie (2001) examines part of speech and syllable stress. He observes that secondary stress within the word slightly favors monophthongization and reports that nouns, adverbs, and verbs favor monophthongization.

Hay, Jannedy, and Mendoza-Denton (1999) find word frequency, which they set as greater than or fewer than five in their corpus, to be a significant predictor of [aɪ] monophthongization. Frequent words are prone to monophthongization.

EXPLORING THE INTERSECTION OF INTERNAL AND EXTERNAL VARIABLES

Discussions of several of the external variables above identified differences in [aɪ] variation: older speakers monophthongize more than younger, men more than women. However, when the incidence of [aɪ] monophthongization is considered in relation only to a following environment of voiceless obstruents (e.g., when [aɪ] is followed by the sounds in words such as *pipe, bite, like, life, scythe, mice, Elisha,* and *righteous*), another picture emerges.

As mentioned above, older speakers have been shown generally to use the monophthongized form more than younger speakers do. However, research in Texas (Bailey and Bernstein 1989) and Appalachia (Bailey and Tillery 1996) suggests that monophthongization before voiceless obstruents is more likely in younger speakers. These researchers have interpreted this finding as evidence for change in progress. Thomas (2001) also discusses monophthongization of [aɪ] before voiceless obstruents as a newer pattern, predominating in Southern Appalachia, and Anderson (2002) has discussed a similar change as characteristic of African American Detroiters who have forged a relationship with Appalachian whites in Detroit. Turning to the variable of gender, Bailey and Bernstein (1989), looking at Texas, found women to be leading the change in monophthongization before voiceless obstruents (cf. Bowie's 2001 finding that women in southern Maryland are moving away from monophthongization). Obviously, researchers must look at all the variables, internal and external, to understand seemingly conflicting results.

MONOPHTHONGIZATION OF [aɪ] IN ELBA

From my interviewees' stories of floods in Elba, Alabama, I collected data pertinent to the variation of [aɪ] and [aː]. I coded the data (i.e., gave it codes for statistical analysis) based on the variables reviewed above and performed analyses using a statistical software package called JMP IN 4.0. The results of my analysis yielded several conclusions (for complete results, see Head 2003). First and foremost, the rate of monophthongization in Elba, Alabama, is quite high. Eighty-two percent of [aɪ]s among the speakers sampled were pronounced as monophthongs [aː].

THE BEARING OF EXTERNAL VARIABLES ON RESULTS

Of the external or social factors tested in this study, age contributed most significantly to the monophthongization of [aɪ] in Elba, Alabama. As consistent with other studies, older speakers monophthongized at a statistically significant higher frequency than did younger speakers. Additionally, in Elba, unlike in some locations (see above), there is no evidence of increasing monophthongization before voiceless obstruents among the younger speakers (for example *right* pronounced [raːt] "raht"). However, the data set represents only three speakers between the ages of eleven and twenty and only seven speakers between twenty-one and thirty-nine. Future research should include additional speakers in these age groups for verification of the findings.

Contrary to research focusing on [aɪ] variation in other locales, my 2003 study did not reveal ethnicity to significantly contribute to monophthongization. However, this corpus represents eighteen African American research participants and twenty-four European American research participants, and several of the African American speakers provided shorter narratives. Thus, subsequent research may benefit from interviewing additional African American speakers.

Similarly, though socioeconomic status (SES) was not found to be a significant factor in monophthongization, this study included only ten working-class research participants. Adding additional working-class speakers might provide a better test of the relevance of SES to the monophthongization of [aɪ] in Elba.

As with ethnicity and SES, and contrary to previous research, this study did not identify gender as significantly conditioning monophthongization. One of the most consistent findings in the sociolinguistic literature is that women are more sensitive to stylistic constraints than men, and thus are more likely to use standard variants in interviews. My female participants may have been disinclined to shift to a more formal style and avoidance of variants considered less standard because of both the topic the research participants discussed and my previous relationship with them, as discussed earlier. This hypothesis could be tested in a subsequent study by asking participants to read a paragraph and a word list, since these language situations will promote a more formal style that has been shown to disfavor monophthongization. (See Doxsey's essay in this volume for discussion of the influence of more formal styles of speech on the incidence of monophthongization.)

THE BEARING OF INTERNAL VARIABLES ON RESULTS

Consistent with the research literature, the sound environment following [aɪ] had the greatest impact on monophthongization. Also as suggested in several studies, voiceless obstruents inhibited monophthongization. However, the corpus contained relatively few instances in which [aɪ] or [aː] was followed by a vowel or a glide. For future study, the environments would need to be equally represented.

Part of speech was also significant in this study. Statistical analysis found words of all parts of speech to favor monophthongization, which is contrary to Bowie (2001), who finds nouns, verbs, and adverbs to favor monophthongization and adjectives and all others to disfavor monophthongization. For future study, more pronouns (other than *I* and *my*) should be collected. (For my 2003 study I removed *I*, *I'll*, *I'm*, *I'd*, *I've*, and *my*, as these words were repeatedly monophthongized, and in an analysis of linguistic variation, the presence of items in which "variability has almost disappeared" [Labov 1984, 141] skews the results.)

CONCLUSIONS

I conducted my 2003 study to describe the monophthongization of [aɪ] in a non-urban Southeast Alabama municipality, informed by previous research on this characteristic variable of Southern English. In conducting a community study, I intended to expand the body of research on the monophthongization of [aɪ], Alabama English, and Southern English. As Dorrill notes, "There is still much to know about the [sound systems] of English in the Southern United States" (2003, 125). Although this study laid a foundation for research on the English of Elba, my community study showed me that there is also much to learn about the sounds even in one's own backyard.[2]

Notes

1. As required for all research involving human research participants, a protocol was submitted to the Auburn University Human Subjects Institutional Review Board (IRB). The project was approved at Minimum Risk.

2. For my dissertation research, which I completed after the research informing this essay, I collected additional interviews concerning racial integration and analyzed two more variables: [ɔɪ] (the sound "oh-ee," especially in words like *oil*, which for many Southerners is pronounced like "awl," and -ing versus -in' ([ŋ] versus [n], inaccurately called "dropping the g"), in addition to [aɪ]. My findings based on comparing African American and European American speakers in three age cohorts suggest the complexity of linguistic choices made by speakers, both as individuals and as members of social groups in response to social change, especially the integration of the Elba environs starting in the 1960s. See Head (2012).

8

To [a:] or Not to [a:] on the Gulf Coast of Alabama

Jocelyn Doxsey

The Southern region of the United States is often described as a separate region of the country, based on differing cultural practices, geography, history and, especially, linguistic features. In their monumental *Atlas of North American English*, Labov, Ash, and Boberg (2005) note that while Americans tend to be generally unknowledgeable about regional dialects, almost every non-Southern American can reproduce a Southern accent on some level by manipulating the stereotypical features of White Southern English. Perhaps the most salient of these features is the Southern Vowel, the pronunciation of the Standard American English vowel [aɪ] as [a:]; that is, pronouncing the diphthong (two-part) vowel in a word like *ride* "rah-eed" so that the word sounds something like "rahd," with a lengthened, single sound (monophthong; see appendices A and B in this volume for explanations of phonetic symbols and the Southern monophthongization of the the [aɪ] diphthong and for definitions of terms such as *obstruent* below). This variant, while stigmatized in Standard American English, is common throughout most of the South and has been present in the dialect since at least the end of the nineteenth century (Bailey and Tillery 1996; Evans 1935).

However, the incidence of pronouncing [aɪ] as [a:] also differs for speakers of the two main Southern dialects associated with South Alabama and North Alabama (see the essays by Nunnally, Davies, and Nunnally and Bailey in this volume). In general, speakers of Coastal Southern (stretching from the Atlantic Coast to East Texas) monophthongize [aɪ] into [a:] only when it occurs either at the end of a word or before a sonorant and voiced obstruent, that is, in words like *my, mine, mile, rise*, and *ride*. When [aɪ] occurs before a voiceless obstruent, that is, in words like *mice* and *right*, speakers of Coastal Southern do not as a rule monophthongize it to [a:] but keep the diphthong [aɪ]. Speakers of Inland Southern, on the other hand, may monophthongize [aɪ] to [a:] (or unlengthened [a]) in all sound environments, that is, in both *ride* and *right*. For Coastal Southern speakers, the [a:] variant is stigmatized when it appears before a voiceless obstruent (in words like *mice* and *right*); production of the monophthong in this phonological context is linked to less education and working-class status. However, among speakers of Inland Southern, [aɪ] may be monophthongized to [aː] in all sound environments without these negative reactions (see Nunnally and Bailey in this volume for interaction of these variants in North Alabama and other areas of the state).

This essay reports summaries of findings from my research investigating the [aɪ] variable along the Gulf Coast (defined in this essay as Mobile and Baldwin Counties) of Alabama to understand its prevalence in the region and to compare it with recent and sometimes conflicting studies (Doxsey 2007). In fieldwork locations in Anniston, Alabama, and rural Georgia, respectively, Feagin (2000) and Melancon and Wise (2005) found evidence that [aː] is disappearing from the dialects of younger speakers. Studies in Texas, however, indicate an increase in use of the [aː] variant for younger, rural, white Texans but a decrease in its use for younger, urban, white Texans (E. Thomas 2001, 144). Furthermore, there is disagreement as to whether this change is related to age alone or to age and social class. My research explores the speech of the Gulf Coast Alabamians to answer the following questions:

- Who is using [aː]?
- Are younger speakers moving away from [aː] (and can anything be said about their social class)?
- Is the [aː] variant present before voiceless obstruents (i.e., before sounds usually spelled -p, -t, -k, -f, -th, -s, -sh, -ch) in this region? If it is present before voiceless obstruents, is its distribution in this environment sensitive to any social factors?
- Do levels of formality in style of speech have a bearing on variation?

THE GULF COAST: HISTORY, ECONOMY, AND PEOPLE

Several linguistic studies have focused on Southern English (for example, Montgomery and Johnson 2007; Nagle and Sanders 2003; Bernstein, Nunnally, and Sabino 1997; Montgomery and Bailey 1986; and Picone and Davies 2015) and Alabama English more specifically (Feagin 1979). Thus, why focus on the Gulf Coast of Alabama? The Alabama Gulf Coast has a different social, geographic, and linguistic history from the rest of Alabama. Furthermore, since these differences are maintained currently, it is reasonable to expect them to be reflected in the language of speakers along the Gulf Coast (similarly, see the essays by Allbritten, Feagin, and Spence in this volume for studies of other unique Alabama areas).

HISTORY

Mobile, the major city in the Gulf Coast of Alabama, was settled in 1702 by the French (though Hernando de Soto first explored the region in 1540; Higginbotham 2001). It is the oldest colonial city in the state. The area's proximity to the Mississippi River Basin and its position on the Gulf of Mexico offered long-range strategic value to the French: access to native peoples via the waterways and a future harbor for seagoing ships (Higginbotham 2001). Thus the French founded

Mobile. The Gulf Coast region of Alabama remained politically separate later as a British and then a Spanish territory until 1819, when Alabama was admitted to the Union. Rogers, Ward, Atkins, and Flynt (1994) illustrate the region's uniqueness by stating that with Mobile's "French and Spanish heritage, the city became the cultural center of Alabama" (1994, 133). The combination of coastline and Spanish and French occupation (until the early 1800s) made Mobile and the Gulf Coast historically distinct from the rest of the state (see Picone's essay for the multilingual history of this area).

Geographic and Linguistic Boundaries

The southernmost area of Alabama has been treated as a distinctive region in linguistic mapping studies as well as in other academic disciplines such as history. Benson (2003, 309), in a study of dialect boundaries in the South, shows that residents of the state perceive the Gulf Coast of Alabama as linguistically different from other regions in the state. Furthermore, in the TELSUR project, a survey of linguistic changes in progress in North American English conducted by Labov, Ash, and Boberg (2005), Alabama is sampled in four locations: Mobile, Linden, Montgomery, and Birmingham.

Labov, Ash, and Boberg (2005) find that these areas differ linguistically, showing Birmingham to have more Southern Vowel Shift features (including high rates of monophthongization) and to be a member of the subcategory "the Inland South" (2006, 130; for more on the Southern Vowel Shift, see Allbritten's essay and appendix A). Mobile, on the other hand, showed the lowest rates of monophthongization of the four Alabama sites (Labov, Ash, and Boberg 2005, 130). The divisions made in both Labov, Ash, and Boberg (2006) and Benson (2003) line up with geographic distinctions. Encyclopedias and geological reference works divide Alabama into four main regions characterized by differing geographic features: North Alabama, or the Tennessee Valley (marked by the Cumberland Plateau and the Great Appalachian Valley); Central Alabama (Birmingham area; the Appalachian Valley extends to this area); the Piedmont area, or Black Belt (located below Birmingham and noted for its rich soil); and finally the Gulf Coast (marked by water access to the Gulf of Mexico as well as the Mississippi River).

Economy

The Gulf Coast also differs economically from the rest of the state. Perhaps the most prominent economic difference in this area is the reliance on the shipping industry. According to the City of Mobile website, the deep-sea Port of Mobile ranks among the top dozen US seaports. It has the world's largest forest products terminal and is first in the nation for wood pulp export and second for forest products (2006). Access to water has given rise to a tourism industry, which is located primarily along the coast of Baldwin County. These two industries, tourism and shipping, have given the Gulf Coast area a different economic landscape from the other metropolitan areas in the state.

PEOPLE

One final factor is relevant to the discussion of the Gulf Coast—its people, specifically the people who comprise this sample (this study was limited to white Alabamians; therefore, Gulf Coast African American English will not be discussed). Informants were asked to share their feelings about living in the South, specifically: 1) if they liked living on the Gulf Coast; 2) if they felt the Gulf Coast was different in any way from the rest of the state; and 3) if they identified themselves as being "Southern." Of the twenty-six informants, all responded positively toward questions about the Gulf Coast, Alabama, and the South in general. Furthermore, most informants noted differences between the Gulf Coast and the rest of the state, as in this description by Margaret (twenty-three, college-educated, female):[1]

> um just because like when I lived in Troy[2] like the people that live in Troy they are like COUNTRY . . . and people have this set idea about how they think the people in Alabama are but people down here are not like that . . . they don't talk real slow ([tɑːk riːl sloː]) if you grew up down here and you went off somewhere it's less likely that they'll be like "oh you're from Alabama" maybe it's like there's this line like and it stops at Baldwin County . . . cause there's all these little places . . . like I knew this one guy he moved to Daphne from Slapout the city is called SLAPOUT . . . and he was he was COUNTRY and after he lived here for awhile—the people here are not country

Edward (twenty-five, graduate education, male) gives a less linguistic reason for the differences in the Gulf Coast area and remarks that the Gulf Coast of Alabama is perfect for the following reasons: "The only place in the country where you— you're thirty minutes from saltwater fishing thirty minutes from freshwater fishing and you can go any type of hunting you want."

DATA COLLECTION

My experience with the Gulf Coast began in 1991, when my parents moved to Daphne from the Los Angeles area. Although I attended local schools from sixth grade to my senior year, before leaving for Ohio State University, I was not strongly involved with aspects of the community other than my school peers. When I returned for my first research visit in the summer of 2005, I spent three months on the Gulf Coast working and developing relationships with people in the community (through a job at a restaurant, church attendance, my parents, my high school-teachers, a local retirement home, etc.). Following this initial visit, I returned in December and began asking people if they would participate in a study about the Gulf Coast of Alabama. Individuals were told that my interviews with them would be recorded and that they would be part of a greater corpus (*body* of collected language) of Gulf Coast English. I informed those who were interested that in March 2006 and then in May/June 2006 I would be coming back to interview them.

The twenty-six informants were stratified by sex, age, and education. Because much previous research has shown that the level of formality of speech influences the speaker's speech production (see Wolfram and Schilling-Estes 2006, 278), each informant participated in an interview process designed to elicit responses in three styles reflecting three levels of formality: making conversation to elicit an informal style, reading a set passage to elicit a more formal style than conversation, and reading a list of words to elicit the most formal style.

Words containing [aɪ] could be expected to occur naturally in conversation, but I also pre-edited the reading passage and the word list to include words where [aɪ] appeared before voiced sounds (like *ride*) and words where [aɪ] occurred before voiceless obstruents (like *right*). In these ways, the variation of [aɪ] and [aː] could be analyzed over three stylistic dimensions.

Results

Monophthongization of [aɪ] was present for each informant before both voiced and voiceless segments (that is, in words like *prize* and *price*). Rates of [aː] were higher in the prevoiced environment, confirming results found in other studies (Evans 1935; Sledd 1966; Labov 1991; Fridland 1998; Feagin 2000; Hazen 2000; Labov, Ash, and Boberg 2005; tables of data supporting my findings are available in Doxsey 2007 but are omitted in this report).

The data in this study suggest that [aɪ] is monophthongized before voiced segments in tautosyllabic environments (that is, occurring in the same syllable), a result found in Hazen (2000). This finding shows that the following phonological environment does not affect the [aɪ] vowel across boundaries of words and grammatical endings. Thus, [maː sit] for *my seat* may not be stigmatized in Gulf Coast speech, even though [aː] comes before the voiceless sound [s] in the next word, but [naːs waːt raːs] for *nice white rice* is stigmatized when the [aː] forms come before voiceless sounds ([s] or [t] here) within the same syllables.

Of particular importance are the results for [aː] in prevoiceless environments. Though voiceless obstruents generally disfavor monophthongization in Coastal Southern dialect regions, all informants in this corpus produced [aː] before voiceless obstruents. Some of the words included: *tight, nice, white, right, fright.* This variant has been called the shibboleth for class status in non–Inland South regions (Feagin 2000, 342) and is recognized in this Gulf Coast community as such. Many informants commented explicitly on this stigmatized variant, and most informants insisted that they did not use this variant in their speech (illustrating why linguistic researchers do not take speakers' perceptions of their own speech at face value). This denial of using [aː] in words like *right* and *nice* is especially interesting when we look at the frequencies for the informants as well as the results for style. Conversational style favored [aː] in prevoiceless environments, while reading-passage style and word-list style, with their greater formality calling forth more self-monitoring, disfavored it.

The passages below show two different speakers explicitly discussing [aː] in prevoiceless environments during their interviews. To illustrate the stigmatized use of [aː] before voiceless obstruents, Rachel monophthongizes [aɪ] in *white, might, night* and *sight*, and Elizabeth does the same in *ice, might, bite, right, white,* and *rice.*

> . . . some of these words now and in normal conversation I may say to you is that a [waːt] blouse you got on I may say [waːt] and we [maːt] be going out Friday [naːt] [LAUGH] and was it love at first [saːt] [LAUGH] so normal conversation I . . . that may be what I say and it probably is a lot of times um not as much as my sister my sister was in Georgia for a long time and they really talk like that (Rachel, forty-six, high school education)

> . . . do you want me to make those [aːz] . . . [maːt] [baːt] [raːt] you know my uh other grand uh daughter my other daughter lives in North Alabama and when she moved up there we had thought uh that she would keep her South Alabama accent but she has picked up that [waːt] [raːt] [raːs] and talks just like them up there (Elizabeth, seventy, college education)

The transcriptions above show that the [aː] before voiceless obstruents is a stigmatized variant in this community that is representative of membership in a "different" part of Alabama or the South more broadly (both informants give examples of this variant and label it as either being northern Alabamian or Georgian).

Though informants were sensitive to [aː] before voiceless consonants and referred to it (as the above transcripts note), they did not make any specific reference to [aː] before voiced segments. This finding indicates that [aː] before voiced segments (for example, in *rize* and opposed to *rice)* is not as salient in the community as [aː] before voiceless obstruents and does not arouse disapproval or label one as an outsider.

Men were found to use [aː] more than women, a finding that comes as no surprise, as men in general use stigmatized variants more than women (Eckert 1989). However, the men's higher rate was apparent only when all the [aɪ] words were taken together, those in both prevoiced and prevoiceless contexts. Results for [aː] in prevoiceless environments do not show an effect for sex.

Results for education followed a canonical pattern in the two phonological contexts, with some surprising variations. Informants with a high school education favored [aː] in both prevoiced and prevoiceless environments; this is an expected result. Informants with a college education disfavored [aː] in both phonological contexts; this is also an expected result. The surprise came when results showed that in the prevoiceless context informants with graduate educations favored [aː] (in the prevoiced context informants neither favored nor disfavored [aː]). I was not expecting to see informants with graduate educations align, at least linguistically, with high school–educated informants; however, my results show that indeed these two groups of informants are behaving similarly in their use of [aː] (specifically in the prevoiceless environment). These results, plus the statements about Southern speech (e.g., see the passages above) by some of the college-educated informants, suggest that the college-educated informants may be exhibiting some linguistic insecurity (see Hasty's essay in this volume). Many of the college-educated informants indicated that they felt as though they did not have a "Southern" accent.

One informant, John (twenty-five, college education), mentioned several times that he did not have a Southern accent. In this excerpt from his interview he describes several occasions where he was mistaken as not being from the South.

> me not having an accent **I've** been mistaken for being from several other places [Interviewer: really?] well when I was working down at the Grand[3] in room service **I** was mistaken for being from uh Australia because I said "g'day" to someone . . . and then we had quite a few people from Czech and Turkey working there so **I** got mistaken for being from Europe somewhere in Europe . . . **I** guess they they expect that Southern accent and if you don't have it they don't see you as being from this area

Before the interview began, John made it clear to me that he did not have a Southern accent and wanted to know if I was studying the Gulf Coast because its residents "don't have Southern accents." It is interesting to note that while John was describing his "accent-less" speech, he was using the "Southern Vowel" [aː]. In the above passage his [aː] in place of [aɪ] is indicated by the bold "I." His overall rate of monophthongization was 40 percent, or 60 out of 149 opportunities to monophthongize [aɪ] during the interview.[4]

My research question concerning age was answered in the affirmative: younger speakers use less of the [aː] variant, while older speakers use the [aː] variant the most. However, this finding is true for [aː] only when [aɪ] is in a prevoiced environment. The findings for age ([aː] before voiced and voiceless environments) corroborate claims made by other scholars (Feagin 2000; Melancon and Wise 2005) that the rate of monophthongization is declining. In contrast, [aː] in prevoiceless environments indicates that age is not significant with respect to monophthongization. This result is not attested in the literature. While scholars agree that [aː] before voiceless segments is highly stigmatized for Coastal Southern speakers, none make any claims about age. The results from this study suggest that Gulf Coast Alabamians of all ages show some monophthongization in prevoiceless environments (see Doxsey 2007 for full details).

Finally, the incidence of [aɪ] monophthongization correlated in interesting ways with the three styles elicited in the interviews. In fact, this study's results according to style demonstrate the importance of isolating a variant within various phonological contexts, in this case, prevoiced and prevoiceless environments. Comparing the results for style across these two phonological contexts highlights the double duty that [aː] plays as a stigmatized variant. First, while it is true that [aː] is stigmatized in all phonological environments in Standard American English, crucially it is salient for the speakers in this corpus only in the word-list style, where they tried to avoid it. Second, [aː] in prevoiceless contexts is an especially stigmatized variant for Southerners ([aː] in this environment is disfavored in both reading passage and word list styles). These results show that a linguistic variable can vary in its degree of stigmatization within a geographic region and that style is not a simple adjustment of the *frequency* of sociolinguistic variants but is strongly sensitive to the *evaluation* of individual variants.

CONCLUSIONS AND SUGGESTIONS FOR FURTHER RESEARCH

The purpose of this study was to describe the status of [aɪ] on the Gulf Coast of Alabama both linguistically and socially. The data from the Gulf Coast corpus indicate that [aɪ] monophthongization is still a robust feature of White Southern English (at least the version spoken on the Gulf Coast). Though [aː] is used by all speakers, it is used significantly less by those speakers in the youngest age category. This decrease in [aː] usage may be indicative of a change in progress. This claim supports Feagin's (2000) suggestion that [aː] is receding in the speech of young Southerners. In this way, the Gulf Coast corpus is patterning with other parts of Alabama. The Gulf Coast differs from Feagin's data (2000) in that young speakers still retain [aː] throughout their speech, not just in "I" and "my."

Results from the TELSUR study show the Mobile area as having the lowest rates of monophthongization (compared with the rest of the state) in both voiced and voiceless contexts (Labov, Ash, and Boberg 2005). The data from this study, particularly in the prevoiceless contexts, show similar results to those of Labov, Ash, and Boberg (2005), which indicate that there is a dialectal difference between Northern Alabama and Coastal Alabama. Furthermore, this difference is most likely seen in the rates of [aː] before voiceless obstruents (Labov, Ash, and Boberg 2005 note that Northern Alabama has higher rates of [aː] before voiceless segments than does Coastal Alabama). Nevertheless, it is important to note that [aː] before voiceless segments was present in every interview in this corpus (albeit at lower rates than before voiced segments).

The presence of [aː] before voiced segments within White Southern English is not entirely surprising. Though all speakers used this variant and did not explicitly comment on [aː] before voiced segments, the fact that they did not monophthongize [aɪ] in word-list style suggests that they were still sensitive to it as a nonstandard feature of American English.

Findings from this study suggest that the Gulf Coast of Alabama may be undergoing a change in progress. The data from this study show that this change is accomplished by avoidance of the nonstigmatized variant ([aː] in prevoiced contexts), demonstrated by the diminished rates of use in the speech of younger speakers. This finding patterns with other studies that show [aː] diminishing in the speech of younger speakers. However, it is important to note that the stigmatized variant ([aː] in prevoiceless environments) continues to have low and unchanged rates of use across apparent time (for more on "apparent time," see appendix B and the essays by Nunnally and Bailey and Allbritten in this volume). If it is the case that White Southern English as a whole is undergoing a change in progress, then this study adds further support for that claim. Furthermore, a change in progress may have implications for the Southern Vowel Shift as a whole (see Allbritten's essay in this volume). If, as Labov (1991) suggests, [aɪ] monophthongization is the initial step in the Southern Vowel Shift, then a reversal of that step may cause changes in other vowels as well. However, if [aɪ] monophthongization is simply part of an "early" step in the Southern Vowel Shift, as Fridland (2000) suggests, then there may not be any effect on other vowels. To make a claim either way about change in the vowels involved in the Southern Vowel Shift will necessitate a full examination of all the relevant vowels in a corpus more representative of the White Southern English speakers of the Gulf Coast.

In conclusion, this study has attempted to describe the presence of [aː] on the Gulf Coast of Alabama. The results from this study will add to the greater body of work on White Southern English as well as the greater body of work on sociolinguistic variation in any dialect. This study has shown that style varies and is sensitive to individual sociolinguistic variants. The more opportunities we have to describe language variation, the better able we will be to make claims about language change and its relation to the community at large.

NOTES

1. Names of informants have been changed to protect identities.
2. Troy is a small college town located in southeastern Alabama.
3. The Grand Hotel is located on Mobile Bay.
4. John's speech also exhibits another highly salient feature of Southern English, the "*pen/pin* merger," wherein [ɛ] ("short e") and [ɪ] ("short i") before nasal consonants both sound like [ɪ], for example, *ten* and *tin* both sound like *tin*. Out of five -en tokens in the passage, *accent, been, when, then,* and *accent* once more, John pronounces only *then* with [ɛn] and the rest with the Southern [ɪn]. This difference between John's concept of his accent and its reality is in no way uncommon and illustrates the difficulty speakers have with self-monitoring the less accessible parts of their language systems, such as phonology, as opposed to monitoring word choice, for example.

9

"They Sound Better Than We Do"

Language Attitudes in Alabama

J. Daniel Hasty

In the Southern United States and especially the Deep South—Alabama, Mississippi, and Louisiana—people talk in a distinctive way. In fact, the South has been called "the most distinctive speech region of the United States" (Montgomery 1989, 761). This distinctiveness, however, is not necessarily a positive in the minds of many people. While Southern United States English (SUSE) is the most recognized and distinctive dialect in America, Preston has shown through perceptual dialect mapping experiments[1] that in the United States "areas perceived as least correct have greatest distinctiveness" and that "pejorative notions of an area's speech enhance that area's salience as a distinct linguistic region" (1996, 306). A speech region, then, will stand out because it is viewed as being less correct. Part of the reason for these perceptions is that what is known as Standard English in America is not actually labeled as such by the way it sounds; rather, as Wolfram and Schilling-Estes highlight (2006, 12–13), Standard English is known by a lack of features that are perceived as being incorrect. The Southern dialect, viewed by many people as the regional dialect[2] containing the most incorrect features, is therefore recognized as the most nonstandard or incorrect dialect of American English.

This negative view of SUSE is not necessarily held only by people outside the South; many Southern speakers themselves have this opinion. This self-deprecating view can be explained by a concept known in sociolinguistics as the *linguistic inferiority principle*: "The speech of a socially subordinate group will be [self-]interpreted as inadequate by comparison with that of the socially dominate group" (Wolfram and Schilling-Estes 2006, 7). People in the South have internalized many of the pejorative attitudes toward Southerners and Southern speech that outsiders hold, and, as this essay will illustrate, this linguistic insecurity reveals itself most clearly in a highly negative view of a fellow Southern speaker's intelligence. That is, Southerners hearing a speaker with a Southern accent will often think that the person sounds dumb, uneducated, ignorant, and lower class. However, Southerners' attitudes toward the way they speak are complicated. These negative language attitudes[3] are balanced with positive feelings, because many people in the South are proud of their origins and proud to live in the South. These positive feelings are expressed in viewing the same Southern speaker—perceived as ignorant and uneducated—as nice, trustworthy, and likeable at the same time. Trudgill (1972) has termed this sort of regional pride in a nonstandard dialect, which often demonstrates itself in assigning greater affection to the nonstandardized variety in certain situations, as *covert prestige*.

In hopes of understanding the issues associated with linguistic insecurity and their interplay with covert prestige, sociolinguists, dialectologists, and social psychologists have been studying the language attitudes of different social groups for several decades. This paper will describe a recent study of the language attitudes of Alabamians toward SUSE in comparison to Northern and Midwestern varieties and will focus specifically on Alabamians' attitudes toward Alabama English compared to another Southern variety.[4]

I surveyed ninety freshmen (forty-nine women; forty-one men) from sections of the second-semester composition class at Auburn University in the spring of 2006.[5] The respondents' ages ranged from nineteen to twenty-four, with 90 percent being nineteen. Most of the respondents were from Alabama originally (68 percent). Georgia (14 percent), Florida (8 percent), Texas (4 percent), and Tennessee (3 percent) were other states of origin. It is important to note that most of the respondents were from Alabama—the heart of the South according to Preston's (1996 and 1997) studies of Southerners' perceptions.

The respondents were exposed to five recordings of speakers from different parts of the country:[6] two from the South (Alabama and Tennessee), two from the North (New York and New Hampshire), and one from the Midwest (Michigan). The five recorded speakers were reading a text; therefore, grammatical and lexical (word-choice) variation were controlled for, and phonology (the speaker's sound system) was isolated as the sole factor educing respondents' perceptions.[7] The respondents were asked to rate each speaker on a semantic differential scale of one to five consisting of seventeen groups of paired, polar-opposite adjectives (adapted from Soukup 2000):

impolite—polite
not self-confident—self-confident
uneducated—educated
unfriendly—friendly
unsociable—sociable
no sense of humor—sense of humor
lazy—industrious
slow—sharp
shy—outgoing

unintelligent—intelligent
bad manners—good manners
not trustworthy—trustworthy
dishonest—honest
not likable—likeable
not helpful—helpful
not open-minded—open-minded
unsuccessful—successful

The adjectives were arranged with the negative adjective closest to the numeral one and the positive adjective closest to the numeral five (e.g., impolite–1–2–3–4–5–polite).

Respondents were also asked three direct questions about each speaker. Because Preston (1997, 314) has pointed to the lack of assurance that respondents were accurately perceiving the location of the sample voices used in previous language attitude studies, the first question—*What state do you think the speaker is from?*—was used to assess the degree to which respondents accurately perceived the origins of the speakers so that reactions toward a particular speaker can be more clearly interpreted as reactions toward a certain speech region.[8] The two other direct questions asked the respondents to identify the speakers' socioeconomic status and education level, respectively. The respondents were given a choice of Upper Class, Upper Middle Class, Middle Class, Upper Working Class, and Lower Working Class for the socioeconomic question and Graduate School, College Degree, Attended Some College, High School Diploma, and Attended Some High School for the education-level question.

Each respondent was also asked to provide demographic information: age, sex, and race, the city and state they were from, and any other city and state they had lived in for a considerable length of time. This allowed for limiting the study to respondents who were from the South, and it provided social information that might affect their responses.

Earlier language attitude studies have shown through statistical factor analysis that there is a "tripartite structure to judgments about language" (Garrett 2001, 628), so for analytical purposes the scores for the adjectives were grouped using the three categories used in Edwards and Jacobsen (1987): Personal Integrity (Trustworthy, Polite, Honest, Helpful, Open-Minded); Competence (Educated, Intelligent, Self-Confident, Industrious, Sharp, Successful); and Social Attractiveness (Friendly, Sociable, Sense of Humor, Outgoing, Likable, Manners).

In the Personal Integrity category, the South was rated the highest of all the speech regions, with an overall mean of 3.62 (on the five-point scale), followed by the Midwest's mean of 3.39 and the North's mean of 2.94.[9] The greatest differences in the adjectives in the Personal Integrity category were for Polite—with the Southern speakers rated substantially higher, at 4.01, compared to the Northern speakers' 2.82 and the Midwestern speakers' 3.41—and for Honest—with the South rated at 3.91 to the North's 2.98 and the Midwest's 3.69. The one adjective for which the South was not rated the highest in the Personal Integrity category was Open-minded, with the Northern speakers' mean of 3.13 and the Midwestern speakers' mean of 3.26 both higher than the Southern speakers' 2.85 (see figure 9.1). The results of the Personal Integrity category are further enlightening when compared with the other category indicative of solidarity, Social Attractiveness.

In Social Attractiveness, the South again was rated higher than the North and the Midwest for all adjectives in that category except Outgoing. The South's combined mean for the category was quite high, at 3.62, in comparison to the North's 2.99 and the Midwest's 3.08. The greatest differences between the speakers were perceived in the Friendly and Likeable adjectives. The South was higher in Friendly, with 4.11 to the North's 2.93 and the Midwest's 3.04, and higher in Likeable, with the South rated 3.83 compared to the North's 2.93 and the Midwest's 3.02 (see figure 9.2). From the combined results of the Personal Integrity and Social Attrac-

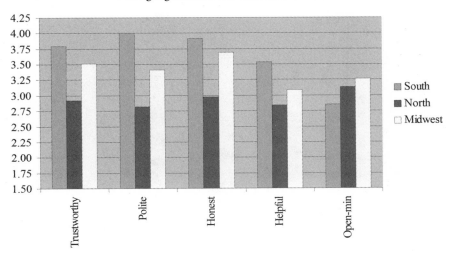

Figure 9.1. Regional Personal Integrity ratings

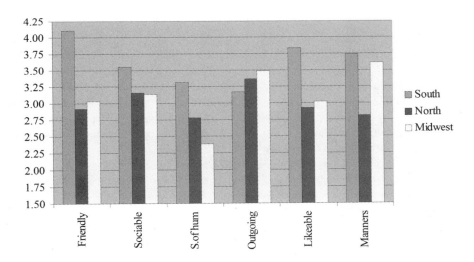

Figure 9.2. Regional Social Attractiveness ratings

tiveness categories, it appears that Southern dialects are perceived by Southerners as being much more desirable on solidarity features than Northern and Midwestern dialects, evidence of the covert prestige Southerners assign to their dialect.

However, in the Competence category, the preference Southerners give to the Southern dialect vanishes. The mean of the respondents' scores from their rating of the two Southern speakers was 2.77, compared to the Northern speakers' 3.41 and the Midwestern speakers' 3.97. There were large differences in all the adjectives. The

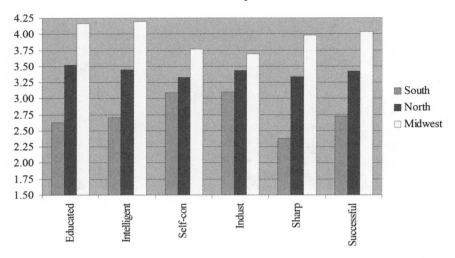

Figure 9.3. Regional Competence ratings

greatest differences were perceived in Sharp, with the South rated 2.38 compared to the North's 3.33 and the Midwest's 3.98, and Educated, with the South rated 2.63 compared to the North's 3.52 and the Midwest's 4.16 (see figure 9.3). These findings suggest that speakers of a Northern or Midwestern dialect are considered by Southerners to be much more educated and intelligent than speakers of a Southern dialect, a clear picture of linguistic insecurity.

The results from the direct questions further reveal how the respondents perceived the Competence of the speakers. For the socioeconomic-status question, the South was the lowest-rated of all the speech regions. Based on the scale assigning Lower Working Class the number 1 and Upper Class the number 5, the South had a considerably lower mean of 2.10 as compared to the Northern and Midwestern means of 2.96 and 3.51, respectively. The Southern speakers were placed in the categories of either the Lower Working Class or the Upper Working Class by 65 percent of the respondents, and only 35 percent put the Southern speakers in the middle classes, with most respondents' placing them in the Middle Class and not the Upper Middle Class. In comparison, the Northern speakers were placed in either the Middle Class or the Upper Middle Class by 71 percent of the respondents, and the Midwestern speaker was placed in either the Middle Class or the Upper Middle Class by 80 percent of the respondents.

For the education-level direct question, the South again was rated the lowest. Based on the scale assigning the number 1 to Attended Some High School and the number 5 to Graduate School, the South had a low mean of 2.38 compared to the 3.32 of the North and the 4.06 of the Midwest. The Southern speakers' highest level of education was perceived by 50 percent of the respondents to be a High School Diploma, and 13 percent even believed the Southern speakers to have only Attended Some High School. Merely 23 percent of the respondents said the Southern speakers had Attended Some College, and only 14 percent responded with College Degree. The Northern speakers, however, were perceived as having a College Degree by 45 percent of the respondents, and when combining that ranking with Attended Some College, the college-educated votes account for 74 percent of the respondents. Further, the Midwestern speaker was placed in the College Degree level by 50 percent of the respondents and in the Graduate School level by 30 percent of the respondents. The direct question data, then, additionally show that Southerners perceive speakers of their own dialect as particularly low in both social class and formal education.

Because two Southern speakers (one from Alabama and one from Tennessee) were used in this language attitude study, the responses can be further broken down to reveal respondents' attitudes toward subregional areas of the South. This level of subregional analysis has been absent from previous language attitude research, where, in efforts to understandably make broader generalizations of the language attitudes held by one group toward another, an individual speaker from one area inside a larger geographic speech region is often taken to represent a regional dialect in a monolithic way, thus erasing further interregional variation. In this study, however, since almost 70 percent of the respondents were from Alabama, the responses given to the Alabama speaker compared to the Tennessee speaker provide an even more enlightening picture of how respondents from a subregion in the South view their own local speech variety. Such knowledge, as will be discussed below, is essential in developing ways to combat the intense negative language attitudes experienced in the South.

Initially, it is important to look at the perceived state of origin of the Alabama and Tennessee speakers to see if there was actually a perceived difference in the separate dialects of the two Southern speakers. For both speakers, the state of origin most often given was Alabama, with 38 percent of the respondents for the Alabama speaker and 27 percent of the respondents for the Tennessee speaker. From this finding, it would at first appear that both speakers were perceived as being from the same state and thus the same local speech region, but upon looking at the percentages of other states given, a distinction appears. For the Alabama speaker, the second highest state given by the respondents was Mississippi, with 27 percent of the respondents, followed by Georgia, with 10 percent. From these ratings, it is apparent that the respondents perceived the Alabama speaker as coming from the Deep South, which in fact he does. For the Tennessee speaker, however, the second highest state given was Tennessee, with 19 percent of the respondents, followed by Georgia, with 16 percent. These data begin to point to a perceived difference in the two Southern speakers. Looking at the other states given for the Tennessee speaker, such as North Carolina and South Carolina, which were not given at all for the Alabama speaker, it seems that the respondents did perceive a difference in the dialect of the two speakers, feeling that the Tennessee speaker had more of a Mid-South dialect.

Having established that there was a difference in the perceived state of origin of the two Southern speakers, it is interesting to compare the ratings on the paired adjectives for these two speakers to see if these speakers are rated differently. Though

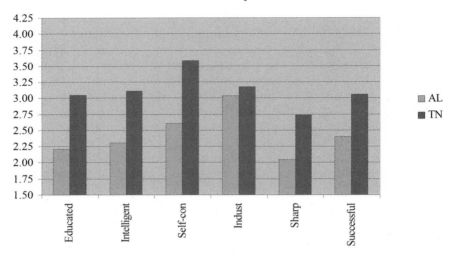

Figure 9.4. Alabama to Tennessee Competence ratings

there were only slight differences in the two categories registering solidarity, a significant difference was seen between the Alabama and Tennessee speakers in the Competence category. The Tennessee speaker's mean of 3.13 for the Competence category is much higher than the Alabama speaker's mean of 2.43. The greatest differences were in the rating for the Self-Confident adjective, with the Tennessee speaker's mean of 3.58 being higher than the Alabama speaker's 2.61. Educated (Alabama 2.21 and Tennessee 3.05) and Intelligent (Alabama 2.30 and Tennessee 3.12) were other notably large differences (see figure 9.4). From these ratings, it is apparent that for these Alabamian respondents, the Tennessee Mid-South dialect is substantially preferred in Competence features over the home Deep South Alabama dialect. The higher scores of the Tennessee speaker, however, are still substantially lower than Competence ratings for both the Northern speakers and the Midwestern speaker, so it would be more descriptive to say that these Alabamian respondents perceived the Tennessee speaker's dialect to be *not as low* in Competence factors as in their own dialect.[10]

For both the socioeconomic-status and the education-level direct questions, the Alabama speaker was again rated lower than the Tennessee speaker. For social status, the Alabama speaker was given a mean of 1.84 to the Tennessee speaker's 2.37. The Alabama speaker was placed in the Lower Working Class by 43 percent of the respondents, while only 15 percent of the respondents placed the Tennessee speaker in that class. In fact, 76 percent of the respondents placed the Alabama speaker in one of the two working classes, while that percentage is only 55 percent for the Tennessee speaker. In education level, the differences between the Southern speakers are further defined. The Alabama speaker was given a mean of 2.12 compared to the Tennessee speaker's 2.64. The Alabama speaker was rated as either Attended Some

High School or High School Diploma by 73 percent of the respondents, while that percentage is only 51 percent for the Tennessee speaker.

This study demonstrates that Alabamians have an extremely low view of their dialect as compared to Northern and Midwestern varieties; further, with the intra-regional comparison, this study reveals that these mostly Alabamian respondents rate a Deep South speaker of Alabama English lower than a fellow Southerner from the Mid-South. The results of this study highlight the prevalence of linguistic insecurity in the South and particularly in Alabama, and it is my hope that studies of this type would open our eyes to our own linguistic prejudices—prejudices that we may be directing toward our neighbors and even ourselves.

While Southerners in this study were shown to have a particularly low view of the intelligence of fellow Southern speakers, the high ratings that were assigned to the Personal Integrity and Social Attractiveness attributes of a Southern dialect are encouraging. I believe that encouraging and increasing this covert prestige may help Alabamians and other speakers of nonprestige dialects be less self-conscious about their own language. Further, I believe that findings from language attitude studies in specific speech regions could be used to inform the development of programs that encourage dialect awareness and appreciation like those instituted in the Ocracoke community and other areas in North Carolina by Walt Wolfram and colleagues.[11] It may be possible that programs of this sort could increase covert prestige to the point that these positive language attitudes can make inroads into the intense linguistic insecurity experienced by Southern speakers in Alabama.

NOTES

1. Respondents were given maps of the United States with only state borders marked and were asked to draw boundaries around the areas where people spoke the same. To determine respondents' attitudes toward different dialects, the respondents were also asked to rate the fifty states plus New York City and Washington, DC, for both correctness and pleasantness of speech.

2. The term *regional dialect* is used because a good case could be made that African American English, an ethnic dialect that is not confined to a region, is perceived as the most stigmatized and nonstandard single dialect of American English.

3. The definition of *language attitude* used in this paper follows Ryan, Giles, and Sebastian's use of the term "in a broad, flexible sense as an affective, cognitive or behavioural index of evaluative reactions toward different language varieties or their speakers" (1982, 7). The last phrase, "or their speakers," is important to note, for these attitudes are not actually based on a language variety but on the speakers of a certain variety. Niedzielski and Preston highlight this distinction, stating that "a language attitude is, after all, not really an attitude to a language feature; it is an awakening of a set of beliefs about individuals or sorts of individuals through the filter of a linguistic performance" (2000, 9).

4. See Hasty (2006) for a complete discussion of this study.

5. To control for ethnicity (see Tucker and Lambert 1969; Frazier 1973), the scores

from the surveys taken by African American respondents were not included in the tabulations of the results.

6. The recordings used in this survey were downloaded from the International Dialects of English Archive (IDEA), founded by Paul Meier and located at www .dialectsarchive.com. The speakers used in this study, by state and identifying number of each, were Alabama 5 (white male, born 1980, Brewton, Alabama), Tennessee 3 (white male, born 1947, Madison, Tennessee), Michigan 3 (white male, born 1957, Trenton, MI), New York 7 (white male, born 1940, Bronx, NY), and New Hampshire 3 (white male, age 25, no date of birth given, Sandown, New Hampshire).

7. IDEA provided minimal background information for the recordings besides state of origin, so the actual socioeconomic status and education level of the speakers are unknown. Since grammatical variation has been shown to be most salient in overtly denoting social class rather than region (see Schneider 2003, 27) and since the recorded speakers were all reading a passage to control for grammatical variation, the respondents' responses are assumed to represent their perceptions of and reactions to the speech regions that the speakers represent. The statistical difference in the respondents' response to the dialects of the Alabama and Tennessee speakers discussed below further suggests that respondents' reactions were based on regional variation and not on socioeconomic differences (if there were any) between the speakers.

8. In this study, the mental maps of dialect boundaries generated by Southerners in Preston (1996, 1997) were used to determine which states belong to the perceived speech regions of the respondents. For instance, if a respondent placed the Alabama speaker in Mississippi, the rating would be taken as correct, but if a respondent placed the Alabama speaker in Indiana, this would be counted as incorrect because Indiana is not included as part of the South in Southern folk-dialect maps. If a respondent misidentified a speaker's region, then their scores for that speaker were not counted, since these perceptions cannot truly be said to apply to speakers of that region.

9. All differences in mean scores discussed in this paper were determined to be statistically significant at $p < 0.05$ through paired t-tests.

10. Hasty (2006) discusses the importance of further determining whether the respondents identify or do not identify with the South. These findings suggest that respondents not identifying with the South have an even more negative view of the Competence of the speaker from Alabama compared to that of the Tennessee speaker.

11. See Wolfram, Adger, and Christian (1999) and Wolfram's foreword in this volume for a discussion of the importance of dialect awareness programs in the classroom.

Code-Switching between African American and Standard English

The Rules, the Roles, and the Rub

Kimberly Johnson with Thomas E. Nunnally

The American Dream proclaims that anyone who works hard enough and perseveres can accomplish any goal. This belief rings true. But within this dream there has always been a problem of fairness. Dreams of success and accomplishment are feasible and attainable, but the playing field is not level. Many minorities who chase the American Dream are faced with obstacles that many mainstream white Americans do not have to overcome. One major obstacle is Standard English (SE). Competency in speaking and writing SE is a nonissue for those who grew up in cultures whose mother tongue is close to it, but it can be a mountain in the way of success for others.

Debates and arguments over the role of standardization of English have continued for decades. While many argue that society should accept the wide range of dialects as a part of the diversity of America, negative connotations and attitudes are still associated with nonstandard English speakers in mainstream America. Marcyliena Morgan says in *Language, Discourse and Power in African American Culture* that "both social class and racial discrimination affect the larger society's attitude toward African American English" (2000, 70). She affirms that in the past, communication in a style that is not the dominant culture's is a sign of poverty and "at times—ignorance." Malcolm X, painfully aware of this, writes in his autobiography, "In the street, I had been the most articulate hustler out there—I had commanded attention when I said something. But now, trying to write simple English, I not only wasn't articulate, I wasn't even functional. How would I sound writing in slang, the way I would *say* it" (Malcolm X 1965, 171).

Among a majority of African Americans, young and old, who are struggling to fit into or coexist within mainstream America, this feeling of inadequacy is common. Studies have shown that African American students may become depressed and self-conscious because of low self-esteem originating from social and linguistic backgrounds. The case study presented in *Standard English, Black English, and Bidialectalism: A Controversy* concerns a first-generation college student from a predominantly African American neighborhood (Taylor 1989). The subject of this case study felt that his nonuse of SE left the perception that he had "missing skills" rather than a cultural and linguistic difference.

This essay grew out of my own experience as an African American student/ parent/educator who has faced the dilemma of using language to succeed in more than one culture. As you read, please know that I am by no means a linguist, but through postgraduate work in that field I was exposed to knowledge enabling me to take a scholarly look at African American English. Like most people who gain new understanding, I tried to make sense of it through my own life.

I view myself as a regular person with many hats. The hats I wear at present (I am nearing my mid-thirties as of this writing) identify me as a member of an extended family, a wife, a parent, a public schoolteacher, and, yet again, a graduate student. One thing I can say is that even with my self-perceived regularity of person, I also view myself as passionate and goal-oriented—which can be good and bad, depending on my goals at the time. I want the best for my children and myself in all my roles. As I look at my children, every day I ponder who and what they will become. I want happiness and success for them. I want that promise of the American Dream.

I graduated from the University of Alabama with a degree in communications, but soon after graduating I entered a fifth-year master's program to become a schoolteacher. I have been an eighth-grade schoolteacher for more than a decade now. Over this time, I've taught in a predominantly white North Alabama school system and a predominantly white South Alabama school system. I've also been elected Teacher of the Year by my peers in both places, and I am a Nationally Board Certified Teacher. I am always seeking to expand myself and my knowledge. Because of this quest, I ended up back in graduate school working on yet another degree. And this is where I begin—trying to make sense of new knowledge.

TERMINOLOGY

Understanding any field of knowledge means grasping its terminology and theoretical backgrounds. The concepts below (adapted from *Do You Speak American?* 2005 unless otherwise noted) were especially important to me as I began to understand the functions of my various language varieties. They should help readers of this essay as well.

Speech Community—a group of people who share language characteristics and ways of speaking. They may be located close to one another geographically, or they may share social characteristics such as age, gender, or socioeconomic class. The notion of speech community is useful for studying how nonlinguistic features such as geographical location and socioeconomic status are related to language use.

Standard English (SE)—the variety of English that with respect to spelling, grammar, pronunciation, and vocabulary is substantially uniform (*Merriam-Webster Online* 2005); the variety of English spoken in the United States that is considered by most Americans to seem right. In the United States, the Midland (i.e., Midwest) area is most often pointed to as the location where standard or mainstream English is spoken. SE is the language variety that is taught in school and is considered necessary for participation and success in American society. Other terms for the same: General English (GE), Mainstream American English.

Dialect—any language variety associated with a particular region or social group. As used by linguists, the term *dialect* involves no judgment of the value of a language variety. No variety is inherently superior to any other. When used by the public, this term often refers to a language variety that is considered inferior to the standard or mainstream variety.

African American English (AAE)—Geneva Smitherman calls AAE "an African-ized form of English reflecting [African Americans'] linguistic-cultural African heritage and the conditions of servitude, oppression, and life in America. [African American] language is Euro-American speech with an [African American] meaning, nuance, tone, and gesture" (1977, 2). Besides differences in the grammar system, words, and pronunciation, it includes its own rich rhetorical tradition, or African American Verbal Tradition (AAVT) (Smitherman 1995, 227–28). It is probably "used by 80 to 90 percent of [African Americans], at least some of the time" (Smitherman 1977, 2). Other terms conveying much the same meaning are Black English Vernacular, Ebonics, African American Dialect, and African American Idiom, but the term *African American Vernacular English (AAVE)* designates the variety of AAE that departs most strongly from Standard English.

Bidialectalism—facility in using two dialects of the same language; also, the teaching of Standard English to pupils who normally use a nonstandard dialect. Those who are truly bidialectal perceive the contrasts between vernacular language varieties and standard varieties of a language and can shift between them.

Code-switching—usually defined as changing from one dialect to another (or from one language to another for bilinguals) when speaking. Code-switching takes place whenever there are groups of people who speak the same two (or more) dialects.

Why Code-Switch?

For most African Americans, Standard English is a second dialect of English, not their home language. In many cases the ability to translate into or use SE, or code-switch, is related to socioeconomic standards or level of education. There is an ongoing debate about the necessity for African Americans to switch from the use of African American English to SE depending upon their social situations.

Some African Americans oppose the need to switch, feeling that doing so fosters an assimilationist attitude. Other African Americans see the need to code-switch because of the reality of language prejudice (Rahman 2008). Language prejudices are "negative value judgments about a person based on the way he or she speaks, usually directed toward a speaker of a vernacular dialect" (*Do You Speak American? 2005: Viewer's Guide*). Because of these prejudices, those who normally use AAE are also victims of language profiling. Language profiling may have the most adverse effects on a person's social or economic status. Often, decisions we make about people are based on the variety of language they speak. According to the viewer's guide for *Do You Speak American?*, "Language profiling is most prevalent in people in gatekeeping positions: that is, people in positions of power who make decisions about employment, immigration, living arrangements, and so forth. This process is very closely related to racial and economic profiling."

Due to language prejudices and profiling, many African Americans have immersed themselves in or created their own bidialectal speech communities. This was the case in the affluent biracial community of Shaker Heights, Ohio. Research found that the majority of the African American community found it necessary to code-switch, which may have had some effect on reading and writing scores. As the author of the study explains, "There are separate cultural rules governing speaking (a) [African American] English, and (b) standard . . . English within the African-American speech community. During their language socialization, [African American] children learn [African American] English and the cultural rules for using it as their mother tongue; they also learn standard English and the rules in their speech community for using it" (Ogbu 2003, 182).

Ogbu found that each dialect (AAE and SE) has a separate function and is used for a different purpose. African Americans within the speech community know and accept the separate functions. They identified their need to speak "'proper' English" in contexts of "education, jobs, and communication with 'outsiders'" (182).

The study identified and explicated the cultural rules for using African American English and Standard English.

Rules for African American English—African American students "used AAE among themselves, in the family and community" or in informal discussions at school.

Rules for Standard English—"Most students understood that they should speak SE at school, especially during lessons." African American students generally recognized SE at school as important, they understood it was required and expected at school, and they tried to follow that rule.

Using African American English out of Place—"Students criticized others who spoke [AAE] where it was not appropriate to do so. There were two kinds of students who broke the rule and were criticized." One was the group who could not competently code-switch to SE; the other was the transfers from other areas.

Speaking Standard English Out of Place—Using SE "at home and in the community amounted to breaking the cultural rule of SE and was criticized by some [African Americans] as acting white." Those who used SE outside the classroom complained of being ridiculed by other African American students (Ogbu 2003, 184–87).

In this bidialectal speech community, "no adult or student African American said that he or she was opposed to [SE]." Opposition occurred only when the variety was used out of place (187). This study further validates the ideas of language prejudices and language profiling. Many equate the ability to be successful and "accepted" in mainstream America with the ability to speak Standard English. It also shows the importance of AAE as a unifying cultural part of African American life and why AAE is not going away soon.

A Case (Self-)Study

I believe, as an African American, that there should be a respect for acculturation in America. However, some view the "melting pot" theory with the suspicion that it destroys African American culture, so there will be continued resistance to SE. When mastery of SE is considered within a context of bidialectalism, it is important for the minority group or individuals to retain their culture even with entrance into the mainstream. Understanding this need to maintain an identity within my culture, I have examined the incidence of code-switching engaged in by myself and family members, some of whom code-switch and some of whom do not.

My History as a Code-Switcher

I am from a medium-sized town in central Alabama. My parents grew up in the same neighborhood and "went together" since the eighth grade. They are both from two-parent, blue-collar homes. Four of my uncles joined the military, and all but one returned to his home area after completing their enlistments. No one from my immediate family left home to go to college—except my mother. I'm pretty sure money was their major deterrent. My mother went away to Alabama A&M University, a historically black university in Huntsville, but returned home within two years to marry my father, who did not go to college. I was the first grandchild on my mom's side and the first girl in a generation on my father's side (he is the youngest of three boys). Even though many family members now have white-collar jobs, my generation, even in the extended family, was basically the first to leave home and graduate from college.

Children from my neighborhood were bused to a predominantly white elementary school, while my church and social settings were completely segregated. I recognized the need and gained the ability to code-switch in elementary school, quickly learning to speak like the white children in my class. I did not interact with white people at all in my life outside of school. Many of the other African American kids did not learn as easily as I did, so I was more readily accepted by the white and, interestingly, African American teachers, because of my high level of reading and my ability to "adapt." But I paid the price with my African American speech community. I was not like the other kids and was somewhat of an outsider. Unlike in the Shaker Heights community in Ohio discussed above, code-switching even during school was "acting white." The concept of "oppositional culture" helps explain why my desire to succeed in school resulted in a degree of ostracism:

> Differential access to opportunities triggers community forces among minority groups. . . . Motivation for maximizing school achievement results from the belief that more education leads to better jobs, higher wages, higher

social status, and more self-esteem. When members of minority groups en-counter barriers within the opportunity structure—the system by which people acquire resources that determine their socioeconomic mobility (up or down)—they develop the perception that they receive lower rewards for education than the dominant group. These perceptions give rise to commu-nity and individual-level forces characterized by an oppositional culture that includes resisting educational goals. . . . A cultural inversion . . . takes place whereby some minority groups define certain behaviors, in this case achieve-ment, as inappropriate for them because they are the domain of their op-pressors. This repudiation is marked by truancy, lack of serious efforts and attitudes toward school, delinquency, and even early school withdrawal al-together. (A. Harris 2008)

By the end of high school, I had discovered my own identity within this speech community. My mother always stressed to me the importance of an education. Furthermore, because she, a generation earlier, had been limited in the choices of where an African American could even attend college, she would not allow me to attend, as many of my friends did, a historically black institution like Alabama A&M, Alabama State University, or even Tuskegee University. She felt that I had to learn to live in a "white world" and needed to immerse myself in a more inte-grated society. Therefore, I chose to attend the University of Alabama in Tusca-loosa. Hence, the ability to code-switch and fit in, in her eyes, gave me a better op-portunity for success.

At the University of Alabama, I remember ridiculing an African American girl in my dorm who either refused to or could not speak AAE. She spoke Southern En-glish, but without the African American vernacular features combined with it. We, the other African American students who were code-switchers, did not consider her cool and thought that she "acted white" even though her friends and boyfriend from her home in North Alabama were African American. As I reflect upon this, I realize now that she did not act differently as much as she spoke differently. We projected her speech onto her personality, which was a misconception on our part.

Code-switching was important; it enabled me to fit within the integrated so-ciety that I was working to become a part of, as well as within my own larger cul-tural and smaller social groups. Added to these earlier functions, I also still find code-switching useful with my students, both African American and white. I code-switch to AAE to come across as genuine to my African American students, while my AAE also works to increase my authority with white students. I usually switch in classroom management situations, not academic ones. I'll use catchy phrases or statements. For example, if the room is messy or the students don't pick up after themselves, I'll say something like, "I'm not cha maid or ya mama, so clean up!" or "You don't even wanna go there!" or "Chill out!" It gives me authority and au-thenticity with the kids. However, I notice that I do not use the features of AAVE ("I ain't yo maid . . .") so much as I do the features of the African American Verbal Tradition and AAE's "nuance, tone, and gesture," as mentioned above.

Table 10.1. K and A's informal Standard English speech

Context: Informal but professional conversation with Euro-American colleague A during work at middle school.
Features: Lacks defining features of AAE. Contains features of informal SE such as contractions (How's, I'm, I'll)

K: Hey A, how's it going?

A: Hi, how are you?

K: Fine, I'm tired though. That field trip wore me out (laughs).

A: I know, but I think things went really well . . . except for VVV.

K: I know. . . . I wanted to strangle her. I should call her mom.

A: We probably should . . . just to let her know . . .

K: I'll give her a call tomorrow, or I'll tell Mrs. WWW to send an email, since I don't teach her.

K: Ummm. Do you have our new room assignments?

A: Oh yes. XXX is going to put you across the hall in YYY's room.

K: Oh, no.

A: What? Is something wrong?

K: No . . . um . . . not really . . . well . . . I think ZZZ really wanted to be in that room. It doesn't matter to me, though.

RESEARCH INTO MY CODE-SWITCHING

To better understand my code-switching, I recorded short conversations between myself and three individuals in one-on-one contexts: a white fellow teacher and team leader at our school; a female African American cousin who teaches in a large metropolitan area in Alabama; and my eighty-year-old grandfather. Tables 10.1 through 10.3 present transcriptions of the conversations (most names are changed or replaced by letters for the sake of anonymity). While my conversation with "A" at school (table 10.1) lacks features of AAE, the conversations with both my cousin (table 10.2) and my grandfather (table 10.3) exhibit AAE features, with the most features occurring in table 10.3, my AAVE style.[1]

I analyzed the motivations for my code-switching in those conversations with the help of research cited by H. Samy Alim in *You Know My Steez: An Ethnographic Study of Styleshifting in a Black American Speech Community*. Alim explains that the protocol for switching, or shifting, consists of three categories (2004, 55):

- Speakers assess the personal characteristics of their addressees and design their style to suit.
- Speakers assess the general level of their addressees' speech and shift relative to it.
- Speakers assess their addressees' levels for specific linguistic variables and shift relative to those levels.

Table 10.2. K and Q's African American English with grammatical and phono-logical features and an intonational feature of the African American Verbal Tradition

Context: Phone conversation with African American cousin. Q worked in retail in large metropolitan malls during college. She is six years younger than K, a teacher in a large metropolitan school system in Alabama, and, like K, is pursuing a graduate degree.

Features: Non-SE contractions, "haven't" and "aren't" contracted to "ain't"; strong intonational change (dramatic change in pitch) derived from AAVT, denoted by bold type; variable replacement of R with vowel sound (denoted by spellings); replacement of -ing with -in for present participles; and variable auxiliary-verb deletion, denoted by *, with deleted item in brackets at end of passage.

K: Hello?

Q: Hey, girl . . . (laughs) I ain't heard from you in a while.

K: (interrupts) I know . . . I * been busy.   ['ve]

Q: Doin what?

K: Everything—work, Will, kids, grad school . . . You didn't know? I'm supuhwoman (laughs).

Q: (laughing) I heard yah Mama * been sick.   ['s]

K: Oh yeah, feet problems, gout—she didn't start havin problems until the kids left spring break.

Q: Girl . . . ain't you glad? (laughs)

K: Don't you know? How's your ghetto school?

Q: Fine, security had to come up in theh today (laughs).

K: Girl . . . **why?** . . . Fight?

Q: No, honey, pink slip day . . .

K: Uh un . . . * You serious? (laughing)   [are]

Q: Yes, it was **not** a pretty sight.

Categories one and two of the protocol make it no surprise that I spoke SE with my white professional colleague and AAE with my cousin and my grandfather. In-terestingly, however, I discovered that my AAE varied between my conversation with my cousin and my conversation with my grandfather. With both these African American family members, category three is important: I was assessing their "levels for specific linguistic variables" and shifting "relative to those levels." Not only do I code-switch with someone outside of my cultural speech community, my white colleague, but I style-shift within AAE depending on whom I am speaking with.

During the conversation with my cousin, who was twenty-seven at the time, our AAE retained more SE features, as we talked about things that we had in com-mon, mostly work and graduate school. Looking back on my conversation with my grandfather, then eighty years old, I saw that I style-shifted to talk more like him and the others who still live in the community. The style in table 10.3 contains the

Table 10.3. K and Butter's African American English with additional features not in table 10.2 conversation

Context: K's conversation with her grandfather, Butter (pronounced as Budduh, without "r" sound) at Butter's place. Butter, eighty, grew up very poor but completed high school while in the military. He worked at a foundry for many years, then as a custodian, full-time at a military base and part-time at their church. Bug is Butter's name for K, Little Bug is K's daughter, and Dayton is her son.

Features: Non-SE contractions, "I'm going to" contracted to "I'ma"; strong intonational change (dramatic change in pitch) derived from AAVT, denoted by bold type; variable replacement of R with a vowel sound (denoted by spellings); replacement of -ing with -in for present participles; variable auxiliary verb deletion, denoted by *, with deleted item in brackets at end of passage; variable substitution of "d" for voiced "th" sound [ð] at beginning of words; variable reduction of consonant clusters into single sounds, "chilren," "jus."

K: Hey, Budduh!

B: Hey, Bug. Wheh * my little Bug at?   ['s]

K: She * in dere (laughs). She * been askin to see you. Dayton too . . . * **You wanna babysit?!**   ['s] twice, [do]

B: Nooooo . . . Dayton is too much . . . I'll keep Bug, dough . . . you * got those two chilren spoiled!   ['ve]

K: No! Not me! **You** did that!

B: What * dey do?   [do]

K: He won't sit still! He * got me runnin all over da place! **See**, he * jumpin on your bed, now! (laughing)   ['s] twice

K: Stop that, Dayton. I'ma make Budduh give you a whippin . . .

B: Nooooo. You bettuh not touch dat boy. He * jus bein a boy–I mean it. I bettuh not catch you hittin him.   ['s]

K: **See what I mean?** Spoiled. . . . (laughing)

AAE features of the style in table 10.2, but it moves farther away from SE and includes additional features of AAE—those associated with AAVE, such as deletion of the forms of the verb "be" and substitution of "d" for "th" in words like *there*.

For comparative purposes, I also reconsidered my conversation with my white coworker. What if I had refused or not learned to code-switch between SE and AAE? How would the conversation have changed—on my part, as I cannot speak for the other speaker? Table 10.4 converts my passages of the conversation into the AAVE style of AAE that I use with my grandfather. While conversion to AAVE leaves the meaning of my parts of the dialogue unchanged, the truth is that I would feel as strange talking in that style while wearing my educator hat in my integrated world of work as I would using SE to speak with my grandfather. The codes would be inappropriate in each case, and each conversation would probably produce dismal results because of the baggage that each style would bring into the relationship.

Table 10.4. K's informal SE speech with A (table 10.1) converted from K's SE into into AAVE style of table 10.3

Original conversation with colleague at work	K's conversation modified to include probable features of K's AAVE style of AAE
K: Hey A, how's it going?	Hey, what's goin on? How you doin'?
A: Hi, how are you?	
K: Fine, I'm tired, though. That field trip wore me out (laughs)	Good . . . ti'ed. That field trip was **too much.**
A: I know, but I think things went really well . . . except for VVV.	
K: I know . . . I wanted to strangle her. I should call her mom.	I know . . . I coulda choked her. I'ma call her mama.
A: We probably should . . . just to let her know . . .	
K: I'll give her a call tomorrow or I'll tell Mrs. WWW to send an email since I don't teach her.	I'll do it tomorrow or I'll jus tell Miz WWW to send an email. I don't teach her anyways.
K: Ummm. Do you have our new room assignments?	Ummm. You have the new room numbers?
A: Oh yes. XXX is going to put you across the hall in YYY's room.	
K: Oh no.	**Uh oh.**
A: What? Is something wrong?	
K: No . . . um . . . not really . . . well . . . I think ZZZ really wanted to be in that room. It doesn't matter to me, though.	I don't guess so . . . ya know ZZZ wanted dat room. I don't care, dough.

CONCLUSION

Although AAE, and especially AAVE, are stigmatized in American mainstream culture, they are spoken by millions of people. Within the community, AAE is an important component of group identity. In this sense, using AAE in the community can be as valuable and important as using SE in professional situations. An inability to switch to SE can lead to feelings of inadequacy for those struggling to fit into mainstream America, but is it also possible for African Americans purposely to resist learning SE because of fear of loss of cultural identity? Geneva Smitherman explains these conflicting desires in her description of what she terms "push-pull": even as African slaves became Americanized away from their African roots, taking up white Americans' "religion, culture, customs, and, of course, language," there were also "strong resistance movements against enslavement and the oppressive ways of white folks." Thus African American culture exhibits "*pushing* toward white American culture while simultaneously *pulling* away from it" (1977, 10). Looking at language, she continues, "The dynamics of push-pull can help to illuminate the complex sociolinguistic situation that continues to exist in Black America. That is, while some blacks speak very Black English, there are others who speak very White English, and still others who are competent in both linguistic systems" (11–12).

Smitherman does not mention it in this passage, but my look at my own code-switching shows that African Americans can also change their language to be more "black" or more "white" as the need arises. As Rahman expresses it, "In the course of their day-to-day affairs, speakers normally express various aspects of identity. Their language may change for different situations, audiences, and attitudes or moods that they wish to express. Frequently, these changes are intradialectal, with speakers strengthening or weakening features, or inserting idiosyncratic features for effect in the construction of personae" (2008, 171). The effect, Renn and Terry explain, is that "in choosing to use or exclude certain linguistic features, speakers indicate group membership and personal identity. Thus, a speaker's style is the consequence of his or her own choices in seeking to promote a particular persona" (2009, 375). African Americans who possess more education and wider social experience will, of course, tend to be more proficient in switching to Standard English.

Personally, I think that those whose goals require them to integrate into mainstream America will find success more difficult if they lack the ability to code-switch (unless it is in the entertainment/sports community, where SE is not a primary aspect of the job description). I perceive acquiring this skill as necessary for being accepted in both worlds.

Be that as it may, with my parent hat on, I often worry aloud to my husband that my daughter won't be accepted by her African American peers. She is growing up in an environment different from the one I grew up in: an integrated community where many of her friends are white or, just like her, are African Americans who speak standard Southern English with few features of AAE. I can sometimes tell when she has spent time at my parents' home, as she shifts slightly. But often many of my old friends, and even college friends, comment to me about how "white" she sounds. Will she be judged as I judged my college peer? Will she make African American friends who are only like her? Do I *teach* her AAE? I am left with questions and worries that will probably continue to be with me for a while.

NOTES

Although this essay is jointly written, the authors chose to present the research in Kimberly's voice to capture the sense of her unique experience.

1. Listings and explanations of the grammatical, phonological, semantic, and discourse features of African American English, especially of African American Vernacular English, are widely available. See, for example, Morgan (2002, 77); chapter 7 in Wolfram and Schilling-Estes 2006; the website *Do You Speak American?* 2005; and other websites listed in appendix C in this volume.

11

College Writers as Alabama Storytellers

Cultural Effects on Academic Writing

Charlotte Brammer

My interest in Southern storytelling probably began when I was a child growing up in South Carolina. When I was four or five years old, I distinctly remember sitting in my great grandmother's lavender bedroom, sometimes on the fuzzy rug beside her bed, other times on the chenille bedspread beside her, listening to "Little Granny" tell about her childhood exploits. Sometimes she would tell me stories about how my mother or grandmother had ignored some rule or warning and, as a consequence, gotten hurt. In short, I was encouraged to obey my mother and my grandmother lest I too get hurt.

While I never lost interest in Southern storytelling, I developed a new curiosity about how Southerners use stories during my doctoral work on dialect features in writing.[1] Storytelling is an art that thrives in the South, and Alabamians love to hear and to tell good stories. The late Kathryn Tucker Windham of Selma is but one acclaimed Alabama storyteller. Her stories about Jeffrey, the ghost who haunts her house and is blamed for all manner of mischief that occurs there, have entertained listeners for more than forty years (Windham and Figh 1969; Windham 1973, 1974), but stories don't just serve to entertain. To Southerners, including Alabamians, stories, like the ones Windham tells and my great grandmother told, serve multiple purposes.[2] They help us identify with or relate to one another, developing intimacy among tellers and listeners, and sometimes they can convince us more than "objective" evidence can. In another sense the stories become Southern not just because of structure but also because of the nuances of Southern speech. Regional dialects and accents can have positive and persuasive effects on listeners even in business contexts (e.g., Mai and Hoffman 2011; Heaton and Nygaard 2011).

In this essay, I will use my experience with as well as research about Southern storytelling and Southern dialect to discuss how some college students employ both types of Southern flavoring in their writing: features *of* Southern storytelling and Southern features *in* their storytelling. I will end by considering the need for writing programs to bridge the gap between such regional resources and mainstream academic writing.

In my experience as a lifelong Southerner and longtime resident of Alabama,

I've discovered that Southerners value personal experience. If we need medical care, we want to "know" or at least "know of" someone who has similar pains. We seem to want someone with whom to compare symptoms, treatment, and outcomes. We also enjoy sharing our experiences—thus, a pregnant woman who ventures out in public (to the grocery store, church, work, etc.) is likely to hear uninvited stories wherein narrators detail either their own or a friend's/wife's/sister's labor and delivery. Few of these stories offer real comfort or encouragement to the pregnant woman. Instead, they generally describe unimaginably long and painful labors wherein epidurals are not possible or births that occur en route to the hospital, usually during hurricanes or aberrant snowstorms. From my experience, such stories are generally accompanied by comments to the effect *I hope you have a better time of it than my friend Joyce did; she . . .* or *You probably won't have any problems like this, but let me tell you about. . . .* At times, these stories of labor and delivery compare with "fish stories," in which one speaker tries to outperform another.

Such stories generally adhere to specific patterns that Shirley Brice Heath identified in *Ways with Words* (1983), in which she describes the language use of residents in three groups in the Piedmont region of South Carolina: the African American working-class community of "Trackton," the white working-class community of "Roadville," and bridging both locations, African American and white middle-class or higher "Townspeople," also described as "mainstreamers." According to Heath, there is much variability in the ways Townspeople use stories. Some parents are very creative, weaving outlandish tales of fantasy in which their children are the heroes, while others scaffold stories for their children by asking questions that children are expected to answer in very specific ways (e.g., asking whether the child would like to have participated in the events of a particular story with the intention of having the child elaborate on why); whatever the form of these interchanges, the motive of Townspeople, according to Heath, is to prepare their children for academic success, because these practices are used in many classrooms. Less conducive to academic success are the features of storytelling in working-class Trackton and Roadville, though the features themselves differ from each other.

In African American Trackton, stories are highly imaginative, resist formulaic introductions and structure, even chronicity, and often show how the speaker or protagonist exhibited super strength to emerge victorious over some fantastic obstacle: "Stories do not teach lessons about proper behavior; they tell of individuals who excel by outwitting the rules of conventional behavior" (187). Heath found that, in contrast to Trackton storytelling, stories in the white community of Roadville are expected to be "factual" and adhere to "strict chronicity, with direct discourse reported, and no explicit exposition of meaning or direct expression of evaluation of the behavior of the main character allowed" (185). Such stories give an accurate accounting of some event, and storytellers "qualify exaggeration and hedge if they might seem to be veering from an accurate reporting of events." Furthermore, stories often expose the teller's (or the main character's) weaknesses and are intended to teach lessons about appropriate behavior. Biblical references are common as a way for "Roadville members [to] reaffirm their commitment to community and church values by giving factual accounts of their own weaknesses and the lessons learned in overcoming them" (185).

To provide an example of Roadville storytelling, Heath prints one of "Sue's" stories about cooking mishaps. In this story, Sue recalls an incident where she does not adhere to the recipe because she takes a phone call and fails to pay attention to her task. The story is very loosely organized, in terms of theme, and includes numerous elaborations and asides, but adheres to a step-by-step recounting of events, including "quoting" from other people involved in the story. To conclude, Sue states the moral: "Guess I'll learn to keep my mind on my own business and off other folks." Heath explains Sue's story as "an occasion in which all recognize their common, but unspoken, Christian ideal of disciplined tongue" (154). I would add that Sue's story should remind most Southerners, even non-Christian Southerners, of Christ's admonition as recorded in Matthew 7:3, "And why beholdest thou the mote that is in thy brother's eye, but considerest not the beam that is in thine own eye?"

Heath's findings can be corroborated by looking at the storytelling patterns of Southern storytellers, even celebrated ones such as Windham. As Johnstone points out, "Southerners have often been characterized as particularly artistic with language, skilled in speechmaking, preaching, storytelling, and writing" (2003b, 196). Part of this artistry may result from the post–Civil War oral culture that encouraged Southern speakers "to cultivate ways of adding and improvising as they spoke" to retain their audience's attention (197). One method that Windham uses for "adding and improvising" is "digression." According to Davies (2008), Windham's use of digression privileges "an associative process with a meditative quality" over a "tightly linear, goal-oriented cognitive pattern" (176). Thus, Windham may begin a story about why she "was almost late" and then move to various digressions about buzzards, a regional myth (or colloquially an "ol' wives' tale"), and a childhood rhyme and do so while embellishing with specific detail. Davies suggests that Windham's digressions meet a pragmatic expectation of Southern storytelling as "a rich and complex experience of entertainment" (176). Equally important, Davies posits that a more direct and linearly organized pattern may be perceived as "intrusive and even insulting to the intelligence of the listener, for whom, presumably, part of the aesthetic pleasure of the discourse is derived from the cognitive activity of making the connections" (177; also see Davies 2015 for more on Southern storytelling).

In my own collecting and analyzing of stories, I have discovered that the teller of a labor/delivery story—or nightmare—will usually begin with a brief history of the person, often identifying some character flaw (*She didn't know nothing about having a baby and had no idea what a labor pain meant*) followed swiftly by the standard Southernism, *bless her heart*. The teller will begin the story a day or so before the main event, describing activities in order of occurrence and sometimes digressing by relating details that serve as clues to the impending climax of the story, clues that parallel common beliefs about women's intuition and cultural myths about pregnancy that the listener should know, unless of course the listener "doesn't know anything about having a baby." Dialogue is important to the teller, and thus, it is reported—she said this and then he said that. Such details and careful construction render the story believable or authentic and help make it a cautionary tale in the grocery-store checkout line.

Given the importance of stories to Southern communication, we should not be surprised to find stories woven into students' writing, even in college. I will discuss three examples of informal student writing, and in keeping with disciplinary practice, I have not edited the original texts. The students attended a large, public university in Alabama at the time they wrote these responses. To protect their anonymity, I refer to them by the pseudonyms "Chad," "Beth Anne," and "John." Chad was born and raised in Jefferson County, Alabama, spending most of his time in a small rural town just north of Birmingham. Chad is the first person in his family to pursue a four-year degree and is somewhat typical of a white Southern working-class male who sees education as a way to improve his socioeconomic circumstances. He is married and works full-time, attending school on a part-time basis and fitting in classes around his work schedule. Like Chad, Beth Anne is a Southerner, born and raised in Tuscaloosa, Alabama. She too works full time and takes classes part-time. She exhibits a strong work ethic that tends to be representative of individuals with her rural white, working-class background. John, a white male, is also a native Alabamian. He has lived his entire life in Jasper, Alabama, a town of fourteen thousand about forty miles northwest of Birmingham, but unlike Chad and Beth Anne, who hail from working-class backgrounds (similar to Heath's Roadville residents), John self-identifies as middle class (similar to the Heath's Townspeople or mainstreamers).

As part of a course on human resources management, the students were asked to define either good service or bad service in an informal journal assignment (they were not expected to edit their entries carefully). In response, some students chose to define by example, that is, by means of stories that explained exceptionally good or bad service. Analyzing the entries uncovered two areas of Southernness that were overtly reflected in some of the stories: structure, as discussed above, and features of Southern speech and cultural expectations. Interestingly, cultural expectations covertly influence student writing, even when other aspects of Southern storytelling are not present.

Chad, introduced above, wrote a story that clearly displays Southern vernacular linguistic and rhetorical structure. His complete and unedited story follows.

The Time I Received Exceptionally Good Service

In the fall of 1998, I was on my way to work, as I normally do, when I noticed that my power steering had become not so powerful. Worried, I then noticed my instrument panel started lighting up like it was the Forth of July with the check engine light being the grand finale. I thought that this could make me have to pull over on that old lonesome highway where the rest of the commuters would no[t] dare waste their time to try to help a stranded stranger. I, however, was determined not to be one of those people.

I, determinely, drove my troubled truck on down the highway to at last I came to the Heaven sent exit that could lead me to the refuge of the life-line of every troubled motorist, a South Central Bell telephone. I pulled off the exit not knowing if this, until now reliable, troubled truck could make it to a service station up on the next hill from where I exited.

As I began to reach that service station of refuge, I began to become excited. If I could just make it there I could call home for help. When I finally turned into the service station I had a joyous feeling of relief that came over me. I got out of my truck and started walking toward the phone when, as I was digging into my pocket, I noticed I didn't have any money on me. My heart sank into my stomach as I was pondering what to do. I went back to my truck and looked under my hood to see if the problem was maybe a loose wire or something simple that I could fix. My heart sank further into the pit of my stomach. My fan, power steering and alternator belt had broken.

My day was shot. I now was late for work and didn't have a dime to my name to make a phone call. I thought of giving up hope, when out from the service station came an attendant to come to my rescue. He had saw that I was having car trouble and came to offer assistance to a wounded traveler. I told him my belt had broke and I didn't have any money on me to call home or work. This Good Samaritan decided to help me with my problems. He allowed me to call work and tell them I would be late for work. What a relief! I was about to call home to have somebody come and carry me the rest of the way to work when the attendant said "I'll carry [you] over to the auto parts store and loan you the money to get the fan belt." I said "thank you, but I don't have the tools or knowledge to put one on." He said, "don't worry. I can help you put one on." The attendant told his coworker what the situation was and allowed him to leave temporarily to go to the auto parts store.

When we returned the attendant helped me put on the fan belt and got my truck running. The extra mile that the attendant went through to help me in my time of need was a surprise and a blessing. I wished everybody could be this generous.

I returned the next day and tried to pay the attendant some exta money for helping me, but he would not take any additional money. From then on I have tried to give as mush business to that service station as I could give.

"Chad," Service Journal for Human Resources Management Course

Chad's informal written response relates loosely connected details that follow a close chronological order of his thinking during the event; his linguistic variations act to enrich the story in ways like that of other Alabama storytellers (see, for example, Bragg 1997 and any of Windham's stories). He carefully recounts his thoughts and emotions during the ordeal and seems to faithfully report dialogue from the attendant who helped him. Additionally, and in line with Heath's observation of biblical references discussed above, Chad includes the direct biblical references *Heaven sent, Good Samaritan, extra mile, blessing*, and *station of refuge*. We may assume that Chad expects these direct Christian references to resonate with many Bible Belt Southerners. Many would identify also with the religious parallel of the *joyous feeling of relief* from "finding salvation" in the service station and the minor challenges to that salvation that are resolved by the "savior" or attendant. In keeping with the salvation motif, Chad must accept his fate and his shortcomings (lack of money, tools, and skill to rectify his situation) and graciously accept the attendant's helping hand. Aside from his religious training of dependence on Christ, such a capitulation of his male-gendered role of control and self-reliance would be unacceptable. Through his story, Chad equates good service with the Golden Rule: "Do unto others as you would have them do unto you." The Southern linguistic features, such as the use of the verb *carry* (meaning "to take"), the verb + double particle in **drove** *my troubled truck* **on down**, and the nuance of grammatical constructions such as *began to become excited*, add charm to the story. More importantly, these dialect features help build solidarity with his assumed Southern readers.[3]

Emphasis on certain rituals and forms of politeness during interaction is associated with Southern dialect: Southerners are known for their politeness (see Davies' essay in this volume) as well as for their personal interest in others (some non-Southerners would say "nosiness").[4] Storytelling may serve to increase the level of politeness, or rather lessen the risk of offending others. As Johnstone notes, "Deferential negative politeness (as opposed to friendly expressions of 'positive' solidarity) is especially important when there are potential threats to negative face [a sociological concept meaning *"one's desire and right not to be imposed upon and have freedom restricted"*]—when it is especially likely that people might offend or bother one another" (2003b, 195). In simplest terms, the linguistic notion of *face* (*positive* or *negative*) suggests that individuals behave and use language in ways to be appreciated by others (that is, to protect or enhance *positive face*) and in ways to avoid embarrassment or threats to personal autonomy (that is, to protect or enhance *negative face*). Through storytelling, individuals can obliquely make comments that might otherwise insult listeners. As one example, we will look at a story that Beth Anne, introduced earlier, wrote in her attempt to define good service.

Poor Service Experience
The worse experience I have had was with my new car. The place I bought it from had a great sales department but their service department needed a lot of work. They could greatly improve on their listening and communication skills. The sales guy I got my car from was really nice and understanding, he tried to help me everyway he could. The problem started when my car only had 500 miles on it. I had driven it to the beach and I was going to let my windows down in the back and they would not roll down. Also on the way home I kept hearing this rattle. I could hold my hand on the headliner of my car and it would stop. So Monday morning when I got home I took my car to the service department, I got there early so I could be near the front of the line because I had school that day. I waited for about 15 minutes. The service guy said what is your problem and I started to tell him, when I said the windows wont roll down he said "are you sure" I said yes, he then said "let me see". Sure enough he could not roll the windows down either. Then I started telling him about the rattle and how I could hold my hand on the headliner and it would stop. He did write down rattle in roof of car on the paper. I got my car back 2 weeks later and the rattle was still there. So I took

it back and got another service man, he wrote it down. That afternoon I got the call that my car was fixed. I drove it home and it was still rattling. Well the fourth time I had my dad to take the car back. This time they heard the noise and could fix it that day. Well, that afternoon I picked up my car the rattle was gone but the quality of work the service department did was awful. I had grease all over the inside of my car and the headliner was not put back right. The problem was the manufacture and not installed the metal bar that held wires in place.

This simple problem took too long to fix due to the service people not listening and doing their job right. Quality and workmanship build a company and without these the company will get a bad rep. I know this is true because many people have complained about the same company.

"Beth Anne," Service Journal for Human Resources Management Course

Beth Anne's story shares many of the features that Heath (1983) describes and that are present in Chad's story, namely, chronology, asides, and reported dialogue. Rather than using biblical imagery, however, Beth Anne alludes to myths (that is, in the scholarly sense of the word *myth*, deeply held, defining cultural beliefs, not "untruths") that resonate with working-class Southerners, much as Windham does in her stories (see Braden 1983, for how Southern speakers use allusions to cultural myths to establish solidarity with their audience). For example, in retelling her actions, she emphasizes the self-sufficiency of her attempts to identify and correct the problem (*I could hold my hand on the headliner of my car and it would stop*); her respectable and traditional work ethic, reflecting the agrarian adage "early to bed, early to rise" (*I got there early so I could be near the front of the line because I had school that day*); and the overall importance of maintaining a good reputation. Indeed, the moral of her story is directed toward businesses' need to maintain their reputations: *Quality and workmanship build a company and without these the company will get a bad rep.*

Prescribed gender roles continue to characterize parts of the South and are evident in this story. First, Beth Anne is apparently interrupted by the male service attendant, who must verify that indeed the car's rear windows will not "roll down." While his actions and incredulity could be explained simply as surprise that the windows would not open, his actions may also suggest that the "little lady just didn't know how to roll them down." As a Southern "lady," Beth Anne must accept his behavior and then ask for his help.[5] Similarly, only Beth Anne's father, the masculine protector and "fixer," is able to get the service department to recognize the problem: *This time* **they heard the noise** *and could fix it that day.* This retelling includes an embedded threat: the service department had no choice but to appease the father. The understood context is that her father would have accepted no other outcome, an implicit threat to the service representative's negative face. Moreover, Beth Anne must acknowledge her father's success in this quest in order to protect his face, and thus she notes that *Well, that afternoon I picked up my car the rattle was gone but the quality of work the service department did was awful. I had grease all over the inside of my car and the headliner was not put back right.* At least one implication is that her father is not responsible for the service department's lack of care in the cosmetic aspects of fixing her car. Yet, another possibility is to imply subtly that her father also had limited control over and success with the situation.

In the very next sentence, Beth Anne redirects her criticism away from the service department: *The problem was the manufacture*[r]. Throughout her story, Beth Anne blames only the service department, specifically stating *They could greatly improve on their listening and communication skills*, and she not only refrains from accusatory remarks against an individual but also is careful to note that each technician *did write down the rattle*. In establishing her ethos of honesty and fairness, by giving a factual and chronological retelling, and by blaming the larger, impersonal manufacturer, Beth Anne creates an implicit opportunity for the reader/listener to interpret blame for her, and while she expects this response to blame the service department, her ethic of polite behavior requires her to leave the situation ambiguous. Her final statement, *I know this is true because many people have complained about the same company*, refers to the custom of valuing others' opinions and experiences, of shared cultural wisdom.

As we saw earlier, the Townspeople in the communities that Heath investigated encouraged literary forms of storytelling that taught and enforced national norms of literacy. Similarly, although middle-class student John still uses an incident to define poor service, essentially a story, he shapes it into a more academically structured account. Nevertheless, we see in his entry that Southerners can adhere to some cultural values of storytelling even while eschewing more easily identifiable Southern euphemisms of politeness and organizational structures.

[no title]

Last year I had a terrible experience with a real estate agency. Throughout the year it seemed as though there was always some issue to resolve. The real estate agency I'm referring to is [name withheld], formerly known as [name withheld]. My roommate and I not only had to deal with problems in the apartment itself, but also with, what I can only assume to be, an incompetent office staff.

As far as the apartment itself goes, there were several inconveniences my roommate and I had to deal with. The initial evaluation of the apartment, done before we moved in, was conducted by one of the agency managers, my roommate and I. The three of us walked through the apartment pointing out any nicks in the paint, spots on the carpet, etc. Apparently the manager forgot to note some things, resulting in a loss of some of our deposit. On one occasion, the water heater was leaking, and ruining the carpet. After calling the office for about a week, they finally decided to come and fix it. Another time water started leaking through the ceiling. We called them, but I guess they did not feel that it was that important. They never responded to us. After a few days the leak stopped on its own, but not until it had left a stain on the carpet. Of course we got billed for that one to.

The office staff would call every other month or so asking about rent money. They would tell us that we had not paid our rent for that month. Sometimes they would ask about the rent for two to three months prior. It was not until we had to take our bank statements, photocopies of our rent checks and handwritten receipts to them before they would acknowledge that we had indeed paid our rent on time and in full. For some reason they would lose all records of us paying rent.

I don't want to sound like I'm whining, but their handling of each of these situations was completely inadequate. Not only was it a nuisance, it costs us money that we shouldn't of had to pay. Now whenever someone asks me about renting from [name withheld], I strongly discourage it because of the awful service I received while renting from them.

"John," Service Journal for Human Resources Management Course

Working within the traditional academic essay format, John begins with a direct thesis, *My roommate and I not only had to deal with problems in the apartment itself, but also with, what I can only assume to be, an incompetent office staff*, and then continues to develop the essay around two points: the apartment had problems, and the staff was inept. This organizational structure is quite different from the chronological retelling of both Chad's and Beth Anne's stories and reflects, if imperfectly, an attempt at shaping the discourse to meet the rhetorical expectations of the classroom. Importantly, John does not include reported dialogue, as both Chad and Beth Anne do, but rather lists problems with the apartment and accuses the apartment staff of being unresponsive to requests for maintenance.

On the surface, this story may come across as rather impolite. After all, John is criticizing the realty company directly. Unlike Beth Anne's complaints, which avoid castigating another individual, John's statements are direct: he explicitly blames the manager and staff of the apartment complex for the poor service he received, for example, *They never responded to us* and *their handling of each of these situations was completely inadequate*. His use of qualifying clauses and phrases (e.g., *what I can only assume to be . . .; Apparently the manager forgot . . .; For some reason . . .*) does little to mediate the impact of his criticism and indeed acts to intensify the manager's and staff's actions as essentially defying common sense, a highly valued characteristic of Southern culture. Making such bald-faced accusations and complaining ("whining") threaten John's positive face, basically his desire to be approved of by his community of readers. To mitigate this threat, John gives evidence to support his case that this realty company is not well managed and may be greedy (and possibly unethical). Additionally, John hedges in the negative face threat: rather than telling people never to rent from this company, he *strongly discourage*[s] it. This hedge prevents John from threatening the autonomy of anyone who might ask him about this realty company, much as Beth Anne's open-ended story encourages the reader (but does not dictate how) to assign blame. While John's hedge fits with cultural notions of politeness, the testimony of poor service he offers reemphasizes the role of personal experience and word of mouth referrals in Southern culture in much the same way as do both Chad's (*From then on I have tried to give as mush business to that service station as I could give*) and Beth Anne's (*Quality and workmanship build a company and without these the company will get a bad rep. I know this is true because many people have complained about the same company).*

John's statements must also balance threats to his masculinity: as a Southern man, he is supposed to be able to "fix things," just as Beth Anne's father was expected to resolve the problem she encountered in getting service for her car. (Chad, though unable to "fix" his predicament and at the mercy of the attendant, cloaks his weakness in a culturally acceptable metaphor of salvation). John's clause *I don't want to sound like I'm whining,* which opens the final paragraph, appeals to Southern stoicism, especially as expected of men, and reinforces the complaint's frame as a response to the staff's inadequacies and possibly to the staff's lack of ethics (why else would the staff *lose all records of us paying rent?*). The story also offers an indirectly stated moral: keep good records, get references, and stand your ground when dealing with realty companies. This moral resonates well with Chad's lesson of the potential hazards of being unprepared with no money, phone, or repair skills.

As the narratives of these students illustrate, stories serve many useful purposes in Southern culture. They can entertain, teach, and argue, all the while helping us preserve a level of politeness that is characteristically Southern. The distinctive linguistic features available in Southern English, including expected literary structures, discourse features of politeness, and dialect features that promote regional solidarity, are thus important resources that storytellers draw upon to make this method of communication effective within some contexts.

Unfortunately, many students, including the three writers presented here, will find that the context of academic writing does not readily accept dialect influence as effective. Instead, dialect influences may mark students as unprepared for college (Brammer 2002a). Although Johnstone (1999, 2003b), Dubois and Horvath (2002), and Mai and Hoffman (2011) describe how individuals can intentionally use dialect features for rhetorical effect, students must first be cognizant of their linguistic options, learning to negotiate linguistic variations and cultural diversity to achieve academic success (see Lee and Anderson 2009). Therefore, educational programs need to develop greater sensitivity to the connections among culture, language use, and identity.[6] With explicit instruction, students can add to their linguistic repertoires (Brammer 2002a, 2002b, and 2009). Our challenge, then, is to find ways to assist college writers, like those featured in this paper, in telling their stories effectively for broader—even academic—audiences.

NOTES

1. As a writer and a writing teacher, I suspected that many of the inappropriate or nonconforming features of my writing and particularly of some of my students' writing stemmed not from lack of concern or ability but rather from dialect and cultural influences, particularly their Southern dialects. For my doctoral research (Brammer 2002a), I identified seven categories of dialect influence on students' writing: (1) Phonological influences occur when speech sound affects writing (e.g., a student may write *would of* instead of the more customary *would have*); (2) Morphological influences include variant or missing inflections of verbs (e.g., missing -*s* on third person singular verbs or copula absence, regularizing of irregular verbs, etc.), among other features, and are

generally regarded very negatively by readers; (3) Semantic influences refer to unique uses of words, including intensifiers (e.g., *real proud about . . .* and *fixing to . . .*); (4) Syntactic influences consist of sentence boundary errors (fragments and run-ons), ambiguous pronoun use, misplaced modifiers, faulty parallelism, unexpected switch/use of tense, and so on; (5) Pragmatics offers insights as to how language is used, and for Southern dialects, pragmatic influences that involve the use of special verbs (including double modals) and pronouns, particularly demonstrative pronouns, often relate to levels of directness and emphasis; (6) Information structure is generally included as part of pragmatics and refers specifically to how writers or speakers present new and given information; and (7) Rhetorical structure attends to the larger discourse issues, including genre expectations, overall organizational structure, appeals, and writer ethos.

2. Research demonstrates that, in addition to entertaining, narratives serve to build rapport among individuals and to help individuals understand ourselves, our community, and our relationship with others in our community. Johnstone 2003a provides an excellent review of "why people tell stories." Lee and Anderson (2009) discuss how language and culture influence social identity.

3. See Feagin's essay in this volume on the solidarity function of the Southern drawl and Johnson and Nunnally's essay in this volume on the solidarity function of African American English; for further discussion of how dialect features build social identity and connections, see Donlon 1995; Gee 1996; Delpit 1995; Wolfram and Schilling-Estes 2006; and Fridland and Bartlett 2006.

4. I refer to notions of politeness and threats to face following Brown and Levinson's (1978, 1987) groundbreaking work. Of course, their work is based largely on Goffman's (1967). Recently, Brown and Levinson's work has been the topic of much research and criticism. Wilson et al. (1991/1992) questions "when do messages become face threatening?" Jary (1998), however, dismisses much of the comprehensive aspects of Brown and Levinson's politeness work and argues that relevance theory, as posited by Sperber and Wilson (1995), offers more clarification for understanding politeness. Terkourafi (2005) attempts to reconcile multiple theories of politeness by exploiting their commonalities and finally by suggesting a "frame-based" method of exploring levels of politeness. Working primarily to distinguish instances of anticipated politeness from those of inferred politeness, Haugh (2003 and 2007) proposes that discourse-based study and theory will increase our understanding of politeness as well as impoliteness. Locher and Watts (2005), working from a discursive stance, argue that Brown and Levinson's work addresses threats to face rather than politeness and furthermore that politeness is primarily a relational act. Other studies have begun to address politeness and face management in intercultural communication (e.g., Holtgraves 1992; Oetzel and Ting-Toomey 2003; Ting-Toomey 2005). An interesting twist on Southern politeness is research that suggests that Southern politeness rituals either reflect (Johnstone 2003b, 195) or possibly encourage violence (Cohen et al. 1999).

5. On the other hand, Southern women can also use the role of the Southern belle as a source of power. See Johnstone (1999, 2003b) and Feagin's essay in this volume.

6. For more detailed discussions of how sociolinguistics can inform language education, see Siegel 2007; Godley et al. 2006; Brown 2009; Brammer 2002a, 2002b, and 2009. Also see Wolfram's foreword to this volume for examples of language arts programs that teach dialect awareness.

12

Tsalagi Language Revitalization and the Echota Cherokee

Robin Sabino

Of the more than three hundred indigenous languages estimated to have been spoken in North America before the arrival of Europeans, linguists predict that only twenty will remain by 2050 (Hansen 2015). With the loss of each language, we lose centuries of accumulated insight into the human condition. Cherokee, Creek, and Choctaw, three languages once spoken in what is now Alabama, are among the indigenous languages that survive today.

The story of the present-day descendants of Alabama's indigenous people is one of resilience. *Access Genealogy* (2004–2007) lists thirty-seven distinct Indian communities once living in what is now our state. Many of these groups, such as the Alabama, the Biloxi, the Koasati, the Natchez, and the Yuchi, are gone (Americans.net 1996–2005). Existing tribes survived the initial European encounter, subsequent repopulation of their lands, and detribalization. Like the MOWA Choctaw described by Cormier, et al. (2006), the several state-recognized Cherokee tribes in Alabama descend from Indian people who escaped removal, enduring hardship and discrimination and often publicly denying their Indian heritage to protect it privately and thereby remain on land to which they are spiritually connected.

Passing as non-Indians was possible because contact, first with Europeans and later with American settlers, resulted in rapid cultural change for southeastern tribes. During this period, some Creek, Chickasaw, and Cherokee women took white husbands (Walker and Marshall 2005). Although an individual's status with the tribe was determined matrilineally, from a Western perspective, at the turn of the century, tribal leadership was described as mixed.

In 1803, the Reverend Patrick Wilson, traveling along a former Indian route, reported a "rapid increase in the settler population" in what is now Mississippi (Hathorn and Sabino 2001, 215–16). Traveling north through what is now Alabama, Wilson encountered the Chickamauga Cherokee,[1] from whom the Echota Cherokee descend. Praising the success of the federal government's recently initiated "civilization" efforts, Wilson also documents the retention of Cherokee cultural patterns, remarking on cooperative work details and use of a traditional eating utensil. In the Chickamauga capital, Wilson reports on a "prosperous, culturally mixed population" (Hathorn and Sabino 2001, 211). Since he comments only once on communication difficulties—indicating he needed a translator to converse with a monolingual tavern keeper in Hiwassee, a town formerly located south of Knoxville—we can infer that by this time, bilingualism was well-established in the Cherokee capital and farther south.

The mid-nineteenth century saw the emergence of a nationwide English-only education program aimed at eradicating the traditional languages (and thus the traditional cultures) of indigenous peoples living in what had become the United States. It was not until the passage of the Civil Rights Act in 1968 that it "bec[a]me legal to be Indian and live in Alabama" (Walker and Marshall 2005, 7). This legacy of cultural repression lingers still: a former tribal chairman and tribal chief of the Echota Cherokee reports that as late as the 1990s elderly Native Americans often voiced concern that admitting to "Indian blood will only bring me trouble" (Charlotte Hallmark, personal communication).

The widespread impact of shameful federally mandated detribalization policies is apparent today on the Indian languages once spoken in what is now the United States. For example, according to the *Ethnologue*, about 14 percent of federally recognized Cherokees are native speakers, and the majority of these people are elderly and bilingual. The *Ethnologue* also reports only 130 monolingual Cherokee (Lewis, Simons, and Fennig 2013); however, Picone (in this volume) cites the 2008 American Community Survey of the US Census Bureau as reporting 269 self-identified Cherokee speakers in Alabama. Additionally, a number of individuals are attempting to teach or relearn their heritage language.

Four of the southeastern historically termed Five Civilized Tribes—the Creek, the Seminole, the Chickasaw, and the Choctaw—spoke Muscogean languages. Cherokee is an Iroquoian language. Reasons for the migration of the people named Tsalagi by their southeastern neighbors (the Cherokee call themselves *ani ya-wi ya*) and renamed Cherokee by Europeans are still not understood. Subsequent division and displacement has resulted in the creation of Tsalagi dialects: Elati (also called Lower/Eastern Cherokee, now classified by linguists as extinct), Giduwa (Middle Cherokee), and Otali (Upper/Western/ Overhill Cherokee).

The approximately twenty-two thousand Echota Cherokee (Hathorn 1997) are one of four Alabama state-recognized tribes with Cherokee membership; the Alabama Indian Affairs Commission website also lists the Cher-o-Creek Intra Tribal Indians, the Cherokee Tribe of Northeast Alabama, and the United Cherokee Ani-Yun-Wiya Nation. There also are groups, such as the Bird Clan, whose members include people of Cherokee descent but who have not sought formal recognition.

The Echota are governed by a tribal council that administers communal land, sponsors annual powwows, and publishes a bimonthly newsletter. Part of the Echotas' program of cultural preservation and renewal is reacquisition of Tsalagi. This desire provided the motivation for the Echota Tsalagi Language Revitalization Project, available at http://auburn.edu/outreach/dl/echota/index.html.[2] An early step toward realizing this goal was a tribal language survey conducted by Stacye Hathorn in the 1990s. The survey instrument explored existing linguistic resources among the Echota and the symbolic meaning of Tsalagi for Echota cultural identity.

Although survey results revealed no self-identified, native Tsalagi speakers among the Echota, it did document Tsalagi being spoken in tribal members' homes within living memory. The survey also documented the Echota's enthusiasm and willingness to work for cultural revitalization and the anticipated social and personal rewards that reacquisition of Tsalagi would bring.

The Echota Tsalagi language revitalization website is the only free-access, self-instructional resource sponsored by an Alabama institution of higher education. The project began in the early 1990s, when tribal member Pat Edwards Ortega requested help with language revitalization. After several unsuccessful attempts to interest funding agencies in a large-scale project to collect language data, a Ford Foundation grant was secured by Paula Backscheider, Auburn University's Philpott-Stevens Eminent Scholar, to develop the web skills of area university faculty. Participation in the grant workshops led to the realization that the World Wide Web provided an inexpensive means of reaching a wide audience, in Alabama and beyond. Over the years, the project's web presence has attracted the attention of competent Tsalagi speakers who have generously contributed to the project's linguistic resources.

Development of the revitalization project was advanced substantially by the addition to the project team of Bradley Morgan, a web designer and programmer then working with Auburn University's Distance Learning and Outreach Technology. The first version of the website was officially launched at a workshop in May 2002 attended by officers of the Echota Tribe and administrators and instructors in the federally funded Title IV Indian Education program. The workshop, which was supported by the Auburn University College of Liberal Arts and the Department of English, was held in a computer lab on campus. By October 2003 there had been more than 5,400 visitors to the website. Additional funding from Auburn University's Office of the Vice President for Research and from Auburn University Outreach in 2004 supported substantial site development. This resulted in an updated design, with faster loads. Another redesign by Vignesh Vellimalaipattinam Si, supported by Distance Learning and the Department of English at Auburn University, further improved the website, which has received more than 100,000 hits.

The current home page for the Echota Tsalagi Language Revitalization Project is shown in figure 12.1. Appropriately, it is graced by the portrait of Sequoyah (d. 1843) holding the syllabary writing system that he devised for Tsalagi (see Picone's essay in this volume for an illustration and the history of Sequoyah's syllabary). Although the website provides a wealth of information through its menus and links, the language lessons are obviously of greatest importance. Due to the current level of the Echota's Tsalagi language resources, the Tsalagi Revitalization website contains mainly vocabulary items. At present, there are more than two thousand lexical entries distributed over nearly three hundred word lessons. These represent topics such as colors, numbers, material objects, weather, and natural phenomena. Because there are learners of both the Otali and Giduwa dialects among the Echota, the website lists and, when possible, identifies dialect variants.

Each word entry minimally contains the Tsalagi word, written in both the Ro-

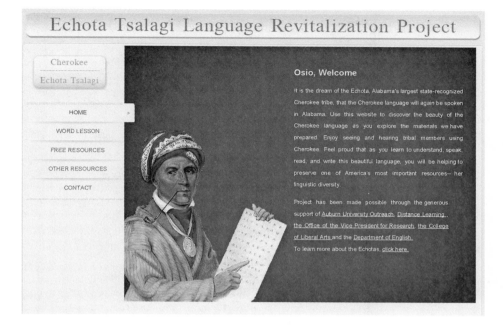

Figure 12.1. Homepage for the Echota Tsalagi Language Revitalization Project (formerly http://auburn.edu/outreach/dl/echota/index.html)

man alphabet and the Tsalagi syllabary, and an English translation.[3] Many word entries also contain sound files and images. The sound files were recorded by Shy Eagle, an Echota who is a fluent second-language speaker of Tsalagi. A second set of sound files has been recorded by a former tribal chief, John Berryhill. These await insertion into the website. Since relying on translation inhibits a learner's language acquisition, the columns in each row are ordered to minimize translation from Tsalagi to English. The most successful users of the website will be those who associate the sound, visual representation, and image for each Tsalagi word without recourse to the English meaning.

Figure 12.2 shows four words from the DEER word lesson. The first column contains sound files. The second column shows the spelling of the Tsalagi word in both Roman and Tsalagi. The third column contains images. The last column shows an English translation. Links connecting the word lessons encourage website users to create individualized learning paths through the word lessons, as they select the proportion of audio, video, textual, and graphic instructional materials that best suits their learning styles. For example, *a-wi* "deer" is linked to the ANIMALS word lesson. *A-ni ka-wi* "Deer Clan" is linked to the lesson on *ANI* "plural marker used with nouns that name living things." *A-wi (a)-k(a)-ta* "black-eyed susan" is linked to the EYE lesson. *A-wi e-kwo* "elk," literally "deer big," is linked to the BIG word

	a-wi D Ө		'deer'
	a-ni ka-wi D h Ꝺ Ө	No Picture	'deer clan'
	a-wi (a)-k(a)-ta D Ө D Ꝺ Ѡ		'black-eyed susan'
	a-wi e-kwo D Ө R Ꝩ		'elk'

Figure 12.2. Selected entries from the DEER Word Lesson from the Echota Tsalagi Language Revitalization Project

lesson. By thinking about the similarities and differences among Tsalagi words like these, learners can discover grammatical relations such as the position of the animate plural marker or the adjective with respect to the noun.

The most popular word lesson has been ANIMALS. The BIRDS word lesson has been accessed more than 1,500 times. The website's sound files have been played nearly twenty-five thousand times. A word-recognition game that reinforces vocabulary recognition also has proven popular.

The website (see figure 12.1) enhances the word lessons with links that offer additional language study and that contextualize Tsalagi within Cherokee history and culture. The official website of the Echota Cherokee Tribe of Alabama presents an array of information about the tribe and its clans, the role of women, the history of gaining state recognition, legends, US military service of tribe members, and much more. The "Free Resources" menu broadens the base of information to Cherokee tribes nationwide, including a link to the online independent newspaper the *Cherokee Observer*, literature in translation, music, and other language resources. Finally, the "Other Resources" menu allows users to pursue further language and cultural study by purchasing audiovisual and print materials.

An unexpected but exciting benefit of the revitalization project is that, because the word lessons are populated by a database, it also has been possible to initiate similar self-instructional websites for Arabic and Mandarin. These projects document the applicability of the programming to other languages and scripts. Our hope is that members of communities interested in creating their own noncommercial heritage language materials will be able to use the programming developed for the Echota Tsalagi Language Revitalization website.

NOTES

1. Unwilling to relinquish additional territory to the United States, the Chickamauga seceded from the Cherokee Nation in 1777. The US government officially recognized the Chickamauga Cherokee in 1817. This was only twelve years before the Alabama state leg-

islature outlawed Native American governments, voided contracts made with and canceled debts to indigenous peoples, and declared testimony against whites to be invalid.

2. This link may become inactive by the time of this essay's publication. In 2017, the federal government enacted revised federal guidelines on accessibility of web content (WCAG 2.0 and the Americans with Disabilities Act) that require compliance in 2018. Under the new regulations, Auburn University will be unable to continue hosting the Echota Tsalagi Language Revitalization Project website and will remove the website from its server. Auburn University has freely granted all rights and given all website files to the Echota, and it is hoped that the tribe will update and host the program on their home page soon. If a search for Echota Tsalagi language information returns cached files of the removed program with pages containing the text © 2003 Auburn University, please be advised that these files are no longer hosted by or under copyright to Auburn University.

3. The Tsalagi writing system is syllabic rather than alphabetical. That is, each symbol represents a syllable such as *wi* or *tla*. When represented in Roman orthography as a guide to pronunciation, syllables within lexical units are separated by hyphens. When a word is composed of two or more lexical units, the lexical units are separated by a space.

Afterword

Some Thoughts about Ways Ahead

Michael B. Montgomery

It is a privilege and a pleasure to contribute a few thoughts, primarily for the future, to a volume of essays on the languages of Alabama, a volume any state would envy for its own languages. In contributing an array of current research and synopses of existing information, this assemblage builds upon a foundation of scholarship already second to none in the South. In focusing on many issues of social import and interest, it will fortify future scholars and ensure that their work will be well-informed and concerned with the roles of language and linguistic diversity in public life. The reader who has come this far will appreciate how widely the languages of Alabama—its English, its other European tongues, and its indigenous languages—have engaged contemporary scholars and commentators, but the interest is in fact of long-standing, on the part of both academics and laypeople (in the latter case, especially regarding vocabulary and place-names). That native Alabamians have written so voluminously about the state's English is a testament to an abiding fascination in their home territory and pride in its heritage.

One of this writer's particularly memorable professional friendships was with the late James B. McMillan, native of Talledega, longtime professor of English at the University of Alabama, and founder of the University of Alabama Press. As a student of the English language, McMillan published works as varied as anyone's in his time, writing on lexicology, semantics, usage, lexicography, onomastics, morphology, phonology, and bibliography.[1] His distinguished career editing reference works and *Publication of the American Dialect Society* (the monograph series PADS of the American Dialect Society) for two decades was matched by his modesty and reputation as a sharp commentator on language. He showed how a student and documentarian could, by exercising inborn curiosity and the powers of observing the lively, quirky details of language, tempered with an understanding for history, model these habits in meticulous scholarship, in teaching, and in sharing ideas with colleagues, thereby leaving an exemplary legacy for others. Predictably, anything written by McMillan was scrupulously clear and insightful, impeccably well grounded and thought out, and above all trustworthy. These same qualities are embodied by and form the legacy of Thomas E. Nunnally in his career at Auburn University. As with McMillan, Nunnally's published scholarship has sometimes been slow to emerge but in a stealthy fashion has been born of his instinctive sensitivity about language and its speakers and his concern to write or edit only what will stand the test.

The present volume is a milestone in the record of the languages and language varieties spoken in a medium-sized Southern state tucked somewhat inconspicuously between three neighbors and at first glance having little to distinguish itself from them. Most outsiders know its fanaticism for college football but probably little about its history beyond textbook statements and images. To them what is distinct or characteristic about its geography, people, and certainly its speech will be all vast unknowns. This volume fills many gaps and at the same time shows how Alabama is a typically Southern state. That its speech patterns have been more thoroughly documented than any other state in the South (Rich and Montgomery 1993) is attributable frequently to the dedication, inspiration, and vision of native-born scholars like James McMillan and Thomas Nunnally.

History has been a steady, powerful undercurrent in the literature on the state's languages. The nickname *Heart of Dixie* suggests a vital crossroads, and what appellation could describe Alabama better? Beginning two centuries ago, it was where settlers from states to the east and northeast met, coming into northern Alabama from Tennessee and into the southern half of the state from the Piedmont and Lowcountry of Georgia and South Carolina, and beyond (this writer's maternal great-great-grandfather came from southeastern Virginia). It was Alabama that settlers from the Carolinas had to cross to settle in Mississippi (as did this writer's paternal great-great-grandfather), the eastern panhandle and northern half of Louisiana, and much of East Texas. Most of them made the move in one step, perhaps because so much of Alabama's prime land was taken up by the late 1820s. Alabama is the only state in the South into which prominent rivers flow from each of its neighbors. It would be difficult to imagine that rivers have played such an important role in any other Southern state's development, with the possible exception of Tennessee.

Thus, the settlement and cultural history of Alabama cannot be understood without first taking stock of its landscape. At the very heart of the Deep South are the river systems of Alabama: the Chattahoochee, Tallapoosa, and Coosa entering from Georgia; the Tennessee entering from Tennessee; and the Tombigbee entering from Mississippi. Given the early lack of east-west roads and the fact that the first four rivers named angle southwesterly into Alabama and then turn south, many people and goods came by water rather than overland (Abernethy 1922). Taken with the reinforcing fact that the three having headwaters in Georgia flowed far south of the Tennessee and that from the south the rivers of Alabama were fully navigable only so far as the mid-state fall line, the stage was set inevitably for producing different settlement populations that has resulted in continuing linguistic contrasts, sectional rivalries, and an instinctive if vague sense of a cultural divide bisecting the state. Not surprisingly, the extent to which a boundary might be mapped for individual lexical contrasts (e.g., *chigger* versus *red bug*) and then generalized has been the focus of several studies. Foscue (1966; based on her own survey), Wood (1971), Carver (1987; using data collected by the *Dictionary of American Regional*

English [DARE]), and Fitts (1989, 1998; using data collected by the *Linguistic Atlas of the Gulf States [LAGS]*) have posited slightly different lines from their data, all collected the better part of half a century ago and mainly from rural and small-town Alabamians. With huge demographic changes having subsequently taken place, especially the growth of suburbia, the reconfiguration of speech communities, and the depopulation of rural areas throughout the South, the question of boundary is ripe for revisiting with a new collection of data in hand. Comparison across generations will be facilitated by the fact that Foscue and Fitts compared two generations of speakers. We will return to these matters further below.

DOCUMENTARY RESOURCES

Alabama can boast of being one of very few states for which substantial linguistic evidence, much of it still in manuscript, exists for its first fifty years of existence. Coming largely from people not born in the state and to date hardly mined, this material can attest input patterns to sketch much of the first hundred years of the state's English. Some documentation is in the form of manuscripts whose transcriptions are tucked away in little-known publications. For example, Jacob Hartsell, born in Pennsylvania but reared in northeast Tennessee, kept a diary while serving in Creek War campaigns in Alabama under General Andrew Jackson in 1813–14 (McCowan 1939–40). Though he did not subsequently remove to Alabama, many other East Tennesseans whose speech must have been similar to Hartsell's did settle in the northern tier of the state. The following examples illustrate two features of American Midland speech attested in the diary that Hartsell left behind: the adjective phrase *all* "the only" and the verb *nicker* "whinny":

> [H]e was *all the* purson that Dyed out of our ridgement yet (1814: McCowan 1940, 143)
> I fetched a verey large load of cane for the horses, and came throw the incampment and some horses lay there, and as I pased throw the horses *nickered* for my cane tell my hart aked for them. (1813; McCowan 1939, 103)

An equally lengthy but unpublished diary is that of John G. Traylor of Lowndes County, south of Montgomery. Traylor was born in Edgefield District, in the Piedmont region of South Carolina, and was one of many moving from farther east for better prospects in South Alabama. From January 1, 1834, to April 16, 1847, Traylor kept an almost daily record of his activities, for most of which period he worked as a plantation overseer.[2] Traylor frequently used *give* and *come* as past-tense forms, and he always used *done* (as seen below) as the past-tense main verb form of *do* (but only *did* as the auxiliary):

> Cloudy an rainy all day an *dun* nothin (April 4, 1837)

In its spellings, the diary of the indifferently schooled Traylor offers tantalizing clues to his pronunciation that raise questions of theoretical linguistic interest, especially relating to final consonant clusters. As shown above, Traylor typically omits the final *d* of *and*. His *bornd* seems to suggest either a compensatory, hyper-correct insertion of the consonant or an articulatory process whereby nasalization ends prior to voicing, thereby producing what is heard—perhaps only as a trace—as a final *d*. The latter process is arguably at the root of why in Southern speech *drown* is sometimes produced as *drownd*, giving rise to the frequently attested bisyllabic past-tense form *drownded* (of which the *LAGS* survey collected examples from 361 speakers in the South). However, the situation for Traylor is more complex, and multiple processes may be involved, because he also produced such highly unusual past-tense forms as *rainded, rolded, pulded,* and *kilded,* for *rained, rolled, pulled,* and *killed*. None of these presumably bisyllabic pronunciations is recorded in either *LAGS* or *DARE*. Did Traylor lack some final consonant clusters in his mental lexicon? Historians of earlier English have long used variant spellings recorded in manuscripts to reconstruct phonological developments (e.g., the Great Vowel Shift), but research of this kind on American English is extremely rare. Regarding the English of the American South, one of the few substantial studies is Stephenson (1958).

Diaries from the early nineteenth century written by commoners and having a wealth of idiosyncratic spellings and diagnostic linguistic forms are quite rare, so for two to exist relevant to Alabama speech represents a windfall for those who would study the state's early English. Nor is Traylor's diary the only writing by overseers. Men who managed plantations at some distance from their owners were required to keep owners informed by periodic reports in the form of letters. Though these documents were of a business nature, dealing with the progress of crops and similarly mundane subjects, the men who wrote them often had relatively little formal schooling and wrote "by ear," thus giving clues to speech patterns. There are, for example, two dozen letters written from Alabama contained in the *Southern Plantation Overseer Corpus* (*SPOC*) (see Schneider and Montgomery 2001). Twenty-one of these were from John Long of Cherokee County, written between 1853 and 1857.[3]

In the way of private correspondence that reveals the state's familiar English, nothing remotely approaches the volume, breadth, or human interest of letters written during the Civil War (1861–1865). The enlistment or conscription of unprecedented numbers of young men who had never been away from their families naturally produced aching homesickness, compelling many who would never have written a letter in their lives to seize a pen and become steady correspondents. Not all were as eloquent as Coosa County Private Thomas Warrick of Company C, Thirty-Fourth Alabama Infantry, the Confederate soldier from whose letters extensive excerpts were read on Ken Burns's widely viewed television series *The Civil War*, but the lofty sentiments and memorable rhetoric of Warrick's letters when read aloud as in the series camouflage the vernacular language seen in his spellings and grammar. He wrote to his wife, Martha, on January 11, 1863:

> Deare louving wife I set my self down in order to let you know that I am well
> and I hope that this may come saft to your hands and find you and the Chil-

dern all Well and in Good helth Martha I have Got a Grate Deal to say to you at presant and I Recand that you are Gitting anxious to here from me I Can inform you that I have seen the Monkey Show at last and I dont Waunt to see it no more I am satisfide with Ware Martha I Cant tell you how meny ded men I did see men was shot Evey poshinton that you mit Call for thay ware piled up one one another all over the Battel feel the Battel Was a Six days Battel and I was in all off it there was one man Cilled in my Company his name Was John Browen ther Was to Wounded C.T. Walls Was wounded and and a man By the name of handerson it is Getting dark a and I will Quite for to nite I will bee gin a new this morning there was a meny a pore man cilled on the feld of Battel the Report is that the Yankees lost 24 thousand and that we lost 12 thousand But I dont think that meny men was cilled in the field I think that were was about 12 or 14 hundred men killed on the field I did not go all over the Battel field I just was on one wing of the Battel field But I can tell you that there Was a meny a ded man Where I was men Was shot Eney poshinton that you mite Call for Som had there hedes shot of and som ther armes and leges som was shot in too in the midel I Can tell you that I am tirde of Ware I am satisfide if the Ballence is that is one thing shore I dont Waunt to see that site no more.

Like much other surviving Civil War correspondence generated by Alabamians, Warrick's letters are in the Alabama Department of Archives and History (ADAH), in Montgomery. Decades ago in his book *The Life of Johnny Reb* (1943), Bell Wiley introduced readers to the common soldier of the Confederacy, relying heavily on letters already deposited in the ADAH. Whether in institutional collections or in private hands, such documents should receive concentrated attention not only for the stories they tell but also for the language in which they tell them. Tens of thousands have already been digitized online, including the Warrick letters (PDF online at https://www.nps.gov/stri/learn/historyculture/upload/Warrick_Thomas _Letters.pdf), and countless more will doubtless follow. They form the richest and most extensive record of mid-nineteenth-century English in Alabama and every other state in the country.

EARLY LITERATURE

With the end of the Creek War (1813–1814), subsequent land cessions by the Creek, Chickasaw, and Choctaw, and the opening of the Alabama Territory to general settlement in 1816, a rush of population ensued that reached twice that required by 1819, when Alabama became the twenty-second state in the country. It had swelled to nearly a million by the advent of the Civil War. Slaves were the majority in many sections, especially in the Black Belt. Shortly after statehood, travelers from the North and from Europe began including Alabama on their tours through the Old South, very often keeping a diary (Clark 1956). These contributed to a genre of American literature of long-standing (among the best-known early journals about the interior South were those of naturalists John Bartram and William Bartram).

In recording their experiences, many diarists noted local people, their behavior, and occasionally speech with which they were not familiar. Among those who related her extended visit to Alabama from 1817 to 1822 was Anne Royall, sometimes known as "Washington's first muck-raking journalist" and apparently the only person in American history to be tried and convicted as a "common scold." Her experiences, recounted in a series of letters for the press of the nation's capital, were published as *Letters from Alabama, 1817–22* ([1830–31] 1969). Not surprisingly, these are flush with exaggeration and indignation, among other predictable reactions of an Eastern urbanite in the not-always-genteel backcountry world of middle Tennessee and northern Alabama. They also feature extended portrayals of the speech of those she encountered, including one backwoods sermon, that have never been studied for their insights to the language of the day. In her *Sketches of History, Life, and Manners, in the United States* (1826), Royall comments, with wonder and usually disapproval, on the speech of Virginians, taking the tack of many other travel writers of the day.[4] But her *Letters from Alabama* offers an entirely different, and potentially as valuable, record of early Southern speech. Other travelers whose antebellum diaries were later published and are of prospective interest are cited in Hitchcock (2002).

We cannot leave prospects for investigating Alabama speech of the mid-nineteenth century without identifying an altogether different type of source: prescriptive schoolbooks (readers, grammars, and rhetorics) produced in the South during Civil War years and having a very definite Confederate orientation. For some years before hostilities, teachers in Southern states had rankled at what they considered unfair and inaccurate portrayals of Southern life by schoolbooks produced in the Northeast, so when the naval blockade of Southern ports imposed in the spring of 1861 prevented shipments of new books, Southern educators and publishers countered by producing and promoting their own. Alabamians took the lead in organizing an annual conference of teachers in the Confederacy, and one enterprising educator in Mobile, Adelaide de Vendel Chaudron, put out a series of texts, including two readers (1863a and 1863b). These featured numerous admonitions about pronunciation, such as the prohibition below against pronouncing words with ŏ (that is, with the sound /ɔ/) as having a diphthong:

> Mark the difference between the ŏ and the diphthong *aw*. *Lŏst*, not lawst; dŏg, not dawg; dŏll, dawl, &c. . . . Some persons carry the drawl in this ŏ to such an extent, that it has the sound ō-ä, thus: lō-äst, dō-äll, &c. In avoiding the drawl, guard against the opposite error, (a British one,) viz: lääst (*lost*), cääffee (*coffee*), dääg (*dog*), gään (*gone*), &c. (Chaudron 1863a, 138)

For language historians, prescriptions like these provide evidence as valuable, if not more so, as renditions of dialect found in the tales of nineteenth-century backwoods humorists like Johnson Jones Hooper, the value of whose work has been shown by Sharp (1981). Prescriptions are usually more straightforward to interpret, within the limits of pronunciation representations by orthography and by diacritics that are sometimes a bit idiosyncratic. Further, such comments imply something about prestige, because forms are singled out only when the writer considers them incorrect or impolite. Literary representation, however suggestive, tends to indicate lack of prestige less explicitly and for a dialect holistically, rather than pinpointing specific forms or features, as schoolbooks do (Montgomery 2015).

Linguistic Atlas of the Gulf States

The data set from the *Linguistic Atlas of the Gulf States*, collected through a lengthy questionnaire in the 1970s and published in various forms between 1986 and 1992, is so vast and multifaceted that an entire essay could be sketched about the usefulness of this in further studying the English of Alabama (see Montgomery 1998b for an overview of the project). Most studies employing *LAGS* would involve research questions of a comparative character because the survey interviewed 135 white and 41 black speakers (for an average of more than five hours, many with sections of free conversation) in mainly rural and small-town communities spread over sixty-two of the state's sixty-seven counties. Each interview is accompanied by more information profiling the speaker (ancestry, social life, work and educational history, etc.) than for any other study ever carried out in the region (Pederson et al. 1986).[5] Its findings have established a foundation for Alabama speech on which future generations of researchers can long build and draw. For example, six of the forty-one African Americans interviewed were born in the 1890s and three in the 1880s. Given researchers' longtime interest in the historical evolution of the speech of African Americans, these records deserve scrutiny. It is unfortunate that so little research has utilized *LAGS* data to date (exceptions include the work of Bailey and Maynor 1985a, 1985b; Montgomery 1998a; Pederson 1996; Schneider 1998; and now Nunnally and Bailey in this volume). Studies comparing white and black pronunciation in Alabama could begin by using *LAGS* idiolect synopses to chart vowel patterns, along the lines of what Dorrill (1986) did for North Carolina, Virginia, and Maryland, using data from the *Linguistic Atlas of the Middle and South Atlantic States* (*LAMSAS*). Nor has the vocabulary of Alabama black populations been examined for whether it patterns within the state similarly to that of its white populations. The studies of Foscue and others cited earlier either did not consider black speech separately or did not include black interviewees in their surveys. In an intensive study in Tuscaloosa, Foley (1969) found that the speech of black Alabamians tended to match that of southern Alabama, while that of white Alabamians matched that of the northern part of the state. While this finding is intriguing, Foley surveyed only five black speakers.

Data from LAGS have helped linguists understand many geographical dimensions of Alabama's long-standing sectional divide, but it remains unutilized for exploring social ones (by comparing races, sexes, age groups, etc.) Geographically speaking, the regional scope of both *LAGS* and *LAMSAS* enables subregional comparison of Alabama to its northern and eastern neighbors a century and a half after migration into the state: How close did the speech of North Alabama remain to that of East Tennessee, of Northern Georgia, of Upstate South Carolina?[6] Or that of South Alabama to that of Southern Georgia and Lower South Carolina?

Given that the generally westward course of antebellum migration into Alabama was complicated by the direction of rivers, one can use *LAGS* to explore whether migrants treated rivers as highways, preferring them to overland routes. The issue is of course a relative one, because any investigation must be accompanied by the local history of roads, the ease of river crossings at various points, and other considerations. When people moved west from Macon, Georgia, for example, did they tend to go to the Chattahoochee River and cross it or go downstream? If the latter, did they fan out along both sides of the river, taking up alluvial land, or did they largely move onward into Alabama? In an exemplary study, Schneider (1998) considers whether the lower two-thirds of the Chattahoochee forms a linguistic boundary, using *LAGS* data to test the views of Wood (1971) and Carver (1987) that it does. Schneider finds minimal support for such a boundary and posits that one in central Alabama (presumably along the Alabama River) is far more consistent with linguistic evidence from *LAGS*. Not only can *LAGS* be used to outline population movement and subsequent cultural influence along any number of southern rivers, but its data is easy to access for researchers to test their own hypotheses, just as Nunnally and Bailey (in this volume) do. They make it clear that questions should sometimes be approached from a local (i.e., county or subcounty) level and that by doing so one can unravel puzzles of atypical areas within larger landscapes. Caution against overly broad questions is surely wise, but *LAGS* data can easily accommodate analysis from either above or below. To conclude, *LAGS* can be used to confirm or expand a wide range of issues concerning language variation and change in Alabama and seven other southern states.

When a broad geographical survey of language such as *LAGS* has the limitation that its coverage is too thin, recorded oral history interviews can often compensate, most notably in providing 1) the extended conversation that linguists need in order to ascertain intraspeaker variation and to conduct quantitative analysis, especially for pronunciation; and 2) extended speech of Alabamians of a wide range of backgrounds. Many of the interviews employed by Flynt in his *Poor but Proud* (1989), now archived at Samford University, the University of North Carolina, and elsewhere, were conducted with people of rural working-class origins.

DEMOGRAPHY AND LINGUISTIC CHANGE

Alabama's population has rarely experienced a time when it was not in the throes of economic instability, due to rampant development or, more often, hardship or necessity. Within two generations of settlement came a ravaging war that on the home front drastically reduced the white population of many areas through casualties of war or destitution. The conflict freed several hundred thousand slaves, who often had nowhere to go and effectively became refugees. In the last quarter of the nineteenth century, industrialization, especially in north-central Alabama, was arguably more pronounced than anywhere else in the South. Millhanding, mining, factory work, and other occupations drew large workforces of the poor and landless from farming into cash-based economies that often provided mixed blessings. Life may have become more predictable for them, but it also became far more dangerous. Early decades of the twentieth century saw countless landless black Alabamians leave the state for parts north, usually cities like Detroit or Chicago, but not a few were recruited to bring their experience in coal mining to Kentucky and West Virginia. The period following World War II has seen steady, rapid growth of urban areas in Alabama, with the populations of four of them now surpassing four hundred thousand and these alone accounting for more than half the state's population. Inasmuch as recent urbanization has involved mainly younger-age cohorts migrating for white-collar professions, this process means that populations in and surrounding cities are changing in their social makeup and geographical origins. To what extent do speakers in these emergent burgeoning communities reflect the speech of their less-schooled forebears versus that of those who have arrived from out of state?

The foregoing chronicle is well-known to the state's social and economic historians. The population shifts identified and others must be having significant linguistic consequences, though for all intents and purposes these have received little mention in linguistic studies, so constant has attention to nineteenth-century settlement history been. Whether or how patterns of socioeconomic migration can help us understand language change (regarding varieties and usages of English) and language shift (regarding the arrival and spread of languages other than English) in Alabama are questions that linguists can no longer ignore. They should begin by learning to read and interpret census data intelligently, for both macro and micro perspectives. This is not only because the 2010 federal census shows that Alabama, like many other states in the region, has seen its Hispanic population double, but more importantly and more generally, Alabama will almost certainly have become an increasingly multilingual place in many ways (see Picone's essay in this volume). How can we describe the emerging speech communities, both rural and urban, in the Alabama of today as compared to a generation ago? Shifts in population and language are primary developments but far from the only ones. In many places, speech networks have changed radically as well. For Hispanics, *where* people are moving may be more important than *how many* are moving. Are Spanish speakers settling mainly in pockets vacated by rural whites and blacks who have left for cities and suburbia? To what extent are speakers of Spanish moving into towns and thereby more likely increasing their contact with English? The latter is probably the prime ongoing issue to watch.

Within the limitations of a single volume, the essays herein collectively fill in the linguistic landscape of the state rather well. Picone's essay, perhaps the jewel in the collection, shows that even in the early days of settlement, several European languages were to be found. Even if one ignores enslaved Africans and what some of them may still have known of the many languages they brought to American shores, the idea that Alabama was ever "English only" has little historical validity. Perhaps it is the multilingual heritage of the state that has long made the study of its place-names so compelling and so prominent (Read 1937, Foscue 1989). Nearly half the published commentary identified in McMillan and Montgomery's *Annotated Bibliography of Southern American English* (1989) concerns them, the great majority of which are of indigenous origin. In few states have place-name researchers worked so closely with archaeologists to document the pre-European-derived toponymy.

For investigating sound changes in progress and other aspects of pronunciation, as well as choices between lexical items, it is, as elsewhere in the country, in urbanized locales where the competition for supremacy takes place. In Alabama, as Allbritten (in this volume) shows, the rivalry often takes the form of a series of shifts in vowels, but the evolving pronunciation of single words, such as place-names, can also index changes in social prestige or the perception of it. The name *Talledega* was once a shibboleth, with natives usually pronouncing the third syllable with the vowel of *dig* rather than *leg* (Foscue 1989, a definitive work, cites only the former), but the latter pronunciation has so penetrated the speech of NASCAR drivers, fandom, and broadcasters that it is the only one known to most Americans. I am informed that Birmingham sportscasters hesitate *not* to use *Tal-la-deg-a*, apprehensive about sounding out of tune and not promoting the state's signature stock-car race. Whether this trend in pronunciation is taking place and who and where its leaders are can easily be explored in student projects. Since *Talladega* names a town and a county as well as a race, do natives say all three the same way, whichever vowel they choose, or is only the name of the race giving way? How does one pronounce the name of Alabama's capital city, Montgomery, that is, does one pronounce the *t* at the end of the first syllable? This writer wavers between using the *t* for his surname (which would scandalize his mother, a native of the Conecuh County town of Evergreen) but not for the capital city. And what about designating the state's residents: are they "Alabamians" or "Alabamans"? Most older residents would probably be no more likely to say "Alabaman" than to say "Floridan," but those under thirty seem increasingly to be more laissez-faire in usage and acceptance. If a disproportion of those who choose "Alabaman" were born outside the state, what does this imply about the "linguistic insecurity" of Alabam(i)ans?

Will Alabamians continue to be intrigued by the language(s) of their state as it moves into a new decade? More than likely, yes. The stage could be ripe for a newspaper column dealing with issues of variation and change. A testimony or two regarding the three issues of pronunciation just outlined would likely prompt quick and plentiful replies and complaints, because older folks still do read newspapers. To take stock of the state's distinctive vocabulary, one could begin with the term *Yankee dime*, which this writer learned from his great aunts in South Alabama, who often used it in the promise "do that for me, and I'll give you a Yankee dime."[7] When the *Dictionary of American Regional English* conducted its nationwide survey in the late 1960s, ten of the twenty speakers using *Yankee dime* turned out to be from Alabama. To what extent is this expression remembered, and do those who recall it agree on its connotations? *DARE* has designated a number of other terms as concentrated in Alabama (sometimes along with other states), including the following:

> *butt-head* "a cow (or less frequently a goat or deer) that has no horns."
> *Cajun* "resident of the hilly areas of Washington, Mobile, or Clarke Counties, by fanciful resemblance to the Acadians of Louisiana."
> *dog fly* "a biting fly that arrives in the fall."

fiddle worm "a large worm up to a foot long."
flip "a slingshot made with a forked stick."
gooselock "to pick cotton ineptly so that part of the tuft is left in the boll."
guinea squat "a children's game, played in a ring."
key "used to remove a hook from a wood-burning stove."
marionette "the buffelheaded Duck."
mellow bug "a whirligig beetle having a sweetish smell."
pullet bone "a wishbone."
river shrimp "a freshwater shrimp."
rusty lizard "a fence lizard."

The geographical labels given by *DARE* are based on evidence from its survey and also on more than a century and a half of quotations taken from published works, but they may or may not be entirely definitive. Although most Alabamians will not be familiar with most terms on the list above because they are specialized ones, each item still has a story to tell, and it would be interesting to know what currency or recognition each may have. Of the fourteen items above, over half relate to flora or fauna and so may be unknown to urbanites unless they are hunters, fishers, or consumers of cookbooks, menus, or the like. Since many appear to relate mainly to the Gulf end of the state, how much more familiar would a survey find them in Mobile than in Huntsville or Gadsden? Are any of the terms changing in meaning as they become less widely known? A survey exploring specialized terminology might thus be fruitful or intriguing to pursue. This is to take nothing away from exploring the continuing livelihood of traditional Southern terms in Alabama, whether *hey!* as a familiar greeting, *y'all* versus *you all* or *you guys* to indicate second-person, and many others, each of which will have a life of its own.

As stated at the beginning, my aim has been to present a few thoughts on observing and documenting the course of Alabama speech. The prospects and possibilities are still far more numerous, but I consider my mission accomplished. More than that, I trust that my words will convince skeptics of the intrinsic interest of the subject and will suffice to show that I may have learned from gentlemen like Jim McMillan and Tom Nunnally.

NOTES

1. For a full bibliography of McMillan's publications, see Raymond and Russell (1977: xiv–xvii).

2. A typescript of this 43,000-word document is on deposit at the Alabama Department of Archives and History, in Montgomery, where there is no record of its manuscript original. John Getzen Traylor's father, Thomas G. Traylor, was born in Virginia circa 1775. John G. Traylor died in Dallas County, Alabama, near the beginning of 1850. He owned twelve slaves at the time of his death. I am grateful to Michael Ellis for extracting this information from US census records.

3. These letters are among the Benjamin Cuckworth Yancey Papers at the Southern Historical Collection, University of North Carolina at Chapel Hill.

4. An extract of this work was published in Mathews (1931).

5. This degree of documentation and accountability has been standard practice for all projects conducted under the auspices of the Linguistic Atlas of the United States and Canada.

6. Pederson et al. (1990, 1991) features many maps, showing the distribution of one or two linguistic items per map, but does not provide a comprehensive statement.

7. That is, a kiss.

Appendix A

The Sounds of English and Southern English

Readers may better enjoy this volume not only by knowing some of the working principles of linguistics regarding language variation (see Nunnally, "Exploring") but also by understanding something about the science of sound description, particularly of vowels, which are the heart of every word. This discussion covers the basics of the study of speech sounds (technically called phonetics and phonology) to help with reading the essays. It should be noted that other descriptive systems disagree on some minor points or use slightly different symbols for some sounds (see the note to Feagin's essay in this volume for her use of vowel symbols that work better to explain the Southern drawl). But it is hoped that this information will increase the accessibility of the essays that discuss sound technically.

The International Phonetic Alphabet: One Sound, One Symbol

Linguists have developed special alphabets to represent each speech sound by one, and only one, symbol. Any symbol could have been used for any sound, but because of the world dominance of Europe and the United States, the alphabet of their languages, based on the Latin alphabet, became the basis of the International Phonetic Alphabet (IPA).

Most of the IPA symbols for consonants correspond to their usual values in English, so that, for instance, the consonant symbols [m] and [t] in *mate* and *meet* look and sound familiar (the brackets [ ] around phonetic spellings distinguish them from regular letters). Several consonant sounds have special symbols, however, to exclude spellings, in English, for example, that use two letters for one sound (th, ch, ng) and that use two sounds for one letter (c, g, x) or to add sounds for which there is no spelling letter in English. These special symbols for a few English consonants include [θ] for the th- in *thin* and [ð] for the th- in *then*; [š] for the "sh" sound in *shy, sugar,* and *action,* and [ž] for the sound in the middle of *measure*; [ǰ] for the beginning and ending sound in *judge* and [č] for the ch- in *child*;

[ŋ] for the sound spelled -ng in *long* and *going,* and [ʔ] for the pause in *uh-oh.* (These are listed with key words in figure A.1. In the list I am using the phonetic symbols that most American linguists prefer. The IPA uses alternatives for some of them, such as [j] for the *y* sound in *yes.*) Each consonant symbol may be associated with a class of consonant sounds as to its place and manner of articulation in the mouth. For example, the sound [b] is 1) "bilabial," made with the "two lips," 2) a type of sound called a "stop," meaning the sound requires interruption of the airstream, and 3) "voiced," meaning the vocal chords vibrate when [b] is produced (see below for more on voicing). This appendix will not fully explain the features of consonants, as it is not necessary for reading this volume, but the chart (figure A.1) provides basic information for those who are interested (see the web sources in appendix C for further study).

Unfortunately for English speakers, the IPA symbols for vowels do not correspond to most vowel spellings in English. They look the same but do not represent the same sounds. The IPA symbols [ɑ], [e], [i], etc., represent the vowel-spelling sounds of European languages such as German, French, and Spanish; that is, [ɑ], [e], [i] represent the sounds "ah, ay, ee." Therefore, we must "unlearn" our normal equation of the IPA *symbols* [ɑ], [e], [i] with our familiar *letters* that "say" the so-called long and short sounds found in, for example, the words *mate, mat, Pete, pet, light, lit.* Basically, it means learning to read all over again. The trick is not letting the IPA vowel symbols deceive us when we read the transcriptions [met] and [mit] (and if you just read these transcribed words as *met* and *mitt* instead of *mate* and *meet,* you now see what I mean. As I warned my students, "Don't be seduced by spelling!").

The International Phonetic Alphabet also fixes the problematic practice in English teaching of calling completely different vowel sounds by the same name plus the designation "short" or "long." For example, when learning to read, we are taught that the vowels in *mat* and *mate* are "short a" in *mat* and "long a" in *mate.* In fact, length of the sound (how many milliseconds it takes to utter it) has nothing to do with differentiating these sounds. The so-called short a and long a are formed in very different parts of the mouth and therefore sound completely different (see the vowel chart below). Do we have long and short vowels, that is, do we hold some longer than others? In a sense, yes, but not to tell different vowels apart. For example, the IPA symbol [æ] represents (or spells) the so-called short a vowel sound in *mat* and *mad.* In normal pronunciation, the [æ] in *mad* is actually held longer than the [æ] in *mat,* but the sound is still basically the same, whether held longer [mæ:d] or shorter [mæt] (the colon means the sound is held longer, or lengthened). In the same way, the IPA symbol [e] spells our "long a" sound in both *mate* and *made,* though the [e] sound in *made* [me:d] is also held longer than the [e] sound in *mate* [met].

It takes us longer to say *mad* and *made* than to say *mat* and *mate* because of the sounds that follow the vowels, the consonants [d] and [t]. This phenomenon brings us to another important linguistic concept: voicing. We say that [t], a voiceless consonant, does not affect the length (in milliseconds) of [æ] in [mæt], while

ENGLISH CONSONANTS

	Bilabial	Labio-dental	Inter-dental	Alveolar	Alveo-Palatal	Velar	Glottal
Stops--voiceless	p			t		k	ʔ
voiced	b			d		g	
Fricatives--voiceless		f	θ	s	š		h
voiced		v	ð	z	ž		
Affricates--voiceless					č		
voiced					ǰ		
Nasals	m			n		ŋ	
Liquids--lateral				l			
retroflex				r			
Glides	w				y		

Key Words for Special Symbols
[ʔ] uh-oh   [ž] measure
[θ] thin   [č] child
[ð] then   [ǰ] judge
[š] shy   [ŋ] long

Figure A.1. Consonant articulation by manner and location, IPA symbols (chart adapted from www.wright.edu/~henry.limouze/ling/conson.htm; used by permission of Henry S. Limouze).

[d], a voiced consonant, does add length to the [æ] in [mæ:d]. But since you can hear both the [t] and the [d], how, you may ask, is [t] voiceless?

Voiced and Voiceless Sounds

Voicing doesn't have to do with audibility but with whether the vocal cords are vibrating during the production of a sound. The easiest way to understand voiced and unvoiced sounds is to put your finger on your Adam's apple (larynx) or use your fingers to close your ears and then alternate making the sounds sssss and zzzzzz. The extra vibration or buzzing you will feel and hear with zzzzzz is the vibrating of the vocal chords because [z] is a voiced sound. All our vowels are voiced, as are the consonant sounds that we spell with the letters m, n, ng, l, r. But the other consonants are either voiced like [z] or voiceless like [s]. This distinction is of major importance, since voicing is the only difference between many pairs of sounds, as our demonstration with zzzz and sssss showed. For one more illustration, slowly say the words *lazy* [lezi] and *lacy* [lesi] to feel that [z] and [s] are made in the same place in the mouth and in the same manner except for the voicing, the vocal-chord vibrating, of [z].

Therefore, consonant sounds separate into voiced and voiceless groups. But since some groups of consonants are more vowel-like in their production (e.g., [l], [m], [n]), the terms *vowel* and *consonant* fail to address the voiced/voiceless contrast adequately. Linguists have found it more helpful to classify language sounds into two classes. **Sonorants** are all the vowels and those vowel-like consonant sounds that can "continue to sound" almost like vowels (like llllll, mmmmmm, nnnnn). **Obstruents** are the rest of the consonants, usually forming pairs of sounds that differ only in being voiced or voiceless, as seen above with the [s] and [z] in *lacy* and *lazy*. The obstruents include three types of consonants: sounds called *stops* that cannot be continued (like the voiceless/voiced pairs [p]/[b] and [t]/[d]) and sounds called *fricatives* and *affricates* that can continue to sound but set up air turbulence in the mouth (like the voiceless/voiced pairs [f]/[v] and [s]/[z]) (you can review the consonant chart in figure A.1 above to see where these are made in the mouth).

Putting Words in Your Mouth, Literally

Understanding sonorants and obstruents is important for understanding a major feature of Southern English Dialects, the pronunciation of *lie*, *line*, and (for only some Southern speakers) *like*, as something like "lah," "lahn," "lahk," to be discussed below. For now, however, we return to vowels and the IPA. The IPA symbols for vowels of English (including the two-sound, or "gliding," vowels called diphthongs) are listed in table A.1 along with a theme word to cue pronunciation and some additional information. Some of these vowels are produced with much more tension of the mouth and tongue muscles, so that the descriptors *tense* and *lax* help identify sounds. Also, some vowels produced in the back of the mouth are accompanied by lip-rounding. Finally, diphthongs start with a sound produced in one place in the mouth and move (glide) to another sound, necessitating a two-part description.

The vowel symbols can be arranged in a diagram to suggest their points of production in the mouth. Figure A.2, a typical chart, suggests a cross section of the mouth cavity as if one is looking at a face in left profile. Each vowel symbol appears in relation to the position of the jaw and tongue for production of the sound, identified by the height of the tongue and jaw (high, mid, low) and where the tongue is forming the sound, the front, center, or back of the mouth.

The illustrations in figure A.3 place the two-part vowels, or diphthongs, [aɪ] [aʊ] [ɔɪ] in the vowel chart (suggesting placement in the mouth) to show three things; where these sounds begin, the path of the "glide" denoted by the arrow, and where they end.

Now that we have presented the system, it is time to remember that these descriptions of vowel placements and sounds are standardized—a homogenized fiction, as it were. First, some speakers of American English don't use all the sounds

Table A.1. The vowels of English, symbols, transcription, features

IPA symbol	Theme word	Transcription	Tense, Lax, or Non-applicable	Rounded Lips
[i]	*leek*	[lik]	Tense	No
[ɪ]	*lick*	[lɪk]	Lax	No
[e]	*late*	[let]	Tense	No
[ɛ]	*let*	[lɛt]	Lax	No
[æ]	*lack*	[læk]	N/A	No
[ʌ]*	*above*	[əbʌv]	N/A	No
[ə]*	*above*	[əbʌv]	N/A	No
[a]	So. English *lie*	[la]	N/A	No
[u]	*Luke*	[luk]	Tense	Yes
[ʊ]	*look*	[lʊk]	Lax	Yes
[o]	*low*	[lo]	Tense	Yes
[ɔ]**	*law*	[lɔ]	Lax	Yes
[ɑ]	*lock*	[lɑk]	N/A	No

Dipththong vowels (American English)***

IPA symbol	Theme word	Transcription	Glide Movement in Mouth
[aɪ]	*like*	[laɪk]	low central [a] to high front [ɪ]
[aʊ]	*loud*	[laʊd]	low central [a] to high back [ʊ]
[ɔɪ]	*loin*	[lɔɪn]	mid back [ɔ] to high front [ɪ]

Notes:

*[ʌ] (called caret) and [ə] (called schwa) are basically the same sound, a middle-of-the-mouth "uh" sound (often called the neutral vowel), but [ʌ] is used to transcribe stressed syllables, while [ə] is used to transcribe unstressed syllables, and for a good reason. [ʌ] is an actual sound that differentiates one word from another, *rug* and *rag* ([rʌg] and [ræg]), and has a limited number of spellings: <o> in *love, money, come*, etc.; <u> in *rug, munch*, etc. The schwa [ə], on the other hand, is a reduced sound found in unstressed English syllables, and it can be spelled many ways: <a> in *sofa*, <e> in *dozen*, <i> in *majority*, <o> in *symptom*. (The symbols < > are used to enclose spellings.)

**Many American dialects exhibit the "low back merger" in which [ɔ] merges with [ɑ], so that *caught* and *cot* sound the same. This merger is a change in progress and is making inroads in the South, especially in urban areas.

***Some American treatments use different phonetic spellings for these diphthongs using [j] for the front glide in [aj] and [ɔj] and [w] for the back glide in [aw]. Some scholars also write the tense vowels of American English as diphthongs, writing [i], [e], [u], and [o] as [iy], [ey], [uw], and [ow], since their research concerns gliding in general and the tongue and jaw do move in these tense vowels just as in the three diphthongs proper. Treatments of British English list up to nine diphthongs since certain vowel + -r combinations are usually diphthongs (*peer* [ɪə], *pair* [eə], *poor* [ʊə]).

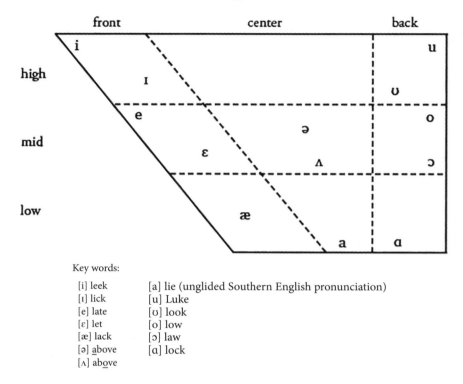

Key words:

[i] leek   [a] lie (unglided Southern English pronunciation)
[ɪ] lick   [u] Luke
[e] late   [ʊ] look
[ɛ] let   [o] low
[æ] lack   [ɔ] law
[ə] a̱bove   [ɑ] lock
[ʌ] abo̱ve

Figure A.2. Location of vowel production in the mouth and key words for sounds of IPA symbols

on this chart. Many Northern, Western, and urban Southern speakers speak forms of English that have undergone the "low back merger," that is, they pronounce [ɔ] and [ɑ] the same, so that *caught* and *cot* are both pronounced as *cot*, using the [ɑ] sound. Such speakers' crows say, "Cah, cah, cah" instead of "Caw, caw, caw." We also saw above how voiced consonants like [d] tend to cause lengthening of preceding vowels in made [me:d] versus mate [met]. Other processes change one's production of vowels as well, so much so that we all produce the "same" vowel in a variety of slightly different ways. Acoustic equipment and computer programs can now graph a person's vowel production in a grid that mimics the chart of the mouth shown in figure A.2. Figure A.4 presents such a graph. Laboratory equipment plotted the vowels of an eighty-one-year-old North Carolinian male (Thomas 2001, 120). The arrows indicate the expected gliding of the three diphthongs as seen in figure A.3 above (spelled here as ai, au, and oi), but the chart shows that nondiphthong vowels glide around as well. You will notice that some of the IPA vowel symbols, such as [i] and [e] (think eee and ay), appear in more than one place, though usually near the standard placement on the vowel chart in figure A.2 above. These multiple, slightly different productions of the "same" vowel illustrate how standard

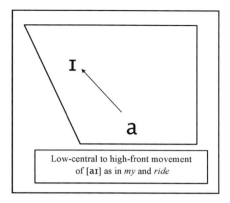

Low-central to high-front movement
of [aɪ] as in *my* and *ride*

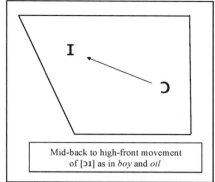

Mid-back to high-front movement
of [ɔɪ] as in *boy* and *oil*

Functional Diphthongs versus Gliding Vowels:
All the tense vowels of American English
move the tongue and the jaw. For example,
[e] as in *bait* glides up to [i], and [o] as in
hoe glides up to [u], but we have no words
that differ only by the gliding part alone
of such vowels, no pair like "hoe" versus
"hoe-uuu." However, the diphthongal vowels
in this chart are word-identifying (contrastive) sounds allowing English word pairs like
ha and *hi* [haɪ], *caw* and *coy* [kɔɪ], and *pa*
and *pow* [paʊ]

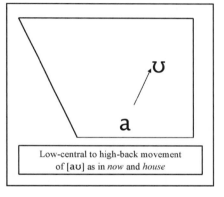

Low-central to high-back movement
of [aʊ] as in *now* and *house*

Figure A.3. Start and end positions of the three diphthongs of English

vowel charts are generalizations of data rather than reflections of reality (for more
explanation and illustrations of acoustic analysis, see Feagin's essay).

Putting Sounds in Your Head: Phonemes and Allophones

In general, the essays in this volume focus on physical sounds rather than phonological theory, but it may be helpful to present a short explanation of two important terms central to such theory: phoneme and allophone. In discussing figure A.4, I remarked that the grid shows the "same" sound in several locations, that
is, being pronounced in slightly different ways. One may well ask, how is it possible for sounds to be both the same and different? The answer to this interesting
question has to do with how our minds treat language sounds. Tackling this subject obliquely, we'll first look at how our minds treat other things that are the same
but also different.

As we experience the world around us, we learn that a dog is not a cat. These
are contrastive mental entities or categories, which I will represent as DOG and

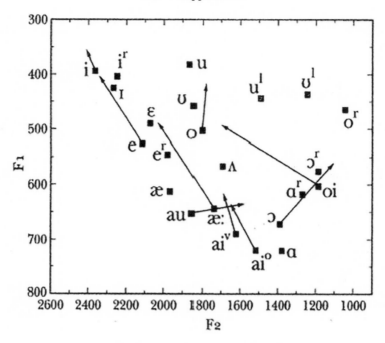

Figure A.4. Plotted vowels of eighty-one-year-old North Carolinian male (Thomas 2001, 120. Copyright 2001, the American Dialect Society. All rights reserved. Republished by permission of the copyright holder, and the present publisher, Duke University Press, www.dukeupress.edu)

CAT. But note that there is no such thing as DOG, only kinds of dogs. If I were to ask you to mentally picture DOG, you could not do so, as you would have to imagine some actual pooch, perhaps one of the varieties in figure A.5. Yet you really do know what DOG is, in spite of the fact that there is no such physical thing. You created that mental concept of DOG from all the different actual dogs you became aware of, all sharing enough of the features of dogginess to keep them separate from cattiness. They are different *dogs*, but each is equally an embodiment of the mental concept DOG. At that level of abstraction, they are the same, or to use *allo-*, a Greek word for "same," they are ALLO-DOGS. Note that once that abstract concept is part of your knowledge base, you would never say, "No, Fido is not a dog; he's a retriever." Furthermore, as hostile as our DOG concept is to our CAT concept, DOG is flexible enough to include Brutus the St. Bernard and Chico the Chihuahua without missing a beat.

Similarly, when we were acquiring our language in the first years of life, we discovered what sounds can create different words—technically, what sounds "contrast" with one another. For example, the vowel in *bit* and the vowel in *bet* are the sole differences that create these different words. Linguists say that these vowels

Figure A.5. ALLO-DOGS of the concept DOG

with the sounds [ɪ] and [ɛ] are **phonemes** of English and write them within slants, /ɪ/ and /ɛ/, to denote their phonemic status (the sounds symbolized in figure A.1 and table A.1 above constitute all the phonemes of English and could be written in / /). But as we, as children, pluck the phonemes of our language out of the air (the language spoken around us), we unconsciously come to understand that the same sound can be made in slightly differently ways. For example, consider the vowel in *bid* and *bit*. If you pause to pronounce them one after the other, you will notice that, just as we saw for *mad* and *mat* above, the [ɪ] in [bɪːd] (colon shows lengthening) is held longer than the [ɪ] in [bɪt]. Acoustic analysis would prove that they are different sounds in the sense that one is held longer (in milliseconds) than the other.

In some languages, just such a length difference in a sound creates two words, as in Finnish *taakka* "burden" and *takka* "fireplace" where [ɑː] and [ɑ] are produced the same way in the mouth but the first syllable in *taakka* is held longer: to Finnish speakers the longer-held [ɑː] and the shorter-held [ɑ] are two completely different sounds, capable of making different words by their contrast alone (Rentz 1997). If a Finn yawned while saying *takka* "fireplace," changing [ɑ] to [ɑː], she would change it into a *taakka* "burden." Yet English speakers don't think of [ɪː] in bid and [ɪ] in bit as two sounds but as one, since the two sounds [ɪː] and [ɪ] NEVER create different words. Even if I artificially prolong the [ɪ] sound in *bit* to [bɪːːːt], it is still just the word *bit*, and even if I rapidly pronounce *bid* as [bɪd] without the normally lengthened [ɪː], it is still just the word *bid*. As we acquired English, we categorized [ɪː] and [ɪ] as the same sound, though they differ slightly. The pronunciations of the vowels in *bid* and *bit*, that is, [ɪː] and [ɪ], are physically different in length, but they are also "the same" in that we don't think of them as separate sounds.

We unconsciously have grouped such slightly different sounds as versions of a sound (and we even cease to hear the physical differences). Each of these versions of the "same" sound is called an ***allophone*** ("same" + "sound"), and all the allophones taken together make up a specific mental entity, a ***phoneme***, which is an abstract, idealized sound that is different from all the other phonemes in the language. As noted above, figure A.1 and table A.1 present all the phonemes of American English. Besides using slants to enclose phonemes, like /ɪ/, linguists use brackets to enclose allophones, the physically produced versions of the phoneme, like regular-length [ɪ] in *bit* or lengthened [ɪː] in *bid*.

To pull the discussions together, we see that DOG is, therefore, just like a phoneme, an abstract entity known to the mind but expressed only in the various physical manifestations of DOG, such as poodle or golden retriever, each of which might be termed an ALLO-DOG in analogy with an allophone. In the same way, the phoneme /ɪ/ gives rise to allophones [ɪː] in *bid* and [ɪ] in *bit* during the vocal production of words. Since we must choose some symbol for the phoneme, the basic symbol is used for identification purposes only, as in /ɪ/, but that idealized /ɪ/, to be pronounced, must manifest itself as one of its allophones, [ɪː] or [ɪ] or others (and for some Southerners, "ee-uh" as in "That dog bee-uht me"; see Southern Vowel Shift below and Feagin's and Allbritten's essays in this volume). We barely scratch the surface of phonology here, but this explanation may help below when we treat the Southern English allophones of the phoneme /ai/ (*my eye* sounding similar to "mah ah" and *rice* to "rahce").

Sound Change within Regions

With all the variation cropping up in an individual's speech (review figure A.4) and with all individuals having to re-create the language in their own minds from what is spoken around them (i.e., having to acquire it), is it any wonder that all languages slowly change over time? At present, two major changes in American English vowel systems are well underway. One set of changes, called the Northern Cities Chain Shift, centers in American cities near the Great Lakes, and another set of changes, called the Southern Vowel Shift, is occurring over large areas of the South. (We will return to the Southern Vowel Shift below.) While one might expect Americans to talk more alike from the influence of the communications media, these vowel shifts are moving the dialects of Northerners and Southerners farther apart, not closer together.

But an earlier vowel change differentiating Southern and non-Southern Englishes is generally recognized as the phonological (sound) feature of Southern English that stands out the most: the pronunciation of the diphthong [aɪ] as the single sound [aː] (*lie* pronounced something like "lah," as mentioned above).

The Confederate A: From Diphthong to Monophthong

The [aɪ] as [aː] Southern speech feature, discussed repeatedly in the essays in this volume and in almost any discussion of Southern speech, deserves special attention. As mentioned above, the sound often called "long i" is actually a type of vowel sound called a diphthong (from Greek for *di* "two" + *phthong* "sound") and symbolized phonetically as [aɪ] (phonemically, it is often symbolized as /ai/). Say "eye" carefully and slowly in Standard English while looking in a mirror and you will both hear, feel, and see your jaw and tongue move (or "glide") from a low position for the first sound to a higher jaw and tongue position for the second sound. Now, say "eye" carefully again, but do not let your tongue or jaw move past the first part of the sound. You have just "smoothed," or "unglided," or "monophthongized" [aɪ] and turned it into the single sound [aː], a *monophthong* (Greek for one sound), and if you listen carefully, you will probably also hear that you did not say the "ah" sound of ah. Southern English revels in this variation of [aɪ] that reduces or even deletes the second part of the diphthong.

This monophthongized or unglided [aɪ], that is, [aɪ] pronounced as [aː], is so familiar as a hallmark of Southern speech that it has even been called the "Confederate a." But the name "Confederate a" is a misnomer in that research has suggested that its broad adoption across the Southern states occurred *after*, not before, the Confederacy. It is one of the features, along with the merger of /ɪ/ and /ɛ/ before nasal sounds (e.g., *pen* and *pin* both pronounced as [pɪn]), that belongs to the era of the New South (see Nunnally and Bailey in this volume; Bailey 1997; and Schneider 2003) and that is a feature (as I discussed in Nunnally, "Exploring," in this volume) of the South's "linguistic secession."

As sociolinguistics has shown us, the occurrence of a linguistic variable is more often a case of frequency rather than absence versus presence. Pronouncing the phrase *my eye*, for example, a native Alabamian like me might say [maː aː], [maɪ aɪ], [maɪ aː], or [maː aɪ]! That is why results are usually presented as percentages in the essays in this volume examining the variation between Standard English [aɪ] and Southern English [aː] (and in Feagin's essay on the Southern drawl). In other words, when a number of words containing [aɪ] are present in a speech sample, we ask, in what percentage did the speaker use the monophthongized [aː] form instead of the [aɪ] form? (To phrase the question phonologically using the discussion above, the English sound system contains the phoneme /ai/. Besides realizing this abstract, contrastive sound entity with the diphthongal pronunciation, that is, as the allophone [aɪ], most speakers of Southern English have acquired an unglided or monophthongized allophone, that is, [aː], which they employ variably.)

The question becomes more interesting when researchers try to find out what correlates with the [aː] usage in two areas: the sound characteristics of the words themselves (linguistic variables), and the characteristics of the speakers, such as socioeconomic level, educational attainment, ethnicity, gender, and regional affili-

Table A.2. Monophthongization of *ride* and *right* in three dialects

Dialect	[aɪ] before voiced obstruent as in the word *ride*	[aɪ] before voiceless obstruent as in the word *right*
Non-Southern	[raɪd]	[raɪt]
Coastal Southern	[ra:d]	[raɪt]
Inland Southern	[ra:d]	[rat]

ation (nonlinguistic variables). The authors of several essays in this volume present examples of the interaction of a speech feature with linguistic and non-linguistic variables (see the essays by Nunnally and Bailey, Feagin, Allbritten, Spence, and Doxsey).

Particularly, one linguistic variable of supreme importance for understanding why [aɪ] is or is not pronounced [a:] concerns whether [aɪ] comes before a "voiced" or "voiceless" sound, bringing us back to our terms *sonorant* and *obstruent* and to the major linguistic divide of Alabama dialects into Coastal/Lowland Southern and Inland/Upland Southern (see essays by Davies and Nunnally and Bailey). For various reasons, such as shifting to a more formal style, Southerners may not monophthongize [aɪ]. But if they do monophthongize [aɪ] to [a:], Alabama's Coastal Southern dialect speakers and its Inland Southern dialect speakers play by a slightly different set of rules. Whether the sound following [aɪ] is voiced or voiceless (as discussed above) will influence speakers of Coastal Southern but not speakers of Inland Southern. Table A.2 divides the question of [aɪ] monophthongization to [a:] into three options, non-Southern English, Coastal Southern, and Inland Southern, using the words *ride* and *right*. Both *ride* and *right* end in obstruents, not sonorants, but note that in *ride* [raɪd] the [aɪ] precedes the voiced obstruent [d] whereas in *right* [raɪt] the [aɪ] precedes the voiceless obstruent [t].

As the essays by Bernstein (2006) and by Davies, Nunnally and Bailey, and Doxsey in this volume bear witness, Alabama speakers of Coastal Southern often assign lower social status to speakers who monophthongize [aɪ] before voiceless obstruents (e.g., "white rice" pronounced as [wa:t ra:s]). The pronunciation may be called a shibboleth, that is, a use of language that distinguishes one group from another (see the story in Judges 12:6). But since two-term Governor Bob Riley (2003–2010), who speaks Inland Southern ([ra:d] [rat]), defeated Coastal Southern speakers ([ra:d] [raɪt]) in both his campaigns, it is anyone's guess as to whether [rat] is increasing in prestige throughout the state.

THE SOUTHERN VOWEL SHIFT

While [aɪ] monophthongization may be the major differentiating feature of Southern (and thus Alabama) English, pronunciations of other interconnected vowels in a major sound shift mentioned above are also adding to the linguistic distinctiveness of the South. This sound shift, called the Southern Vowel Shift by researchers, occasions comment in many of the chapters in this volume and is the major topic

The square approximates the mouth in cross section as viewed from the left side. The arrows DO NOT denote tongue movement during production (as in diphthong glides) but the new places to which vowel production has migrated within the mouth in connection with this sound shift.

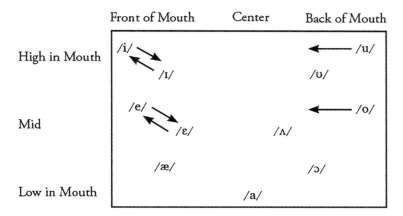

As the diagram shows, there are a number of shifts among the vowels:

- the tense-vowel sound /i/ in words such as *meet* is shifting back and downward to sound like muh-eet
- the lax-vowel sound /ɪ/ in words such as *mitt* is shifting upward and forward, often becoming diphthongized, as is common among tense vowels in Standard English to sound like meeyuht
- the tense-vowel sound /e/ in words such as *mate* is shifting back and downward to sound like mah-ate
- the lax-vowel sound /ɛ/ in words such as *met* is shifting upward and forward, becoming diphthongized, as is common among tense vowels in Standard English to sound like may-et
- the tense-vowel sounds /u/ and /o/ in words such as *moot* and *mote* are shifting forward to be pronounced without the lips being rounded to sound like muh-oot and muh-oat

Notes:
1. This chart does not distinguish between low-back [ɑ] and low-central [a], crucial to understanding the Southern monophthongized /ai/ diphthong. See Davies and appendix A for more information.
2. The chart's enclosure of vowel symbols in / / rather than [ ] denotes important linguistic status of the sounds but can be ignored for this survey without harm. For help with the phonetic symbols and the terms such as tense vowel, refer to discussions in appendix A.

—Adapted and expanded by Thomas Nunnally from the Language Samples Project, Southern Vowel Shift, http://www.ic.arizona.edu/~lsp/Features/SVS.html. (Courtesy of Norma Mendoza-Denton, Sean Hendricks, and the Regents of the University of Arizona.) Used and adapted by permission.

Figure A.6. The Southern Vowel Shift

in Allbritten's essay. Figure A.6 will help you gather the main points as well as tune your ears to listening for evidence of it in the language varieties you hear every day.

Although language variations besides the phonological ones that I have discussed distinguish Southern and non-Southern Englishes and give Alabamians their own voices (see the essays by Davies and Brammer), nothing matches the power of pronunciation to mark out allegiances. I hope, therefore, that this overview has offered sufficient insight for comprehension of the phonological research findings appearing within the volume.

Thomas E. Nunnally

Appendix B

A Glossary of Select Linguistic Terms

NOTE: This glossary presents definitions of technical linguistic terms appearing in the volume. Definitions were written by comparing the editor's understanding of the terms in their contexts to standard definitions found in multiple sources in print and on the web and adapted as necessary.

accent—An imprecise term meaning 1) the marking of a syllable with prominence (e.g., the accent is on the first syllable in the word *apple*), 2) speech marked with a cluster of recognizable features carried over from one's native language (e.g., speaking English with a French accent) or 3) (often used dismissively) a dialect varying considerably from the conception of the standard form of a language (e.g., speaking with a Southern accent). See **stress**.

accommodation—The speaker's attempt, largely unconscious, to sound more like the person he or she is conversing with.

acoustic formants—Bands of resonance within a sound that can be illustrated by acoustic measurements. These formants give vowels the qualities that differentiate them to our hearing, especially the F_1, the first, and F_2, the second, formants.

amplitude—The height and depth of a sound wave as graphed by acoustic equipment. The greater the amplitude, the more energy in the production of the wave.

apparent-time analysis—A method for studying language change by comparing the language of people of different ages at the same point in time. For example, in 2000 one might compare pronunciations of eighty-year-olds (b. 1920) and thirty-year-olds (b. 1970). The assumption is that the eighty-year-olds' pronunciations have remained basically the same since their youth. If the thirty-year-olds' pronunciations are different, it is assumed, all other things being equal, that the difference reflects language change within the fifty-year period. For instance, if for the word *farmer* an eighty-year-old upper-class man says "fahmah" while a thirty-year-old upper-class man of similar background says "farmer," the implication is that traditional Southern r-less speech (not pronouncing the r sound after vowels) is giving way to r-full speech. See **change in progress**.

audience design—The concept that the speaker's understanding of the communicative needs of his or her audience is a major factor in the choices made about the features of the communication.

bidialectal—Descriptive of a person able to function well in more than one variety of a language, for example, Standard English and African American Vernacular English.

central glide—A gliding or movement of the tongue during vowel production such that the first sound of the vowel shifts or glides to a sound produced in the mid-center of the mouth, the schwa, as in the word *them* pronounced as "thee-yum" [ðiəm]; also called schwa glide.

change in progress—An assumption that when linguistic data is collected from older and younger speakers and analyzed to show a clear difference based on the ages of the speakers, the change is change in progress. For example, suppose urban, upper-middle-class Alabamians over fifty say "caught" and "cot" differently, but urban, upper-middle-class Alabamians under twenty-five say both words as "cot." This generational difference, all other things being equal, would denote a change in progress called the "low back vowel merger." See **apparent-time analysis**.

code-switching/shifting, style-shifting—A speaker's changing of his or her variety of language or dialect (a "code") for specific purposes. In bilingual countries, one language may be deemed appropriate for work and business while another may be deemed appropriate for domestic communication. Similarly, a speaker may shift to different styles or dialects of one language as associated with topics or uses.

cohort—A generational group as defined in demographics, statistics, or certain kinds of research.

conditioning factors—Influences that cause variation in language usage. These may be linguistic, that is, conditioning factors arising from "inside" the language itself, or social, that is, conditioning factors arising from "outside" the language per se. For example, in the Southern English of many speakers, the sound "eh" is linguistically conditioned to be pronounced "ih" when it occurs before the sounds m and n, as in *pen* being pronounced just like *pin*. Use of double negatives ("I ain't got no money"), however, is a product of one's socioeconomic background and speech community, and thus is socially conditioned.

corpus—A collected "body" of data for linguistic research designed to yield meaningful results when analyzed, for example, a set of taped interviews or a collection of texts of an era and type.

covert prestige—Assignment of prestige not to standard forms (overt prestige), as is expected, but to nonstandard forms because of their power to act as in-group markers and to invoke pride and solidarity among nonstandard speakers, to show nonconformity, or to identify with "cool" groups (e.g., use of AAVE "What up?" among middle-class white youngsters as a greeting).

creole—When not capitalized, not a specific language such as Louisiana Creole but a native language (i.e., a language that children acquire in the normal way) that developed from a pidgin or trade language formed from an elementary form of two or more languages mixed together for simplified communication. See **pidgin**.

deictic, adj.; deixis, n.—Concept for words in discourse that provide orientation or "point" outside the discourse in reference to person (*You* are a friend of *ours*), time (I went *yesterday*), or space (Put the book *over there*) or point inside the discourse to another part of it (As I said *above*).

dialect—A term relating to a form of a language. In linguistic understanding, every form of a language is a dialect, and a language is composed of the sum of its dialects. In societal practice, however, one dialectal form, that of the powerful and influential, is perceived as the correct or "real" language and is enhanced in its written form with additional normative features; the other dialectal forms are judged as more standard or as less standard, compared to that now nonspoken standard variety. Besides national standards, languages develop regional standards that also allow deviation from the privileged variety of a region to be regarded negatively as "dialects."

diphthong, n.; diphthongize, v.—A two-sound (complex) vowel written with two IPA symbols, the starting sound and the ending sound. American English is said to have three contrastive diphthongs, the so-called long i in *pie* [aɪ], the sound in *pout*, [aʊ], and the sound in *point*, [ɔɪ]; that is, their pronunciation is distinctive enough to contrast with other vowel sounds, making the hearer able to distinguish one word from another, as in *light* versus *lot*, *loud* versus *laud*, and *roil* versus *role*. Other two-part sounds are also sometimes called diphthongs because of the presence of glides, such as the "long o" in *home*, but these phonetic diphthongs are not contrastive. Whether one says "hohm," "ho-uum," "hah-uum" or "heh-uum," the word is still *home*. Different linguistic traditions represent the three contrastive or phonemic diphthongs with slightly different phonetic symbols (e.g., [ai], [ay], [aj] variously for "long i"), but each representation still shows the complex vowel starting with the tongue at one position (making one sound) and ending by gliding to another position (making the second sound). To make a one-sound vowel into a two-sound vowel is to diphthongize it, as in the drawled pronunciation of *yes* as "yay-yus," but this does not create a contrastive diphthong as explained above. See **monophthong**. See appendix A for a basic introduction to phonology.

environment—In linguistics, the sounds surrounding another sound that influence its production; for example, preceding environment is important for conditioning the lack of consonantal pronunciation of -r by some speakers (e.g., "fahmah" for *farmer*) who do say -r if it starts a word, and following environment is important for conditioning the monophthongization (smoothing) of the "long i" sound [ai] into [a:] for some speakers ("mahn" for *mine*).

formant—A frequency at which the vocal tract resonates. The F1 formant tends to shift with the height of the tongue body, with a low F1 signifying a high tongue body. The F2 formant tends to shift with the backness of the tongue body, with the difference between F2 and F1 indicating relative backness of the tongue body. A low value (F2 minus F1) signifies that the body of the tongue is located in the back of the mouth.

fricatives—Hissy consonant sounds formed by near closures of parts of the vocal tract to make turbulence, i.e., in English the sounds [f], [v], [θ], [ð], [š], [ž], [h] in *foe, vie, thin, thy, shoo, leisure*, and *he*. Other than for [h], they are in voiced and voiceless pairs, differentiated by whether the vocal fold (or vocal cord) vibrates during the production of the sound, giving it "voice." See appendix A for a basic introduction to phonology.

glide—The second part of a diphthong, as the tongue moves from one sound to the other. Most glides are offglides, following the major sound of the vowel, as in /ai/ ("ah-ee"), but some glides are onglides, like the /i/ before /u/ in the Southern pronunciation of *tune* ("tee-OON"). Offglides may move to the high-front part of the mouth (*hi,* "hah-ee"), the mid-back of the mouth (*how,* "hah-ow"), or the central part of the mouth (*them* when drawled as "thee-yum").

grammatical—In linguistics, a judgment formed by a native speaker's intuition as to whether an utterance in the language is well-formed or defective. This technical use of the term is not the common meaning gleaned from schoolbook grammars or artificially created rules such as "do not split an infinitive."

Great Vowel Shift—A systematic shifting of the long vowels (in milliseconds) of Middle English into different sounding vowels. The high back and high front vowels became diphthongs, while the other long vowels moved higher and sometimes fronter in the mouth, for example, the vowel in the word *sweet* was "ay" for Chaucer (d. 1400) but "ee" by the time of Shakespeare (d. 1616).

idiolect—The personal speech variety of an individual.

intonation—The rising and/or falling of pitch accompanying a sentence or word (a suprasegmental feature), for example, in English the rising of the voice to a higher pitch at the end of an utterance when asking a question, or when talking in California "upspeak" or "uptalk".

jargon—The specialized, usually technical vocabulary of a trade or subject area such as medicine, computer engineering, literary criticism, and so on. Jargon contrasts with the generally nontechnical terms of young in-group communication, that is, slang.

lexical, adj.; lexicon, n.—Having to do with the word-stock of a language, its lexemes, and with external lists of words and definitions (i.e., a dictionary) or internalized knowledge of words (i.e., a mental lexicon).

lingua franca—Any language that is adopted for purposes of common communication by speakers of various languages. For example, many of the Native American tribes of the Southeast such as the Alabama used Mobilian Trade Language for communication within the region.

linguistics—The scientific study of language, containing many subareas.

liquids—Consonants formed by the tongue in the middle of the mouth and having vowel-like qualities, thus in English the lateral liquid sound [l] and the bunched or retroflex liquid [r]. See appendix A for a basic introduction to phonology.

metalinguistic—Language that specifically talks about linguistics, as when interviewed people discuss their own dialects.

monophthong, n; monophthongize, v.; monophthongization, n.—A one-sound vowel written with a single IPA symbol is a monophthong. Monophthongization is the process of dropping or greatly reducing (monophthongizing) the second sound, or glide, of a diphthong, especially in the Southern English pronunciation of [aɪ] as a lengthened [a:] so that *ride* sounds much like "rahd." See **diphthong**.

morphemes—The smallest meaningful units of a language. All words contain at least one morpheme, but not every morpheme is a word. The types of morphemes of English include lexical, grammatical, and derivational morphemes (prefixes and suffixes). For example, the word *king* is a content or lexical morpheme; *kings* contains two morphemes, the lexical morpheme *king*, and the grammatical morpheme "plural" expressed as the sound z (though spelled with an s); *kingly* also contains two morphemes, the lexical morpheme *king* and -*ly*, a derivational morpheme, in this case a suffix, that derives adjectives from nouns.

nasals—Sounds produced by closing off all or part of the mouth so that the sound proceeds mainly from the nose; in English the nasals are [m], formed by stopping sound with the lips, [n], formed by stopping sound in the middle of the mouth, and [ŋ] (spelled -ng), formed by stopping sound at the back of the mouth. See appendix A for a basic introduction to phonology.

observer's paradox—A problem faced by field researchers whereby the presence of observers of language changes the linguistic context and thus possibly the language data collected.

obstruent—In English a large subclass of consonants in which air flow is obstructed, as opposed to the sonorants, the unobstructed consonants [l], [r], [m], [n], and [ŋ], and all the vowels. See appendix A for a basic introduction to phonology.

patois—A nonstandard local dialect, especially used for dialects of French other than Parisian French taken as Standard.

Phonology, n.; phonological, adj. —Branch of linguistics dealing with the study of sounds of languages; also, the part of a language dealing with its sound system, its phonology. See appendix A for a basic introduction to phonology.

pidgin—A simplified language developed from two languages in contact for basic communication; when a pidgin becomes elaborated and is adopted as a native language, it has become a **creole**.

pragmatics—The linguistic study of how meaning is created and decoded in the three-way context of the speaker, the hearer, and the formulation of the message.

prevoiceless and prevoiced—Descriptive of a sound occurring before a voiceless sound or a voiced sound. See **voiced and voiceless**. See appendix A for a basic introduction to phonology.

r-full and r-less speech—Also called rhotic and nonrhotic speech, it is not a reference to lack of all r's in a dialect but to the presence (r-fullness) or absence (r-lessness) of r pronounced as an "rrr" sound in certain environments, predominantly when it occurs after a vocalic (vowel) sound. Received Pronunciation in Great Britain is r-less (*lord* pronounced as *laud*, *here* as "hee-yah"), as are traditional plantation Southern and New England speech. Irish English and most forms of American English are r-full.

real-time analysis—As opposed to apparent-time analysis, linguistic investigation of language change based on language samples collected at different times, for example, tape recordings made in the 1950s and in the 1990s.

segmental—Having to do with the individual sounds or "segments" that make up words

semantic—Having to do with meaning rather than sound (phonology) or grammar (morphology and syntax). Semantics is the branch of linguistics that investigates meaning.

shibboleth—A language usage that differentiates a speaker from other speakers, usually with negative connotations of otherness (see the Book of Judges, chapter 12 in the Bible for the origin of this expression); for example, "boid" for *bird* would be a shibboleth for identifying a stereotypical speaker from the Bronx in New York City.

sociolinguistics—Study of language in relation to society, especially research that correlates particulars of language use with social characteristics of the users; typically, sociolinguists study the correlation of linguistic variables, for example, the use of *-ing* versus *-in* to end verbs such as *walking*, with social factors such as age, socioeconomic class, region, ethnicity, and education.

standard variety (often capitalized)—The dialect of a language that is held as the correct form, usually derived from the dialect of speakers who hold the power and prestige within a speech community.

stress—Also called **accent**, the extra volume or pulse given to a syllable in a word or group of words; thus the emphasis on the first syllable in *lively* but on the second syllable in *alive*.

style-shift—See **code-switch**.

suprasegmental—Having to do with features such as stress, tone, and pitch added to the segments (individual sounds) of words, for example, the rising of the pitch on the last word of a question is a suprasegmental feature, whereas the words of the question are made up of phonetic segments.

syllabary—A writing system that uses symbols to represent commonly occurring syllables rather than single sounds (as an alphabet does), used for languages that construct words out of a limited set of syllables, such as Tsalagi.

tautosyllabic—Referring to sounds occurring within the same syllable, that is, in the word *hit* [h], [ɪ], and [t] are tautosyllabic.

vocal tract—The physical organs used to produce speech, that is, lips, teeth, alveolar ridge, (hard) palate, soft palate, uvula, upper throat, voice box (larynx), tongue tip, tongue blade, tongue body, tongue root.

voiced and voiceless—A sound quality determined by whether the vocal folds or cords are vibrating when a sound is made. Consonants in English are usually in pairs, made essentially in the same way except for "voicing"; thus, for example, the difference in the beginning sounds of the fricative pairs like *fie* and *vie*, the affricates *cheer* and *jeer*, and stop pairs like *tab* and *dab*. See appendix A for a basic introduction to phonology.

Appendix C

Web Sources for Further Study

Davies's essay in this volume provides an annotated list of collateral readings, and the references at the end of the volume provide bibliographical information for citations throughout the book, most of which are print items. Although such sources are essential for research, many helpful linguistic websites exist for the nonspecialist. For example, Wikipedia (wikipedia.org) has information on just about any linguistic question that one can imagine, though one must be cautious regarding the accuracy of every article.[1] The sites discussed below (which omit Wikipedia, both because of the ease of searching it for the topics and in favor of less anonymously created sites) allow further insight into topics in this volume. To list online sites in a printed book brings with it an element of futility (if not irony), because of the tumult of cyberspace. Should specific links become nonfunctioning, the topic areas that are framed below will allow searching for alternatives.

Overviews of Linguistics and Dialects

An excellent nontechnical guide to linguistics in relation to American English is the website based on the PBS series, *Do You Speak American?*: www.pbs.org/speak/. Particularly helpful in conjunction with the essays in this volume are these segments:

Sociolinguistics Basics: www.pbs.org/speak/speech/sociolinguistics/sociolinguistics/
Standard English: www.pbs.org/speak/seatosea/standardamerican/
American Varieties: www.pbs.org/speak/seatosea/americanvarieties/
Rful Southern (far-mer versus fah-muh): www.pbs.org/speak/seatosea/americanvarieties/southern/
Language Prejudice: www.pbs.org/speak/speech/prejudice/
Drawl or Nothin' (Texas accent): www.pbs.org/speak/seatosea/americanvarieties/texan/drawl/

Power of Prose, sub area Voices of the South: www.pbs.org/speak/seatosea/
powerprose/south/

To hear speakers of American English and other national varieties of English
and speakers of other languages, see these links:

http://csumc.wisc.edu/AmericanLanguages/english/eng_us
http://web.ku.edu/idea/

Much closer to home are two episodes on streaming video of the Alabama Public Television series "Journey Proud," one on the speech of South Alabamians and
the other on the speech of North Alabamians. These shows are direct outgrowths
of the Alabama Folklife Association's project that launched the collaboration of
scholars that resulted in this book. Dr. Anna Head Spence, author of an essay in
this volume, joins the host of "Journey Proud," anthropologist Joey Brackner, to
travel east and west and north and south over the state to interview Alabamians
about the way they talk. Readers who have spent time with this book will especially enjoy the episodes on language, but they will also bring linguistic insight to
any other episodes of "Journey Proud" that they watch as they hear Alabamians
talk about Alabama's folkways. Episodes can be found at the Journey Proud link:

https://video.aptv.org/show/journey-proud/

AFRICAN AMERICAN (VERNACULAR) ENGLISH
AND THE EBONICS CONTROVERSY (BASIC)

Jack Sidnell has created a site about African American English that provides a
brief, accessible starting point for learning about lexical (vocabulary), phonological (sound), and grammatical features. The site is currently part of the larger site
Language Varieties.

https://www.hawaii.edu/satocenter/langnet/definitions/aave.html

The Library of Congress *American Memory* collection includes digitalized recordings of twenty-three former slaves interviewed in the 1930s and 1940s. Alabamians may now hear the actual voices of Alabama ex-slaves: Alice Gaston of Gee's
Bend, Isom Mosely of Gee's Bend, and Joe McDonald of Livingston.

http://memory.loc.gov/ammem/collections/voices/index.html

Additional internet resources on AAE include a site from which I quoted Walt
Wolfram in Nunnally, "Exploring," John Baugh's page in *Do You Speak American?*,
and the links Baugh provides therein.

http://linguistlist.org/topics/ebonics/
www.pbs.org/speak/seatosea/americanvarieties/AAVE/ebonics/#baugh

Technically Advanced Sites

For treatments of varieties of English at a more technical level than those in *Do You Speak American?*, visit the *Language Samples Project* website *Varieties of English*, under development at the Anthropology Department of the University of Arizona. Varieties listed include African American English, American Indian English, British English, Canadian English, Chicano English, Northeast US English, and Southern States English. The sites for the varieties listed are in various states of completion and seem to be mainly if not completely devoted to sound (phonological) differences. The section on British English is especially informative for speakers of American English.

www.ic.arizona.edu/~lsp/main.html

The Child Phonology Laboratory at the University of Alberta, Canada, has created an excellent online survey of the Phonological Features of African American Vernacular English (AAVE). Two strengths include a comparison of the scope of each linguistic feature, that is, whether the feature is found in other varieties of English, as is often the case, and an updating of the list of AAVE sound features using recent studies. As the authors explain, "Most commonly referenced descriptions of AAVE phonology are based on data collected in the 1960s from adolescents in northern urban areas. . . . As a result of the dynamic nature of spoken language, these oft-cited descriptions may no longer be accurate for AAVE speakers today or for AAVE speakers in different regions of the US. Using existing literature from sociolinguistics and child language, along with our own data from Memphis AAVE-speaking children and adults and . . . data from Texas AAVE-speakers, we have compiled an updated list of AAVE phonological features [through 2001]."

www.rehabmed.ualberta.ca/spa/phonology/features.htm

The Southern Vowel Shift is a major topic for Allbritten's essay. I explain it in some detail in appendix A but simply mention the equally interesting and important sound shift taking place in the North, called the Northern Cities Shift. William Labov's "Driving Forces in Linguistic Change" treats the Northern Cities Shift within an interconnected theoretical framework of language change, bringing in effects of social class and gender.

www.ling.upenn.edu/~wlabov/Papers/DFLC.htm

Linguistic Study of Speech Sounds

The International Phonetic Association, now more than 125 years old, "provides the academic community world-wide with a notational standard for the phonetic representation of all languages—the International Phonetic Alphabet." Charts of all the sounds of the IPA may be copied from their webpage.

https://www.internationalphoneticassociation.org/content/ipa-chart

For a more practically useful site that plays recordings and presents moving images of the production of sounds in a cross section of the mouth, visit the University of Iowa phonetics site. Two caveats are needed: the Iowa site categorizes the sound [a] as a front vowel instead of a mid vowel and the recorded pronunciation is very close to its back vowel [ɑ]. The [a] you will hear is not the allophone that most Southerners produce when monophthongizing [aɪ]. Also, the dialect of the speaker doing the pronunciations has merged [ɑ] and [ɔ]. Though the pronunciation of the two sounds is a bit different, the [ɔ] is not lip-rounded to my ears. (The plight of the speaker is like that of asking a Southerner who pronounces *pin* and *pen* with the same [ɪ] sound to use the word *ten* to illustrate the [ɛ] sound!)

http://soundsofspeech.uiowa.edu/english/english.html

For a fun and artistic use of phonetic transcription and a look at phonetic transcription following British English practices, see the YouTube video created by "Justinlrb" of jazz greats Ella Fitzgerald and Louis Armstrong singing "Let's Call the Whole Thing Off" (you say *potato* and I say *potahto*, etc.).

www.youtube.com/watch?v=8lJJVrJYvUA

Websites of Some Major Linguistic Projects

The granddaddy of American linguistic projects was begun in 1929 as the Linguistic Atlas of the United States and Canada. Now called Linguistic Atlas Projects (LAP), and appearing not to include Canada, it is housed at the University of Georgia under editor-in-chief William Kretzschmar. The mapping of dialect regions of the United States began in the 1930s and is still underway. Because of the time involved in collecting data and the technological advances in and methodological changes to the study of linguistics, each finished segment of the Linguistic Atlas differs from the ones before it. For example, the Linguistic Atlas of the Gulf States, directed by Lee Pederson, was the first to develop much broader sociolinguistically oriented methodologies. Nevertheless, a certain level of comparability remains between all projects. For information on ten projects, see the UGA website:

http://us.english.uga.edu

The TELSUR Project is a massive TELephone SURvey that collected phonological (sound) information from carefully determined locations across the nation. The project's Atlas of North American English (ANAE) is the culmination of years of important work by William Labov, of the University of Pennsylvania, and allied scholars. Labov has earned the title "father of sociolinguistics" because of his groundbreaking work in relating variation in how people speak to social factors such as socioeconomic class. (Labovian sociolinguistics laid the foundation for the essays by Feagin, Allbritten, Spence, and Doxsey in this volume.) The map based on TELSUR/ANAE DATA in Nunnally's "Exploring" in this volume shows findings from TELSUR being used to determine dialect areas. Although consulting the sumptuous Atlas volume with CD ROM (Labov, Ash, and Boberg 2005) gives fuller appreciation of the project, much can be learned from the authors' and the publisher's websites available as of this writing.

http://www.ling.upenn.edu/phono_atlas/home.html
http://www.atlas.mouton-content.com/

The Language and Life Project at North Carolina State University (earlier, the North Carolina Language and Life Project), founded by Walt Wolfram at North Carolina State University, is a model program for study and documentation of language use, diversity, and change in a state within its cultural contexts. NCLLP has published a series of books and audiovisual materials that bring knowledge of the rich linguistic and cultural resources of North Carolina to a broad audience and also sponsors various educational outreach programs. It is a leader in the battle against language-based prejudice and linguistic security foisted on speakers of nonstandard dialects. Founder Wolfram's foreword in this volume provides an overview of much of its important work and accomplishments. The link below will offer many hours of interesting and moving learning.

https://languageandlife.org/

DARE, The Dictionary of American Regional English, was begun in 1963 by the late Frederic Gomes Cassidy. DARE is the opposite of a dictionary of Standard English in that it "documents words, phrases, and pronunciations that vary from one place to another place across the United States." It collected data on regional words from more than one thousand locations in all fifty states. The six volumes, published between 1985 and 2013, demonstrate that dialect regions in the United States continue to differ by thousands of words. Adding to the print version, a digital version has now been launched. Although full use requires a subscription, visitors have access to many interesting features, including one hundred sample words. Some words will be familiar to many (older?) Alabamians (e.g., the *mulligrubs*, a *play-pretty*), but others will be about as clear as pogonip to them. The first link below is a transcript of an interview with Emerita Chief Editor Joan Houston Hall. The second is the general link to the DARE site.

http://wordsmith.org/chat/dare.html
http://polyglot.lss.wisc.edu/dare/dare.html

NOTE

1. Although caution is enjoined regarding accuracy of the entries in Wikipedia, I have discovered that other websites appearing to be of a scholarly nature contain over-

generalizations and misinformation about Southern Englishes. I caution readers to be skeptical when a website presents certain features and lexical items as emblematic of entire populations of Southern regions, fails to note that many such features are fading and recessive forms, neglects to explain the sound environments for certain features, misunderstands [ɑ] versus [a] (rampant even for trained Northern linguists, as I explain in appendix A), and cites no sources for the information or for many admittedly attractive maps. It is my hope that the information presented in this volume will help readers discern between accurate and inaccurate descriptions of Southern English varieties.

References

Abernethy, Thomas Perkins. 1922. *The Formative Period in Alabama: 1815–1828*. Montgomery, AL: Brown Printing Company. Repr. 1990, University of Alabama Press, Tuscaloosa.

Access Genealogy. 2004–2007. *Alabama Indian Tribes*. http://www.accessgenealogy.com/native/alabama.

Adams, Charles Edward. 2001. *Blocton: The History of an Alabama Coal Mining Town*. Brierfield, AL: Cahaba Trace Commission.

"Alabama History Timeline." n.d. Alabama Department of Archives and History. http://www.archives.state.al.us/timeline/al1801.html.

Alabama Indian Affairs Commission. n.d. *Tribes, Chiefs, and Commissioners*. http://www.aiac.state.al.us/tribes.aspx.

Algeo, John, ed. 2001. *The Cambridge History of the English Language, Vol. 6: English in North America*. Cambridge: Cambridge University Press.

———. 2003. "The Origins of Southern American English." In Nagle and Sanders 2003, 6–16.

Alim, H. Samy. 2004. *You Know My Steez: An Ethnographic and Sociolinguistic Study of Styleshifting in a Black American Speech Community*. Publication of the American Dialect Society 89. Durham: Duke University Press.

Allbritten, Rachael. 2008. "The Southern Vowel Shift in Alabama: The Role of Urban Orientation in Intra-Community Variation." *Journal of Southern Linguistics* 32: 1–38.

———. 2011. "Sounding Southern: Phonetic Features and Dialect Perceptions." PhD diss., Georgetown University.

Americans.net 1996–2005. *Native Languages of the Americas*. http://www.nativelanguages.org/alabama.htm

Anderson, Bridget L. 1999. "Source-Language Transfer and Vowel Accommodation in the Patterning of Cherokee English /ai/ and /oi/." *American Speech* 74: 339–68.

———. 2002. "Dialect Leveling and /ai/ Monophthongization among African American Detroiters." *Journal of Sociolinguistics* 6: 86–98.

Ardery, Julie. 2006. "Changing Church in the South: Religion and Politics in Elba, Alabama." Durham: University of New Hampshire, Carsey Institute. https://carsey.unh.edu/publication/changing-church-south-religion-and-politics-elba-alabama.

Ash, Sharon. n.d. "Sampling Strategy for the Telsur/Atlas Project." http://www.ling.upenn.edu/phono_atlas/sampling.html.

Asselin, Claire, and Anne McLaughlin. 1994. "Les immigrants en Nouvelle-France au XVIIe siècle parlaient-ils français?" In *Les origines du français québécois*, edited by Raymond Mougeon and Edouard Beniak, 101–30. Sainte-Foy: Les Presses de l'Université Laval.

Bailey, Charles-James N. 1968. "Segmental Length in Southern States English: An Instrumental Investigation of a Standard Dialect in South Carolina." PEGS paper No. 20. ERIC/PEGS. Washington, DC: Center for Applied Linguistics.

———. 1969. "An Exploratory Investigation of Variations in the Accented Outputs of Underlying Short Vowels in a Dialect of Southern States English." University of Hawaii Working Papers in Linguistics 1.1.

———. 1985a. "English Phonetic Transcription." Summer Institute of Linguistics and University of Texas at Arlington Series in Linguistics. Dallas: Summer Institute of Linguistics/University of Texas at Arlington.

———. 1985b. "Toward Principles Governing the Progress and Patterning of Phonetological Development." In *Developmental Mechanisms of Language*, edited by Charles-James N. Bailey and Roy Harris, 1–50. Oxford: Pergamon.

Bailey, Guy. 1981. "A Social History of the Gulf States." *LAGS Working Papers* (Second Series), no. 1. Ann Arbor: University Microfilms International.

———. 1997. "When Did Southern American English Begin?" In *Englishes around the World*. Vol. I, edited by Edgar W. Schneider, 255–75. Amsterdam: John Benjamins Publishing Company.

———. 2001. "The Relationship between African American Vernacular English and White Vernaculars in the American South: A Sociocultural History and Some Phonological Evidence." In *Sociocultural and Historical Contexts of African American Vernacular English*, edited by Sonja L. Lanehart, 53–92. Amsterdam: John Benjamins Publishing Company.

———. 2015. "Demography as Destiny? Population Change and the Future of Southern American English." In Picone and Davies 2015, 327–49.

Bailey, Guy, and Cynthia Bernstein. 1989. "Methodology of a Phonological Survey of Texas." *Journal of English Linguistics* 22: 6–16.

Bailey, Guy, and Natalie Maynor. 1985a. "The Present Tense of 'Be' in Southern Black Folk Speech." *American Speech* 60: 195–213.

———. 1985b. "The Present Tense of 'Be' in White Folk Speech of the Southern United States." *English World-Wide* 6: 199–216.

Bailey, Guy, and Jan Tillery. 1996. "The Persistence of Southern American English." *Journal of English Linguistics* 24: 308–21.

———. 2000. "Southern American English." *American Language Review* 4.4: 27–29.

Bailey, Guy, Tom Wikle, and Lori Sand. 1991. "The Focus of Linguistic Innovation in Texas." *English World-Wide* 12: 195–214.

Bailey, Guy, Tom Wikle, Jan Tillery, and Lori Sand. 1993. "Some Patterns of Linguistic Diffusion." *Language Variation and Change* 5: 359–90.

———. 1996. "The Linguistic Consequences of Catastrophic Events: An Example from the Southwest." In *Sociolinguistic Variation: Data, Theory, and Analysis*, edited by Jennifer Arnold, Renee Blake, and Brad Davidson, 435–51. Stanford: CSLI.

Baranowski, Maciej. 2007. *Phonological Variation and Change in the Dialect of Charleston, South Carolina*. Publication of the American Dialect Society 92. Durham: Duke University Press.

Barbaud, Philippe. 1984. *Le choc des patois en Nouvelle-France: Essai sur l'histoire de la francisation au Canada*. Québec: Presses de l'Université du Québec.

Baugh, John. 2000. *Beyond Ebonics: Linguistic Pride and Racial Prejudice*. New York: Oxford University Press.

———. 2005. "Ebony + Phonics." *Do You Speak American?* http://www.pbs.org/speak /seatosea/americanvarieties/AAVE/ebonics/.

Bayley, Robert. 2007. "Recent Immigrant Languages." In Montgomery and Johnson 2007, 72–78.

Bell, Allan. 1984. "Language Style as Audience Design." *Language in Society* 13: 145–204.

Benson, Erica J. 2003. "Folk Linguistic Perceptions and Dialect Boundaries." *American Speech* 78: 307–30.

Bergstresser, Jack. 2008. "Iron and Steel Production in Birmingham." *Encyclopedia of Alabama*. http://www.encyclopediaofalabama.org/face/Article.jsp?id=h-1638.

Bernstein, Cynthia. 2006. "Drawing out the /ai/: Dialect Boundaries and /ai/ Variation." In *Language Variation and Change in the American Midland: A New Look at "Heartland" English*, edited by Thomas E. Murray and Beth Lee Simon, 209–32. Amsterdam: John Benjamins.

Bernstein, Cynthia, Thomas Nunnally, and Robin Sabino, eds. 1997. *Language Variety in the South Revisited*. Tuscaloosa: University of Alabama Press. (LAVIS II).

Blaufarb, Rafe. 2005. *Bonapartists in the Borderlands: French Exiles and Refugees on the Gulf Coast, 1815–1835*. Tuscaloosa: University of Alabama Press.

———. 2006. "Alabama's Vine and Olive Colony: Myth and Fact." *Alabama Heritage* 81: 26–34.

Boersma, Paul, and David Weenink. 2007. *Praat: Doing Phonetics by Computer*. Version 4.5.15. http://www.praat.org.

Bolinger, Dwight. 1979. "The Socially Minded Linguist." *Modern Language Journal* 63: 404–07.

Bowie, David. 2001. "The Diphthongization of /ay/." *Journal of English Linguistics* 29: 329–45.

Braden, Waldo W. 1983. *The Oral Tradition in the South*. Baton Rouge: Louisiana State University Press.

Bragg, Rick. 1997. *All Over but the Shoutin'*. New York: Vintage Books.

Brammer, Charlotte. 2002a. "Identifying Southern Dialect Influences on Business Student Writing." PhD diss., University of Alabama. DAI 63.10A, 3533.

———. 2002b. "Linguistic Cultural Capital and Basic Writers." *Journal of Basic Writing* 21: 16–36.

———. 2009. "Composition and Applied Linguistics: Exploring the Oral/Written Connection." In *Negotiating a Meta-Pedagogy: Learning from Other Disciplines*, edited by Emily Golson and Toni Glover, 152–69. Newcastle upon Tyne, UK: Cambridge Scholars Publishing.

Britain, David. 2003. "Exploring the Importance of the Outlier in Sociolinguistic Dialectology." In *Social Dialectology: In Honour of Peter Trudgill*, edited by David Britain and Jenny Cheshire, 191–208. Amsterdam: John Benjamins.

Brown, David. W. 2009. "Coming to Terms with What It Means to Teach and Learn Grammar." *American Speech* 84: 216–27.

Brown, Penelope, and Stephen C. Levinson. 1987. *Politeness: Some Universals in Language Usage*. New York: Cambridge University Press. First published 1978.

Brown, Vivian R. 1991. "Evolution of the Merger of /ɪ/ and /ɛ/ before Nasals in Tennessee." *American Speech* 66: 303–15.

Brunson, Marion. 1984. *Pea River Reflections: Intimate Glimpses of Area Life during Two Centuries*. Tuscaloosa, AL: Portals.

Cameron, Deborah, Elizabeth Fraser, Penelope Harvey, M.B.H. Rampton, and Kay Richardson. 1992. *Researching Language: Issues of Power and Method*. London/New York: Routledge.

Carsey Institute. n.d. *About Us*. https://carsey.unh.edu/about. (Revised version, 2017.)

Carver, Craig. 1987. *American Regional Dialects: A Word Geography*. Ann Arbor: University of Michigan Press.

Cassidy, Frederic G., and Joan Houston Hall, eds. 1985–2013. *Dictionary of American Regional English*. Cambridge, MA: Belknap.

Chaudron, Adelaide de Vendel. 1863a. *Chaudron's Third Reader*. Mobile, AL: W. G. Clark.

———. 1863b. *The Second Reader, Designed for the Use of Primary Schools*. Mobile, AL: Daily Advertiser and Register.

Childs, Becky, Christine Mallinson, and Jeannine Carpenter. 2010. "Vowel Phonology and Ethnicity in North Carolina." In *African American English Speakers and Their Participation in Local Sound Changes: A Comparative Study*, edited by Malcah Yaeger-Dror and Erik R. Thomas, 23–47. Publication of the American Dialect Society 94. Durham: Duke University Press.

Childs, Becky, Walt Wolfram, and Ellen Fulcher Cloud, producers. 2000. *Ocracoke Speaks*. Raleigh: North Carolina Language and Life Project.

City of Mobile. 2006. *Maps and Facts*. http://www.cityofmobile.org/mapsnfacts/facts.php.

Clark, Thomas Dionysius, ed. 1956. *Travels in the Old South: A Bibliography*. 4 vols. Norman: University of Oklahoma Press.

Clopper, Cynthia. 2000. "Some Acoustic Cues for Categorizing American English Regional Dialects: An Initial Report on Dialect Variation in Production and Perception." *Research on Spoken Language Processing. Progress Report No. 24*: 43–65.

Cobb, James Charles. 2005. *Away down South: A History of Southern Identity*. Oxford: Oxford University Press.

Cohen, Dov, Joseph Vandello, Sylvia Puente, and Adrian Rantilla. 1999. "'When You Call Me That, Smile!': How Norms for Politeness, Interaction Styles, and Aggression Work Together in Southern Culture." *Social Psychology Quarterly* 62: 257–75.

Cook, Ruth Beaumont. 2006. *Guests behind the Barbed Wire: German POWs in America; A True Story of Hope and Friendship*. Birmingham: Crane Hill.

Cormier, Loretta A., Jacqueline A. Matte, Reva Lee Reed, and Cedric Sunray. 2006. "*Yakni*—The Binding Force: Nature and Culture Among the MOWA Choctaw of Alabama." *Tributaries* 9: 42–57.

Coulmas, Florian. 2005. *Sociolinguistics: The Study of Speakers' Choices*. Cambridge: Cambridge University Press.

Cox, Karen L. 2008. "Lost Cause Ideology." *Encyclopedia of Alabama.* http://www.encyclopediaofalabama.org/face/Article.jsp?id=h-1643.

Crane, L. Ben. 1977. "The Social Stratification of /ai/ in Tuscaloosa, Alabama." In Shores and Hines 1977, 189–200.

Crawford, James M. 1978. *The Mobilian Trade Language.* Knoxville: University of Tennessee Press.

DARE. See Cassidy and Hall.

Davies, Catherine Evan. 2007. "Language and Identity in Discourse in the American South: Sociolinguistic Repertoire as Expressive Resource in the Presentation of Self." In *Selves and Identity in Narrative and Discourse,* edited by Michael Bamberg, Anna De Fina, and Deborah Schiffrin, 71–88. Amsterdam: John Benjamins.

———. 2009. "'We Digress': Kathryn Tucker Windham and Southern Storytelling Style." *Storytelling, Self, Society* 4: 167–84.

———. 2015. "Southern Storytelling: Historical and Contemporary Perspectives." In Picone and Davies 2015, 399–421.

Delpit, Lisa. 1995. *Other People's Children: Cultural Conflict in the Classroom.* New York: New Press.

Digital Archive of Southern Speech, digitized recordings of LAGS field recordings (interviews with informants), information at http://www.lap.uga.edu/Site/DASS.html.

Diouf, Sylviane Anna. 1998. *Servants of Allah: African Muslims Enslaved in the Americas.* New York: New York University Press.

———. 2007. *Dreams of Africa in Alabama: The Slave Ship Clotilda and the Story of the Last Africans Brought to America.* Oxford and New York: Oxford University Press.

Disheroon-Green, Suzanne, ed. 2005. *Voices of the American South.* New York: Pearson Longman.

Do You Speak American? 2005. MacNeil/Lehrer Productions. http://www.pbs.org/speak/.

Dodd, Donald B. 1972. *Winston: An Antebellum and Civil War History of a Hill County of North Alabama.* Birmingham: Oxmoor.

Donlon, Jocelyn Hazelwood. 1995. "Hearing Is Believing: Southern Racial Communities and Strategies of Story-Listening in Gloria Naylor and Lee Smith." *Twentieth Century Literature* 41: 16–36.

Dorian, Nancy. 1994. "Varieties of Variation in a Very Small Place: Social Homogeneity, Prestige Norms, and Linguistic Variation." *Language* 70: 631–96.

Dorrill, George T. 1982. *Black and White Speech in the South: Evidence from the Linguistic Atlas of the Middle and South Atlantic States.* Bamberger Beiträge zur Englischen Sprachwissenschaft 19. New York: Peter Lang.

———. 2003. "Sounding Southern: A Look at the Phonology of English in the South." In Nagle and Sanders 2003, 119–25.

Downes, William. 1998. *Language and Society.* 2nd ed. London: Fontana.

Doxsey, Jocelyn. 2007. "/ai/ Monophthongization on the Gulf Coast of Alabama." Master's thesis, New York University.

Drechsel, Emanuel J. 1996. "An Integrated Vocabulary of Mobilian Jargon, a Native American Pidgin of the Mississippi Valley." *Anthropological Linguistics* 38: 248–354.

———. 1997. *Mobilian Jargon: Linguistic and Sociohistorical Aspects of a Native American Pidgin.* Oxford: Clarendon.

Dubois, Sylvie, and Barbara M. Horvath. 2002. "Sounding Cajun: The Rhetorical Use of Dialect in Speech and Writing." *American Speech* 77: 264–87.

Dumont de Montigny, Jean François Benjamin. 1753. *Mémoires historiques sur la Louisiane*. Paris.

Dunaway, Wilma A. 2003. *Slavery in the American Mountain South*. Cambridge: Cambridge University Press.

Dunstan, Stephany Brett, Walt Wolfram, Audrey J. Jaeger, and Rebecca E. Crandall. 2015. "Educating the Educated: Language Diversity in the University Backyard." *American Speech* 90: 266-80.

Dupre, Daniel S. 1997. *Transforming the Cotton Frontier: Madison County, Alabama, 1800–1840*. Baton Rouge: Louisiana State University Press.

Eckert, Penelope. 1989. "The Whole Woman: Sex and Gender Differences in Variation." *Language Variation and Change* 1: 245–67.

———. 1996. "(ay) Goes to the City: Exploring the Expressive Use of Variation." In Gregory R. Guy et al. 1996, 47–68.

———. n.d. "Three Waves of Variation Study: The Emergence of Meaning in the Study of Variation." Ms. available at http://www.stanford.edu/~eckert/PDF/ThreeWavesofVariation.pdf. A condensed version published in 2012 in *Annual Review of Anthropology* 41: 87–100 omits the quotation used in the essay by Nunnally and Bailey in this volume.

Edwards, John, and Maryanne Jacobsen. 1987. "Standard and Regional Standard Speech: Distinctions and Similarities." *Language in Society* 16: 369–80.

Edwards, Walter F. 1997. "The Variable Persistence of Southern Vernacular Sounds in the Speech of Inner-City Black Detroiters." In Bernstein, Nunnally, and Sabino 1997, 76–86.

Evans, Medford. 1935. "Southern 'Long I.'" *American Speech* 10: 188–90.

Feagin, Crawford. 1979. *Variation and Change in Alabama English: A Sociolinguistic Study of the White Community*. Washington, DC: Georgetown University Press.

———. 1987. "A Closer Look at the Southern Drawl: Variation Taken to Extremes." *Variation in Language: NWAVE XV at Stanford*, edited by Keith M. Denning, Sharon Inkelas, Faye C. McNair-Knox, and John R. Rickford, 137–50. Stanford, CA: Department of Linguistics, Stanford University.

———. 1996. "Peaks and Glides in Southern States Short-a." In Gregory R. Guy et al. 1996, 135–60.

———. 2000. "Sound Change in the South." *American Speech* 75: 342–44.

———. 2002. "Entering the Community: Fieldwork." In *The Handbook of Language Variation and Change*, edited by J. K. Chambers, Peter Trudgill, and Natalie Shilling-Estes, 20–39. Malden, MA: Blackwell.

———. 2003. "Vowel Shifting in the Southern States." In Nagle and Sanders 2003, 126–40.

———. 2015. "A Century of Sound Change in Alabama." In Picone and Davies 2015, 353–68.

Fischer, David Hackett. 1989. *Albion's Seed: Four British Folkways in America*. Oxford: Oxford University Press.

Fitts, Anne Malone. 1989. "Words of the Black Belt and Beyond: A Study of Alabama

Lexical Patterns in the Linguistic Atlas of the Gulf States." PhD diss., University of Alabama.

———. 1998. "Dialect Boundaries in Alabama: Evidence from LAGS." In Montgomery and Nunnally 1998, 146–66.

Fitzgerald, Michael. 1988. "Radical Republicanism and the White Yeomanry during Alabama Reconstruction, 1865–1868." *Journal of Southern History* 54: 565–96.

Flanders, Stephen A. 1998. *Atlas of American Migration.* New York: Facts on File.

Flynt, J. Wayne. 1989. *Poor but Proud: Alabama's Poor Whites.* Tuscaloosa: University of Alabama Press.

———. 2005. "Regions of Alabama, Part I." *Southern Spaces.* Online video. http://southernspaces.org/2005/regions-alabama.

Foley, Lawrence M. 1969. "A Phonological and Lexical Study of the Speech of Tuscaloosa County, Alabama." PhD diss., University of Alabama.

Foscue, Virginia Oden. 1966. "Background and Preliminary Survey of the Linguistic Geography of Alabama." 2 vols. PhD diss., University of Wisconsin. Repr. 1971 as *Publication of the American Dialect Society 56.*

———. 1971. *A Preliminary Survey of the Vocabulary of White Alabamians.* Publication of the American Dialect Society Number 56. Tuscaloosa: University of Alabama Press.

———. 1989. *Place Names in Alabama.* Tuscaloosa: University of Alabama Press.

Frazer, Timothy. 2000. "Are Rural Dialects Endangered like Island Dialects?" *American Speech* 75: 347–49.

Frazier, Bruce. 1973. "Some 'Unexpected' Reactions to Various American-English Dialects." In *Language Attitudes: Current Tends and Prospects*, edited by Roger Shuy and Ralph Fasold, 28–35. Washington, DC: Georgetown University Press.

Fridland, Valerie. 1998. "The Southern Vowel Shift: Linguistic and Social Factors." PhD diss., Michigan State University.

———. 2000. "The Southern Vowel Shift in Memphis, Tennessee." *Language Variation and Change* 11: 267–85.

———. 2003. "'Tie, Tied and Tight': The Expansion of /ai/ Monophthongization in African-American and European-American Speech in Memphis, Tennessee." *Journal of Sociolinguistics* 7: 279–98.

Fridland, Valerie, and Kathryn Bartlett. 2006. "Correctness, Pleasantness, and Degree of Difference Ratings across Regions." *American Speech* 81: 358–86.

Galloway, Patricia. 1995. *Choctaw Genesis, 1500–1700.* Lincoln: University of Nebraska Press.

Garrett, Peter. 2001. "Language Attitudes and Sociolinguistics." *Journal of Sociolinguistics* 5: 626–31.

Gee, James P. 1996. *Social Linguistics and Literacies: Ideology in Discourses.* 2nd ed. Bristol, PA: Taylor & Francis.

Godley, Amanda J., Julie Sweetland, Rebecca S. Wheeler, Angela Minnici, and Brian D. Carpenter. 2006. "Preparing Teachers for Dialectally Diverse Classrooms." *Educational Researcher* 35: 30–37.

Goffman, Erving. 1967. *Interaction Ritual: Essays on Face-to-Face Behavior.* Garden City, NY: Anchor.

Gray, Lewis Cecil. 1958. *History of Agriculture in the Southern United States to 1860.* Vol. 2. Gloucester, MA: Peter Smith.

Gruendler, Shelley, and Walt Wolfram. 1997. "The Ocracoke Brogue." An exhibit at the Ocracoke Preservation Society. Ocracoke: North Carolina Language and Life Project.

———. 2001. "Lumbee Language." An exhibit at the Museum of the Native American Resource Center. Pembroke: North Carolina Language and Life Project.

Guy, Gregory R., Crawford Feagin, Deborah Schiffrin, and John Baugh, eds. 1996. *Towards a Social Science of Language: Papers in Honor of William Labov, Vol. 1: Variation and Change in Language and Society.* Amsterdam: John Benjamins.

Habick, Timothy. 1980. "Sound Change in Farmer City: A Socio-linguistic Study Based on Acoustic Data." PhD diss., University of Illinois at Urbana-Champaign.

Hagood, Thomas. 2008. "Territorial Period and Early Statehood." *Encyclopedia of Alabama.* http://www.encyclopediaofalabama.org/face/Article.jsp?id=h-1548.

Hansen, Matt. 2015. "The future of America's endangered languages." *The Week: America in 2050.* http://theweek.com/section/Americain2050.

Hardy, Heather K., and Janine Scancarelli, eds. 2005. *Native Languages of the Southeastern United States.* Lincoln: University of Nebraska Press.

Harris, Angel L. 2008. *Encyclopedia of the Life Course and Human Development*, s.v. "Oppositional Culture Theory." Farmington Hills, MI: Gale/CENGAGE Learning.

Harris, Jim. 2003. "A Study of a Variant Black English Vernacular Developed by African American and White Immigrant Coal Miners in the Coal Mining Camp Towns of Central Alabama." PhD diss., Indiana University of Pennsylvania.

Hasty, James Daniel. 2006. "What Do Y'all Think? A Study of Language Attitudes in the South." Master's thesis, Auburn University.

Hathorn, Stacye. 1997. "The Echota Cherokee Language: Current Use and Opinions About Revival." In *Teaching Indigenous Languages*, edited by John Reyhner. Flagstaff: Northern Arizona University, 228–38. http://jan.ucc.nau.edu/~jar/TIL_19.html.

Hathorn, Stacye, and Robin Sabino. 2001. "Views and Vistas: Traveling through the Choctaw, Chickasaw, and Cherokee Nations in 1803." *Alabama Review* 54: 208–20.

Haugh, Michael. 2003. "Anticipated versus Inferred Politeness." *Multilingua* 22: 397–413.

———. 2007. "The Discursive Challenge to Politeness Research: An Interactional Alternative." *Journal of Politeness Research* 3: 295–317.

Hay, Jennifer, Stefanie Jannedy, and Norma Mendoza-Denton. 1999. "Oprah and /ay/: Lexical Frequency, Referee Design, and Style." *Proceedings of the 14th International Congress of Phonetic Sciences, San Francisco.* http://www.saps.canterbury.ac.nz/jen/documents/icphs.html.

Hazen, Kirk. 2000. "A Methodological Suggestion on /aj/ Ungliding." *American Speech* 75: 221–24.

———. 2005. The West Virginia Dialect Project. http://dialects.english.wvu.edu/.

Head, Anna. 2003. "The Monophthongization of /ai/ in Elba and the Environs." Master's thesis, Auburn University.

———. 2012. "The Sounds of Social Change: Phonology and Identity in Elba, Alabama." PhD diss., Auburn University. Online access through Auburn University's online thesis and dissertation collection.

Heath, Shirley Brice. 1983. *Ways with Words: Language, Life, and Work in Communities and Classrooms*. New York: Cambridge University Press.

Heaton, Hayley, and Lynne C. Nygaard. 2011. "Charm or Harm: Effect of Passage Content on Listener Attitudes toward American English Accents." *Journal of Language and Social Psychology* 30: 202–11.

Hébert, Keith S. 2009. "Slavery." *Encyclopedia of Alabama*. http://www.encyclopediao falabama.org/face/Article.jsp?id=h-2369.

Heller, Monica. 2003. "Globalization, the New Economy, and the Commodification of Language and Identity." *Journal of Sociolinguistics* 7: 473–92.

Higginbotham, Jay. 1977. *Old Mobile: Fort Louis de la Louisiane, 1702–1711*. Tuscaloosa: University of Alabama Press.

———. 2001. "Discovery, Exploration and Colonization of Mobile Bay to 1711." In *Mobile: The New History of Alabama's First City*, edited by Michael Thomason, 3–28. Tuscaloosa: University of Alabama Press.

Hilliard, Sam Bowers. 1984. *Atlas of Antebellum Southern Agriculture*. Baton Rouge: Louisiana State University Press.

Hitchcock, Bert. 2000. Lecture Notes: English 0495, Southern Literature.

———. 2002. *The Companion to Southern Literature: Themes, Genres, Places, People, Movements, and Motifs*, s.v. "The Literature of Alabama." Baton Rouge: Louisiana State University Press.

Holtgraves, Thomas. 1992. "The Linguistic Realization of Face Management: Implications for Language Production and Comprehension, Person Perception, and Cross-Cultural Communication." *Social Psychology Quarterly* 55: 141–59.

Hubbs, Guy Ward. 2005. "A Settlement House in Ensley's Italian District." *Alabama Heritage* 75: 32–40.

Hutcheson, Neal, producer. 2001. *Indian by Birth: The Lumbee Dialect*. Raleigh: North Carolina Language and Life Project.

———, producer. 2004a. *Mountain Talk*. Raleigh: North Carolina Language and Life Project.

———, producer. 2004b. *An Unclouded Day: Stories and Songs of the southern Appalachian Mountains*. Raleigh: North Carolina Language and Life Project.

———, producer. 2005. *Voices of North Carolina*. Raleigh: North Carolina Language and Life Project.

———, producer. 2006. *The Queen Family: Appalachian Tradition and Back Porch Music*. Raleigh: North Carolina Language and Life Project.

———, producer. 2009. *The Carolina Brogue*. Raleigh: North Carolina Language and Life Project.

Hutcheson, Neal, and Danica Cullinan, producers. 2015. *First Language: The Race to Save Cherokee*. Raleigh: Language and Life Project at NC State.

———, producers. 2017. *Talking Black in America: The Story of African American Language*. Raleigh: Language and Life Project at NC State.

Jack, Theodore Henley. 1919. *Sectionalism and Party Politics in Alabama, 1819–1842*. Menasha, WI: Collegiate.

Jary, Mark. 1998. "Relevance Theory and the Communication of Politeness." *Journal of Pragmatics* 30: 1–19.

Jeffries, Hasan Kwame. 2008. "Modern Civil Rights Movement in Alabama." *Encyclopedia of Alabama*. http://encyclopediaofalabama.org/face/Article.jsp?id=h-1580.

Johnson, Ellen. 1996. *Lexical Change and Variation in the Southeastern United States, 1930–1990*. Tuscaloosa: University of Alabama Press.

Johnstone, Barbara. 1999. "Uses of Southern-sounding Speech by Contemporary Texas Women." *Journal of Sociolinguistics* 3: 505–22.

——. 2003a. "Discourse Analysis and Narrative." In *The Handbook of Discourse Analysis*, edited by Deborah Schiffrin, Deborah Tannen, and Heidi E. Hamilton, 635–49. Malden, MA: Blackwell.

——. 2003b. "Features and Uses of Southern Style." In Nagle and Sanders 2003, 189–207.

Jones, Mari C., and Ishtla Singh. 2005. *Exploring Language Change*. New York: Routledge.

Jordan-Bychkov, Terry G. 2003. *The Upland South: The Making of an American Folk Region and Landscape*. Santa Fe, NM: Center for American Places, and Charlottesville: University of Virginia Press.

Keith, LeeAnna. 2011. "Alabama Fever." *Encyclopedia of Alabama*. http://www.encyclopediaofalabama.org/face/Article.jsp?id=h-3155.

Kelley, Charles. 2005. "Maintaining Mexican Identity in Birmingham." *Tributaries* 8: 49–65.

Kersey, Harry A., Jr. 1992. "Seminoles and Miccosukees: A Century in Retrospective." In *Indians of the Southeastern United States in the Late 20th Century*, edited by J. Anthony Paredes, 102–19. Tuscaloosa: University of Alabama Press.

Kniffen, Fred B., Hiram F. Gregory, and George A. Stokes. 1987. *The Historic Indian Tribes of Louisiana from 1542 to the Present*. Baton Rouge: Louisiana State University Press.

Kurath, Hans. 1949. *A Word Geography of the Eastern United States*. Ann Arbor: University of Michigan Press.

Labov, William. 1963. "The Social Motivation of a Sound Change." In *Sociolinguistic Patterns*, edited by William Labov, 1–42. Philadelphia: University of Pennsylvania Press. Repr. 1972.

——. 1966. *The Social Stratification of English in New York City*. Washington, DC: Center for Applied Linguistics.

——. 1972. "Some Principles of Linguistic Methodology." *Language in Society* 1: 97–120.

——. 1984. "The Interpretation of Zeroes." In *Phonologica 1984: Proceedings of the Fifth International Phonology Meeting*, edited by Wolfgang Dressler et al., 135–56. Cambridge: Cambridge University Press.

——. 1991. "The Three Dialects of English." In *New Ways of Analyzing Sound Change*, edited by Penelope Eckert, 1–44. New York: Academic Press.

——. 2010. *Cognitive and Cultural Factors*. Vol. 3 of *Principles of Linguistic Change*. Oxford: Wiley/Blackwell.

Labov, William, and Sharon Ash. 1997. "Understanding Birmingham." In Bernstein, Nunnally, and Sabino 1997, 508–73.

Labov, William, Sharon Ash, and Charles Boberg. 2005. *The Atlas of North American English: Phonetics, Phonology and Sound Change: A Multimedia Reference Tool*. New York: Mouton de Gruyter.

Labov, William, Malcah Yaeger, and Richard Steiner. 1972. *A Quantitative Study of*

Sound Change in Progress. 2 vols. Report on National Science Foundation contract NSF-GS-3287, University of Pennsylvania. Philadelphia: US Regional Survey.

LAGS. *Linguistic Atlas of the Gulf States*, consisting of the following publications (*LAGS*)

  Basic Materials, see Pederson, Billiard, Leas, Bailey, and Bassett, eds. 1981. Microfiche.

  Concordance, see Pederson, McDaniel, and Bassett. 1986. Microfiche.

  Handbook, vol. 1, see Pederson, McDaniel, Bailey, and Bassett, eds. 1986.

  General Index, vol. 2, see Pederson, McDaniel, and Adams, eds. 1988.

  Technical Index, vol. 3, see Pederson, McDaniel, Adams, and Liao, eds. 1989.

  Regional Matrix, vol. 4, see Pederson, McDaniel, Adams, and Montgomery, eds. 1990.

  Regional Pattern, vol. 5, see Pederson, McDaniel, and Adams, eds. 1991.

  Social Matrix, vol. 6, see Pederson, McDaniel, Adams, and Montgomery, eds. 1991.

  Social Pattern, vol. 7, see Pederson and McDaniel, eds. 1992.

Lanehart, Sonja L. 1999. "African American Vernacular English." In *Handbook of Language and Ethnic Identity*, edited by Joshua A. Fishman, 211–25. New York: Oxford University Press.

Lee, Jin Sook, and Kate T. Anderson. 2009. "Negotiating Linguistic and Cultural Identities: Theorizing and Constructing Opportunities and Risks in Education." *Review of Research in Education* 33: 181–211.

Lewis, Herbert J. "Jim." 2007. "Madison County." *Encyclopedia of Alabama.* http://www.encyclopediaofalabama.org/face/Article.jsp?id=h-1168.

Lewis, M. Paul, Gary F. Simons, and Charles D. Fennig, eds. 2013. *Ethnologue: Languages of the World.* 17th ed. Dallas, TX: SIL International. Online version http://www.ethnologue.com.

Lippi-Green, Rosina. 1997. *English with an Accent: Language, Ideology and Discrimination in the United States.* New York: Routledge.

Locher, Miriam A., and Richard J. Watts. 2005. "Politeness Theory and Relational Work." *Journal of Politeness Research* 1: 9–33.

Lockett, James D. 1998. "The Last Ship That Brought Slaves from Africa to America: The Landing of the 'Clotilde' at Mobile in the Autumn of 1859." *Western Journal of Black Studies* 22: 159–63.

Locklear, Hayes Alan, Walt Wolfram, Natalie Schilling-Estes, and Clare Dannenberg. 1999. *A Dialect Dictionary of Lumbee English.* Raleigh: North Carolina Language and Life Project.

Mai, Robert, and Stefan Hoffmann. 2011. "Four Positive Effects of a Salesperson's Regional Dialect in Services Selling." *Journal of Service Research* 14: 460–74.

Mallinson, Christine, Becky Childs, and Zula Cox. 2006. *Voices of Texana.* Texana, NC: Texana Committee on Community History and Preservation.

Marshall, Margaret M. 1991. "The Creole of Mon Louis Island, Alabama, and the Louisiana Connection." *Journal of Pidgin and Creole Languages* 6: 73–87.

Mathews, Mitford M., ed. 1931. *The Beginnings of American English.* Chicago: University of Chicago Press.

McCowan, Mary Hardin. (1813–14) 1939–40. "The 'J. Hartsell Memora': The Journal of a Tennessee Captain in the War of 1812." *East Tennessee Historical Society Publications* 11: 93–115; 12: 118–46.

McKenney, Thomas R., and James Hall. 1854. *History of the Indian Tribes of North America with Biographical Sketches and Anecdotes of the Principal Chiefs.* Philadelphia: D. Rice & A. N. Hart.

McMillan, James B., and Michael B. Montgomery. 1989. *Annotated Bibliography of Southern American English.* Updated and expanded ed. Tuscaloosa: University of Alabama Press.

McWilliams, Richebourg Gaillard, ed. and trans. 1953. *Fleur de Lys and Calumet: Being the Pénicaut Narrative of French Adventure in Louisiana.* Baton Rouge: Louisiana State University Press.

Meinig, D. W. 1993. *The Shaping of America.* Vol. 2 of *Continental America, 1800–1967: A Geographical Perspective on 500 Years of History.* New Haven: Yale University Press.

Melancon, Megan, and Katherine Wise. 2005. "Dialect Shifts in Rural Middle Georgia." Paper presented at New Ways of Analyzing Variation (NWAV) 34. October 20–23.

Merriam-Webster Online. 2008. Merriam-Webster, Incorporated. http://www.merriam-webster.com/.

Metcalf, Allan. 2000. *How We Talk: American Regional English Today.* New York: Houghton Mifflin.

Meyerhoff, Miriam, and Nancy Niedzielski. 2003. "The Globalisation of Vernacular Variation." *Journal of Sociolinguistics* 7: 534–55.

Milroy, Leslie. 1991. *Language and Social Networks.* 2nd ed. Oxford: Basil Blackwell.

Mohl, Raymond A. 2002. "Latinization in the Heart of Dixie: Hispanics in Late-Twentieth-Century Alabama." *Alabama Review* 55: 243–74.

Montgomery, Michael B. 1989. "Language." In *Encyclopedia of Southern Culture,* edited by Charles Reagan Wilson and William Ferris, 757–92. Chapel Hill: University of North Carolina Press.

———. 1993. "Was Welsh the First European Language Spoken in Alabama?" *The SECOL Review* 17: 55–79.

———. 1997. "Language Variety in the South: A Retrospective and Assessment." In Bernstein, Nunnally, and Sabino 1997, 3–20.

———. 1998a. "Multiple Modals in LAGS and LAMSAS." In Montgomery and Nunnally 1998, 90–122.

———. 1998b. "The Treasury of LAGS: Its History, Organization, and Accomplishments." In Montgomery and Nunnally 1998, 7–52.

———. 2015. "The Crucial Century for English in the American South." In Picone and Davies 2015, 97–117.

Montgomery, Michael B., and Guy Bailey, eds. 1986. *Language Variety in the South: Perspectives in Black and White.* Tuscaloosa: University of Alabama Press. (LAVIS I)

Montgomery, Michael B., and Joseph S. Hall. 2004. *Dictionary of Smoky Mountain English.* Knoxville: University of Tennessee Press.

Montgomery, Michael B., and Ellen Johnson, eds. 2007. *Language.* Vol. 5 of *The New Encyclopedia of Southern Culture.* Chapel Hill: University of North Carolina Press.

Montgomery, Michael B., and Thomas E. Nunnally, eds. 1998. *From the Gulf States and Beyond: The Legacy of Lee Pederson and LAGS.* Tuscaloosa: University of Alabama Press.

Morgan, Marcylienna. 2002. *Language, Discourse, and Power in African American Culture.* Cambridge: Cambridge University Press.

Moroni, Girolamo. 1913. "Lo Stato dell'Alabama." *Bollettino dell'Emigrazioni* 1: 34–66.

Mufwene, Salikoko. 2003. "The Shared Ancestry of African-American and American-White Southern Englishes: Some Speculations Dictated by History." In Nagle and Sanders 2003, 64–81.

Munro, Pamela. 2015. "American Indian Languages of the Southeast: An Introduction." In Picone and Davies 2015, 21–42.

Murray, Thomas E., and Beth Lee Simon. 2004. "Colloquial American English: Grammatical Features." In *A Handbook of Varieties of English: A Multimedia Reference Tool, Vol. 2*, edited by Bernd Kortmann and Edgar W. Schneider, 221–44. Berlin: Mouton de Gruyter.

Nagle, Stephen J., and Sara L. Sanders. 2003. *English in the Southern United States*. Cambridge: Cambridge University Press.

New York Times. 1929. *ProQuest Historical Newspapers the New York Times (1851–2004)*. March 15. http://www.proquest.com/en-US/.

Niedzielski, Nancy A., and Dennis R. Preston. 2000. *Folk Linguistics*. Trends in Linguistics: Studies and Monographs 122. New York: Mouton de Gruyter.

Novkov, Julie. 2007. "Segregation." *Encyclopedia of Alabama*. http://www.encyclopediao falabama.org/face/Article.jsp?id=h-1248.

O'Cain, Raymond K. 1972. "A Social Dialect Survey of Charleston, South Carolina." PhD diss., University of Chicago.

Oetzel, John G., and Stella Ting-Toomey. 2003. "Face Concerns in Interpersonal Conflict: A Cross-Cultural Empirical Test of the Face Negotiation Theory." *Communication Research* 30: 599–624.

Ogbu, John U. 2003. *African American Students in an Affluent Suburb: A Study of Academic Disengagement*. Mahwah, NJ: Lawrence Erlbaum.

Olsen, Otto H. 2004. "Historians and the Extent of Slave Ownership in the Southern United States." *Civil War History* 50: 401–17.

Owen, Thomas McAdory. 1921. *History of Alabama and Dictionary of Alabama Biography*. Vols. 1–4. Chicago: S. J. Clarke. Online version. http://digital.archives.alabama .gov/cdm4/browse.php?CISOROOT=/dictionary.

Paredes, J. Anthony. 1992. "Federal Recognition and the Poarch Creek Indians." In *Indians of the Southeastern United States in the Late 20th Century*, edited by J. Anthony Paredes, 120–39. Tuscaloosa: University of Alabama Press.

Pederson, Lee. 1972. "Black Speech, White Speech, and the Al Smith Syndrome." In *Studies in Linguistics in Honor of Raven I. McDavid, Jr.*, edited by Lawrence M. Davis, 123–34. Tuscaloosa: University of Alabama Press.

———. 1993. "An Approach to Linguistic Geography." In *American Dialect Research*, edited by Dennis Preston, 31–92. Amsterdam: John Benjamins.

———. 1996. "Piney Woods Southern." In Schneider 1996, 13–23.

Pederson, Lee, Charles E. Billiard, Susan E. Leas, Guy Bailey, and Marvin Bassett, eds. 1981. *Linguistic Atlas of the Gulf States: The Basic Materials*. Microform collection. Ann Arbor: University Microfilms.

Pederson, Lee, Carol Adams, Marvin Bassett, Guy Bailey, Caisheng Liao, Michael B. Montgomery, Susan Leas McDaniel, eds. 1986–92. *Linguistic Atlas of the Gulf States*. 7 vols. Athens: University of Georgia Press.

Pederson, Lee, and Susan Leas, eds. 1981. "A Compositional Guide to the LAGS Project."

2nd ed. LAGS Working Papers, First Series, Number 5. *Linguistic Atlas of the Gulf States: The Basic Materials*. Microform collection. Ann Arbor: University Microfilms.

Pederson, Lee, and Susan Leas McDaniel, eds. 1992. *Social Pattern*. Vol. 7 of *Linguistic Atlas of the Gulf States*. Athens: University of Georgia Press.

Pederson, Lee, Susan Leas McDaniel, and Carol Adams, eds. 1988. *General Index*. Vol. 2 of *Linguistic Atlas of the Gulf States*. Athens: University of Georgia Press.

———, eds. 1991. *Regional Pattern*. Vol. 5 of *Linguistic Atlas of the Gulf States*. Athens: University of Georgia Press.

Pederson, Lee, Susan Leas McDaniel, Carol Adams, and Caisheng Liao, eds. 1989. *Technical Index*. Vol. 3 of *Linguistic Atlas of the Gulf States*. Athens: University of Georgia Press.

Pederson, Lee, Susan Leas McDaniel, Carol Adams, and Michael B. Montgomery, eds. 1990. *Regional Matrix*. Vol. 4 of *Linguistic Atlas of the Gulf States*. Athens: University of Georgia Press.

———, eds. 1991. *Social Matrix*. Vol. 6 of *Linguistic Atlas of the Gulf States*. Athens: University of Georgia Press.

Pederson, Lee, Susan Leas McDaniel, Guy H. Bailey, and Marvin H. Bassett, eds. 1986. *Handbook*. Vol. 1 of Linguistic Atlas of the Gulf States. Athens: University of Georgia Press.

Pederson, Lee, Susan Leas McDaniel, and Marvin Bassett. 1986. *The Linguistic Atlas of the Gulf States: A Concordance of Basic Materials*. Ann Arbor, MI: University Microfilms.

Phillips, Kenneth E., and Janet Roberts. 2008. "Cotton." *Encyclopedia of Alabama*. http://www.encyclopediaofalabama.org/face/Article.jsp?id=h-1491.

Phillips, William H. 2004. *EH.Net Encyclopedia*, s.v. "The Cotton Gin." http://eh.net/?s=cotton+gin.

Picone, Michael D. 1997. "Enclave Dialect Contraction: An External Overview of Louisiana French." *American Speech* 72: 117–53.

———. 2015. "French Dialects of Louisiana: A Revised Typology." In Picone and Davies 2015, 267–87.

Picone, Michael D., and Catherine Evans Davies, eds. 2015. *Language Variety in the South: Historical and Contemporary Perspectives*. Tuscaloosa: University of Alabama Press. (LAVIS III)

Picone, Michael D., and Amanda LaFleur. 2007. "French." In Montgomery and Johnson 2007, 60–65.

Picone, Michael D., and Albert Valdman. 2005. "La situation du français en Louisiane." In *Le français en Amérique du nord: Etat présent*, edited by Albert Valdman, Julie Auger, and Deborah Piston-Hatlen, 143–65. Québec: Les Presses de l'Université Laval.

Pillsbury, Richard. 2006. *Geography*. Vol. 2 of *The New Encyclopedia of Southern Culture*. Chapel Hill: University of North Caroline Press.

Poirier, Claude. 1994. "La langue parlée en Nouvelle-France: Vers une convergence des explications." In *Les origines du français québécois*, edited by Raymond Mougeon and Edouard Beniak, 237–73. Sainte-Foy: Les Presses de l'Université Laval.

Preston, Dennis R. 1986. "Five Visions of America." *Language in Society* 15: 221–40.

————. 1989. *Perceptual Dialectology: Nonlinguists' Views of Areal Linguistics*. Dordrecht: Foris.

————. 1996. "Where the Worst English Is Spoken." In Schneider 1996, 297–360.

————. 1997. "The South: The Touchstone." In Bernstein, Nunnally, and Sabino, 311–51.

————, ed. 1999. *Handbook of Perceptual Dialectology*. Vol. 1. Amsterdam: John Benjamins.

————. 2005. "What Has Folk Linguistics Done for You Lately?" Paper presented at the Southeastern Conference on Linguistics (SECOL) 72, North Carolina State. April 7–9.

Prévost, Antoine François (l'abbé). 1731. *Histoire du Chevalier des Grieux et de Manon Lescaut*. Paris.

Purnell, Thomas C., and Malcah Yaeger-Dror. 2010. "Accommodation to the Locally Dominant Norm: A Special Issue." *American Speech* 85: 115–20.

Pyles, Thomas, and John Algeo. 1993. *The Origins and Development of the English Language*. 3rd ed. Fort Worth, TX: Harcourt Brace College Publishers.

Rahman, Jacquelyn. 2008. "Middle-Class African Americans: Reactions and Attitudes toward African American English." *American Speech* 83: 141–76.

Raymond, James C., and I. Willis Russell, eds. 1977. *James B. McMillan: Essays in Linguistics by His Friends and Colleagues*. Tuscaloosa: University of Alabama Press.

Read, William Alexander. 1937. *Indian Place-Names in Alabama*. Baton Rouge: Louisiana State University Press. Revised ed., with a foreword, appendix, and index by James B. McMillan, University of Alabama Press. 1984.

Reaser, Jeffrey. 2006. "The Effect of Dialect Awareness on Adolescent Knowledge and Attitudes." PhD diss., Duke University.

Reaser, Jeffrey, Paula Dickerson Boddie, and Walt Wolfram (NCLLP); and DeAnna Locke, Chester Lynn, and Philip Howard (Ocracoke Preservation Society). 2011. *Ocracoke Still Speaks: Reflections Past and Present*. Raleigh: North Carolina Language and Life Project and the Ocracoke Preservation Society.

Reaser, Jeffrey, and Walt Wolfram. 2007a. *Voices of North Carolina: Language and Life from the Atlantic to the Appalachians, Instructor's Manual*. Raleigh: North Carolina Language and Life Project.

————. 2007b. *Voices of North Carolina: Language and Life from the Atlantic to the Appalachians, Student Workbook*. Raleigh: North Carolina Language and Life Project.

Reed, John Shelton. 1993. *Surveying the South*. Columbia: University of Missouri Press.

————. 2003. *Minding the South*. Columbia: University of Missouri Press.

Renn, Jennifer, and J. Michael Terry. 2009. "Operationalizing Style: Quantifying the Use of Style Shift in the Speech of African American Adolescents." *American Speech* 84: 367–90.

Rentz, Päivi. 1997. *Introduction to Finnish*. http://www.ddg.com/LIS/InfoDesignF97/paivir/finnish/page1.html (site discontinued).

Ress, Thomas V. 2009. "Tennessee-Tombigbee Waterway." *Encyclopedia of Alabama*. http://www.encyclopediaofalabama.org/face/Article.jsp?id=h-2365.

Rich, John Stanley, and Michael B. Montgomery. 1993. "A Century of Scholarly Commentary on Alabama English." *SECOL Review* 17: 12–35.

Rickford, John R. 1997. "Unequal Partnership: Sociolinguistics and the African American Speech Community." *Language in Society* 26: 161–98.

Rickford, John R., and Russell J. Rickford. 2000. *Spoken Soul: The Story of Black English.* New York: Wiley.

Rogers, William Warren, Robert David Ward, Leah Rawls Atkins, and Wayne Flynt. 1994. *Alabama: The History of a Deep South State.* Tuscaloosa: University of Alabama Press.

Rojas, David M., Deborah Piston-Hatlen, Kathryn Propst, Madeleine Gonin, and Tamara Lindner, eds. 2003. *A la découverte du français cadien à travers la parole/Discovering Cajun French Through the Spoken Word.* CD ROM. Albert Valdman, project director, in collaboration with Barry Jean Ancelet, Amanda LaFleur, Michael D. Picone, Kevin J. Rottet, and Dominique Ryon. Bloomington: Indiana University Creole Institute.

Romaine, Suzanne. 2005. "Stephen J. Nagle and Sara L. Sanders, editors: *English in the Southern United States.*" Book Review. *Linguistics* 43: 657–62.

Royall, Anne Newton. 1826. *Sketches of History, Life, and Manners, in the United States.* New Haven, CT: Self-published.

———. 1830. *Letters from Alabama on Various Subjects.* Washington, DC: n.p. Digital Google books version available online.

———. (1830–31) 1969. *Letters from Alabama, 1817–1822.* Biographical introduction and notes by Lucille Griffith. Tuscaloosa: University of Alabama Press.

Russell, William Howard. 1863. *My Diary North and South.* Vol. 1. London: Bradbury and Evans.

Ryan, Ellen Bouchard, Howard Giles, and Richard J. Sebastian. 1982. "An Integrative Perspective for the Study of Attitudes toward Language Variation." In *Attitudes Towards Language Variation: Social and Applied Contexts*, edited by Ellen Bouchard Ryan and Howard Giles, 1–19. London: Edward Arnold.

Saussure, Ferdinand de. 1986. *Cours de linguistique génerale.* Paris: Editions Payot. *Course in General Linguistics.* Trans. Roy Harris. LaSalle, Il: Open Court. First published 1916.

Schiffrin, Deborah. 1996. "Narrative as Self-portrait: Sociolinguistic Constructions of Identity." *Language in Society* 25: 167–203.

Schilling-Estes, Natalie. 1997. "Accommodation versus Concentration: Dialect Death in Two Post-Insular Island Communities." *American Speech* 72: 12–32.

Schilling-Estes, Natalie, Chris Estes, and Aida Premilovac. 2002. *Smith Island Voices: A Collection of Stories, Memories, and Slices of Life from Smith Island, Maryland, in the Late 20th and Early 21st Centuries.* Washington, DC: Maryland Historical Trust.

Schilling-Estes, Natalie, and Walt Wolfram. 1999. "Alternative Models of Dialect Death: Dissipation vs. Concentration." *Language* 75: 486–521.

Schmidt, Greg. 2009. "Huntsville." *Encyclopedia of Alabama.* http://www.encyclopediao falabama.org/face/Article.jsp?id=h-2498.

———. 2010. "Athens." *Encyclopedia of Alabama.* http://www.encyclopediaofalabama .org/face/Article.jsp?id=h-2604.

Schneider, Edgar W., ed. 1996. *Focus on the USA.* Amsterdam: John Benjamins.

———. 1998. "The Chattahoochee River: A Linguistic Boundary?" In Montgomery and Nunnally 1998, 123–45.

———. 2003. "Shakespeare in the Coves and Hollows? Toward a History of Southern English." In Nagle and Sanders 2003, 17–35.

———. 2004. "The English Dialect Heritage of the Southern United States." In *Legacies of Colonial English: Studies of Transported Dialects*, edited by Raymond Hickey, 262–309. Cambridge: Cambridge University Press.

Schneider, Edgar W., and Michael B. Montgomery. 2001. "On the Trail of Early Non-standard Grammar: An Electronic Corpus of Southern U.S. Antebellum Overseers' Letters." *American Speech* 79: 388–409.

Sellers, James, producer. 2006. *If They Could Cross the Creek: The Freedmen's Colony of Roanoke Island*. Raleigh: North Carolina Language and Life Project.

Siegel, Jeff. 2007. "Creoles and Minority Dialects in Education: An Update." *Language and Education* 21: 66–86.

Sharp, Ann Wyatt. 1981. "The Literary Dialect in the Simon Suggs Stories of Johnson Jones Hooper." PhD diss., University of Alabama.

Shores, David L., and Carole P. Hines, eds. 1977. *Papers in Language Variation*. Tuscaloosa: University of Alabama Press.

Sledd, James H. 1966. "Breaking, Umlaut, and the Southern Drawl." *Language* 42: 18–41.

Smitherman, Geneva. 1977. *Talkin and Testifyin: The Language of Black America*. Boston: Houghton Mifflin. Repr. Detroit, MI: Wayne State University Press, 1986.

———. 1995. *African American Women Speak Out on Anita Hill-Clarence Thomas*. Detroit: Wayne State University Press.

Soukup, Barbara. 2000. "Y'all Come Back Now, Y' Hear! Language Attitudes in the United States towards Southern American English." Master's thesis, University of Vienna.

Spencer, Thomas. 2006. "Sounds like Alabama." *Birmingham News*, Sunday, November 05, 1E, 4E.

Sperber, Dan, and Deirdre Wilson. 1995. *Relevance: Communication and Cognition*. 2nd ed. Oxford: Blackwell.

Stephens, Elise Hopkins. 1984. *Historic Huntsville: A City of New Beginnings*. Woodland Hills, CA: Windsor Publications.

Stephenson, Edward A. 1958. "Early North Carolina pronunciation." PhD diss., University of North Carolina at Chapel Hill.

———. 1977. "The Beginnings of the Loss of Postvocalic /r/ in North Carolina." In Shores and Hines 1977, 73–92.

Swanton, John Reed. 1911. *Indian Tribes of the Lower Mississippi Valley and Adjacent Coast of the Gulf of Mexico*. Washington, DC: US Government Printing Office.

Tamasi, Susan. 2000. "Linguistic Perceptions of Southern Folk." Paper presented at the annual meeting of the American Dialect Society, San Francisco, CA.

Taylor, Hanni U. 1989. *Standard English, Black English, and Bidialectalism: A Controversy*. New York: Peter Lang.

Terkourafi, Marina. 2005. "Beyond the Micro-Level in Politeness Research." *Journal of Politeness Research* 1: 237–62.

Terry, J. Michael. 2010. "Variation in the Interpretation and Use of the African American English Preverbal *Done* Construction." *American Speech* 85: 3–32.

"The Spread of Cotton and of Slavery, 1790–1860." 1997. American History. Edited by James Mohr and John Nicols. Mapping History Project, University of Oregon. http://mappinghistory.uoregon.edu/english/US/US18-04.html.

Thomas, Daniel H. 1989. *Fort Toulouse: The French Outpost at the Alabamas on the Coosa*. Tuscaloosa: University of Alabama Press.

Thomas, Erik R. 1997. "A Rural/Metropolitan Split in the Speech of Texas Anglos." *Language Variation and Change* 9: 309–32.

———. 2001. *An Acoustic Analysis of Vowel Variation in New World English*. Publication of the American Dialect Society 85. Durham: Duke University Press.

———. 2003. "Secrets Revealed by Southern Vowel Shifting." *American Speech* 78: 150–70.

Thomason, Michael V. R., ed. 2001. *Mobile: The New History of Alabama's First City*. Tuscaloosa: University of Alabama Press.

Thornton, J. Mills, III. 1978. *Politics and Power in a Slave Society: Alabama, 1800–1860*. Baton Rouge: Louisiana State University Press.

———. 2007. "Broad River Group." *Encyclopedia of Alabama*. http://www.encyclopediaofalabama.org/face/Article.jsp?id=h-1137.

Tillery, Jan, and Guy Bailey. 2003. "Urbanization and the Evolution of Southern American English." In Nagle and Sanders 2003, 159–72.

Tillery, Jan, Guy Bailey, and Tom Wikle. 2004. "Demographic Change and American Dialectology in the Twenty-first Century." *American Speech* 79: 227–49.

Ting-Toomey, Stella. 2005. "The Matrix of Face: An Updated Face-Negotiation Theory." In *Theorizing about Intercultural Communication*, edited by William B. Gudykunst, 71–92. Thousand Oaks, CA: Sage.

Trudgill, Peter. 1972. "Sex, Covert Prestige, and Linguistic Change in the Urban English of Norwich." *Language in Society* 1: 171–98.

Tucker, Richard G., and Wallace E. Lambert. 1969. "White and Negro Listeners' Reactions to Various American-English Dialects." *Social Forces* 47: 463–68.

Usner, Daniel H. 1992. *Indians, Settlers, and Slaves in a Frontier Exchange Economy: The Lower Mississippi Valley Before 1783*. Chapel Hill: University of North Carolina Press.

Valdman, Albert, Kevin J. Rottet, Barry Jean Ancelet, Amanda LaFleur, Richard Guidry, Thomas A. Klingler, Tamara Lindner, Michael D. Picone, and Dominique Ryon, eds. 2010. *Dictionary of Louisiana French: As Spoken in Cajun, Creole, and American Indian Communities*. Jackson: University Press of Mississippi.

Vaughn, Charlotte, and Drew Grimes. 2006. "Freedom's Voice: Celebrating the Black Experience on the Outer Banks." An exhibit at the Outer Banks History Center. Roanoke Island: North Carolina Language and Life Project and the Outer Banks History Center.

Vaughn, Charlotte, and Walt Wolfram. 2008. "Celebrating Muzel Bryant." An exhibit at the museum of the Ocracoke Preservation Society. Ocracoke Island: North Carolina Language and Life Project.

Vejnar, Robert J., II. 2008. "Plantation agriculture." *Encyclopedia of Alabama*. http://www.encyclopediaofalabama.org/face/Article.jsp?id=h-1832.

Walker, Ricky Butch, and Lamar Marshall. 2005. *Indian Trails of the Warrior Mountains*. Lawrence County, AL: Lawrence County Schools/Indian Education Program.

Walthall, John A. 1980. *Prehistoric Indians of the Southeast: Archeology of Alabama and the Middle South*. Tuscaloosa: University of Alabama Press.

Warren, Robert Penn. 1961. *The Legacy of the Civil War*. New York: Random House.

Weldon, Tracy L. 2007. "Gullah." In Montgomery and Johnson 2007, 69–72.

Wells, John C. 1982. *Accents of English 3: Beyond the British Isles*. Cambridge: Cambridge University Press.

Werner, Randolph. 2001. "The New South Creed and the Limits of Radicalism: Augusta, Georgia, before the 1890s." *Journal of Southern History* 67: 573–600.

Wiley, Bell Irvin. 1943. *The Life of Johnny Reb: The Common Soldier of the Confederacy*. New York: Bobbs-Merrill.

Wilson, Steven R., Min-Sun Kim, and Hendrika Meischke. 1991/1992. "Evaluating Brown and Levinson's Politeness Theory: A Revised Analysis of Directives and Face." *Research on Language and Social Interaction* 25: 215–52.

Windham, Kathryn Tucker. 1973. *13 Georgia Ghosts and Jeffrey*. Tuscaloosa: University of Alabama Press.

———. 1974. *13 Mississippi Ghosts and Jeffrey*. Tuscaloosa: University of Alabama Press.

Windham, Kathryn Tucker, and Margaret Gillis Figh. 1969. *13 Alabama Ghosts and Jeffrey*. Tuscaloosa: University of Alabama Press.

Winemiller, Terance L. 2008. "Cultural Geography of Alabama." *Encyclopedia of Alabama*. http://www.encyclopediaofalabama.org/face/Article.jsp?id=h-1830.

Winford, Donald. 2000. "*Plus ça Change*: The State of Studies in African American English." *American Speech* 75: 409–11.

Wise, Claude M. 1933. "The Southern American Drawl." *Le Maitre Phonétique*, 3rd series 48.44: 69–71.

Wolfe, Suzanne. 2006. "Vine and Olive: The Unfolding Legacy." *Alabama Heritage* 81: 35.

Wolfram, Walt. 1993. "Ethical Considerations in Language Awareness Programs." *Issues in Applied Linguistics* 4: 225–55.

———. 1996. "Dialect in Society." In *The Handbook of Sociolinguistics*, edited by Florian Coulmas, 107–26. Cambridge: Basil Blackwell.

———. 2007a. "AAE: African American English." Quotation posted on the Linguist List page. http://linguistlist.org/topics/ebonics/.

———. 2007b. "Sociolinguistic Folklore in the Study of African American English." *Language and Linguistic Compass* 1: 292–313.

———. 2007c. "The North Carolina Language and Life Project." In Montgomery and Johnson 2007, 159–61.

Wolfram, Walt, Carolyn Temple Adger, and Donna Christian. 1999. *Dialects in Schools and Communities*. Mahwah, NJ: Lawrence Erlbaum.

Wolfram, Walt, Clare Dannenberg, Stanley Knick, and Linda Oxendine. 2002. *Fine in the World: Lumbee Language in Time and Place*. Raleigh: North Carolina State Humanities Extension/Publications.

Wolfram, Walt, and Jeffrey Reaser. 2014. *Talkin' Tar Heel: How Our Voices Tell the Story of North Carolina*. Chapel Hill: University of North Carolina Press.

Wolfram, Walt, Jeffrey Reaser, and Charlotte Vaughn. 2008. "Operationalizing Linguistic Gratuity: From Principle to Practice." *Language and Linguistic Compass* 2: 1109—34.

Wolfram, Walt, and Natalie Schilling-Estes. 1996. "Dialect Change and Maintenance in a Post-Insular Island Community." In Schneider 1996, 103–48.

———. 1997. *Hoi Toide on the Outer Banks: The Story of the Ocracoke Brogue*. Chapel Hill: University of North Carolina Press.

———. 2006. *American English: Dialects and Variation*. 2nd ed. New York: Blackwell.

Wolfram, Walt, Natalie Schilling-Estes, and Kirk Hazen. 1994. *Dialect Vocabulary in Ocracoke*. Raleigh: North Carolina Language and Life Project.

Wood, Gordon R. 1963. "Dialect Contours in the Southern States." *American Speech* 38: 243–56.

———. 1971. *Vocabulary Change: A Study of Variation in Regional Words in Eight of the Southern States*. Carbondale: Southern Illinois University Press.

X, Malcolm. 1965. *The Autobiography of Malcolm X*. New York: Grove Press.

Yaeger-Dror, Malcah, and Erik R. Thomas. 2010. "Introduction." In *African American English Speakers and Their Participation in Local Sound Changes: A Comparative Study*, edited by Yaeger-Dror and Thomas, 1–20. Publication of the American Dialect Society 94. Durham: Duke University Press.

Contributors

Rachael Allbritten received her PhD in linguistics from Georgetown University in 2011. Her research was primarily in sociolinguistics and English dialectal variation, especially that of the American South. In addition to work on topics such as vowel shifts, her interests focused on acoustic phonetics, language change, and perception of linguistic features by listeners. She is also interested in the role of linguistic resources in constructing long- and short-term personae and vice versa: how a group of speakers' identities and choices shape language. She received her master's degree in computational linguistics from Georgetown University in 2007. Her work in that field concentrated on machine translation and statistically based language models. Rachael received her undergraduate degree from the University of North Alabama in 1999. She currently works as an investigative scientist at the National Science Foundation in Arlington, Virginia.

Guy Bailey is founding president of the University of Texas Rio Grande Valley and has served as a president or provost at several universities since 1998. He maintains an active research agenda focused on the synchronic approach to language change; the relationship between demography and language change; approaches to time in dialectology and sociolinguistics; and the effects of methodology on results. He has published extensively in journals such as *Language Variation and Change, Language in Society*, and *American Speech* and in volumes such as *The Handbook of Dialectology, The Oxford Handbook on African American Language*, and *The Handbook of Varieties of English*. His research was included in the 2004 PBS documentary *Do You Speak American?* and featured in a front-page *New York Times* story in 2003.

Charlotte Brammer is an associate professor of English at Howard College of Arts and Sciences and director of the Communication Resource Center, at Samford University, Birmingham. Her research interests include writing pedagogy, professional communication, and sociolinguistics. Currently, she serves as a reviewer for *Business and Professional Communication Quarterly*. A native of South Carolina, Charlotte has lived in Alabama for twenty-six years and completed her PhD at the University of Alabama.

Catherine Evans Davies (PhD, University of California, Berkeley) is a professor of linguistics in the English Department at the University of Alabama. Her main research interests are in the sociolinguistics and pragmatics of cross-(sub)cultural communication, particularly in relation to Southern discourse. She was coeditor of *English and Ethnicity* (2006) and has published in the *Journal of Pragmatics*, *Multilingua*, *Text*, *Humor*, and *Narrative Inquiry*. She is coeditor with Michael Picone of the third LAVIS volume, *New Perspectives on Language Variety in the South: Historical and Contemporary Approaches* (University of Alabama Press, 2015). She was president of the Southeastern Conference on Linguistics in 2003; as a current member of the Alabama Humanities Foundation's Road Scholars program, she gives a lecture for nonspecialists on language in Alabama that she expanded into an article in this volume.

Jocelyn Doxsey completed her graduate studies in linguistics at New York University. Her work is primarily sociophonetic in nature and deals specifically with American English dialects. Her master's thesis concentrated on Southern American English dialect variation, specifically on the coast of Alabama. Additionally, she has contributed to NYU's ongoing study of dialect variation in New York City English. Jocelyn completed her master's degree in 2007 and currently works in the advertising industry in New York City.

Crawford Feagin, a native of Anniston, specializes in sociolinguistics, particularly the study of variation in the grammar and phonology of Southern States English. Dr. Feagin earned her doctorate at Georgetown University with the University of Pennsylvania's William Labov as advisor. Her book, *Variation and Change in Alabama English: A Sociolinguistic Study of the White Community*, provided the first extended view of the grammar of whites in the American South, with many comparisons to the grammar of African American English as well as other varieties of English, past and present. Her more recent work has centered on phonological change in Alabama English, especially vowel shifting. She was a Fulbright guest professor at the University of Klagenfurt in 1992 and more recently a visiting professor at Georgetown University and the University of Zurich.

J. Daniel Hasty is an associate professor of linguistics in the Department of English at Coastal Carolina University. Daniel is a sociolinguist specializing in syntactic variation, with a focus on Appalachian English and Southern US English. He also studies the subjective reactions and attitudes toward these varieties by both insiders and outsiders with the goal of understanding how speakers use syntactic variants to construct social identities. Additionally, Daniel is interested in Southern identity construction, issues associated with the Standard Language Ideology, and representations of Southern English and Culture in literature, music, and popular culture. He holds a PhD in linguistics from Michigan State University, an MA in English from Auburn University, and a BA in English from Tennessee Technological University.

Kimberly Johnson teaches eighth- and ninth-grade creative writing and reading for at-risk students at Auburn (Alabama) Junior High School. Nationally board-certified in early adolescent language arts in 2004, Kimberly started teaching language arts in 1998 at Cedar Ridge Middle School in Decatur before moving to

Auburn in 2004. Originally from Anniston, she received a degree in communications from the University of Alabama, a master's in language arts education from Alabama A&M University, and an education specialist's degree in English language arts education from Auburn University. She and her husband, Jeff, have three children, Jouri, Jaden, and Jayme, and she serves as a mentor and teacher-leader at Auburn Junior High and with Auburn City Schools.

Michael B. Montgomery (PhD 1979, University of Florida) is Distinguished Professor Emeritus of English and Linguistics at the University of South Carolina, where for twenty years he taught classes mainly in English linguistics. He has authored or edited thirteen books and published nearly two hundred scholarly papers and chapters. At the core of his research and scholarship has long been the English of the American South. With Guy Bailey, he organized the first Language Variety in the South conference in 1981 and coedited the associated volume of essays. He has keynoted subsequent iterations of this once-a-decade stocktaking of all aspects of language in the region. In 1989, he edited (with James B. McMillan) an exhaustive, annotated bibliography of this field, a work that has become a standard reference. In the 1990s, he was assistant editor for two volumes of The Linguistic Atlas of the Gulf States (with Lee Pederson and Susan McDaniel) and in 2007 the *Language* volume of the *New Encyclopedia of Southern Culture* (with Ellen Johnson). For the past twenty-five years, he has pursued archival and other research on the Irish and Scottish connections to American English, which has led among other things to the publications *From Ulster to America: The Scotch-Irish Heritage of American English* (2006, 2nd ed. 2017) and *The Academic Study of Ulster-Scots: Essays for and by Robert J. Gregg* (2006). For fifteen years, he served as honorary president of both the Ulster-Scots Language Society and the Forum for Research on the Languages of Scotland and Ulster. In 1990, Montgomery began a collaboration with Joseph Sargent Hall, which led to a work of historical lexicography, *Dictionary of Smoky Mountain English* (2004) and the forthcoming sequel *Dictionary of Southern Smoky Mountain and Appalachian English*. His work in corpus linguistics includes the Southern Plantation Overseer Corpus (with Edgar Schneider), the Corpus of American Civil War Letters (with Michael Ellis), and the Archive of Traditional Appalachian Speech and Culture. He was also editor of the *Language* section of the *Encyclopedia of Appalachia*. Most recently he has created, with Paul Reed, the website MULTIMO: The Database of Multiple Modals, a New Resource for Researchers.

Thomas E. Nunnally, professor emeritus of English at Auburn University, received his PhD from the University of Georgia. He coorganized and hosted the second Language Variety in the South conference (LAVIS II) in 1993 and coedited the volume of essays from the conference. His special interests are the dynamics of language change in English over the last thousand years, Old English language and literature, and cultural views of language usage. He has contributed to and (co) edited three books of essays in sociolinguistics and dialectology and published in *American Speech*, *Language*, *The SECOL Review*, and other journals. He was president of the Southeastern Conference on Linguistics 1998–99. Honors include two Fulbright awards and NEH Seminar participation.

Michael D. Picone is a professor of French and linguistics at the University of Alabama, where he began teaching in 1988, shortly after earning his doctorate at the Sorbonne (University of Paris). His publications and program of research encompass an assortment of topics, including contemporary and historical profiles of language use in the Gulf South (especially Louisiana and Alabama), languages in contact, literary dialect, French neology, and language in relation to the visual arts (especially in graphic novels). He is author of *Anglicisms, Neologisms, and Dynamic French* (1996), a detailed study of borrowings and other types of lexical creativity in the French of France, and coeditor of the *Dictionary of Louisiana French* (2010). With Catherine Evans Davies, he was coorganizer of the third Language Variety in the South symposium, which resulted in the coedited volume of selected and revised papers, *New Perspectives on Language Variety in the South: Historical and Contemporary Approaches* (University of Alabama Press, 2015).

Robin Sabino (PhD, University of Pennsylvania) is a professor in the English Department at Auburn University, where she directs the department's Undergraduate Studies Program. She is also the director of the Africana Studies Program in the College of Liberal Arts. A current monograph project, Languaging without Languages: Beyond trans-, pluri-, metro-, and multi-, explores implications of language ideology and language variation for grammatical theory. A chapter, "Sociolinguistic Overview of the United States Virgin Islands," is forthcoming in the *Handbook of Caribbean Languages and Linguistics* (Language Science Press).

Anna Head Spence is chair of the division of English, foreign languages, and communication at Enterprise State Community College in Alabama, where she teaches courses in literature and writing. She received her PhD from Auburn University, and her areas of research interest include the language, literature, and history of the American South. Her work on Southern English has focused primarily on speech in the Alabama Wiregrass and, in particular, on the role of integration in shaping speakers' linguistic choices in the community of Elba, Alabama. In 2017, for the Alabama Public Television series "Journey Proud," she cohosted two episodes that explored North Alabama and South Alabama dialects.

Walt Wolfram is William C. Friday Distinguished University Professor at North Carolina State University, where he also directs the Language and Life Project. He has pioneered research on social and ethnic dialects since the 1960s and published more than twenty books and three hundred articles. Over the last two decades, he and his students have conducted more than 2,500 sociolinguistic interviews with residents of North Carolina and beyond. Current research supported by National Science Foundation grants has included the longitudinal development of African American English during the first twenty years of life and the emergence of Hispanicized English in the southeastern United States. Professor Wolfram is particularly interested in the application of sociolinguistic information for public audiences, including the production of a number of television documentaries, the construction of museum exhibits, and the development of an innovative social-studies dialect awareness curricula endorsed by the North Carolina Department of Public Instruction. He has received numerous awards, including the Caldwell

Humanities Laureate from the NC Humanities Council, the Holladay Medal at NC State, and the Linguistics, Language and the Public Award from the Linguistic Society of America, as well as the NC State Alumni Association Research Award, the Graduate Professor Award, and the Extension and Engagement Award. He has also served as president of the Linguistic Society of America, the American Dialect Society, and the Southeastern Conference on Linguistics.

Index